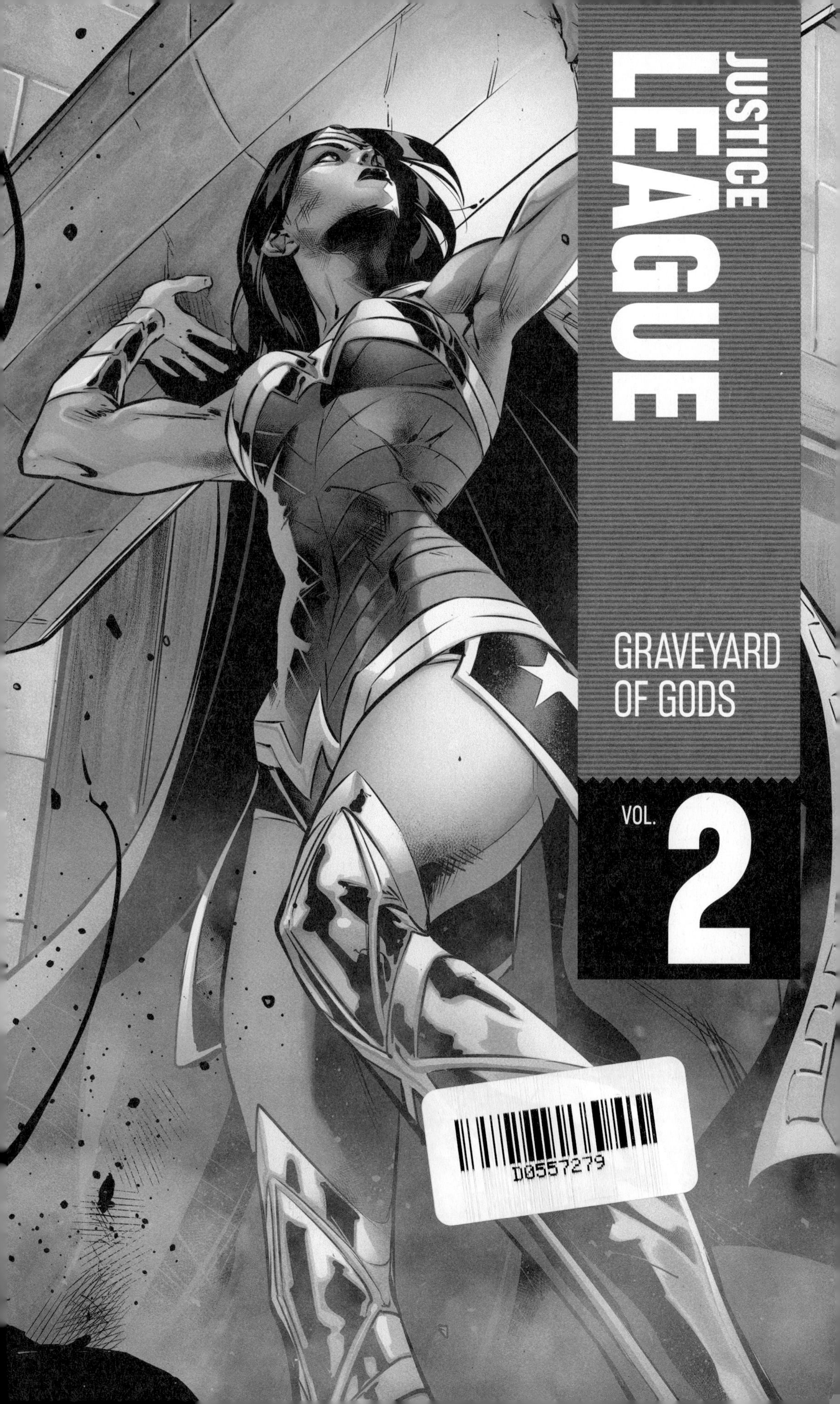

JUSTICE LEAGUE

GRAVEYARD OF GODS

VOL. 2

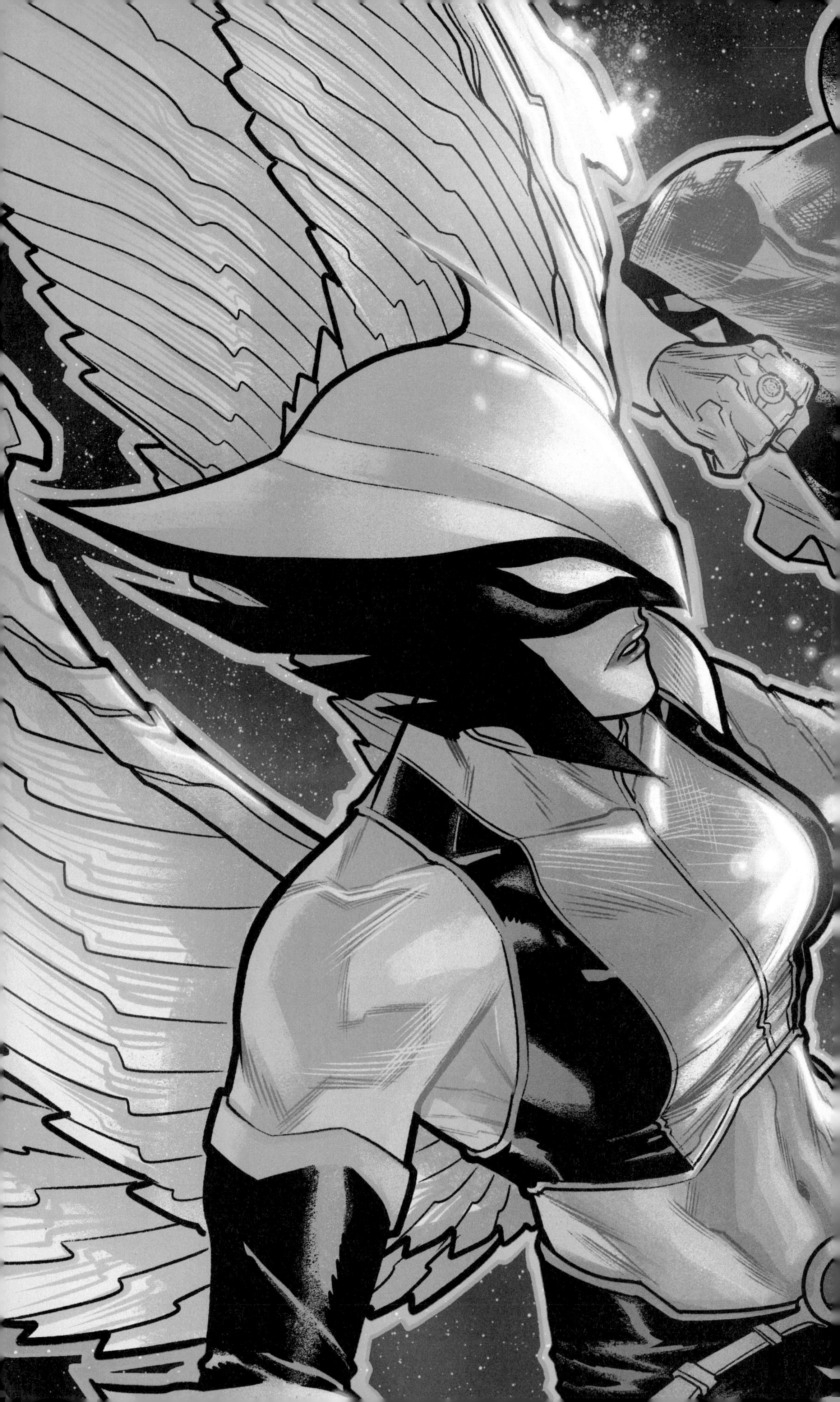

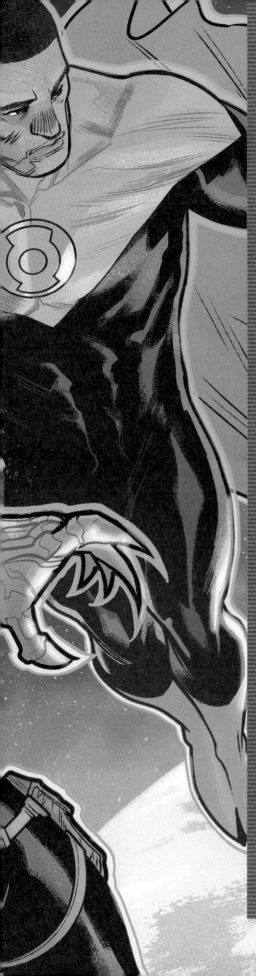

JUSTICE LEAGUE
GRAVEYARD OF GODS

writers
SCOTT SNYDER
JAMES TYNION IV

artists
FRANCIS MANAPUL
HOWARD PORTER
MIKEL JANÍN
JORGE JIMENEZ
FRAZER IRVING
BRUNO REDONDO
SCOTT GODLEWSKI

colorists
FRANCIS MANAPUL
HI-FI
JEROMY COX
ALEJANDRO SANCHEZ
FRAZER IRVING
SUNNY GHO

letterer
TOM NAPOLITANO

collection cover artist
MIKEL JANÍN

AQUAMAN created by PAUL NORRIS
SUPERMAN created by
JERRY SIEGEL and JOE SHUSTER
By special arrangement with
the Jerry Siegel family

VOL.
2

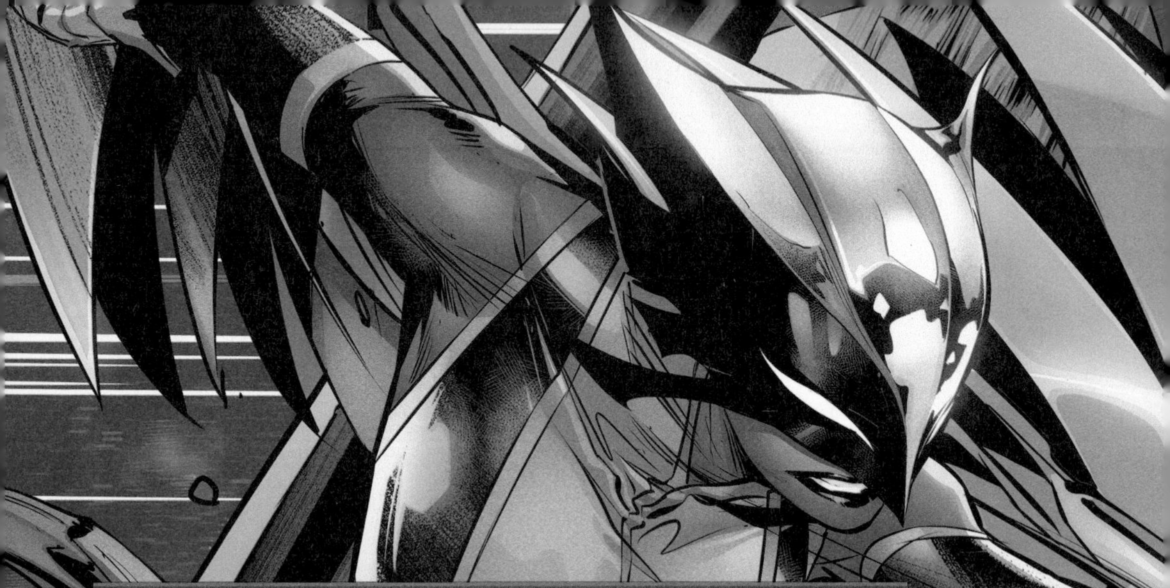

REBECCA TAYLOR PAUL KAMINSKI ALEX ANTONE Editors – Original Series
ROB LEVIN Associate Editor – Original Series
ANDREW MARINO ANDREA SHEA BEN MEARES Assistant Editors – Original Series
JEB WOODARD Group Editor – Collected Editions
ROBIN WILDMAN Editor – Collected Edition
STEVE COOK Design Director – Books
MEGEN BELLERSEN Publication Design

BOB HARRAS Senior VP – Editor-in-Chief, DC Comics
PAT McCALLUM Executive Editor, DC Comics

DAN DiDIO Publisher
JIM LEE Publisher & Chief Creative Officer
AMIT DESAI Executive VP – Business & Marketing Strategy, Direct to Consumer & Global Franchise Management
BOBBIE CHASE VP & Executive Editor, Young Reader & Talent Development
MARK CHIARELLO Senior VP – Art, Design & Collected Editions
JOHN CUNNINGHAM Senior VP – Sales & Trade Marketing
BRIAR DARDEN VP – Business Affairs
ANNE DePIES Senior VP – Business Strategy, Finance & Administration
DON FALLETTI VP – Manufacturing Operations
LAWRENCE GANEM VP – Editorial Administration & Talent Relations
ALISON GILL Senior VP – Manufacturing & Operations
JASON GREENBERG VP – Business Strategy & Finance
HANK KANALZ Senior VP – Editorial Strategy & Administration
JAY KOGAN Senior VP – Legal Affairs
NICK J. NAPOLITANO VP – Manufacturing Administration
LISETTE OSTERLOH VP – Digital Marketing & Events
EDDIE SCANNELL VP – Consumer Marketing
COURTNEY SIMMONS Senior VP – Publicity & Communications
JIM (SKI) SOKOLOWSKI VP – Comic Book Specialty Sales & Trade Marketing
NANCY SPEARS VP – Mass, Book, Digital Sales & Trade Marketing
MICHELE R. WELLS VP – Content Strategy

JUSTICE LEAGUE VOL. 2: GRAVEYARD OF GODS

DC Comics, 2900 West Alameda Ave., Burbank, CA 91505
Printed by LSC Communications, Owensville, MO, USA. 4/5/19. First Printing.
ISBN: 978-1-4012-8849-5

Library of Congress Cataloging-in-Publication Data is available.

PEFC Certified
This product is from sustainably managed forests and controlled sources
PEFC
PEFC/29-31-337
www.pefc.org

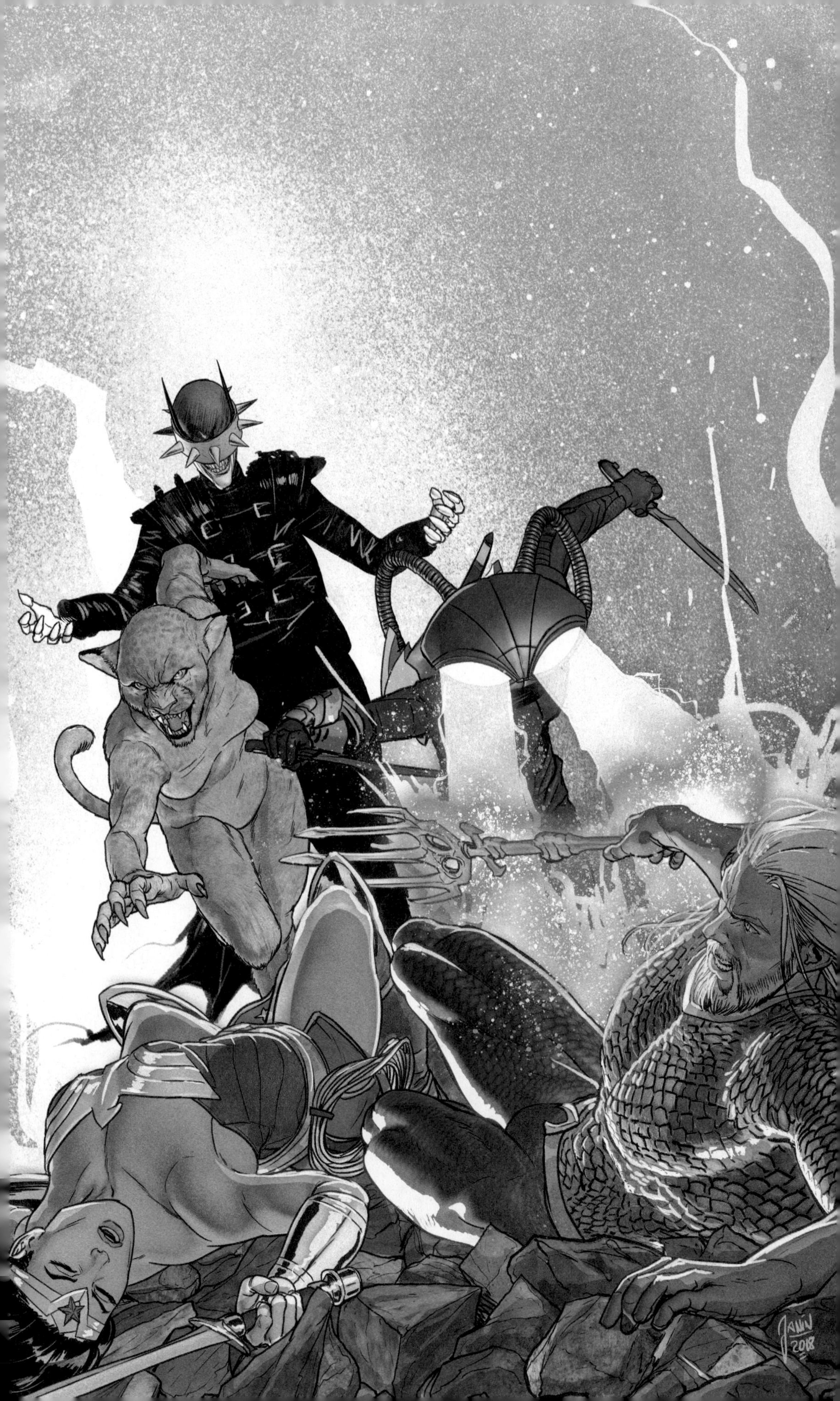

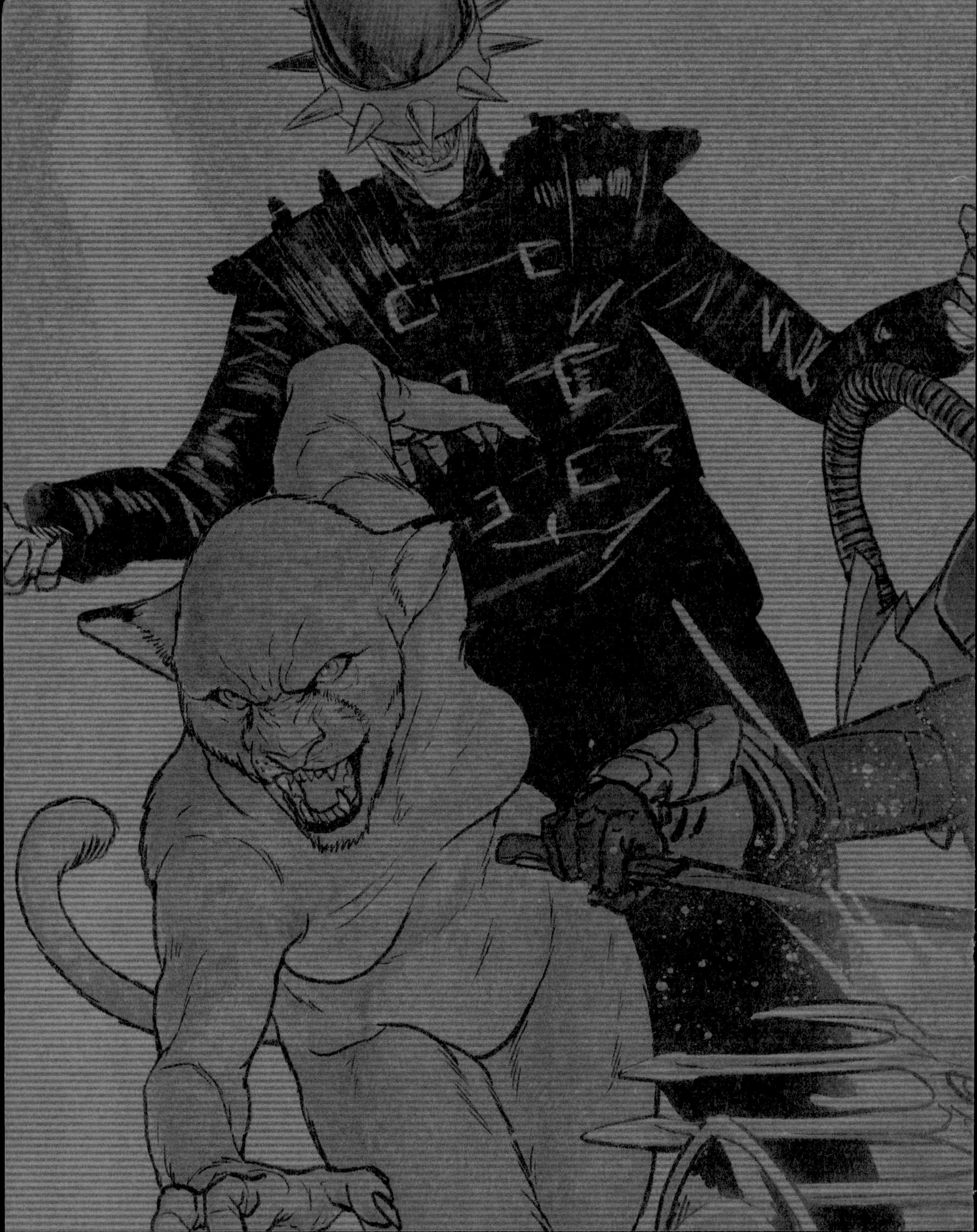

JUSTICE LEAGUE #8

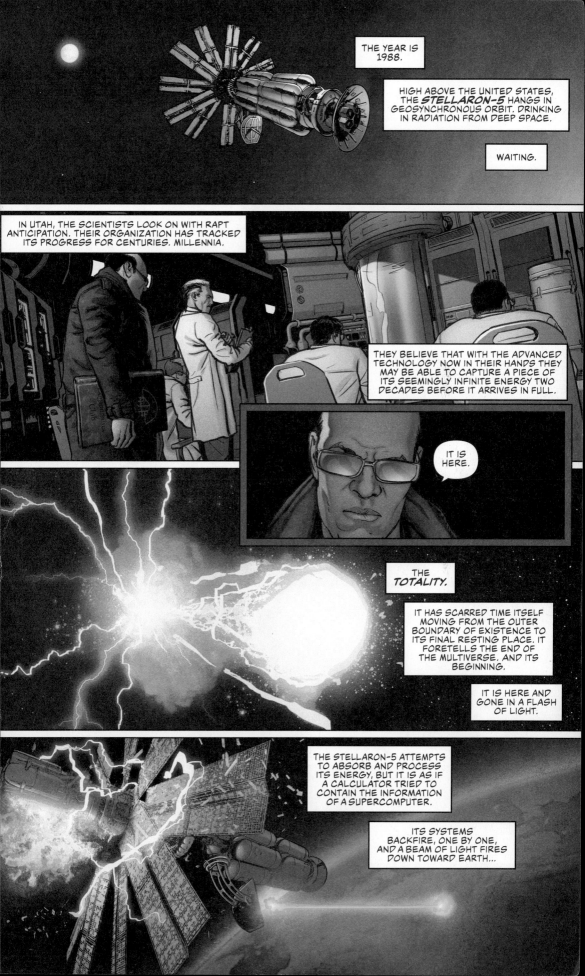

THE YEAR IS 1988.

HIGH ABOVE THE UNITED STATES, THE **STELLARON-5** HANGS IN GEOSYNCHRONOUS ORBIT. DRINKING IN RADIATION FROM DEEP SPACE.

WAITING.

IN UTAH, THE SCIENTISTS LOOK ON WITH RAPT ANTICIPATION. THEIR ORGANIZATION HAS TRACKED ITS PROGRESS FOR CENTURIES. MILLENNIA.

THEY BELIEVE THAT WITH THE ADVANCED TECHNOLOGY NOW IN THEIR HANDS THEY MAY BE ABLE TO CAPTURE A PIECE OF ITS SEEMINGLY INFINITE ENERGY TWO DECADES BEFORE IT ARRIVES IN FULL.

IT IS HERE.

THE **TOTALITY.**

IT HAS SCARRED TIME ITSELF MOVING FROM THE OUTER BOUNDARY OF EXISTENCE TO ITS FINAL RESTING PLACE. IT FORETELLS THE END OF THE MULTIVERSE. AND ITS BEGINNING.

IT IS HERE AND GONE IN A FLASH OF LIGHT.

THE STELLARON-5 ATTEMPTS TO ABSORB AND PROCESS ITS ENERGY, BUT IT IS AS IF A CALCULATOR TRIED TO CONTAIN THE INFORMATION OF A SUPERCOMPUTER.

ITS SYSTEMS BACKFIRE, ONE BY ONE, AND A BEAM OF LIGHT FIRES DOWN TOWARD EARTH...

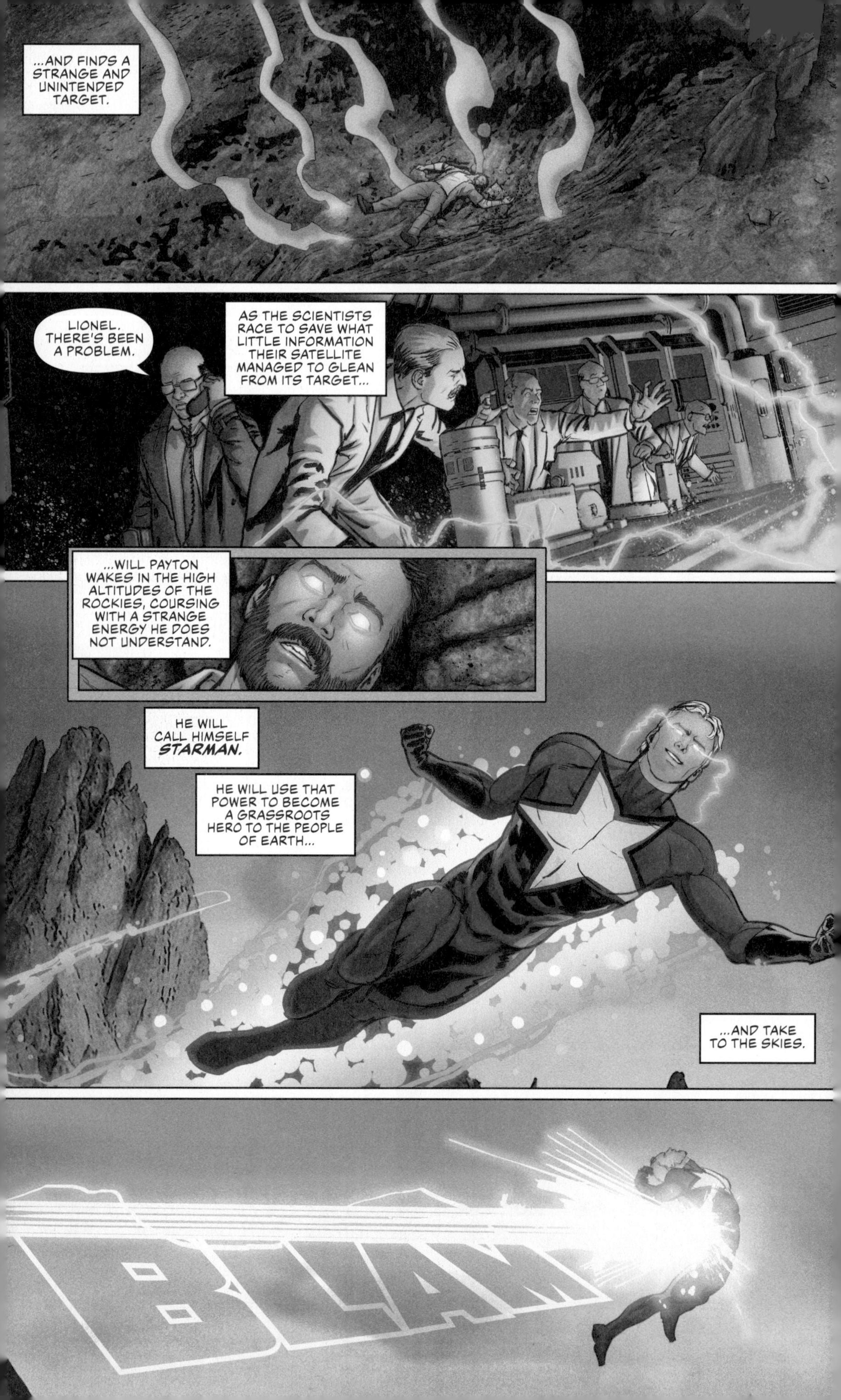
...AND FINDS A STRANGE AND UNINTENDED TARGET.
LIONEL. THERE'S BEEN A PROBLEM.
AS THE SCIENTISTS RACE TO SAVE WHAT LITTLE INFORMATION THEIR SATELLITE MANAGED TO GLEAN FROM ITS TARGET...
...WILL PAYTON WAKES IN THE HIGH ALTITUDES OF THE ROCKIES, COURSING WITH A STRANGE ENERGY HE DOES NOT UNDERSTAND.
HE WILL CALL HIMSELF STARMAN.
HE WILL USE THAT POWER TO BECOME A GRASSROOTS HERO TO THE PEOPLE OF EARTH...
...AND TAKE TO THE SKIES.
BLAM

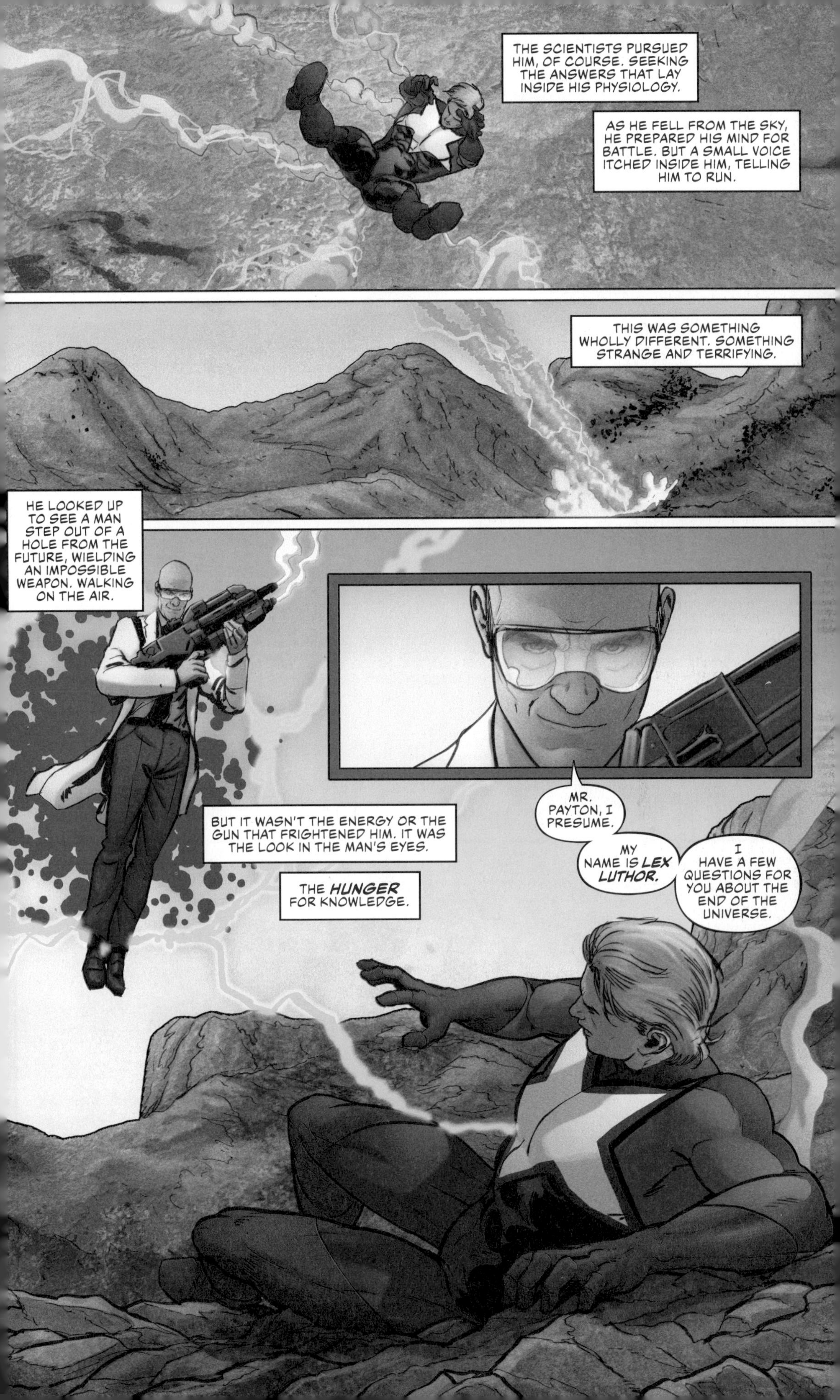
THE SCIENTISTS PURSUED HIM, OF COURSE. SEEKING THE ANSWERS THAT LAY INSIDE HIS PHYSIOLOGY.
AS HE FELL FROM THE SKY, HE PREPARED HIS MIND FOR BATTLE. BUT A SMALL VOICE ITCHED INSIDE HIM, TELLING HIM TO RUN.
THIS WAS SOMETHING WHOLLY DIFFERENT. SOMETHING STRANGE AND TERRIFYING.
HE LOOKED UP TO SEE A MAN STEP OUT OF A HOLE FROM THE FUTURE, WIELDING AN IMPOSSIBLE WEAPON. WALKING ON THE AIR.
MR. PAYTON, I PRESUME.
BUT IT WASN'T THE ENERGY OR THE GUN THAT FRIGHTENED HIM. IT WAS THE LOOK IN THE MAN'S EYES.
THE ***HUNGER*** FOR KNOWLEDGE.
MY NAME IS ***LEX LUTHOR.***
I HAVE A FEW QUESTIONS FOR YOU ABOUT THE END OF THE UNIVERSE.

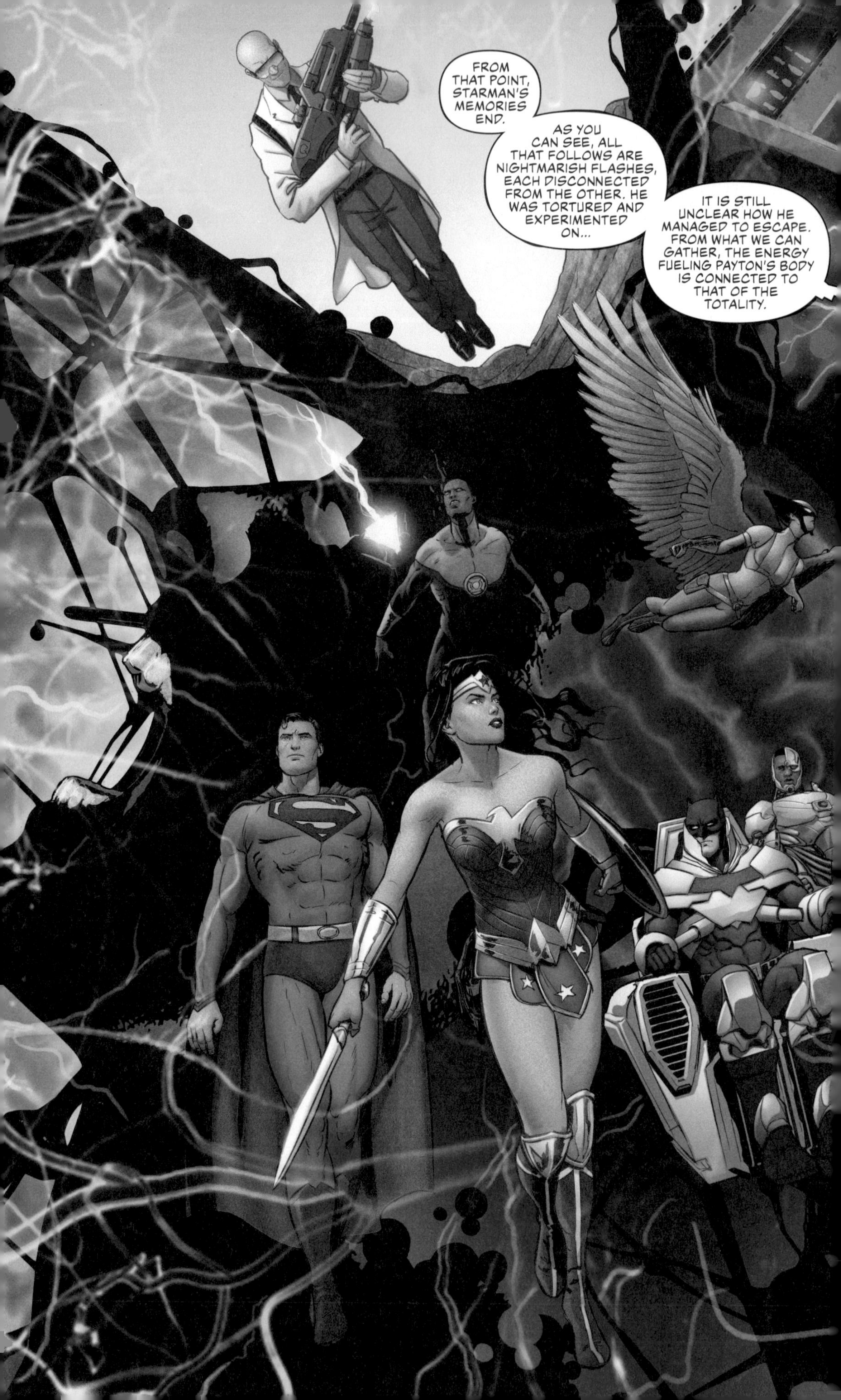
FROM THAT POINT, STARMAN'S MEMORIES END.
AS YOU CAN SEE, ALL THAT FOLLOWS ARE NIGHTMARISH FLASHES, EACH DISCONNECTED FROM THE OTHER. HE WAS TORTURED AND EXPERIMENTED ON...
IT IS STILL UNCLEAR HOW HE MANAGED TO ESCAPE. FROM WHAT WE CAN GATHER, THE ENERGY FUELING PAYTON'S BODY IS CONNECTED TO THAT OF THE TOTALITY.

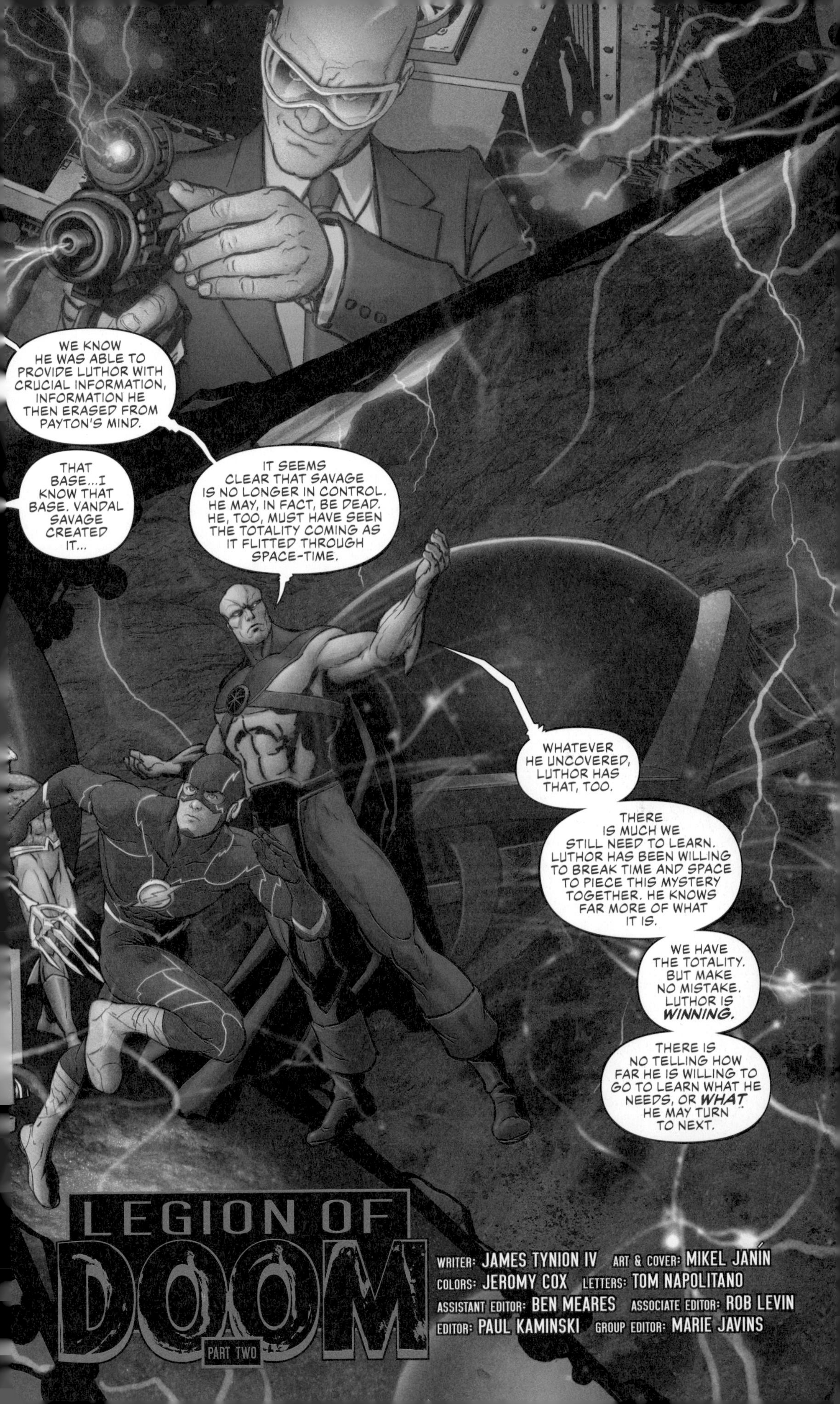

WE KNOW HE WAS ABLE TO PROVIDE LUTHOR WITH CRUCIAL INFORMATION, INFORMATION HE THEN ERASED FROM PAYTON'S MIND.
THAT BASE...I KNOW THAT BASE. VANDAL SAVAGE CREATED IT...
IT SEEMS CLEAR THAT SAVAGE IS NO LONGER IN CONTROL. HE MAY, IN FACT, BE DEAD. HE, TOO, MUST HAVE SEEN THE TOTALITY COMING AS IT FLITTED THROUGH SPACE-TIME.
WHATEVER HE UNCOVERED, LUTHOR HAS THAT, TOO.
THERE IS MUCH WE STILL NEED TO LEARN. LUTHOR HAS BEEN WILLING TO BREAK TIME AND SPACE TO PIECE THIS MYSTERY TOGETHER. HE KNOWS FAR MORE OF WHAT IT IS.
WE HAVE THE TOTALITY. BUT MAKE NO MISTAKE. LUTHOR IS ***WINNING.***
THERE IS NO TELLING HOW FAR HE IS WILLING TO GO TO LEARN WHAT HE NEEDS, OR ***WHAT*** HE MAY TURN TO NEXT.
LEGION OF DOOM
PART TWO
WRITER: JAMES TYNION IV ART & COVER: MIKEL JANÍN
COLORS: JEROMY COX LETTERS: TOM NAPOLITANO
ASSISTANT EDITOR: BEN MEARES ASSOCIATE EDITOR: ROB LEVIN
EDITOR: PAUL KAMINSKI GROUP EDITOR: MARIE JAVINS

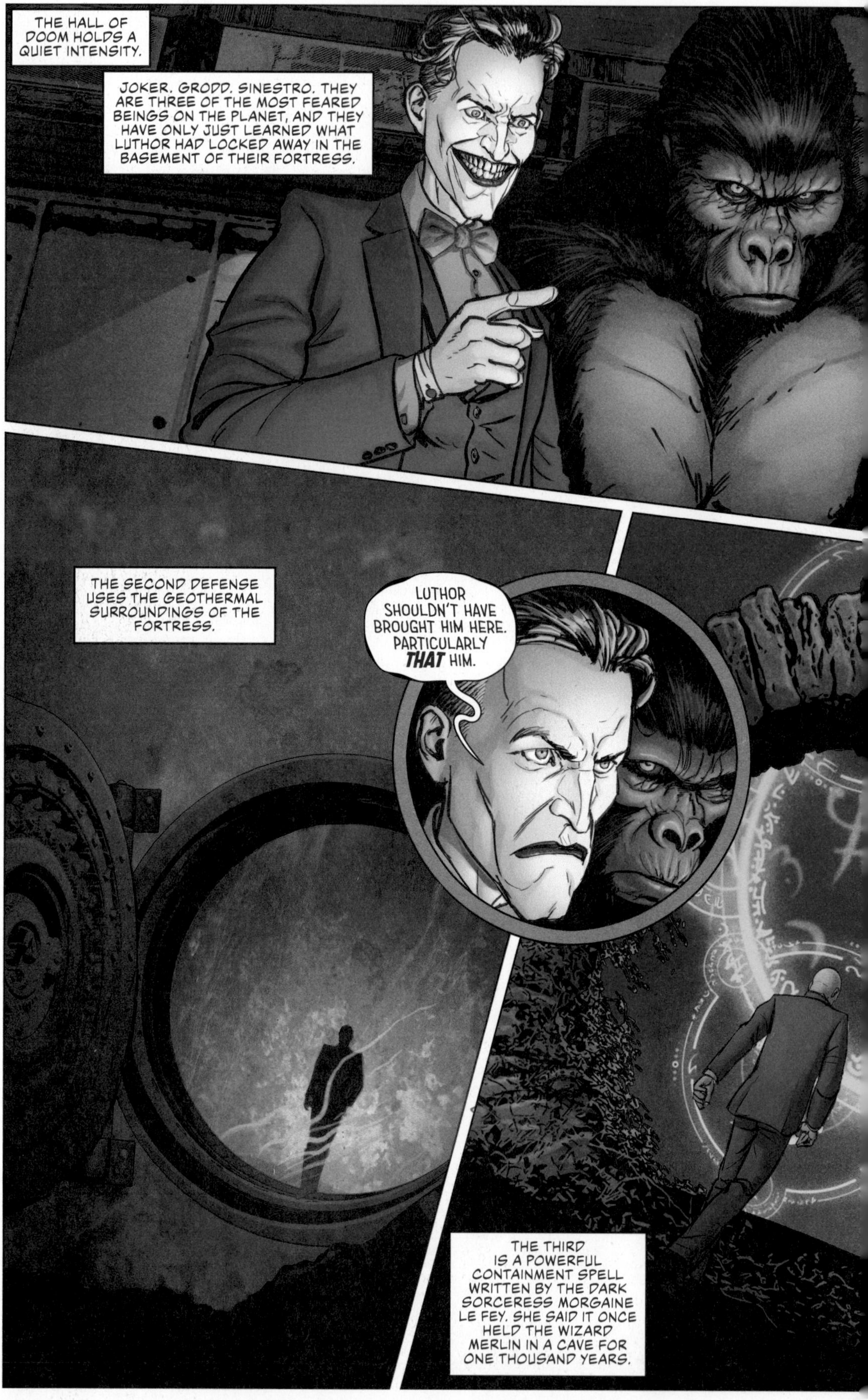

THE HALL OF DOOM HOLDS A QUIET INTENSITY.
JOKER. GRODD. SINESTRO. THEY ARE THREE OF THE MOST FEARED BEINGS ON THE PLANET, AND THEY HAVE ONLY JUST LEARNED WHAT LUTHOR HAD LOCKED AWAY IN THE BASEMENT OF THEIR FORTRESS.
THE SECOND DEFENSE USES THE GEOTHERMAL SURROUNDINGS OF THE FORTRESS.
LUTHOR SHOULDN'T HAVE BROUGHT HIM HERE. PARTICULARLY **THAT** HIM.
THE THIRD IS A POWERFUL CONTAINMENT SPELL WRITTEN BY THE DARK SORCERESS MORGAINE LE FEY. SHE SAID IT ONCE HELD THE WIZARD MERLIN IN A CAVE FOR ONE THOUSAND YEARS.

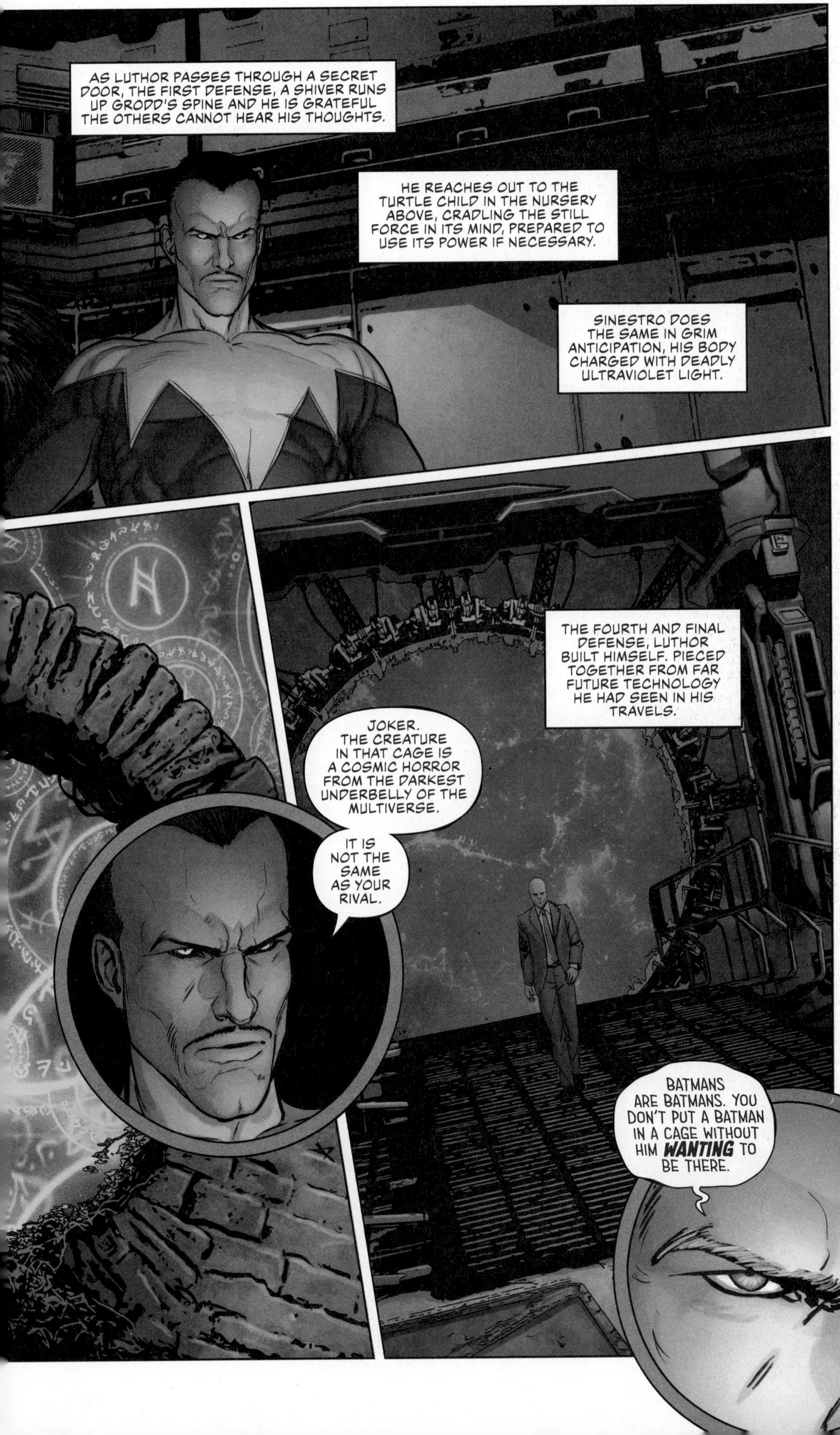
AS LUTHOR PASSES THROUGH A SECRET DOOR, THE FIRST DEFENSE, A SHIVER RUNS UP GRODD'S SPINE AND HE IS GRATEFUL THE OTHERS CANNOT HEAR HIS THOUGHTS.
HE REACHES OUT TO THE TURTLE CHILD IN THE NURSERY ABOVE, CRADLING THE STILL FORCE IN ITS MIND, PREPARED TO USE ITS POWER IF NECESSARY.
SINESTRO DOES THE SAME IN GRIM ANTICIPATION, HIS BODY CHARGED WITH DEADLY ULTRAVIOLET LIGHT.
THE FOURTH AND FINAL DEFENSE, LUTHOR BUILT HIMSELF. PIECED TOGETHER FROM FAR FUTURE TECHNOLOGY HE HAD SEEN IN HIS TRAVELS.
JOKER. THE CREATURE IN THAT CAGE IS A COSMIC HORROR FROM THE DARKEST UNDERBELLY OF THE MULTIVERSE.
IT IS NOT THE SAME AS YOUR RIVAL.
BATMANS ARE BATMANS. YOU DON'T PUT A BATMAN IN A CAGE WITHOUT HIM WANTING TO BE THERE.

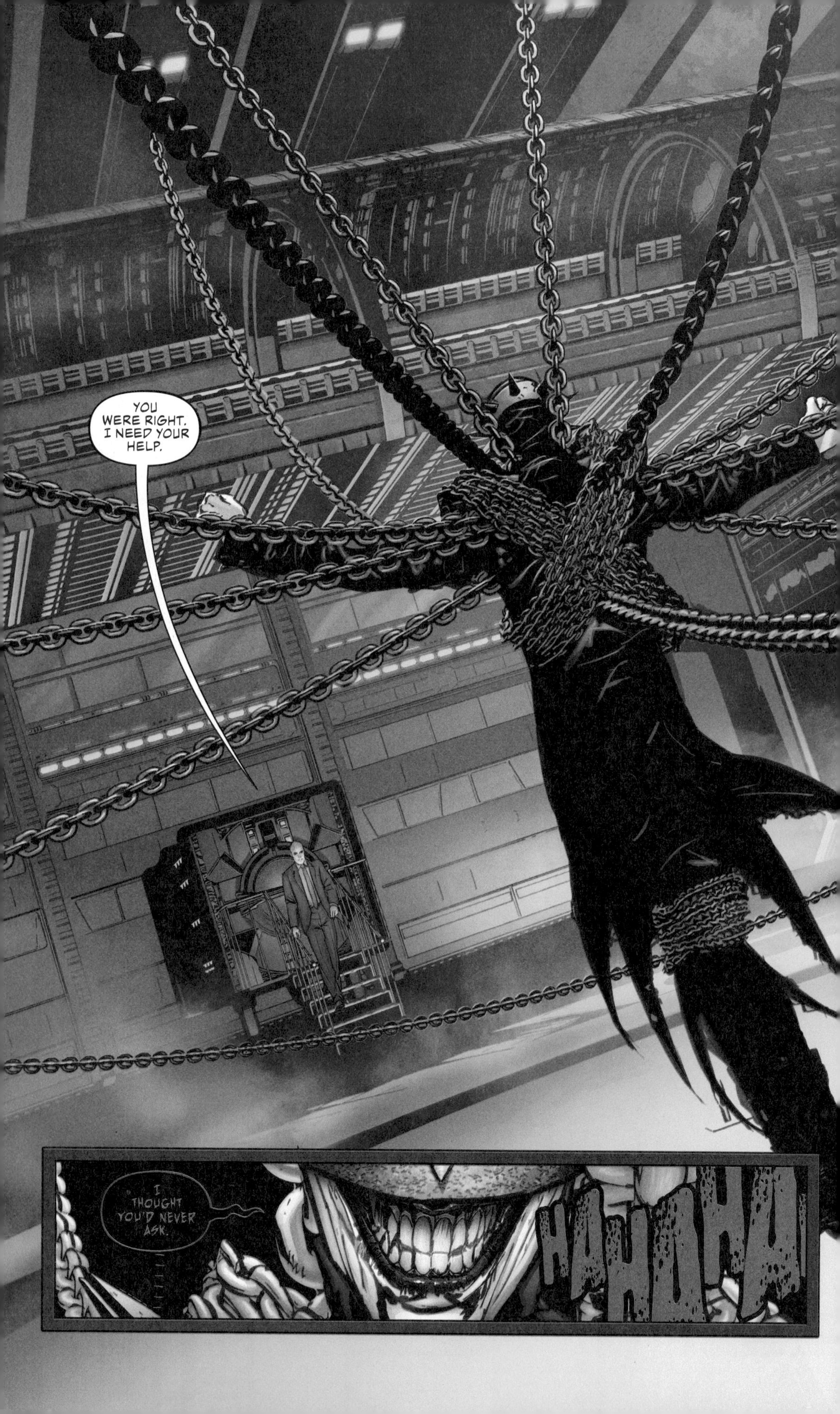
YOU WERE RIGHT. I NEED YOUR HELP.
I THOUGHT YOU'D NEVER ASK.
HAHAHA

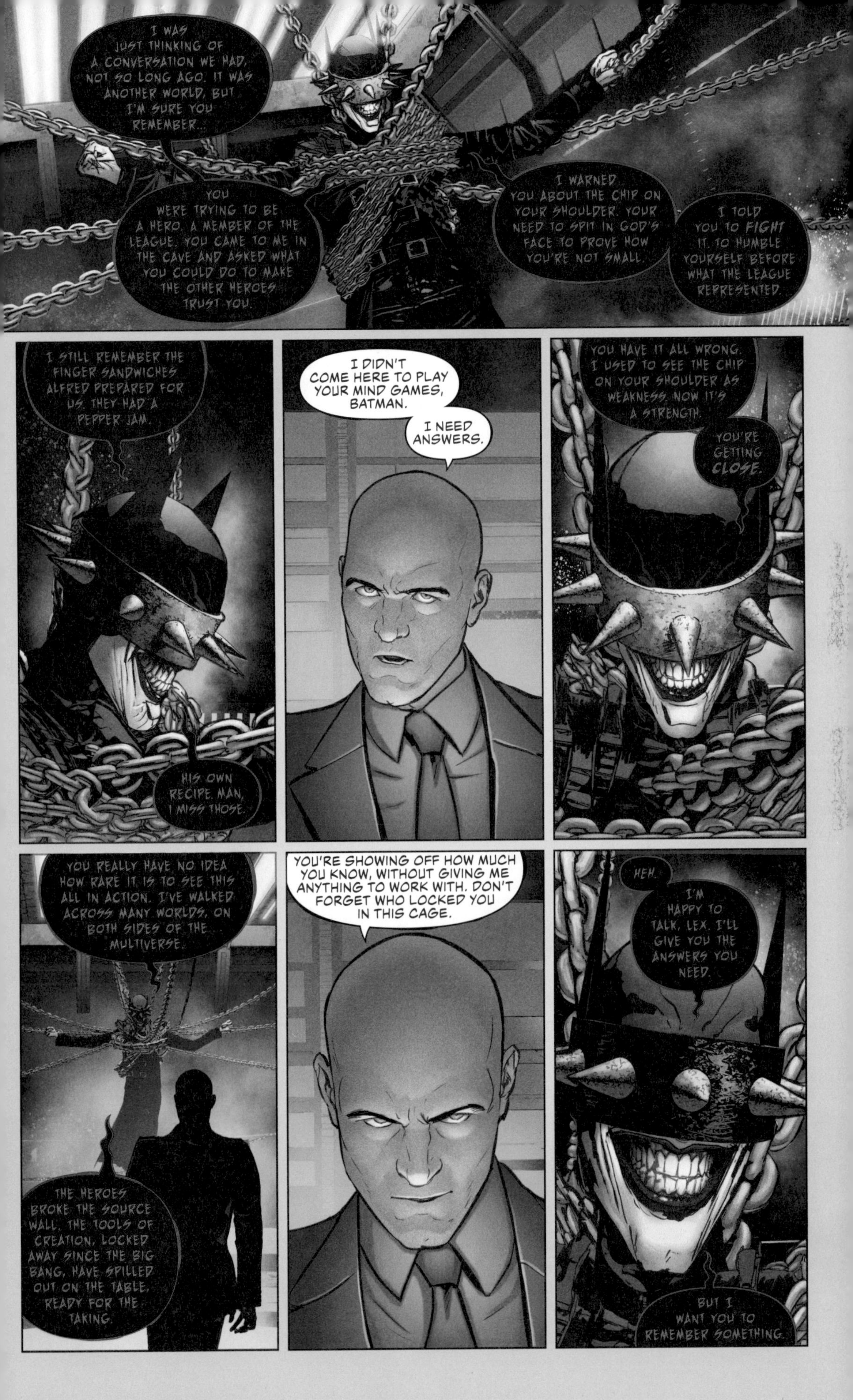
I WAS JUST THINKING OF A CONVERSATION WE HAD, NOT SO LONG AGO. IT WAS ANOTHER WORLD, BUT I'M SURE YOU REMEMBER...
YOU WERE TRYING TO BE A HERO. A MEMBER OF THE LEAGUE. YOU CAME TO ME IN THE CAVE AND ASKED WHAT YOU COULD DO TO MAKE THE OTHER HEROES TRUST YOU.
I WARNED YOU ABOUT THE CHIP ON YOUR SHOULDER. YOUR NEED TO SPIT IN GOD'S FACE TO PROVE HOW YOU'RE NOT SMALL.
I TOLD YOU TO FIGHT IT. TO HUMBLE YOURSELF BEFORE WHAT THE LEAGUE REPRESENTED.
I STILL REMEMBER THE FINGER SANDWICHES ALFRED PREPARED FOR US. THEY HAD A PEPPER JAM.
HIS OWN RECIPE. MAN, I MISS THOSE.
I DIDN'T COME HERE TO PLAY YOUR MIND GAMES, BATMAN.
I NEED ANSWERS.
YOU HAVE IT ALL WRONG. I USED TO SEE THE CHIP ON YOUR SHOULDER AS WEAKNESS. NOW IT'S A STRENGTH.
YOU'RE GETTING CLOSE.
YOU REALLY HAVE NO IDEA HOW RARE IT IS TO SEE THIS ALL IN ACTION. I'VE WALKED ACROSS MANY WORLDS, ON BOTH SIDES OF THE MULTIVERSE.
THE HEROES BROKE THE SOURCE WALL. THE TOOLS OF CREATION, LOCKED AWAY SINCE THE BIG BANG, HAVE SPILLED OUT ON THE TABLE, READY FOR THE TAKING.
YOU'RE SHOWING OFF HOW MUCH YOU KNOW, WITHOUT GIVING ME ANYTHING TO WORK WITH. DON'T FORGET WHO LOCKED YOU IN THIS CAGE.
HEH.
I'M HAPPY TO TALK, LEX. I'LL GIVE YOU THE ANSWERS YOU NEED.
BUT I WANT YOU TO REMEMBER SOMETHING.

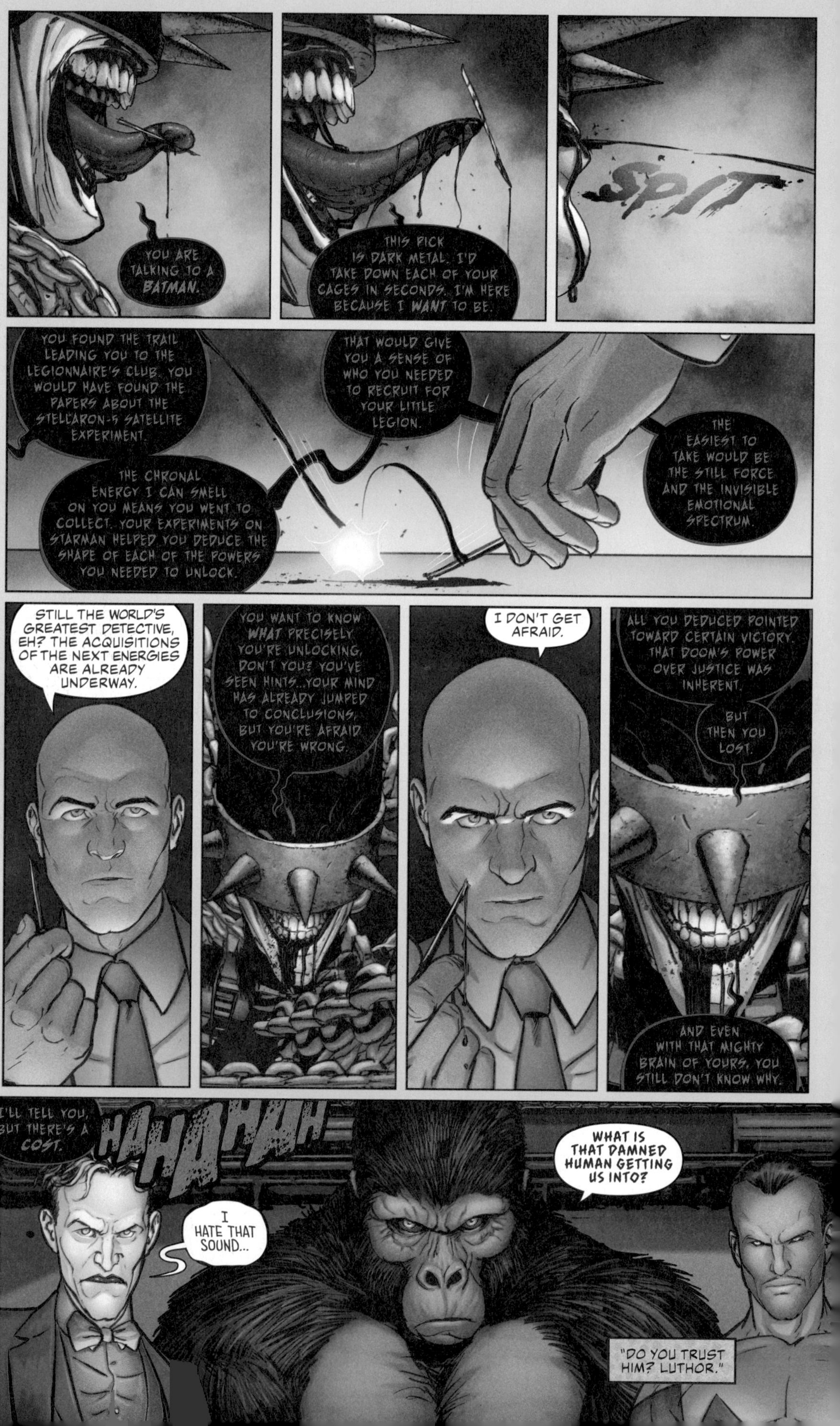

YOU ARE TALKING TO A BATMAN.
THIS PICK IS DARK METAL. I'D TAKE DOWN EACH OF YOUR CAGES IN SECONDS. I'M HERE BECAUSE I WANT TO BE.
SPIT
YOU FOUND THE TRAIL LEADING YOU TO THE LEGIONNAIRE'S CLUB. YOU WOULD HAVE FOUND THE PAPERS ABOUT THE STELLARON-5 SATELLITE EXPERIMENT.
THAT WOULD GIVE YOU A SENSE OF WHO YOU NEEDED TO RECRUIT FOR YOUR LITTLE LEGION.
THE CHRONAL ENERGY I CAN SMELL ON YOU MEANS YOU WENT TO COLLECT. YOUR EXPERIMENTS ON STARMAN HELPED YOU DEDUCE THE SHAPE OF EACH OF THE POWERS YOU NEEDED TO UNLOCK.
THE EASIEST TO TAKE WOULD BE THE STILL FORCE AND THE INVISIBLE EMOTIONAL SPECTRUM.
STILL THE WORLD'S GREATEST DETECTIVE, EH? THE ACQUISITIONS OF THE NEXT ENERGIES ARE ALREADY UNDERWAY.
YOU WANT TO KNOW WHAT PRECISELY YOU'RE UNLOCKING, DON'T YOU? YOU'VE SEEN HINTS...YOUR MIND HAS ALREADY JUMPED TO CONCLUSIONS, BUT YOU'RE AFRAID YOU'RE WRONG.
I DON'T GET AFRAID.
ALL YOU DEDUCED POINTED TOWARD CERTAIN VICTORY. THAT DOOM'S POWER OVER JUSTICE WAS INHERENT.
BUT THEN YOU LOST.
AND EVEN WITH THAT MIGHTY BRAIN OF YOURS, YOU STILL DON'T KNOW WHY.
I'LL TELL YOU, BUT THERE'S A COST.
HAHAHAHH
I HATE THAT SOUND...
WHAT IS THAT DAMNED HUMAN GETTING US INTO?
"DO YOU TRUST HIM? LUTHOR."

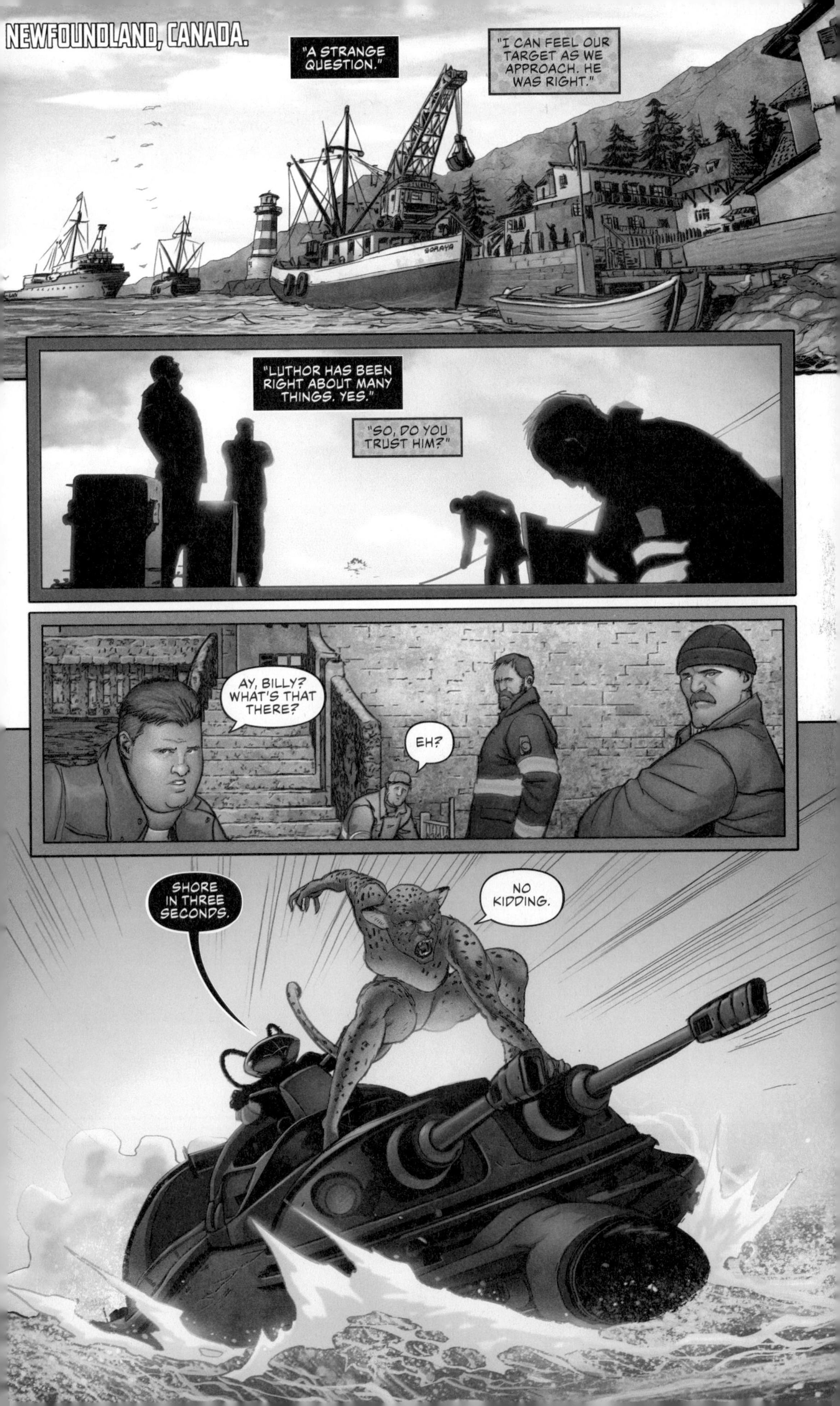
NEWFOUNDLAND, CANADA.
"A STRANGE QUESTION."
"I CAN FEEL OUR TARGET AS WE APPROACH. HE WAS RIGHT."
"LUTHOR HAS BEEN RIGHT ABOUT MANY THINGS. YES."
"SO, DO YOU TRUST HIM?"
AY, BILLY? WHAT'S THAT THERE?
EH?
SHORE IN THREE SECONDS.
NO KIDDING.

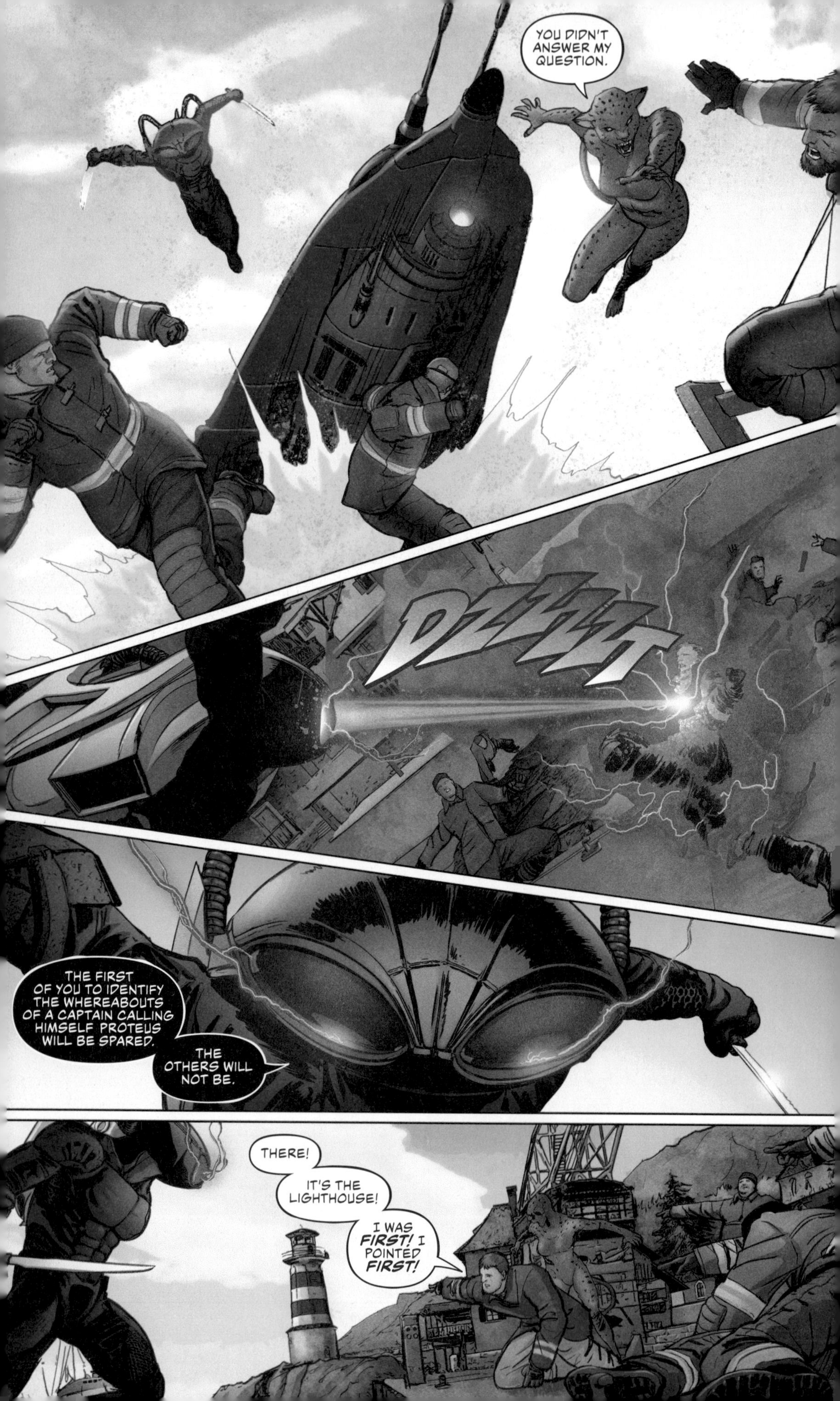
YOU DIDN'T ANSWER MY QUESTION.
DZZZT
THE FIRST OF YOU TO IDENTIFY THE WHEREABOUTS OF A CAPTAIN CALLING HIMSELF PROTEUS WILL BE SPARED.
THE OTHERS WILL NOT BE.
THERE!
IT'S THE LIGHTHOUSE!
I WAS FIRST! I POINTED FIRST!

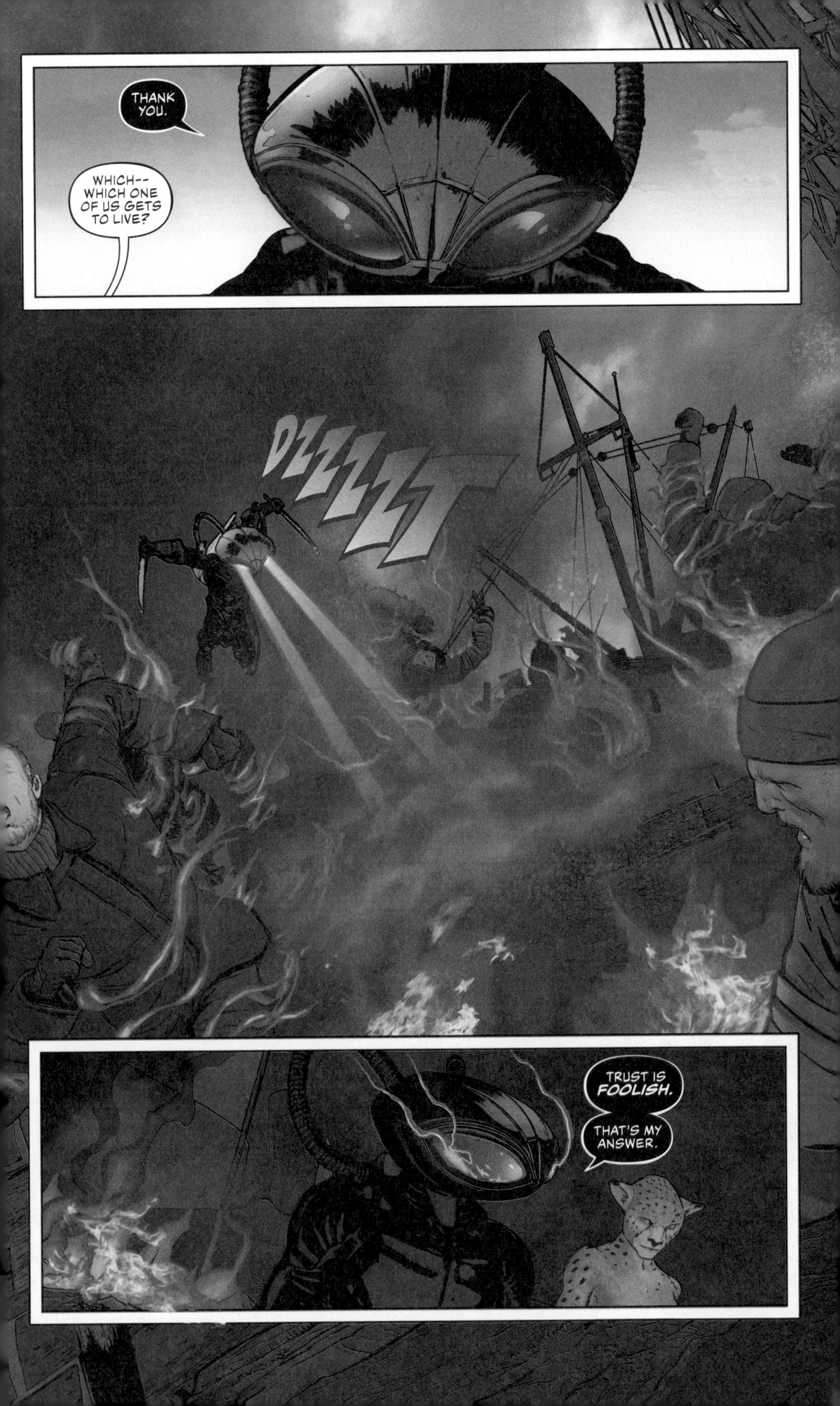
THANK YOU.
WHICH-- WHICH ONE OF US GETS TO LIVE?
DZZZZT
TRUST IS FOOLISH.
THAT'S MY ANSWER.

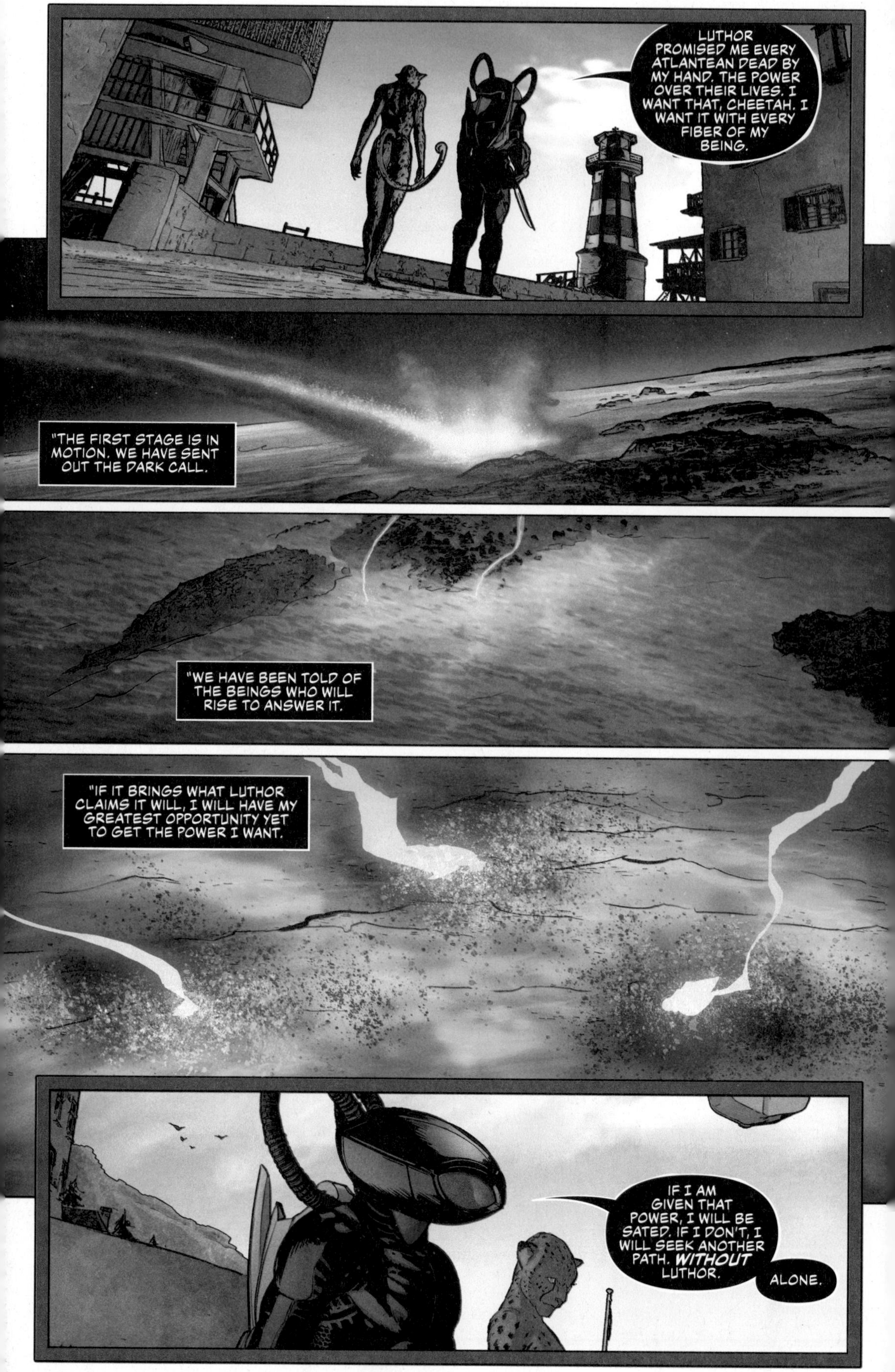
LUTHOR PROMISED ME EVERY ATLANTEAN DEAD BY MY HAND. THE POWER OVER THEIR LIVES. I WANT THAT, CHEETAH. I WANT IT WITH EVERY FIBER OF MY BEING.
"THE FIRST STAGE IS IN MOTION. WE HAVE SENT OUT THE DARK CALL.
"WE HAVE BEEN TOLD OF THE BEINGS WHO WILL RISE TO ANSWER IT.
"IF IT BRINGS WHAT LUTHOR CLAIMS IT WILL, I WILL HAVE MY GREATEST OPPORTUNITY YET TO GET THE POWER I WANT.
IF I AM GIVEN THAT POWER, I WILL BE SATED. IF I DON'T, I WILL SEEK ANOTHER PATH. *WITHOUT* LUTHOR.
ALONE.

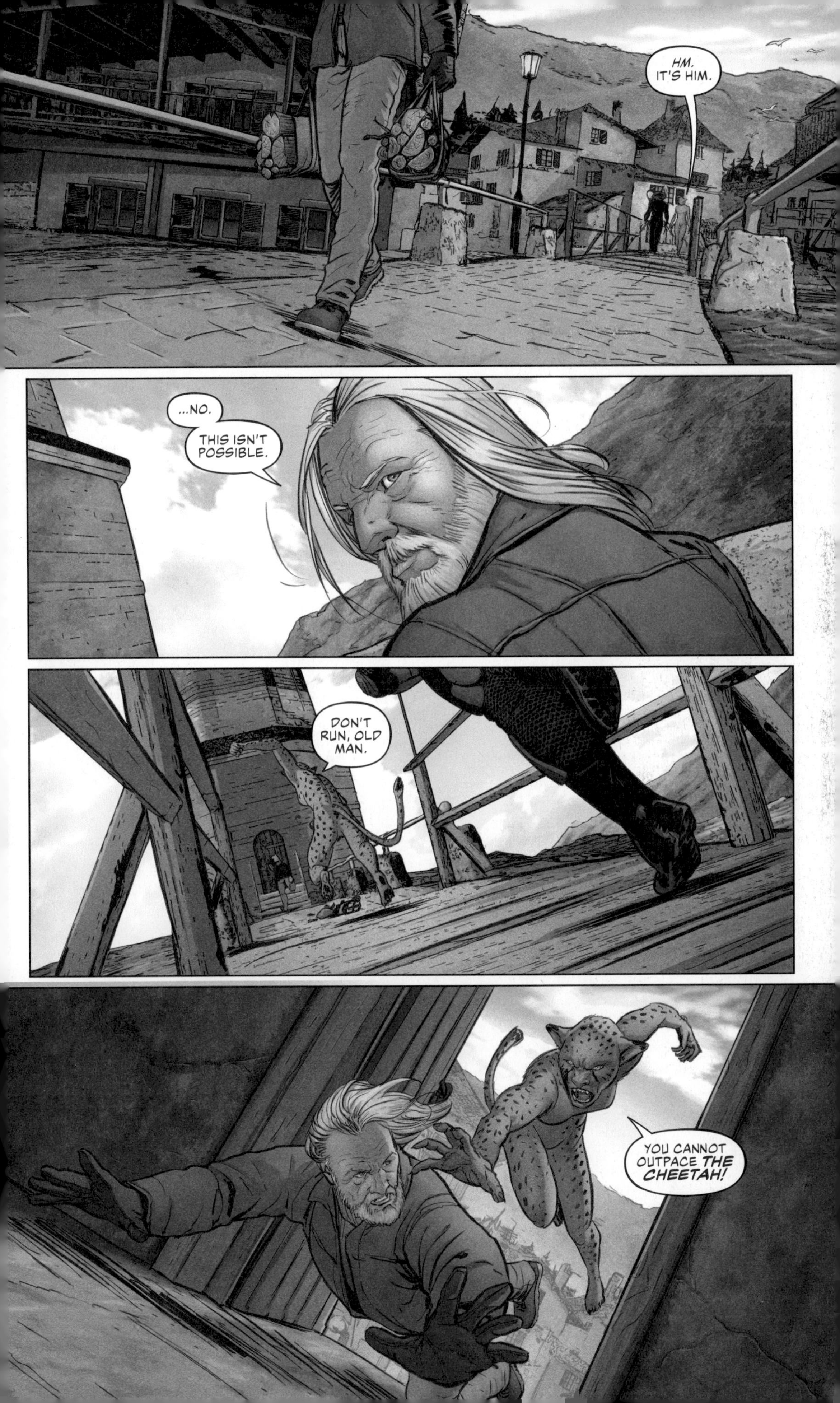
HM. IT'S HIM.
...NO.
THIS ISN'T POSSIBLE.
DON'T RUN, OLD MAN.
YOU CANNOT OUTPACE THE CHEETAH!

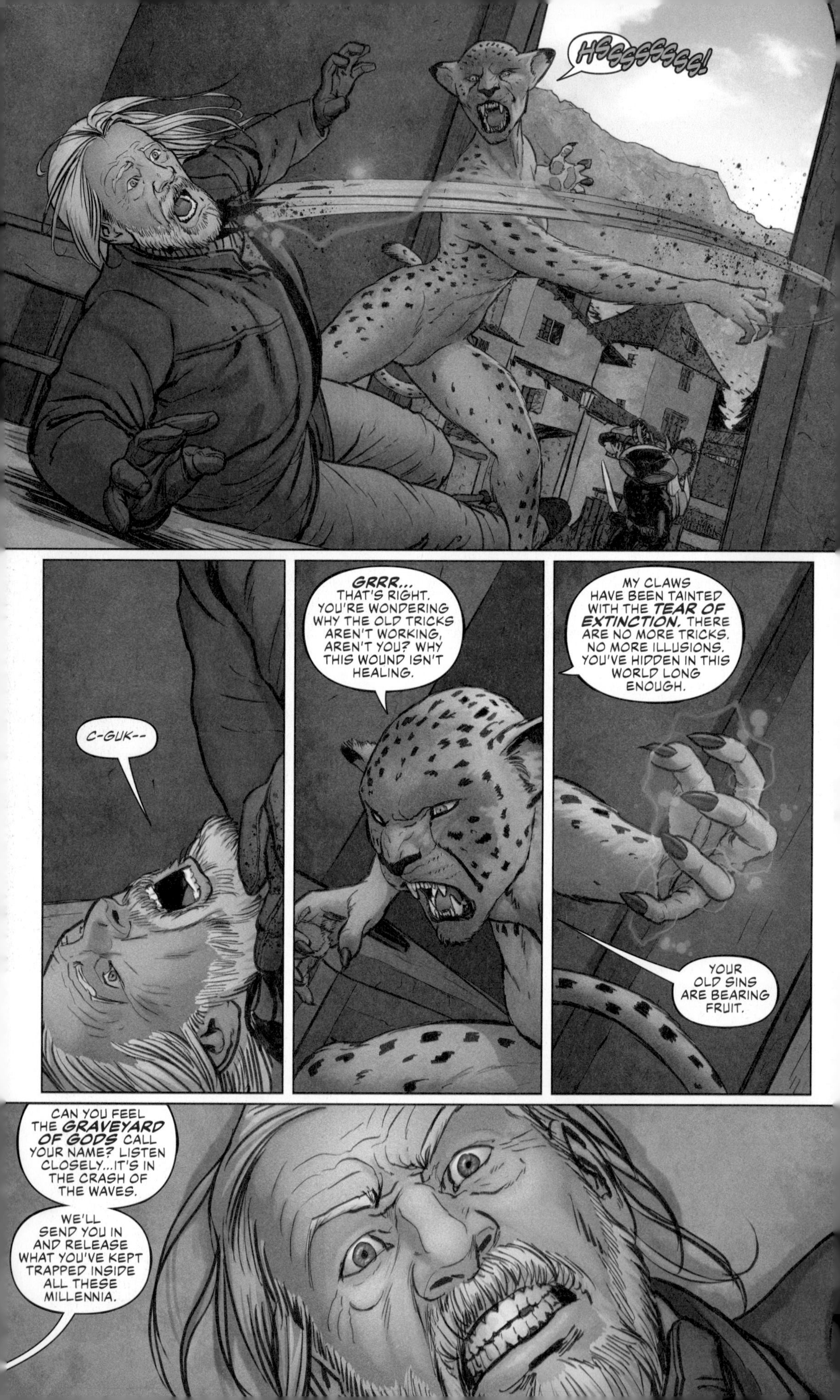
HSSSSSSSS!
C-GUK--
GRRR... THAT'S RIGHT. YOU'RE WONDERING WHY THE OLD TRICKS AREN'T WORKING, AREN'T YOU? WHY THIS WOUND ISN'T HEALING.
MY CLAWS HAVE BEEN TAINTED WITH THE TEAR OF EXTINCTION. THERE ARE NO MORE TRICKS. NO MORE ILLUSIONS. YOU'VE HIDDEN IN THIS WORLD LONG ENOUGH.
YOUR OLD SINS ARE BEARING FRUIT.
CAN YOU FEEL THE GRAVEYARD OF GODS CALL YOUR NAME? LISTEN CLOSELY...IT'S IN THE CRASH OF THE WAVES.
WE'LL SEND YOU IN AND RELEASE WHAT YOU'VE KEPT TRAPPED INSIDE ALL THESE MILLENNIA.

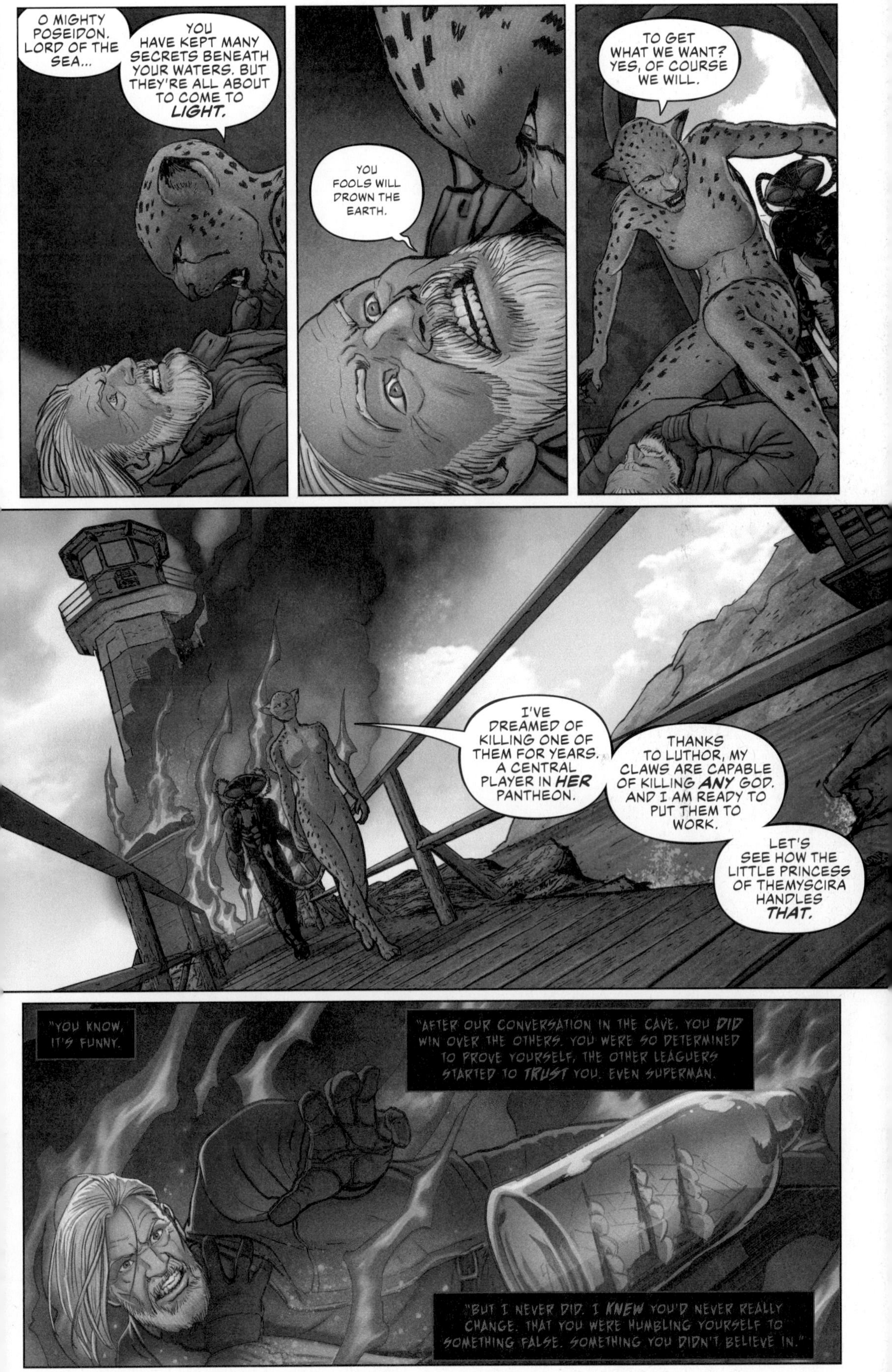
O MIGHTY POSEIDON. LORD OF THE SEA...
YOU HAVE KEPT MANY SECRETS BENEATH YOUR WATERS. BUT THEY'RE ALL ABOUT TO COME TO LIGHT.
YOU FOOLS WILL DROWN THE EARTH.
TO GET WHAT WE WANT? YES, OF COURSE WE WILL.
I'VE DREAMED OF KILLING ONE OF THEM FOR YEARS. A CENTRAL PLAYER IN HER PANTHEON.
THANKS TO LUTHOR, MY CLAWS ARE CAPABLE OF KILLING ANY GOD. AND I AM READY TO PUT THEM TO WORK.
LET'S SEE HOW THE LITTLE PRINCESS OF THEMYSCIRA HANDLES THAT.
"YOU KNOW, IT'S FUNNY.
"AFTER OUR CONVERSATION IN THE CAVE, YOU DID WIN OVER THE OTHERS. YOU WERE SO DETERMINED TO PROVE YOURSELF, THE OTHER LEAGUERS STARTED TO TRUST YOU. EVEN SUPERMAN.
"BUT I NEVER DID. I KNEW YOU'D NEVER REALLY CHANGE. THAT YOU WERE HUMBLING YOURSELF TO SOMETHING FALSE. SOMETHING YOU DIDN'T BELIEVE IN."

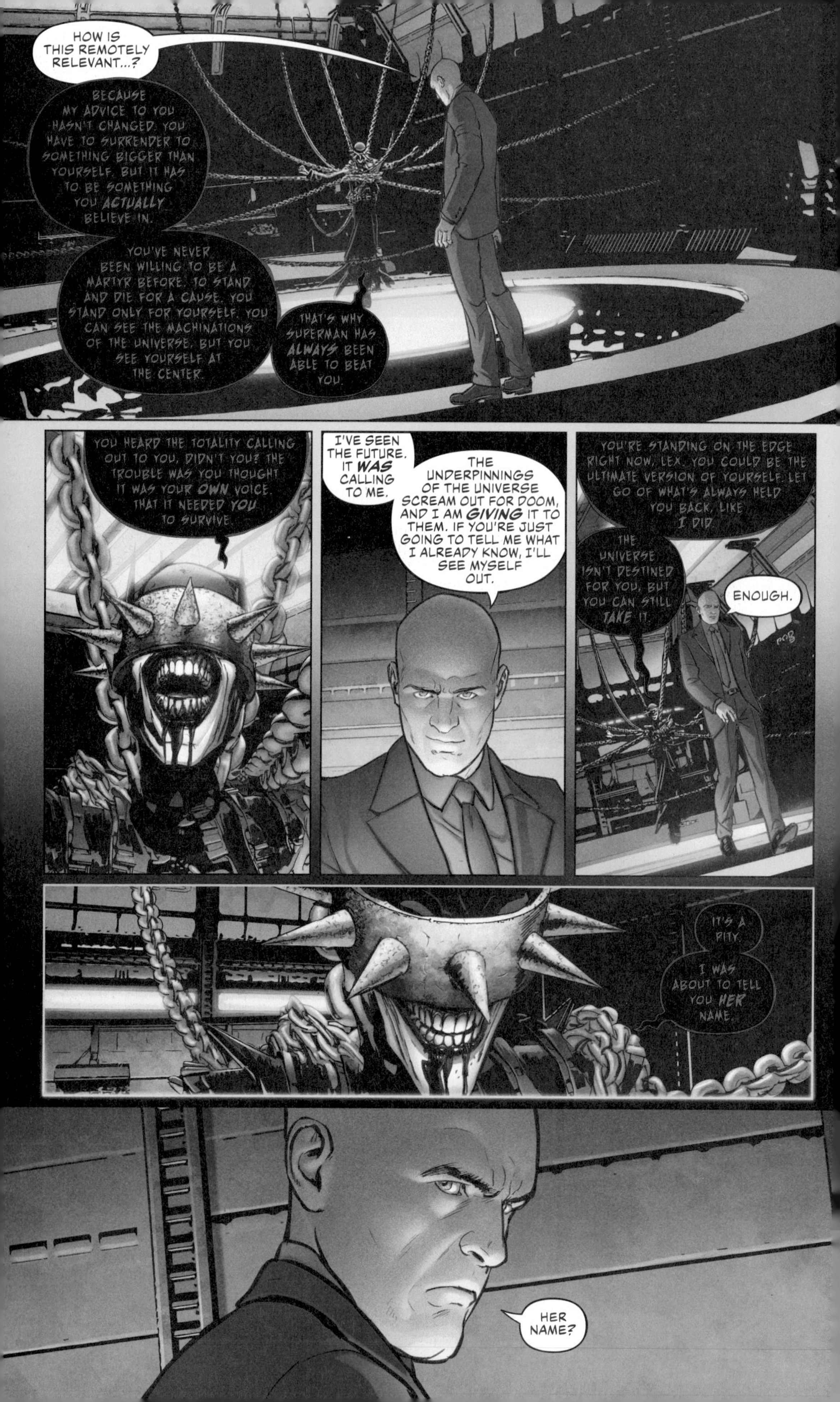

HOW IS THIS REMOTELY RELEVANT...?
BECAUSE MY ADVICE TO YOU HASN'T CHANGED. YOU HAVE TO SURRENDER TO SOMETHING BIGGER THAN YOURSELF. BUT IT HAS TO BE SOMETHING YOU ACTUALLY BELIEVE IN.
YOU'VE NEVER BEEN WILLING TO BE A MARTYR BEFORE. TO STAND AND DIE FOR A CAUSE. YOU STAND ONLY FOR YOURSELF. YOU CAN SEE THE MACHINATIONS OF THE UNIVERSE, BUT YOU SEE YOURSELF AT THE CENTER.
THAT'S WHY SUPERMAN HAS ALWAYS BEEN ABLE TO BEAT YOU.
YOU HEARD THE TOTALITY CALLING OUT TO YOU, DIDN'T YOU? THE TROUBLE WAS YOU THOUGHT IT WAS YOUR OWN VOICE. THAT IT NEEDED YOU TO SURVIVE.
I'VE SEEN THE FUTURE. IT WAS CALLING TO ME.
THE UNDERPINNINGS OF THE UNIVERSE SCREAM OUT FOR DOOM, AND I AM GIVING IT TO THEM. IF YOU'RE JUST GOING TO TELL ME WHAT I ALREADY KNOW, I'LL SEE MYSELF OUT.
YOU'RE STANDING ON THE EDGE RIGHT NOW, LEX. YOU COULD BE THE ULTIMATE VERSION OF YOURSELF. LET GO OF WHAT'S ALWAYS HELD YOU BACK, LIKE I DID.
THE UNIVERSE ISN'T DESTINED FOR YOU, BUT YOU CAN STILL TAKE IT.
ENOUGH.
IT'S A PITY.
I WAS ABOUT TO TELL YOU HER NAME.
HER NAME?

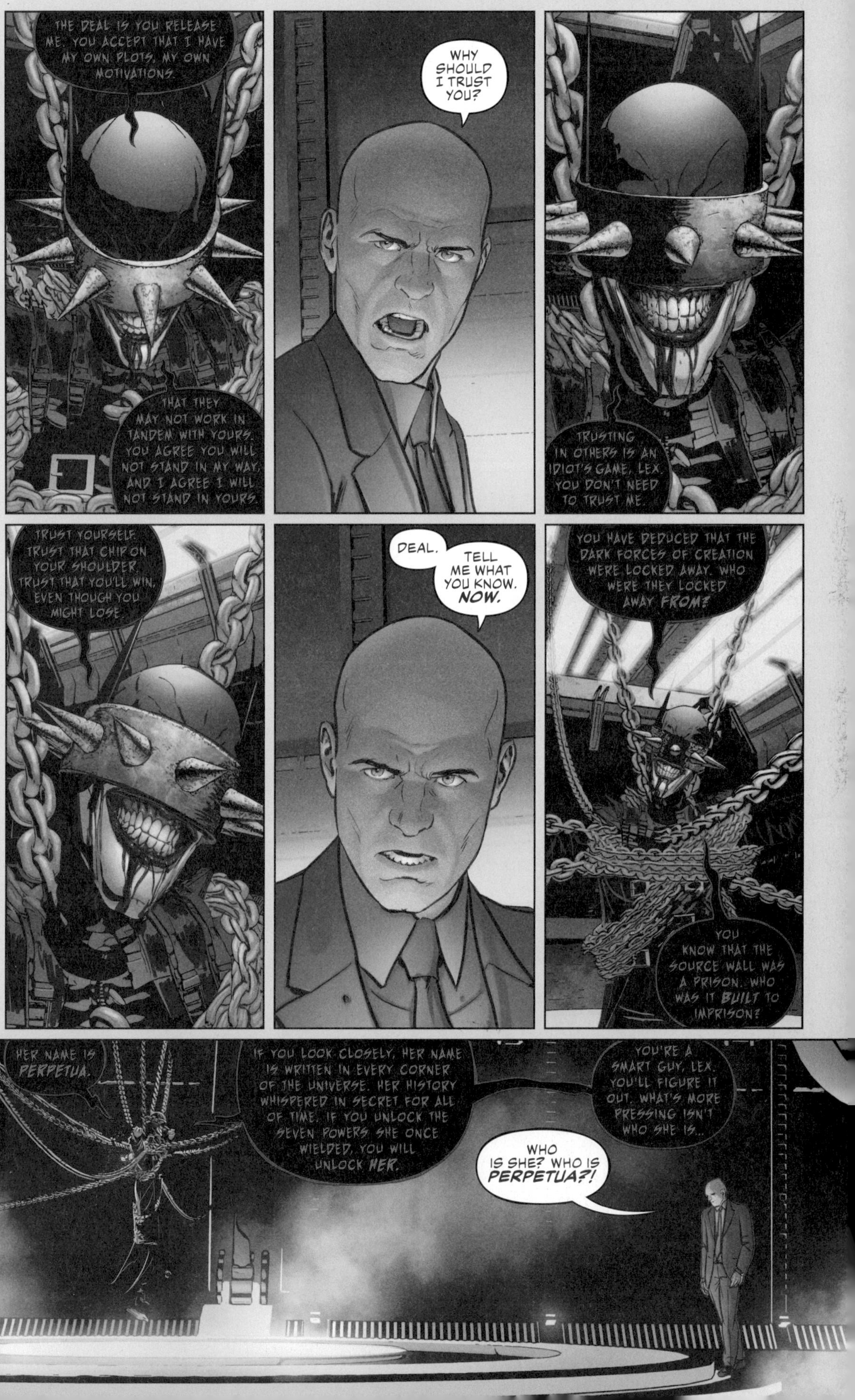

THE DEAL IS YOU RELEASE ME. YOU ACCEPT THAT I HAVE MY OWN PLOTS, MY OWN MOTIVATIONS.
THAT THEY MAY NOT WORK IN TANDEM WITH YOURS. YOU AGREE YOU WILL NOT STAND IN MY WAY, AND I AGREE I WILL NOT STAND IN YOURS.
WHY SHOULD I TRUST YOU?
TRUSTING IN OTHERS IS AN IDIOT'S GAME, LEX. YOU DON'T NEED TO TRUST ME.
TRUST YOURSELF. TRUST THAT CHIP ON YOUR SHOULDER. TRUST THAT YOU'LL WIN, EVEN THOUGH YOU MIGHT LOSE.
DEAL.
TELL ME WHAT YOU KNOW. NOW.
YOU HAVE DEDUCED THAT THE DARK FORCES OF CREATION WERE LOCKED AWAY. WHO WERE THEY LOCKED AWAY FROM?
YOU KNOW THAT THE SOURCE WALL WAS A PRISON. WHO WAS IT BUILT TO IMPRISON?
HER NAME IS PERPETUA.
IF YOU LOOK CLOSELY, HER NAME IS WRITTEN IN EVERY CORNER OF THE UNIVERSE. HER HISTORY WHISPERED IN SECRET FOR ALL OF TIME. IF YOU UNLOCK THE SEVEN POWERS SHE ONCE WIELDED, YOU WILL UNLOCK HER.
WHO IS SHE? WHO IS PERPETUA?!
YOU'RE A SMART GUY, LEX. YOU'LL FIGURE IT OUT. WHAT'S MORE PRESSING ISN'T WHO SHE IS...

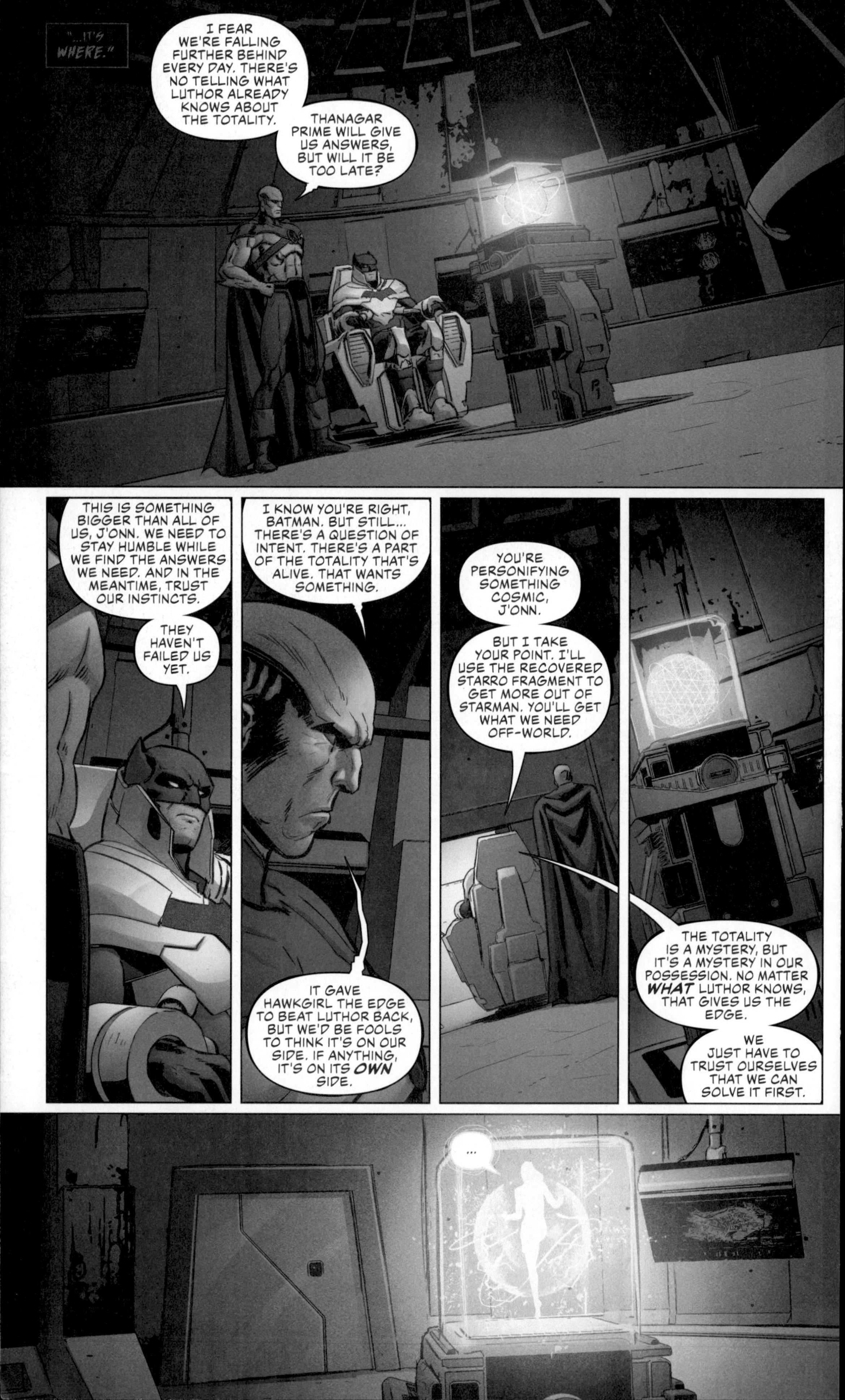
"...IT'S WHERE."
I FEAR WE'RE FALLING FURTHER BEHIND EVERY DAY. THERE'S NO TELLING WHAT LUTHOR ALREADY KNOWS ABOUT THE TOTALITY.
THANAGAR PRIME WILL GIVE US ANSWERS, BUT WILL IT BE TOO LATE?
THIS IS SOMETHING BIGGER THAN ALL OF US, J'ONN. WE NEED TO STAY HUMBLE WHILE WE FIND THE ANSWERS WE NEED. AND IN THE MEANTIME, TRUST OUR INSTINCTS.
THEY HAVEN'T FAILED US YET.
I KNOW YOU'RE RIGHT, BATMAN. BUT STILL... THERE'S A QUESTION OF INTENT. THERE'S A PART OF THE TOTALITY THAT'S ALIVE. THAT WANTS SOMETHING.
IT GAVE HAWKGIRL THE EDGE TO BEAT LUTHOR BACK, BUT WE'D BE FOOLS TO THINK IT'S ON OUR SIDE. IF ANYTHING, IT'S ON ITS OWN SIDE.
YOU'RE PERSONIFYING SOMETHING COSMIC, J'ONN.
BUT I TAKE YOUR POINT. I'LL USE THE RECOVERED STARRO FRAGMENT TO GET MORE OUT OF STARMAN. YOU'LL GET WHAT WE NEED OFF-WORLD.
THE TOTALITY IS A MYSTERY, BUT IT'S A MYSTERY IN OUR POSSESSION. NO MATTER WHAT LUTHOR KNOWS, THAT GIVES US THE EDGE.
WE JUST HAVE TO TRUST OURSELVES THAT WE CAN SOLVE IT FIRST.
...

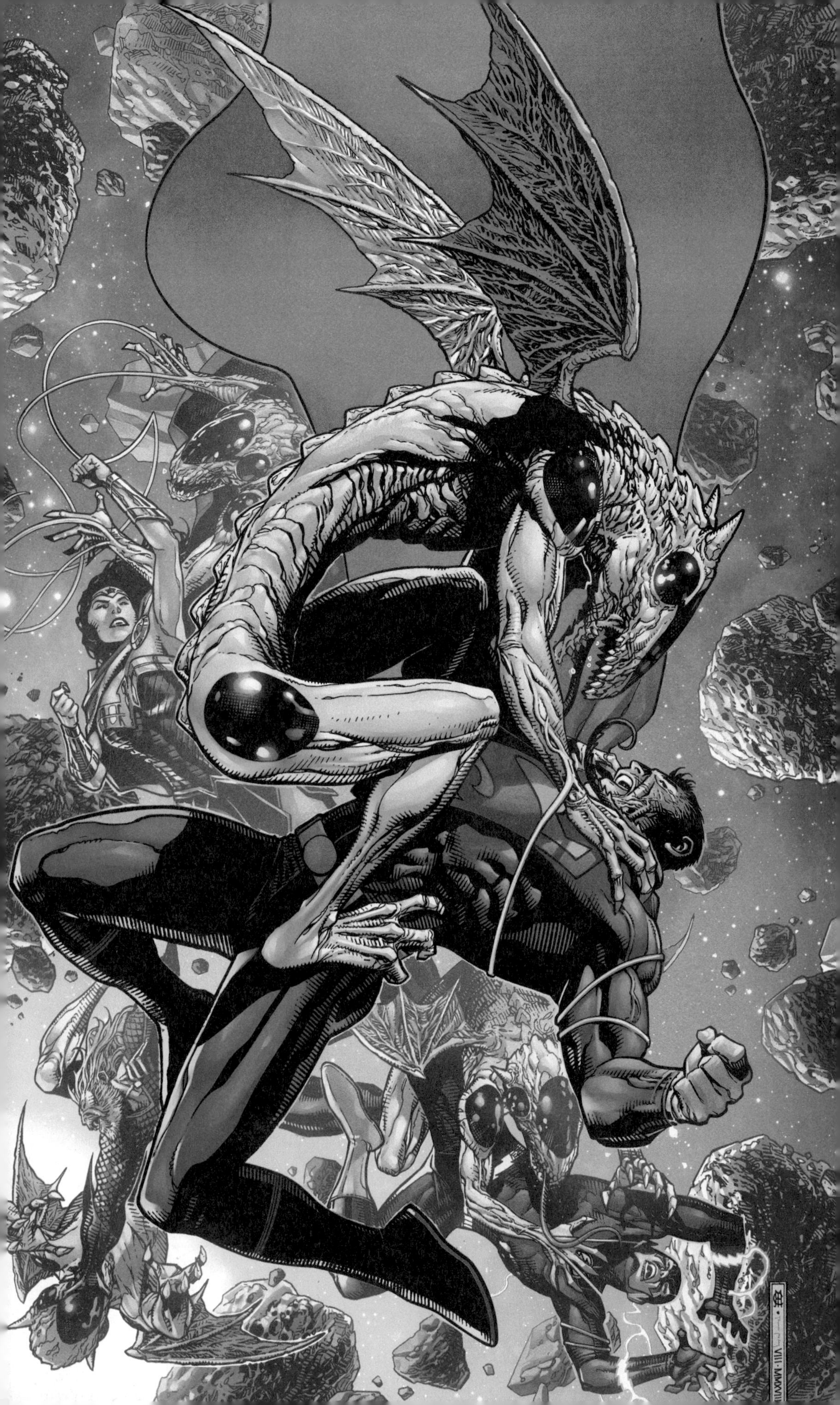

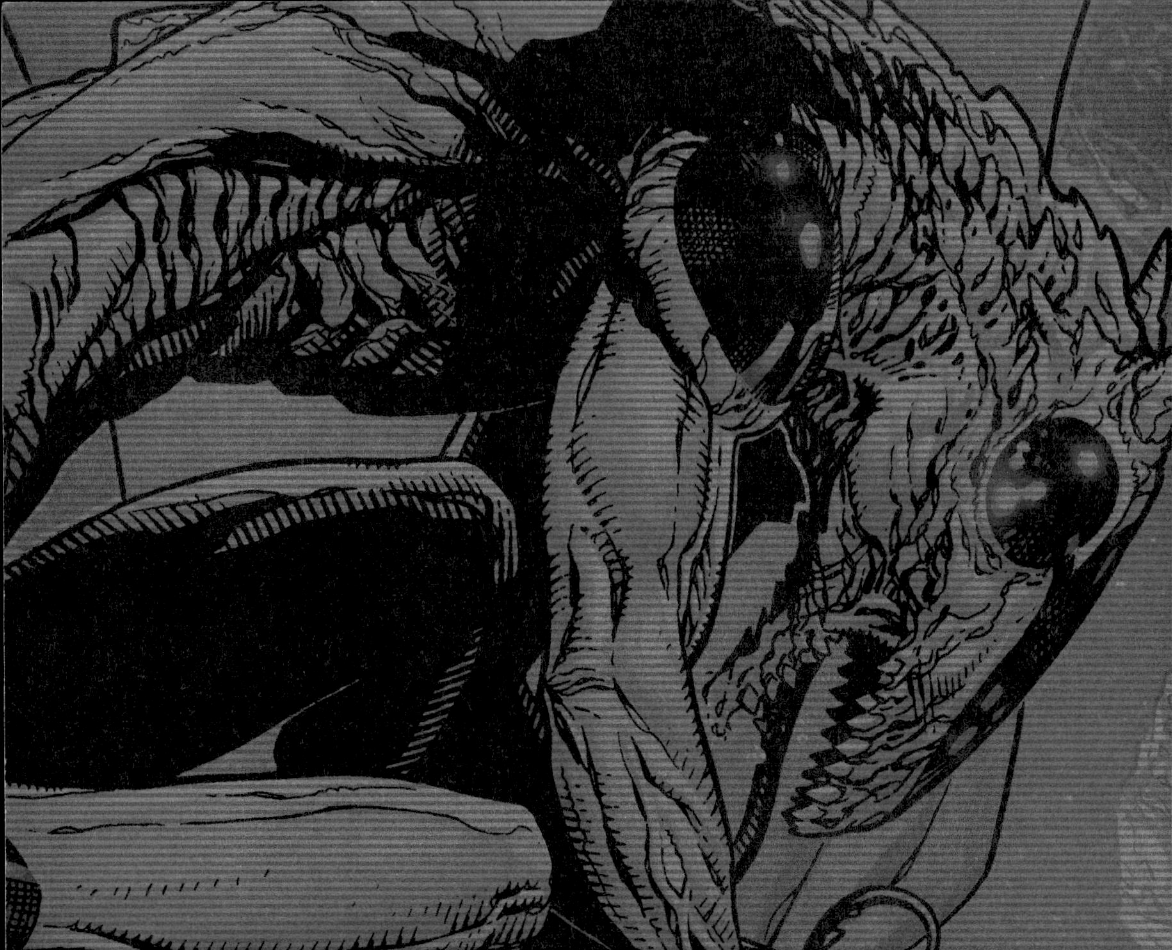

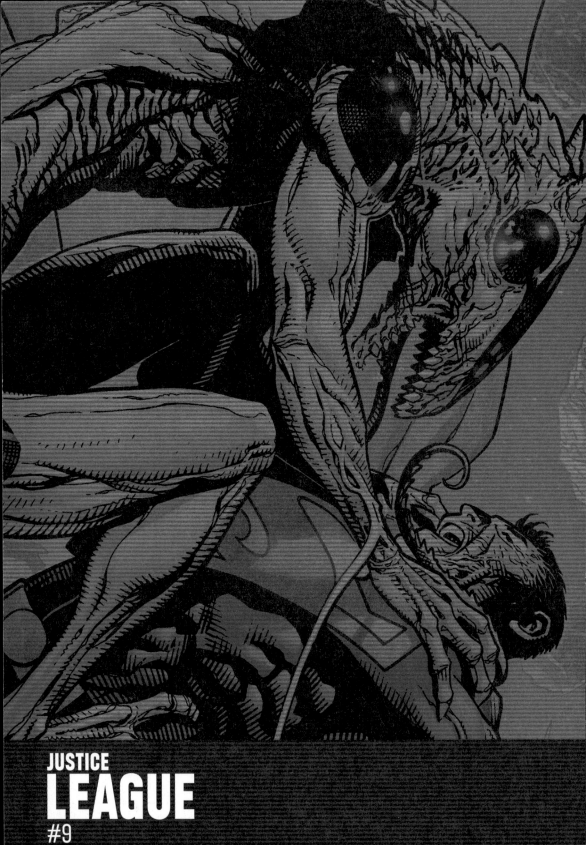

JUSTICE LEAGUE
#9

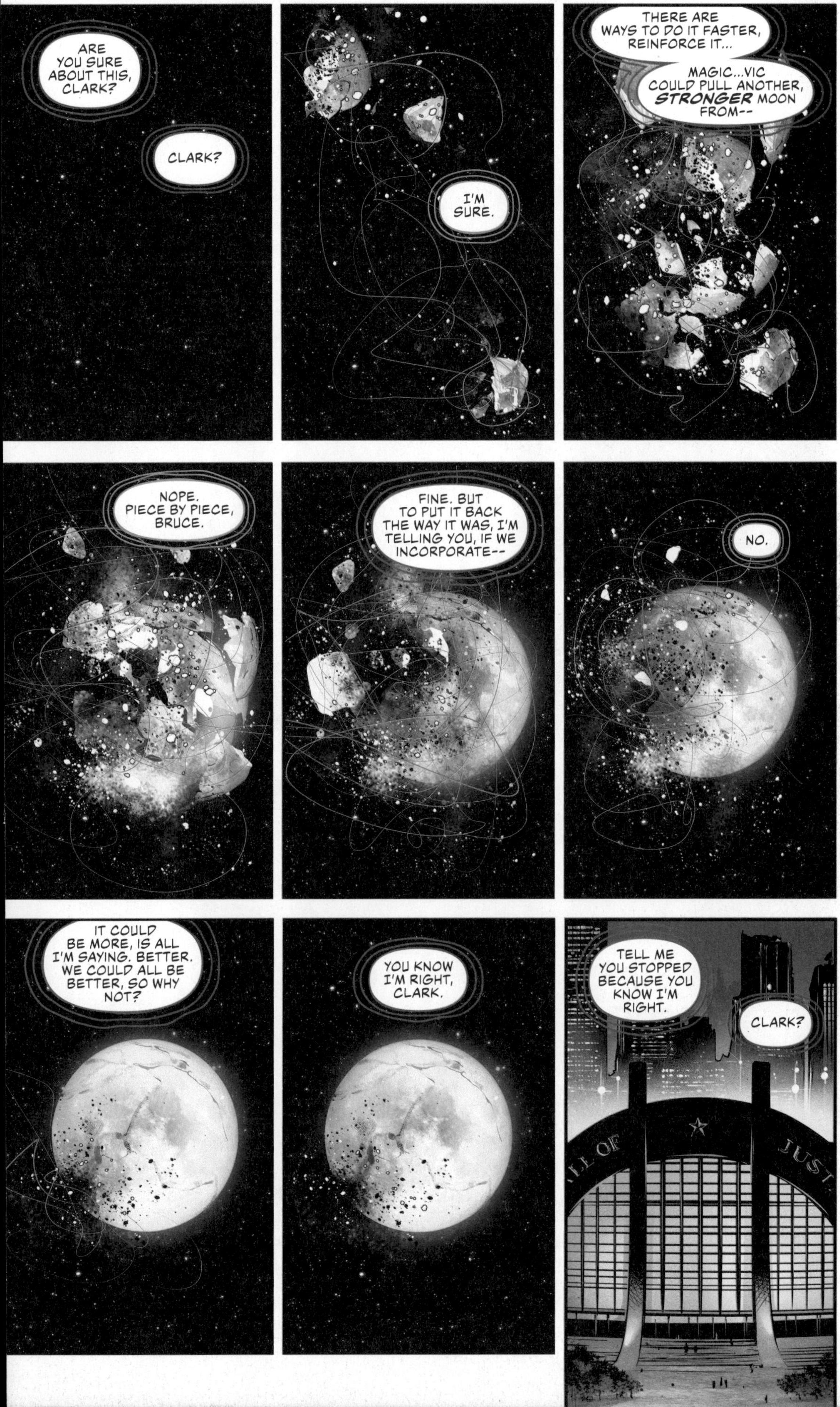
ARE YOU SURE ABOUT THIS, CLARK?
CLARK?
I'M SURE.
THERE ARE WAYS TO DO IT FASTER, REINFORCE IT...
MAGIC...VIC COULD PULL ANOTHER, STRONGER MOON FROM--
NOPE. PIECE BY PIECE, BRUCE.
FINE. BUT TO PUT IT BACK THE WAY IT WAS, I'M TELLING YOU, IF WE INCORPORATE--
NO.
IT COULD BE MORE, IS ALL I'M SAYING. BETTER. WE COULD ALL BE BETTER, SO WHY NOT?
YOU KNOW I'M RIGHT, CLARK.
TELL ME YOU STOPPED BECAUSE YOU KNOW I'M RIGHT.
CLARK?

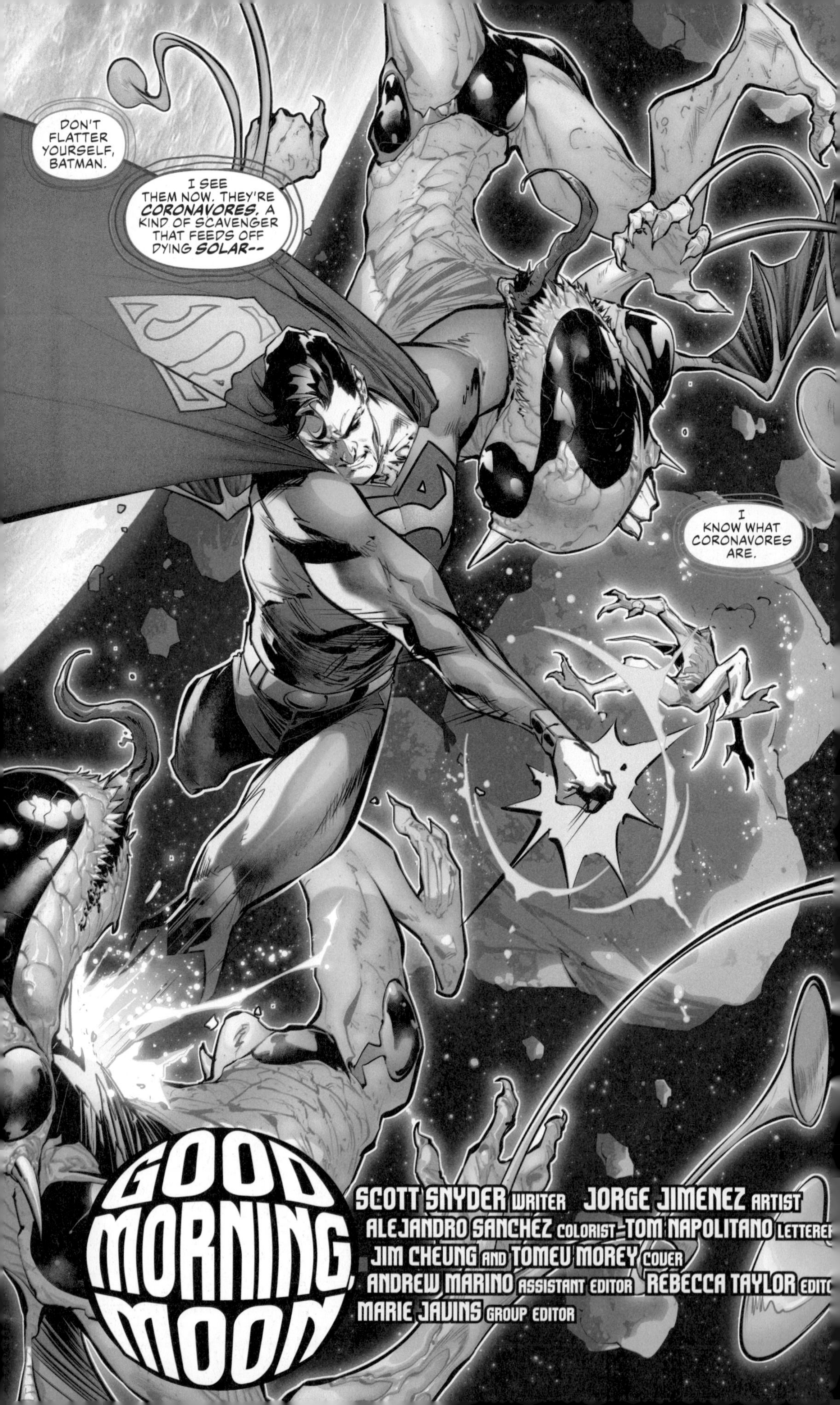
DON'T FLATTER YOURSELF, BATMAN.
I SEE THEM NOW. THEY'RE CORONAVORES, A KIND OF SCAVENGER THAT FEEDS OFF DYING SOLAR--
I KNOW WHAT CORONAVORES ARE.
GOOD MORNING, MOON
SCOTT SNYDER WRITER JORGE JIMENEZ ARTIST
ALEJANDRO SANCHEZ COLORIST TOM NAPOLITANO LETTERER
JIM CHEUNG AND TOMEU MOREY COVER
ANDREW MARINO ASSISTANT EDITOR REBECCA TAYLOR EDITOR
MARIE JAVINS GROUP EDITOR

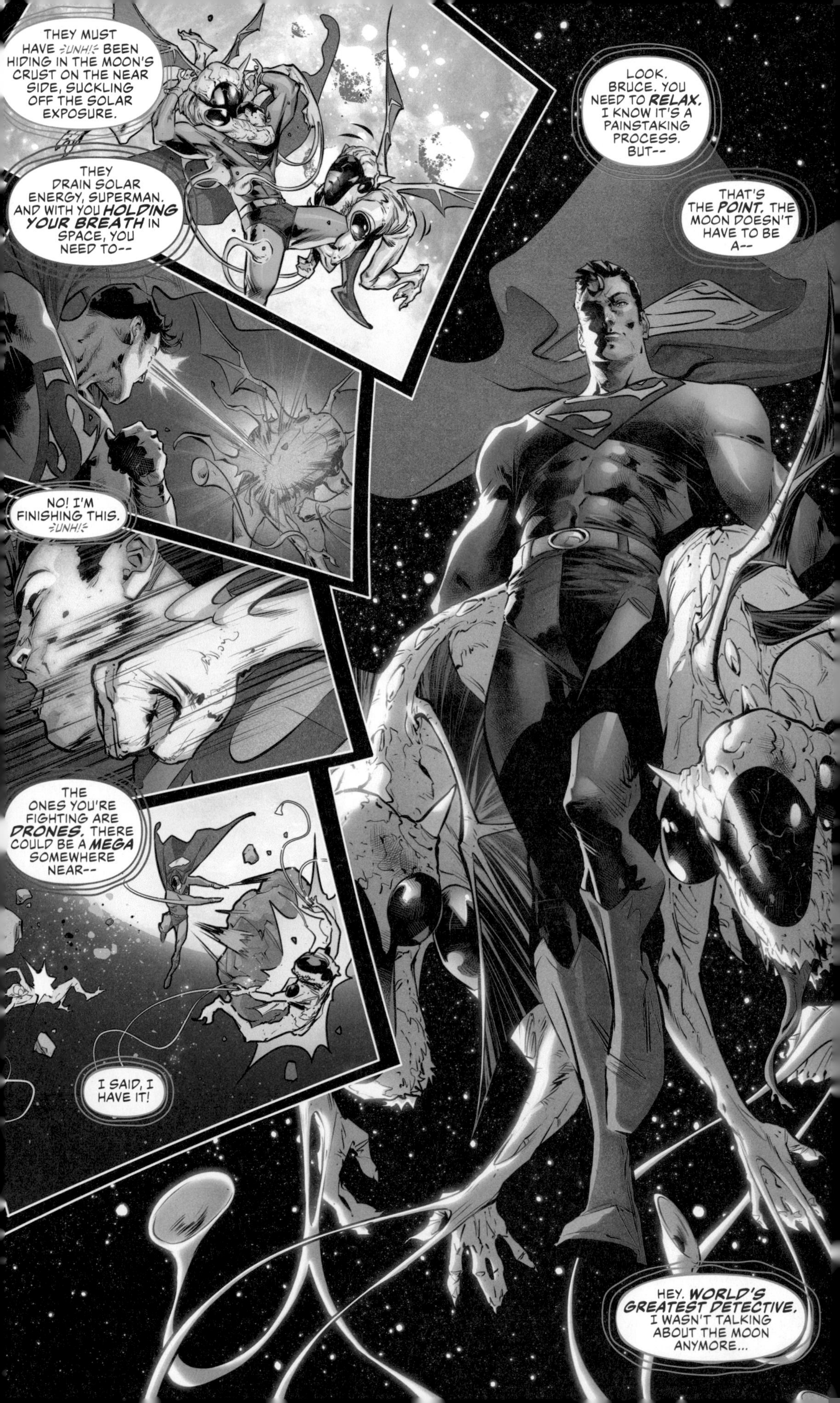

THEY MUST HAVE -UNH!- BEEN HIDING IN THE MOON'S CRUST ON THE NEAR SIDE, SUCKLING OFF THE SOLAR EXPOSURE.
THEY DRAIN SOLAR ENERGY, SUPERMAN. AND WITH YOU HOLDING YOUR BREATH IN SPACE, YOU NEED TO--
NO! I'M FINISHING THIS. -UNH!-
THE ONES YOU'RE FIGHTING ARE DRONES. THERE COULD BE A MEGA SOMEWHERE NEAR--
I SAID, I HAVE IT!
LOOK. BRUCE. YOU NEED TO RELAX. I KNOW IT'S A PAINSTAKING PROCESS. BUT--
THAT'S THE POINT. THE MOON DOESN'T HAVE TO BE A--
HEY. WORLD'S GREATEST DETECTIVE. I WASN'T TALKING ABOUT THE MOON ANYMORE...

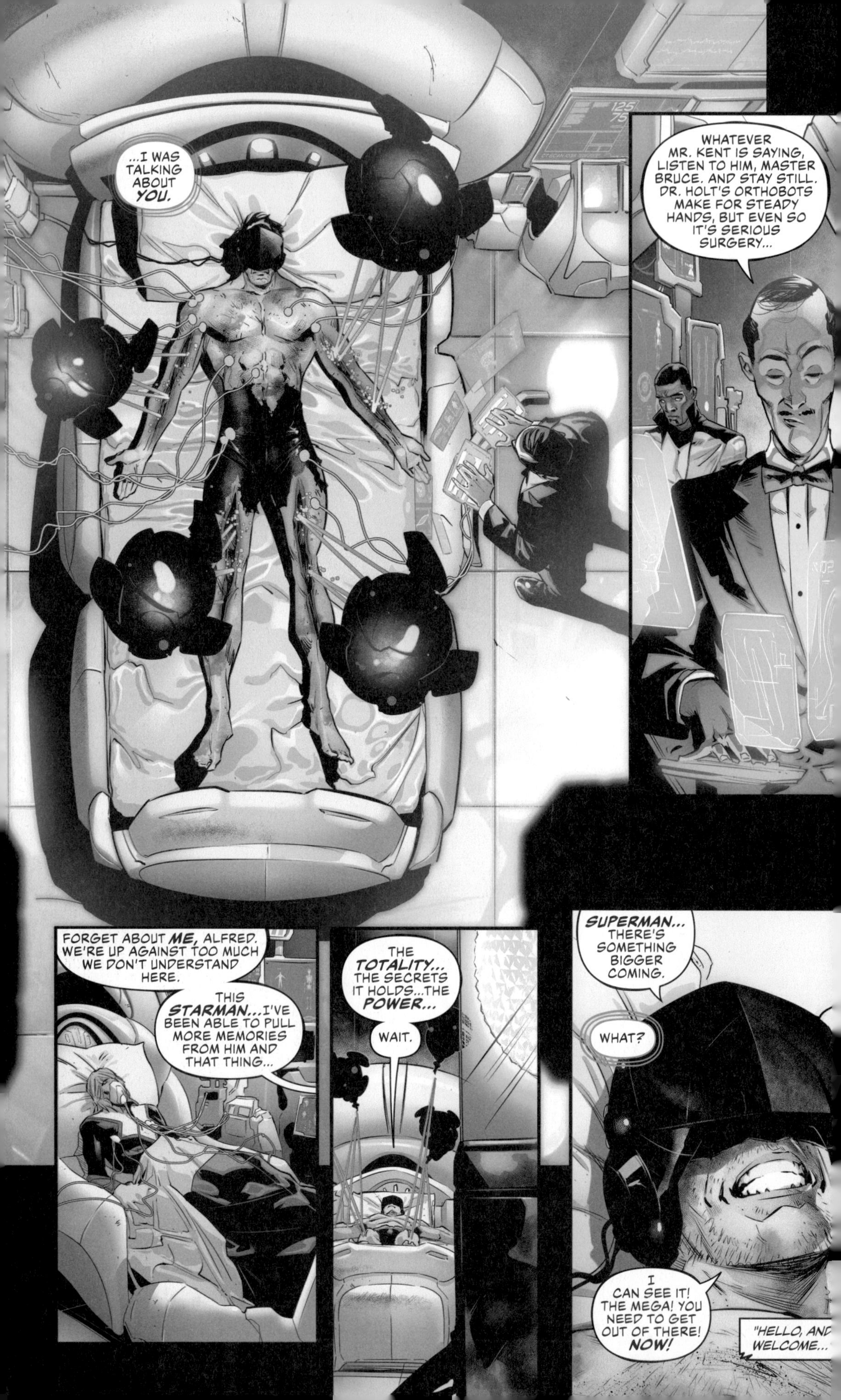

...I WAS TALKING ABOUT YOU.
125
75
WHATEVER MR. KENT IS SAYING, LISTEN TO HIM, MASTER BRUCE. AND STAY STILL. DR. HOLT'S ORTHOBOTS MAKE FOR STEADY HANDS, BUT EVEN SO IT'S SERIOUS SURGERY...
FORGET ABOUT ME, ALFRED. WE'RE UP AGAINST TOO MUCH WE DON'T UNDERSTAND HERE.
THIS STARMAN...I'VE BEEN ABLE TO PULL MORE MEMORIES FROM HIM AND THAT THING...
THE TOTALITY... THE SECRETS IT HOLDS...THE POWER...
WAIT.
SUPERMAN... THERE'S SOMETHING BIGGER COMING.
WHAT?
I CAN SEE IT! THE MEGA! YOU NEED TO GET OUT OF THERE! NOW!
"HELLO, AND WELCOME...

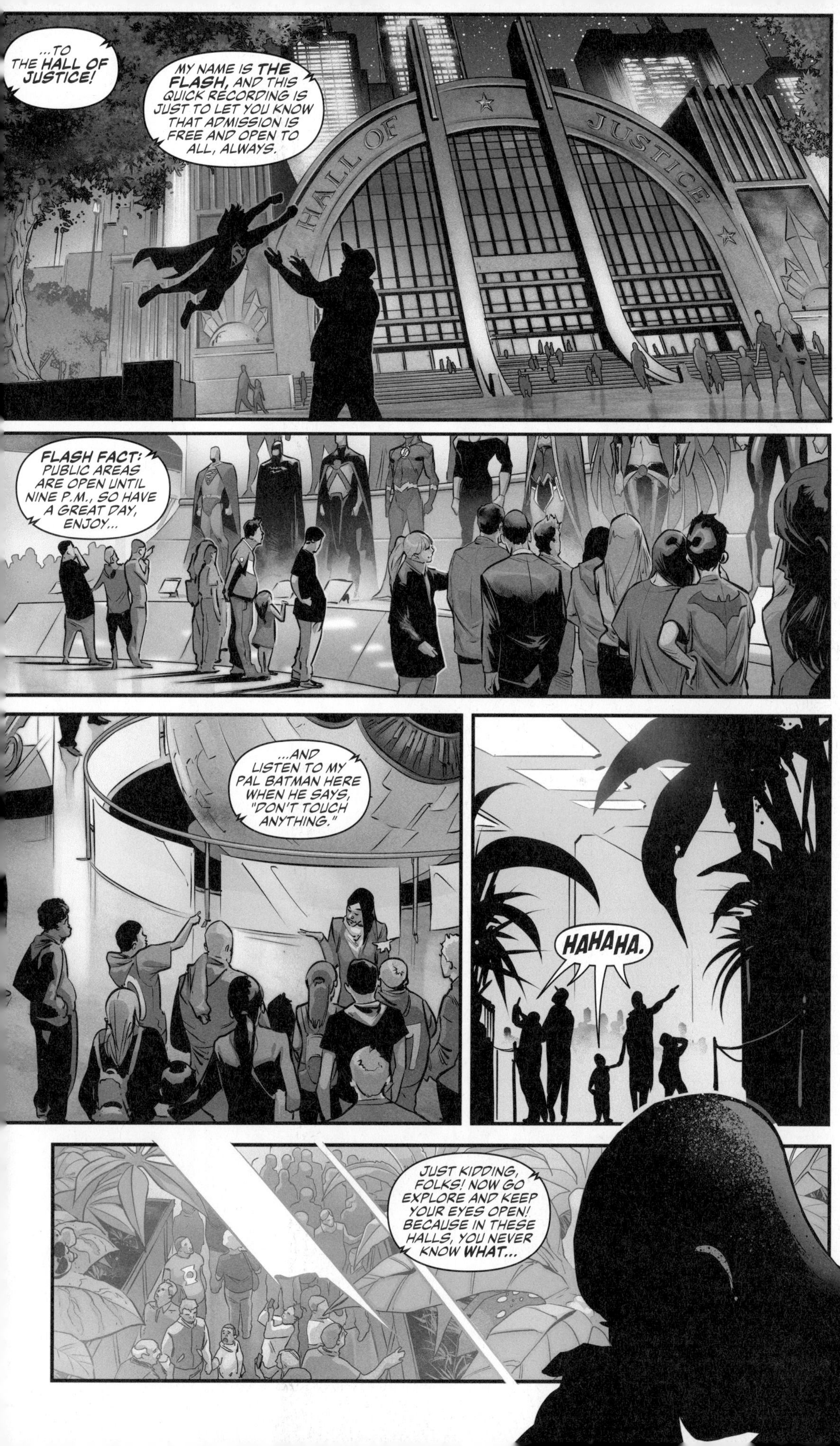
...TO THE HALL OF JUSTICE!
MY NAME IS THE FLASH, AND THIS QUICK RECORDING IS JUST TO LET YOU KNOW THAT ADMISSION IS FREE AND OPEN TO ALL, ALWAYS.
HALL OF JUSTICE
FLASH FACT: PUBLIC AREAS ARE OPEN UNTIL NINE P.M., SO HAVE A GREAT DAY, ENJOY...
...AND LISTEN TO MY PAL BATMAN HERE WHEN HE SAYS, "DON'T TOUCH ANYTHING."
HAHAHA.
JUST KIDDING, FOLKS! NOW GO EXPLORE AND KEEP YOUR EYES OPEN! BECAUSE IN THESE HALLS, YOU NEVER KNOW WHAT...

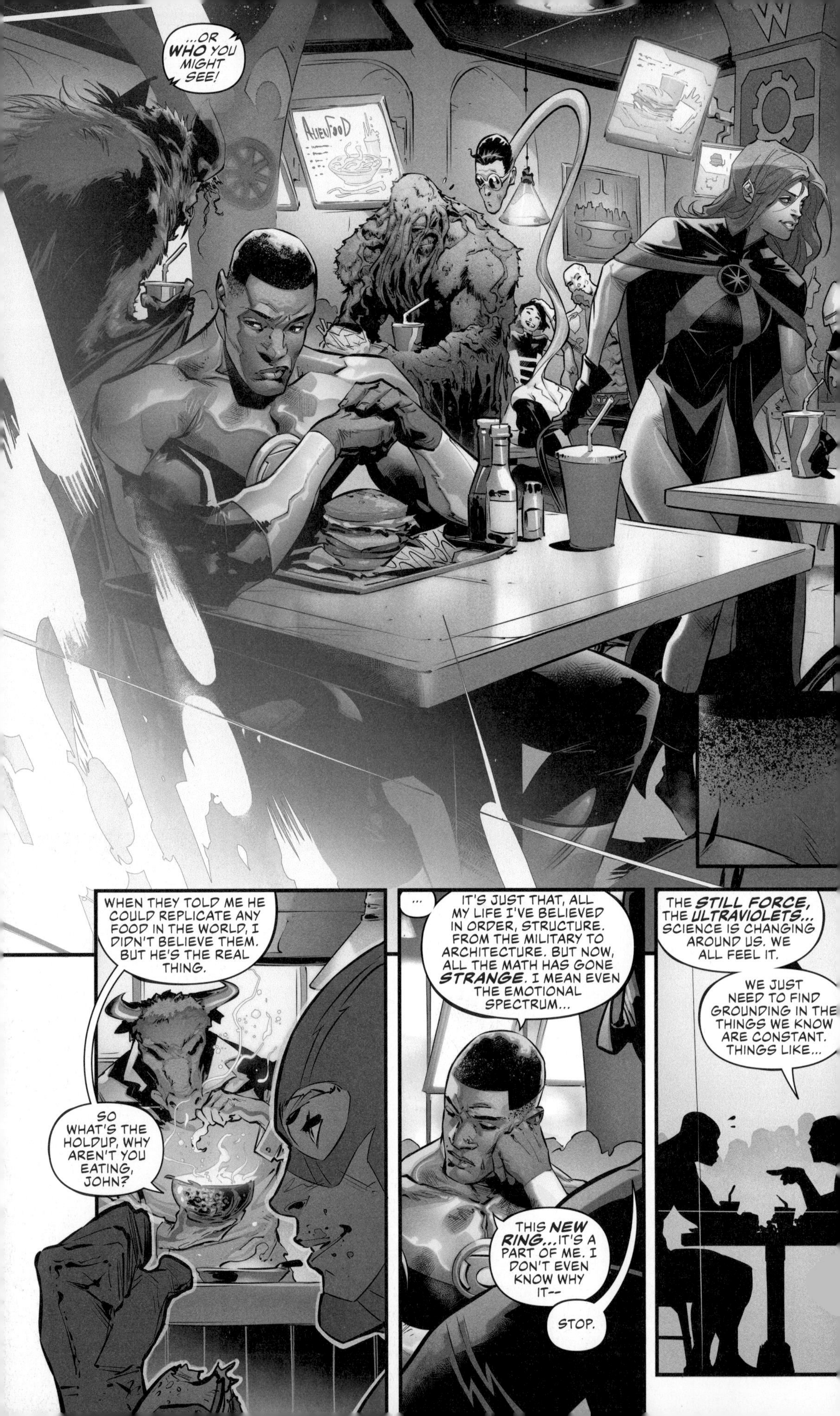
...OR WHO YOU MIGHT SEE!
ALIENFOOD
WHEN THEY TOLD ME HE COULD REPLICATE ANY FOOD IN THE WORLD, I DIDN'T BELIEVE THEM. BUT HE'S THE REAL THING.
SO WHAT'S THE HOLDUP, WHY AREN'T YOU EATING, JOHN?
...
IT'S JUST THAT, ALL MY LIFE I'VE BELIEVED IN ORDER, STRUCTURE. FROM THE MILITARY TO ARCHITECTURE. BUT NOW, ALL THE MATH HAS GONE STRANGE. I MEAN EVEN THE EMOTIONAL SPECTRUM...
THIS NEW RING... IT'S A PART OF ME. I DON'T EVEN KNOW WHY IT--
STOP.
THE STILL FORCE, THE ULTRAVIOLETS... SCIENCE IS CHANGING AROUND US. WE ALL FEEL IT.
WE JUST NEED TO FIND GROUNDING IN THE THINGS WE KNOW ARE CONSTANT. THINGS LIKE...

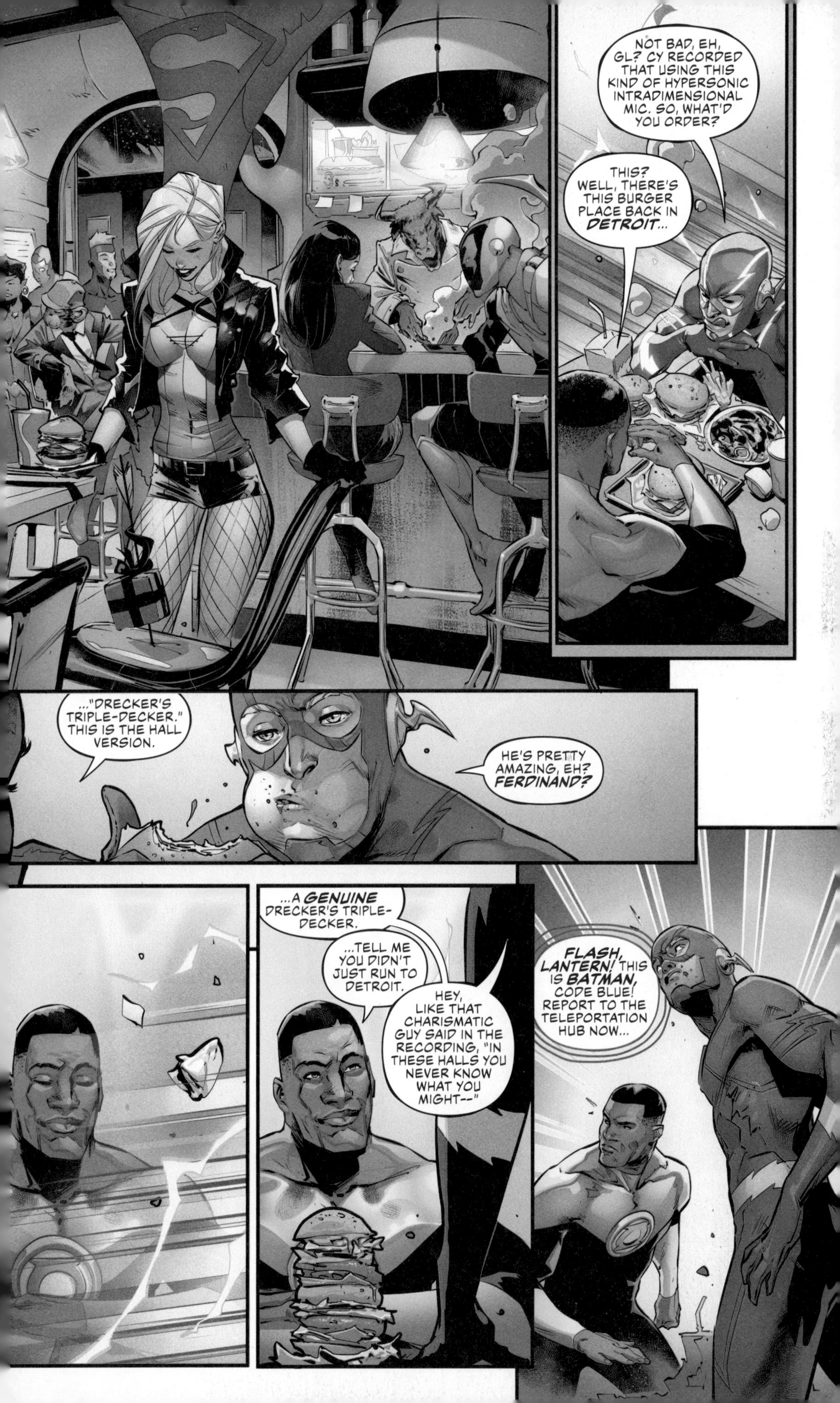
NOT BAD, EH, GL? CY RECORDED THAT USING THIS KIND OF HYPERSONIC INTRADIMENSIONAL MIC. SO, WHAT'D YOU ORDER?
THIS? WELL, THERE'S THIS BURGER PLACE BACK IN DETROIT...
..."DRECKER'S TRIPLE-DECKER." THIS IS THE HALL VERSION.
HE'S PRETTY AMAZING, EH? FERDINAND?
...A GENUINE DRECKER'S TRIPLE-DECKER.
...TELL ME YOU DIDN'T JUST RUN TO DETROIT.
HEY, LIKE THAT CHARISMATIC GUY SAID IN THE RECORDING, "IN THESE HALLS YOU NEVER KNOW WHAT YOU MIGHT--"
FLASH, LANTERN! THIS IS BATMAN, CODE BLUE! REPORT TO THE TELEPORTATION HUB NOW...

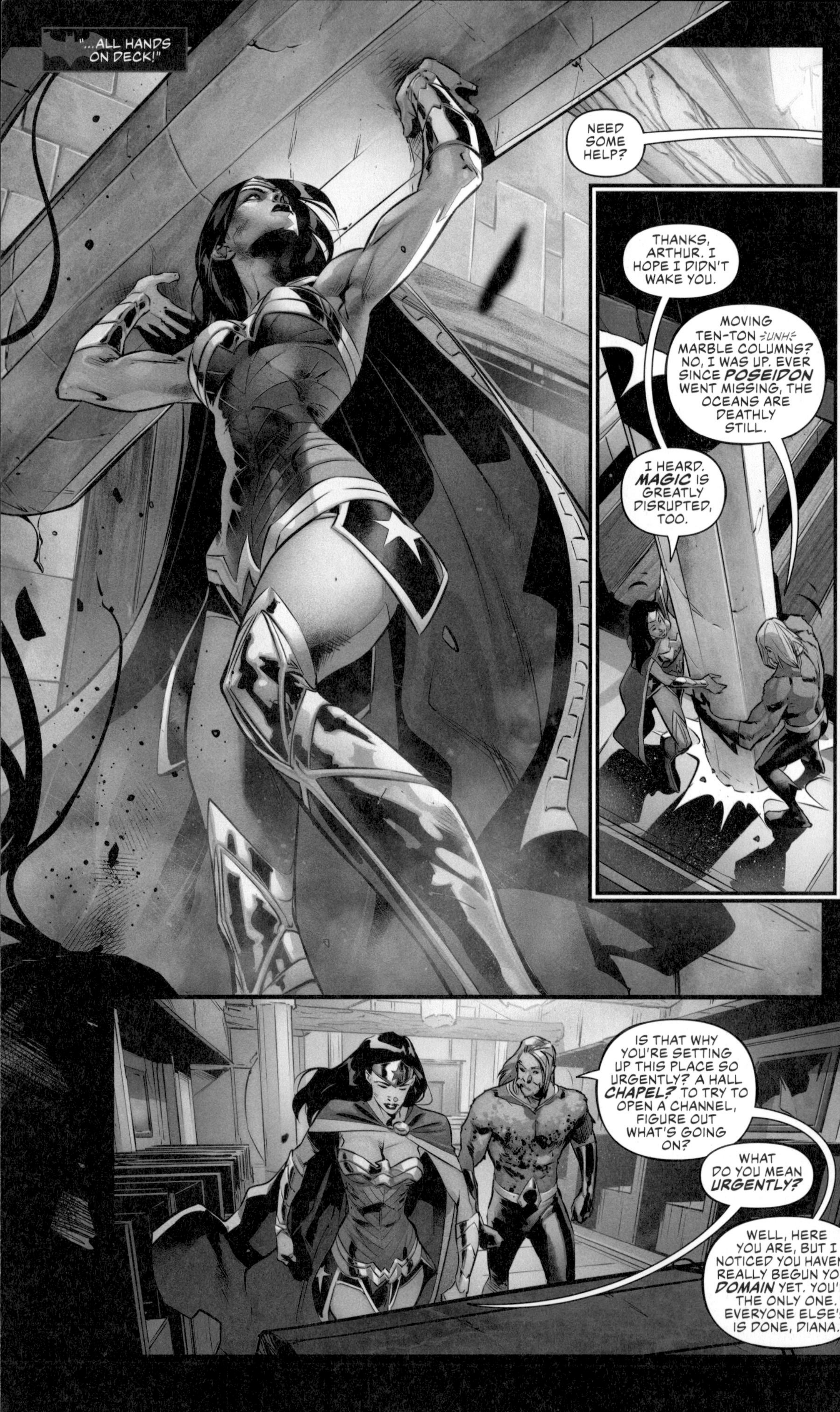
"...ALL HANDS ON DECK!"
NEED SOME HELP?
THANKS, ARTHUR. I HOPE I DIDN'T WAKE YOU.
MOVING TEN-TON ≡UNH≡ MARBLE COLUMNS? NO, I WAS UP. EVER SINCE POSEIDON WENT MISSING, THE OCEANS ARE DEATHLY STILL.
I HEARD. MAGIC IS GREATLY DISRUPTED, TOO.
IS THAT WHY YOU'RE SETTING UP THIS PLACE SO URGENTLY? A HALL CHAPEL? TO TRY TO OPEN A CHANNEL, FIGURE OUT WHAT'S GOING ON?
WHAT DO YOU MEAN URGENTLY?
WELL, HERE YOU ARE, BUT I NOTICED YOU HAVEN REALLY BEGUN YO DOMAIN YET. YOU' THE ONLY ONE. EVERYONE ELSE' IS DONE, DIANA.

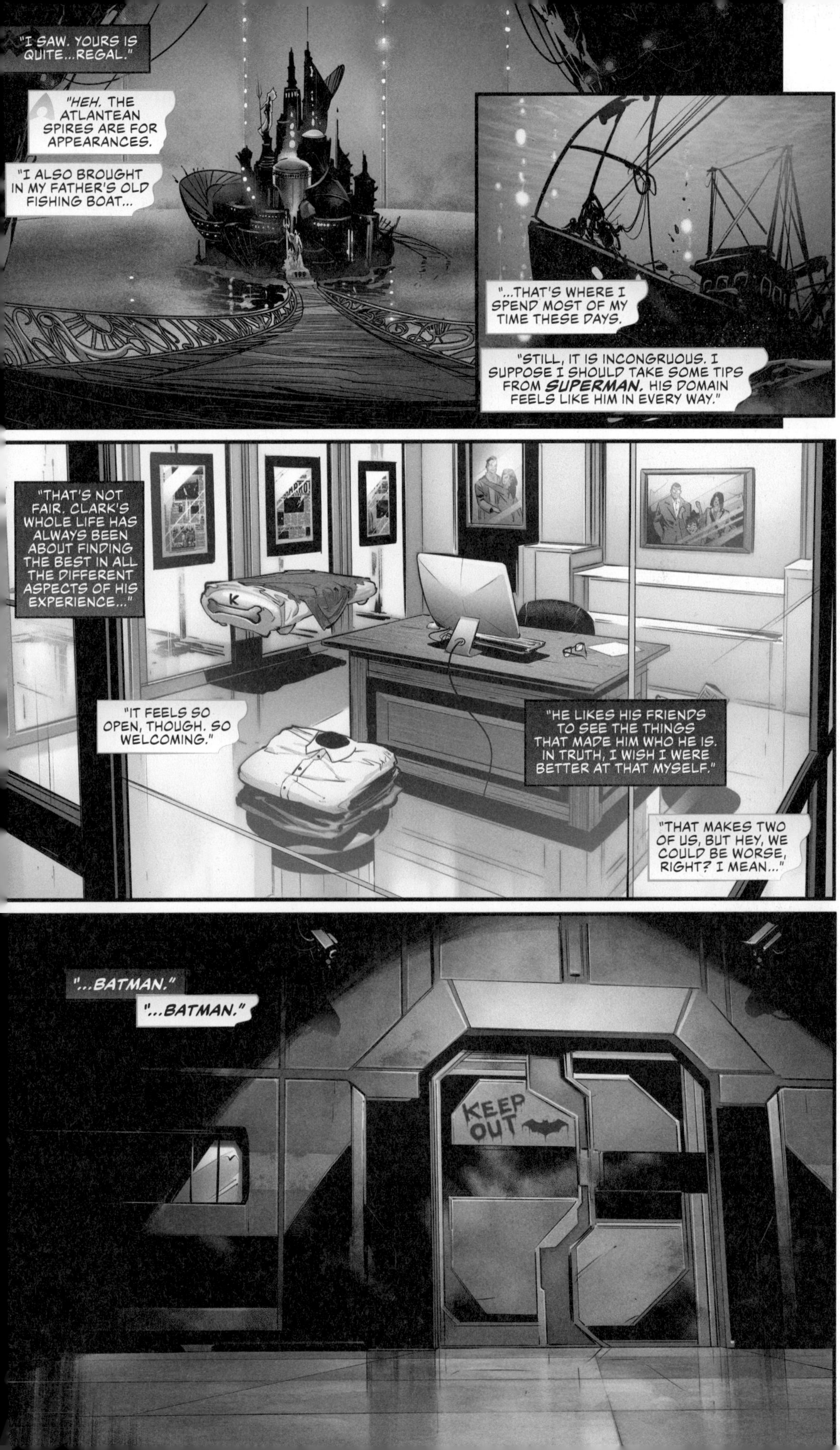
"I SAW. YOURS IS QUITE...REGAL."
"HEH. THE ATLANTEAN SPIRES ARE FOR APPEARANCES.
"I ALSO BROUGHT IN MY FATHER'S OLD FISHING BOAT...
"...THAT'S WHERE I SPEND MOST OF MY TIME THESE DAYS.
"STILL, IT IS INCONGRUOUS. I SUPPOSE I SHOULD TAKE SOME TIPS FROM SUPERMAN. HIS DOMAIN FEELS LIKE HIM IN EVERY WAY."
"THAT'S NOT FAIR. CLARK'S WHOLE LIFE HAS ALWAYS BEEN ABOUT FINDING THE BEST IN ALL THE DIFFERENT ASPECTS OF HIS EXPERIENCE..."
"IT FEELS SO OPEN, THOUGH. SO WELCOMING."
"HE LIKES HIS FRIENDS TO SEE THE THINGS THAT MADE HIM WHO HE IS. IN TRUTH, I WISH I WERE BETTER AT THAT MYSELF."
"THAT MAKES TWO OF US, BUT HEY, WE COULD BE WORSE, RIGHT? I MEAN..."
"...BATMAN."
"...BATMAN."
KEEP OUT

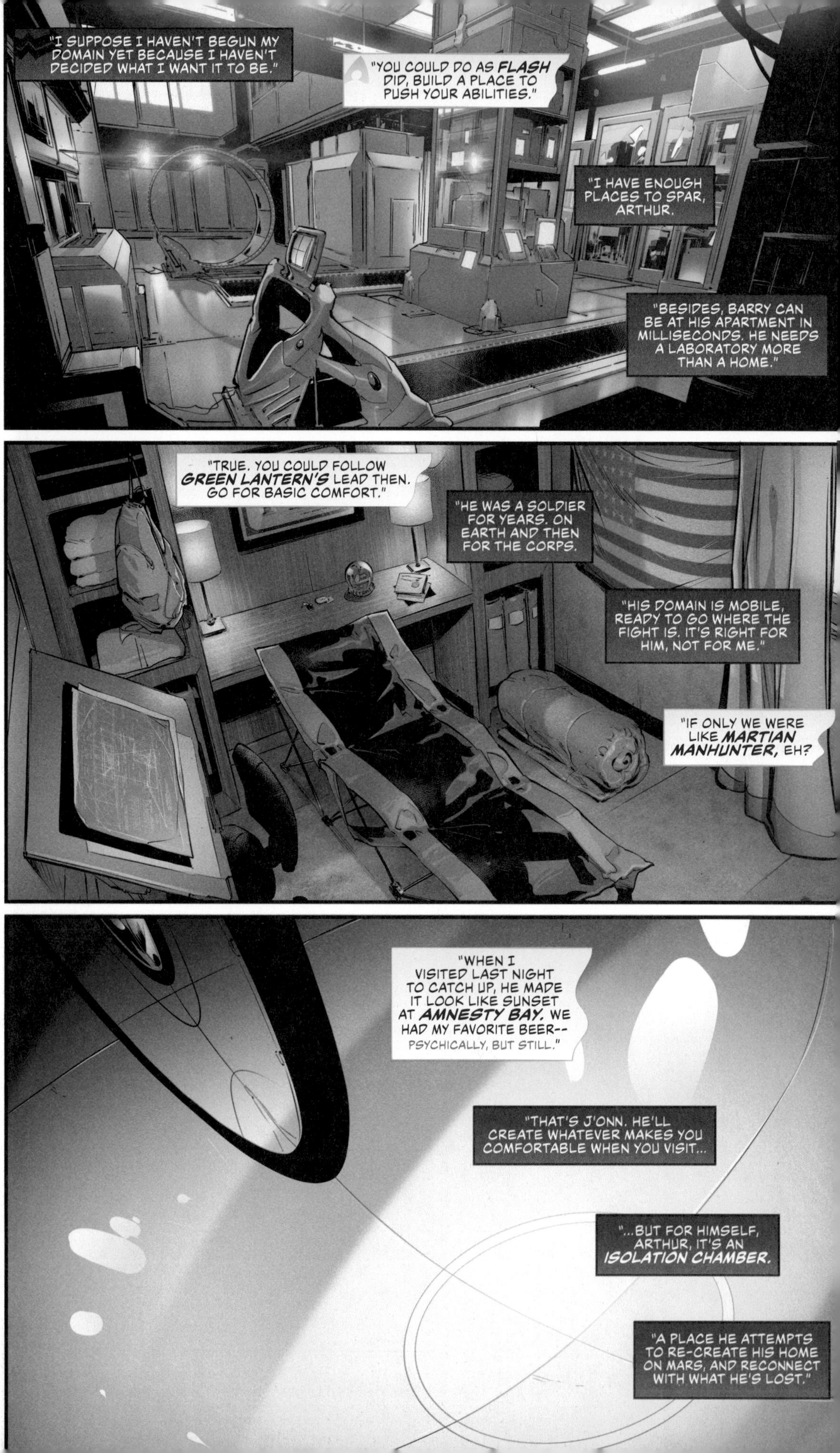
"I SUPPOSE I HAVEN'T BEGUN MY DOMAIN YET BECAUSE I HAVEN'T DECIDED WHAT I WANT IT TO BE."
"YOU COULD DO AS FLASH DID, BUILD A PLACE TO PUSH YOUR ABILITIES."
"I HAVE ENOUGH PLACES TO SPAR, ARTHUR.
"BESIDES, BARRY CAN BE AT HIS APARTMENT IN MILLISECONDS. HE NEEDS A LABORATORY MORE THAN A HOME."
"TRUE. YOU COULD FOLLOW GREEN LANTERN'S LEAD THEN. GO FOR BASIC COMFORT."
"HE WAS A SOLDIER FOR YEARS. ON EARTH AND THEN FOR THE CORPS.
"HIS DOMAIN IS MOBILE, READY TO GO WHERE THE FIGHT IS. IT'S RIGHT FOR HIM, NOT FOR ME."
"IF ONLY WE WERE LIKE MARTIAN MANHUNTER, EH?
"WHEN I VISITED LAST NIGHT TO CATCH UP, HE MADE IT LOOK LIKE SUNSET AT AMNESTY BAY. WE HAD MY FAVORITE BEER-- PSYCHICALLY, BUT STILL."
"THAT'S J'ONN. HE'LL CREATE WHATEVER MAKES YOU COMFORTABLE WHEN YOU VISIT...
"...BUT FOR HIMSELF, ARTHUR, IT'S AN ISOLATION CHAMBER.
"A PLACE HE ATTEMPTS TO RE-CREATE HIS HOME ON MARS, AND RECONNECT WITH WHAT HE'S LOST."

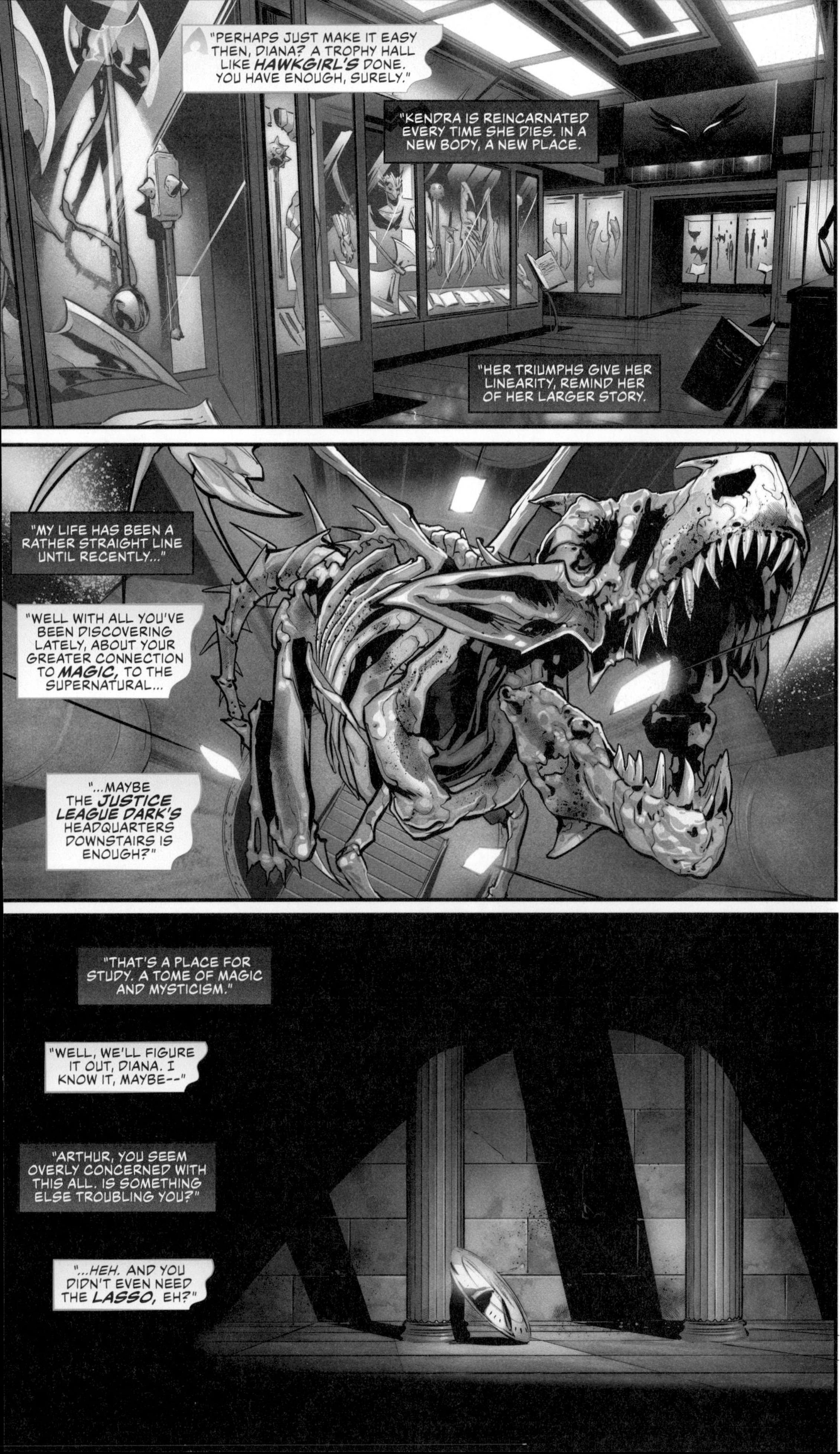
"PERHAPS JUST MAKE IT EASY THEN, DIANA? A TROPHY HALL LIKE HAWKGIRL'S DONE. YOU HAVE ENOUGH, SURELY."
"KENDRA IS REINCARNATED EVERY TIME SHE DIES. IN A NEW BODY, A NEW PLACE.
"HER TRIUMPHS GIVE HER LINEARITY, REMIND HER OF HER LARGER STORY.
"MY LIFE HAS BEEN A RATHER STRAIGHT LINE UNTIL RECENTLY..."
"WELL WITH ALL YOU'VE BEEN DISCOVERING LATELY, ABOUT YOUR GREATER CONNECTION TO MAGIC, TO THE SUPERNATURAL...
"...MAYBE THE JUSTICE LEAGUE DARK'S HEADQUARTERS DOWNSTAIRS IS ENOUGH?"
"THAT'S A PLACE FOR STUDY. A TOME OF MAGIC AND MYSTICISM."
"WELL, WE'LL FIGURE IT OUT, DIANA. I KNOW IT, MAYBE--"
"ARTHUR, YOU SEEM OVERLY CONCERNED WITH THIS ALL. IS SOMETHING ELSE TROUBLING YOU?"
"...HEH. AND YOU DIDN'T EVEN NEED THE LASSO, EH?"

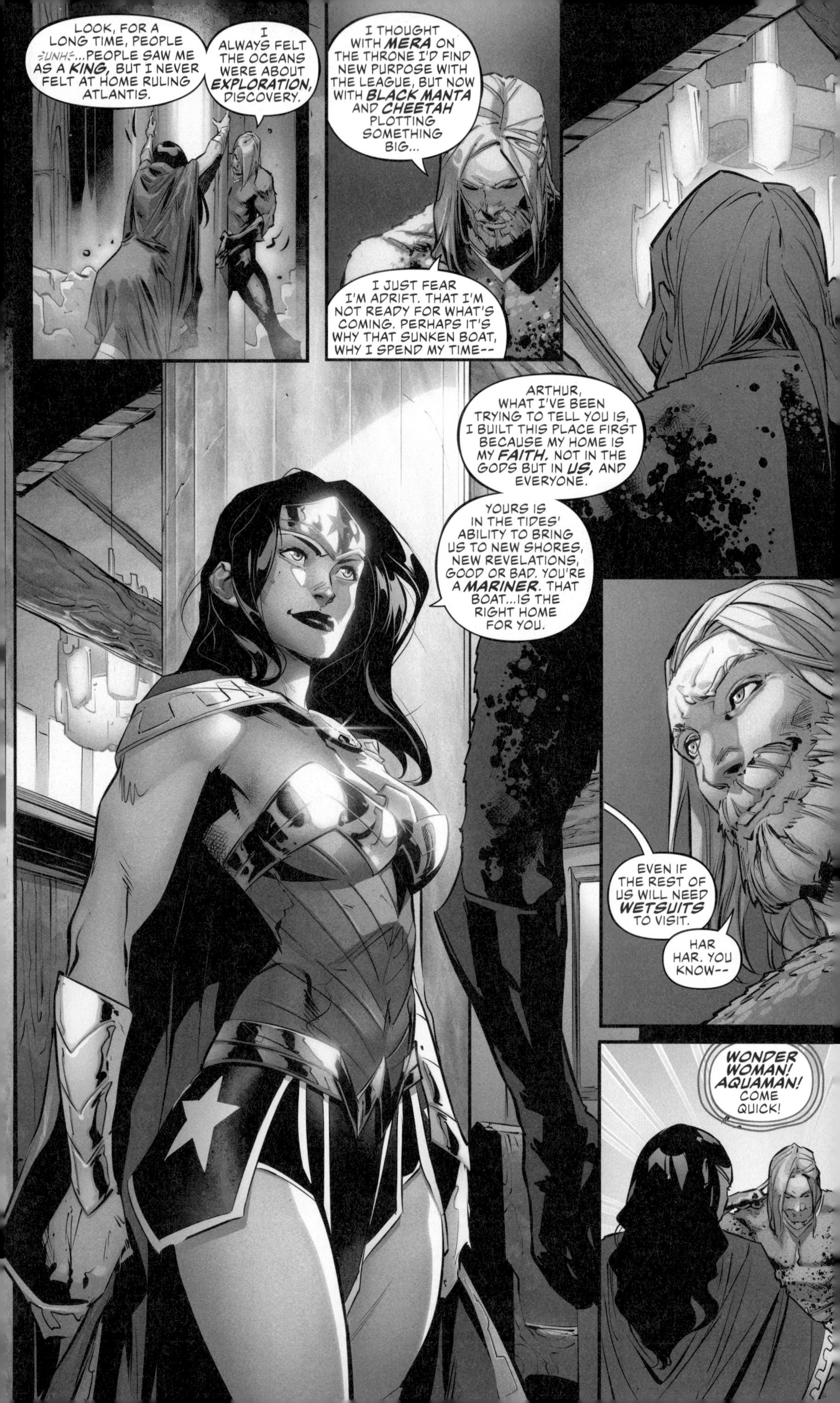

LOOK, FOR A LONG TIME, PEOPLE =UNH=...PEOPLE SAW ME AS A KING, BUT I NEVER FELT AT HOME RULING ATLANTIS.
I ALWAYS FELT THE OCEANS WERE ABOUT EXPLORATION, DISCOVERY.
I THOUGHT WITH MERA ON THE THRONE I'D FIND NEW PURPOSE WITH THE LEAGUE, BUT NOW WITH BLACK MANTA AND CHEETAH PLOTTING SOMETHING BIG...
I JUST FEAR I'M ADRIFT. THAT I'M NOT READY FOR WHAT'S COMING. PERHAPS IT'S WHY THAT SUNKEN BOAT, WHY I SPEND MY TIME--
ARTHUR, WHAT I'VE BEEN TRYING TO TELL YOU IS, I BUILT THIS PLACE FIRST BECAUSE MY HOME IS MY FAITH. NOT IN THE GODS BUT IN US, AND EVERYONE.
YOURS IS IN THE TIDES' ABILITY TO BRING US TO NEW SHORES, NEW REVELATIONS, GOOD OR BAD. YOU'RE A MARINER. THAT BOAT...IS THE RIGHT HOME FOR YOU.
EVEN IF THE REST OF US WILL NEED WETSUITS TO VISIT.
HAR HAR. YOU KNOW--
WONDER WOMAN! AQUAMAN! COME QUICK!

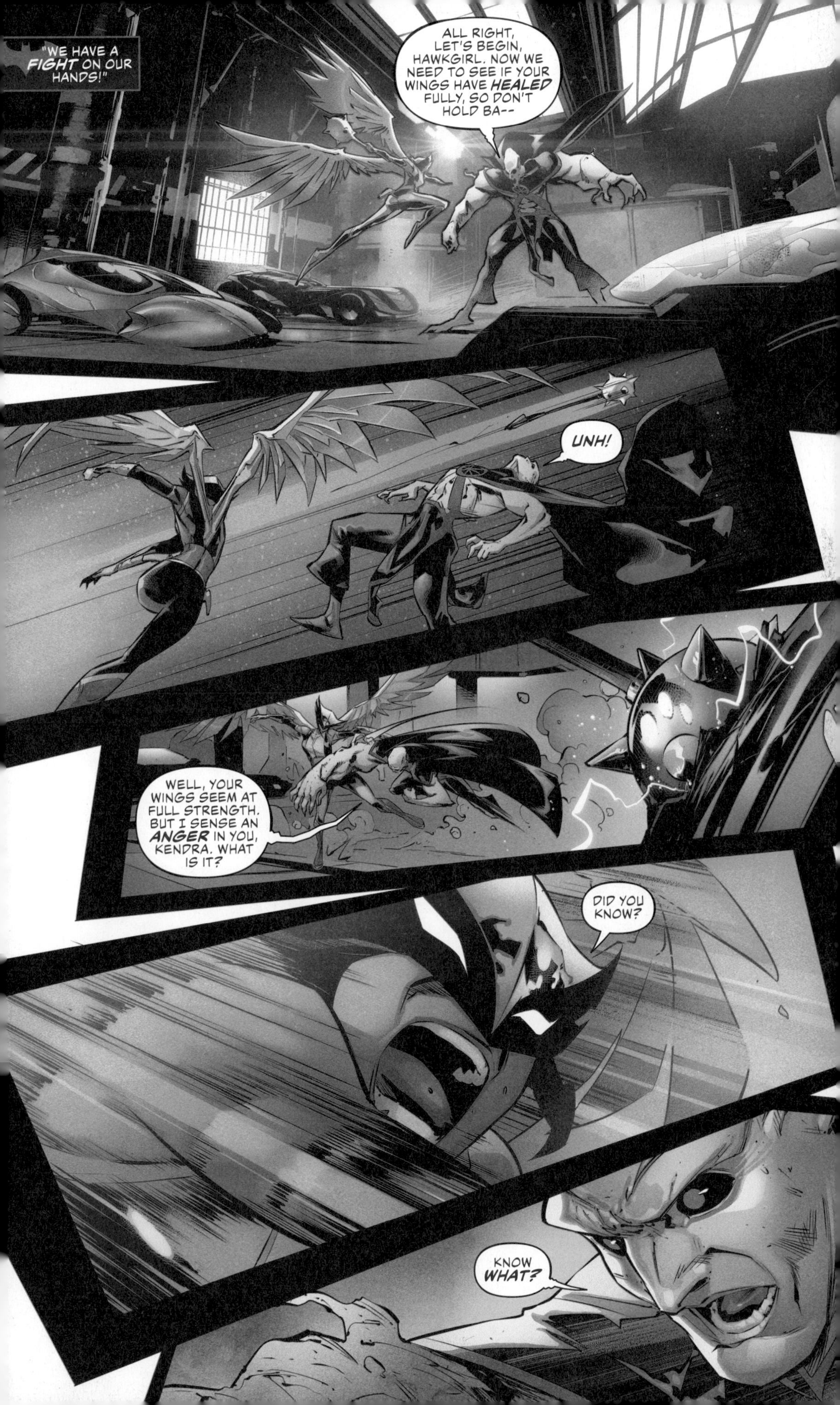
"WE HAVE A FIGHT ON OUR HANDS!"
ALL RIGHT, LET'S BEGIN, HAWKGIRL. NOW WE NEED TO SEE IF YOUR WINGS HAVE HEALED FULLY, SO DON'T HOLD BA--
UNH!
WELL, YOUR WINGS SEEM AT FULL STRENGTH. BUT I SENSE AN ANGER IN YOU, KENDRA. WHAT IS IT?
DID YOU KNOW?
KNOW WHAT?

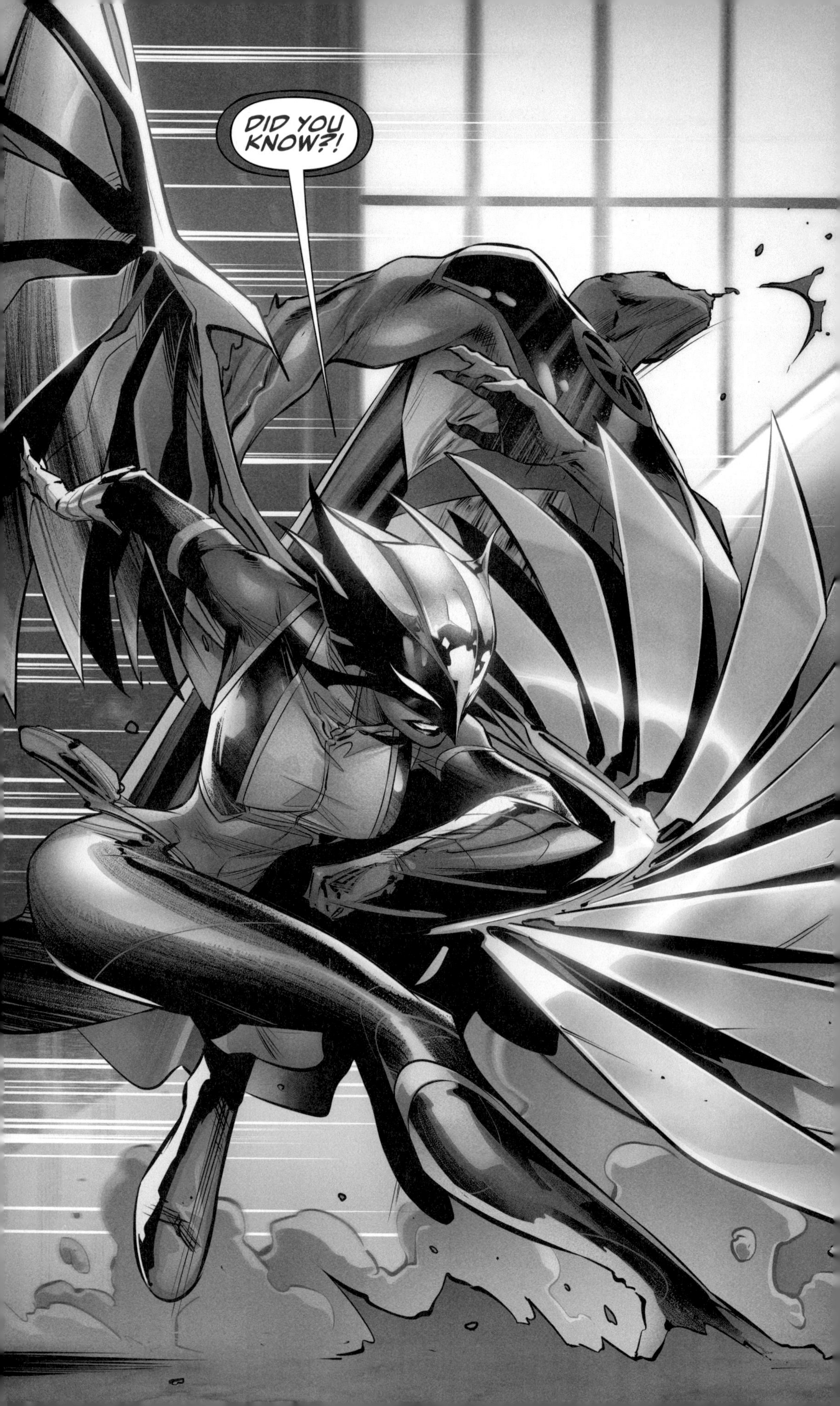
DID YOU KNOW?!

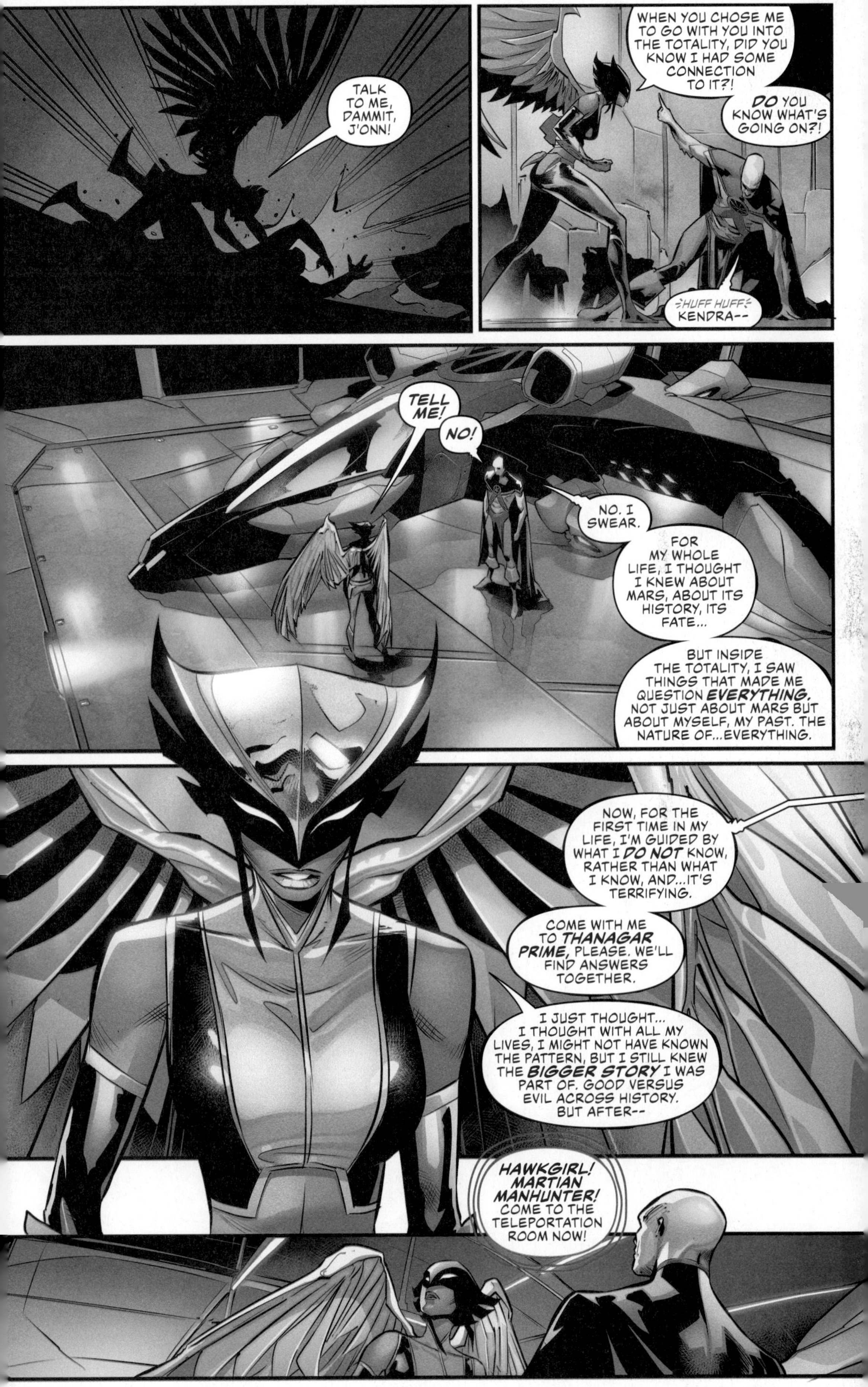

TALK TO ME, DAMMIT, J'ONN!
WHEN YOU CHOSE ME TO GO WITH YOU INTO THE TOTALITY, DID YOU KNOW I HAD SOME CONNECTION TO IT?!
DO YOU KNOW WHAT'S GOING ON?!
HUFF HUFF KENDRA--
TELL ME!
NO!
NO. I SWEAR.
FOR MY WHOLE LIFE, I THOUGHT I KNEW ABOUT MARS, ABOUT ITS HISTORY, ITS FATE...
BUT INSIDE THE TOTALITY, I SAW THINGS THAT MADE ME QUESTION EVERYTHING. NOT JUST ABOUT MARS BUT ABOUT MYSELF, MY PAST. THE NATURE OF...EVERYTHING.
NOW, FOR THE FIRST TIME IN MY LIFE, I'M GUIDED BY WHAT I DO NOT KNOW, RATHER THAN WHAT I KNOW, AND...IT'S TERRIFYING.
COME WITH ME TO THANAGAR PRIME, PLEASE. WE'LL FIND ANSWERS TOGETHER.
I JUST THOUGHT... I THOUGHT WITH ALL MY LIVES, I MIGHT NOT HAVE KNOWN THE PATTERN, BUT I STILL KNEW THE BIGGER STORY I WAS PART OF. GOOD VERSUS EVIL ACROSS HISTORY. BUT AFTER--
HAWKGIRL! MARTIAN MANHUNTER! COME TO THE TELEPORTATION ROOM NOW!

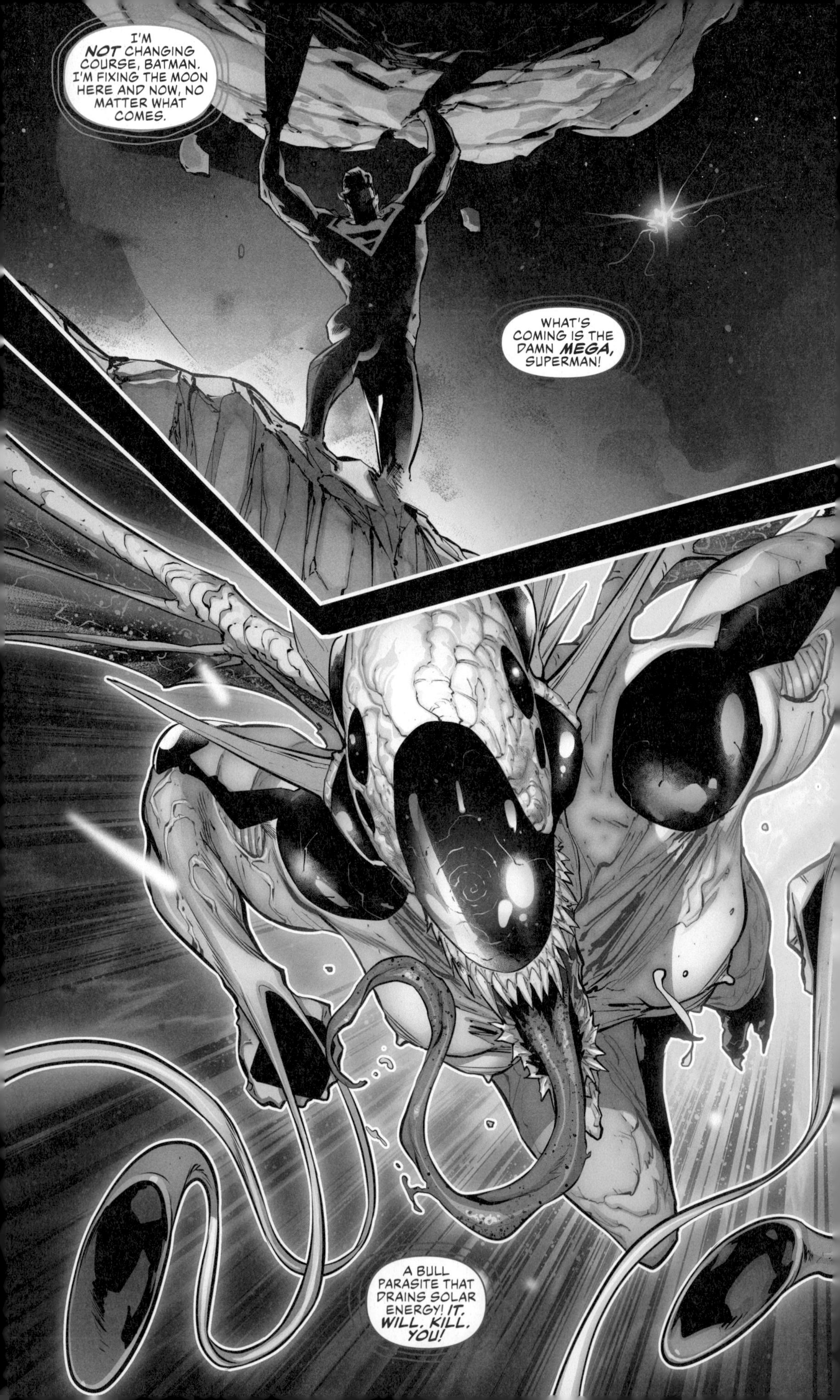

I'M NOT CHANGING COURSE, BATMAN. I'M FIXING THE MOON HERE AND NOW, NO MATTER WHAT COMES.
WHAT'S COMING IS THE DAMN MEGA, SUPERMAN!
A BULL PARASITE THAT DRAINS SOLAR ENERGY! IT. WILL. KILL. YOU!

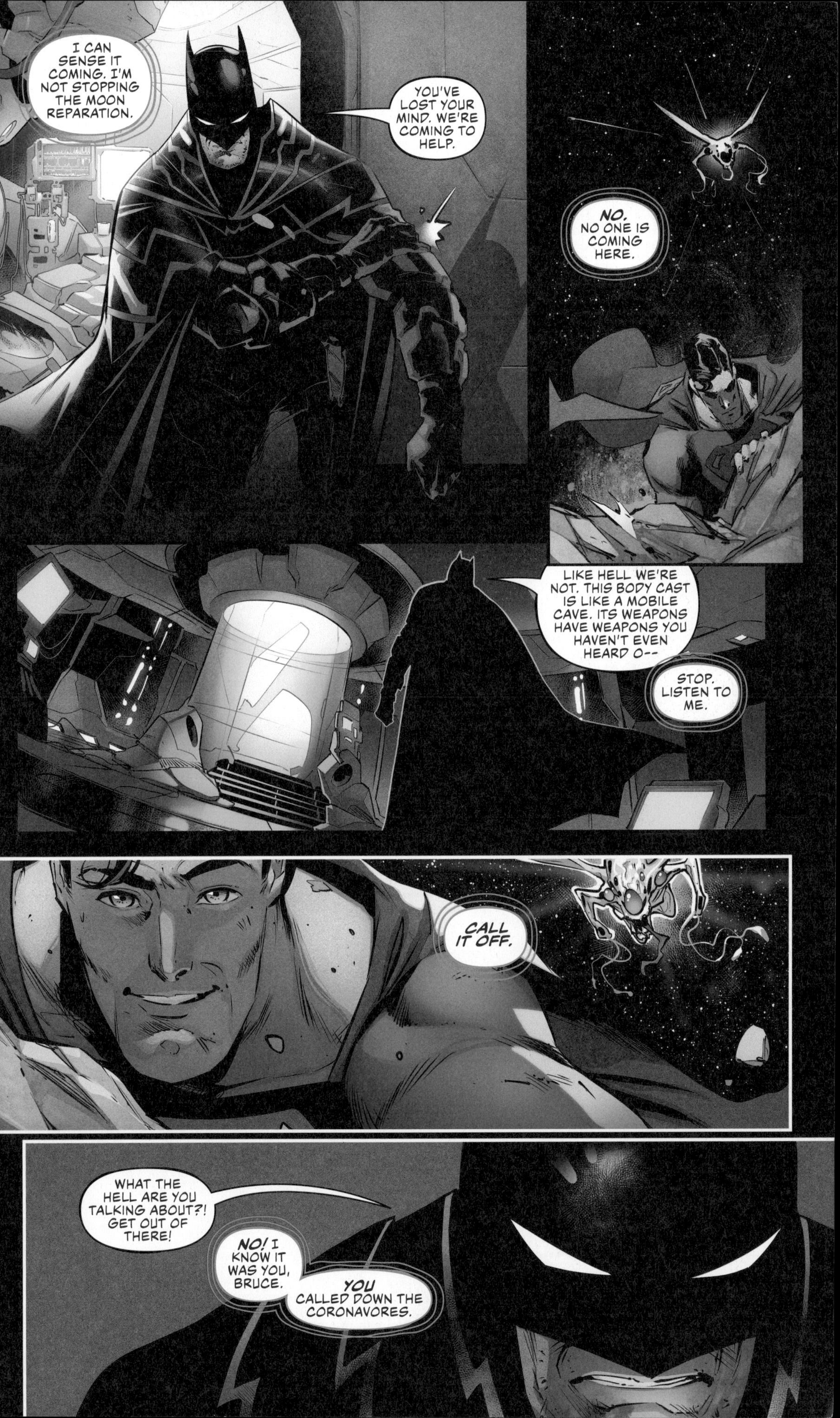
I CAN SENSE IT COMING. I'M NOT STOPPING THE MOON REPARATION.
YOU'VE LOST YOUR MIND. WE'RE COMING TO HELP.
NO. NO ONE IS COMING HERE.
LIKE HELL WE'RE NOT. THIS BODY CAST IS LIKE A MOBILE CAVE. ITS WEAPONS HAVE WEAPONS YOU HAVEN'T EVEN HEARD O--
STOP. LISTEN TO ME.
CALL IT OFF.
WHAT THE HELL ARE YOU TALKING ABOUT?! GET OUT OF THERE!
NO! I KNOW IT WAS YOU, BRUCE.
YOU CALLED DOWN THE CORONAVORES.

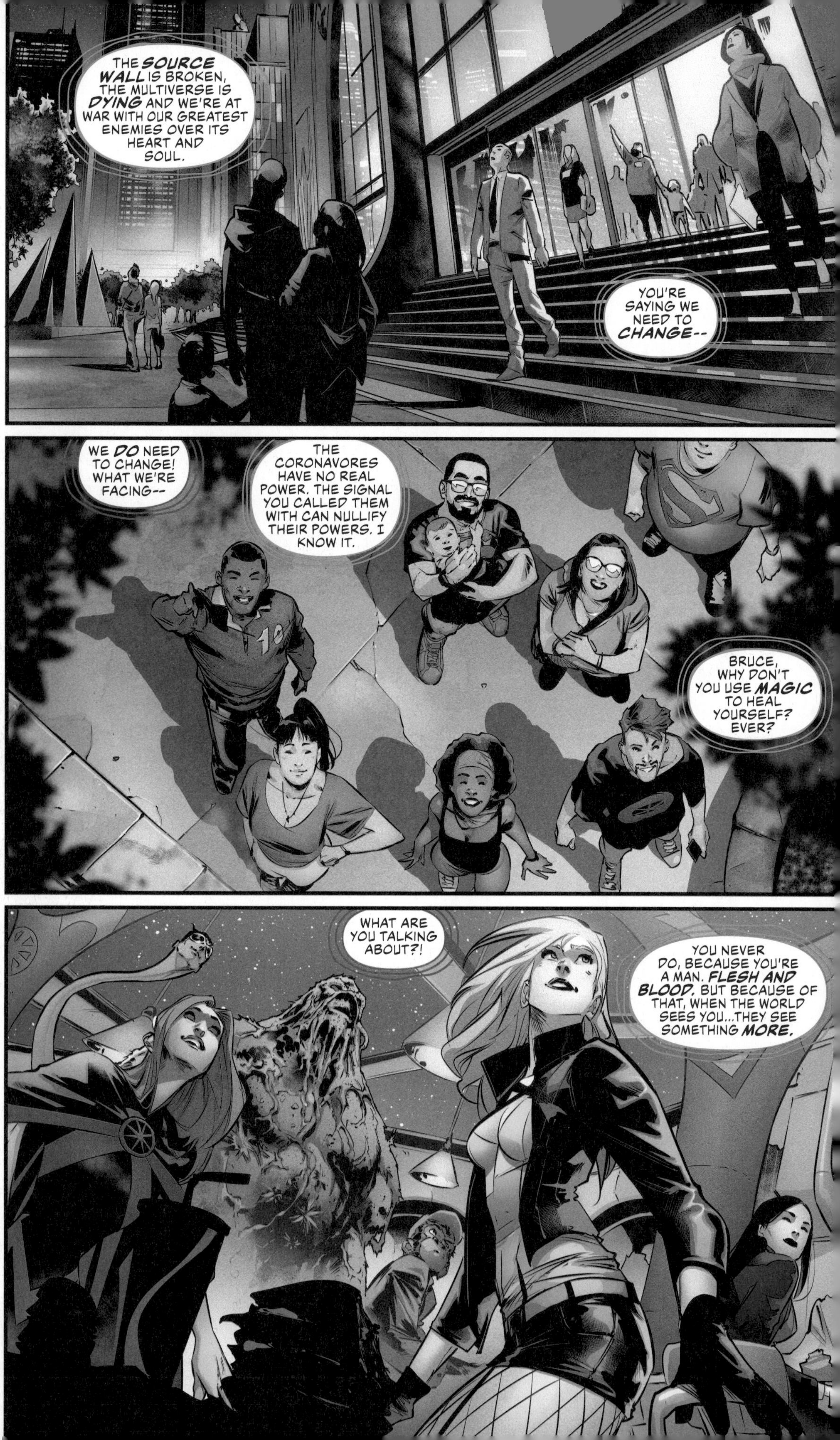
THE SOURCE WALL IS BROKEN, THE MULTIVERSE IS DYING AND WE'RE AT WAR WITH OUR GREATEST ENEMIES OVER ITS HEART AND SOUL.
YOU'RE SAYING WE NEED TO CHANGE--
WE DO NEED TO CHANGE! WHAT WE'RE FACING--
THE CORONAVORES HAVE NO REAL POWER. THE SIGNAL YOU CALLED THEM WITH CAN NULLIFY THEIR POWERS. I KNOW IT.
BRUCE, WHY DON'T YOU USE MAGIC TO HEAL YOURSELF? EVER?
WHAT ARE YOU TALKING ABOUT?!
YOU NEVER DO, BECAUSE YOU'RE A MAN. FLESH AND BLOOD. BUT BECAUSE OF THAT, WHEN THE WORLD SEES YOU...THEY SEE SOMETHING MORE.

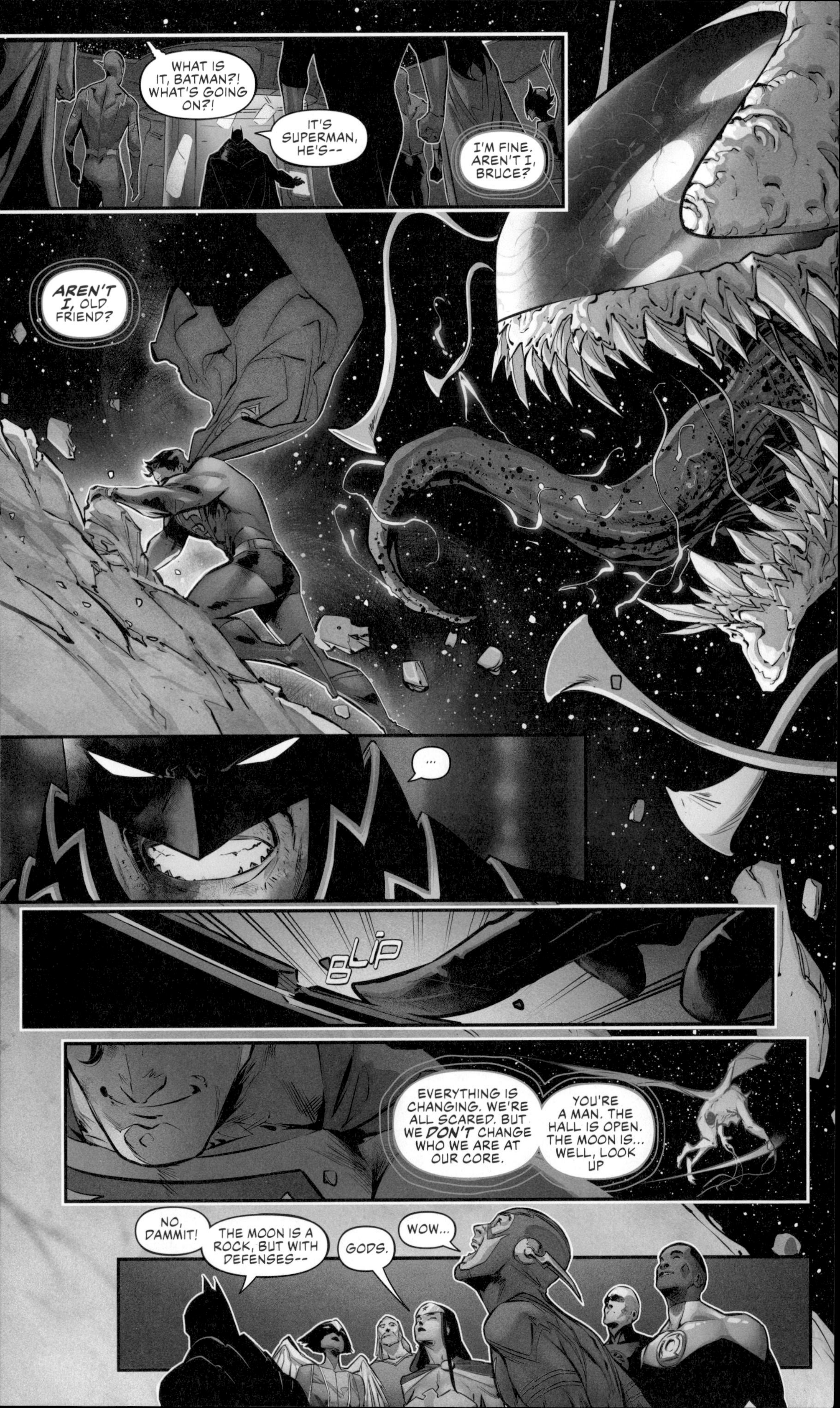
WHAT IS IT, BATMAN?! WHAT'S GOING ON?!
IT'S SUPERMAN, HE'S--
I'M FINE. AREN'T I, BRUCE?
AREN'T I, OLD FRIEND?
...
BLIP
EVERYTHING IS CHANGING. WE'RE ALL SCARED. BUT WE DON'T CHANGE WHO WE ARE AT OUR CORE.
YOU'RE A MAN. THE HALL IS OPEN. THE MOON IS... WELL, LOOK UP
NO, DAMMIT!
THE MOON IS A ROCK, BUT WITH DEFENSES--
GODS.
WOW...

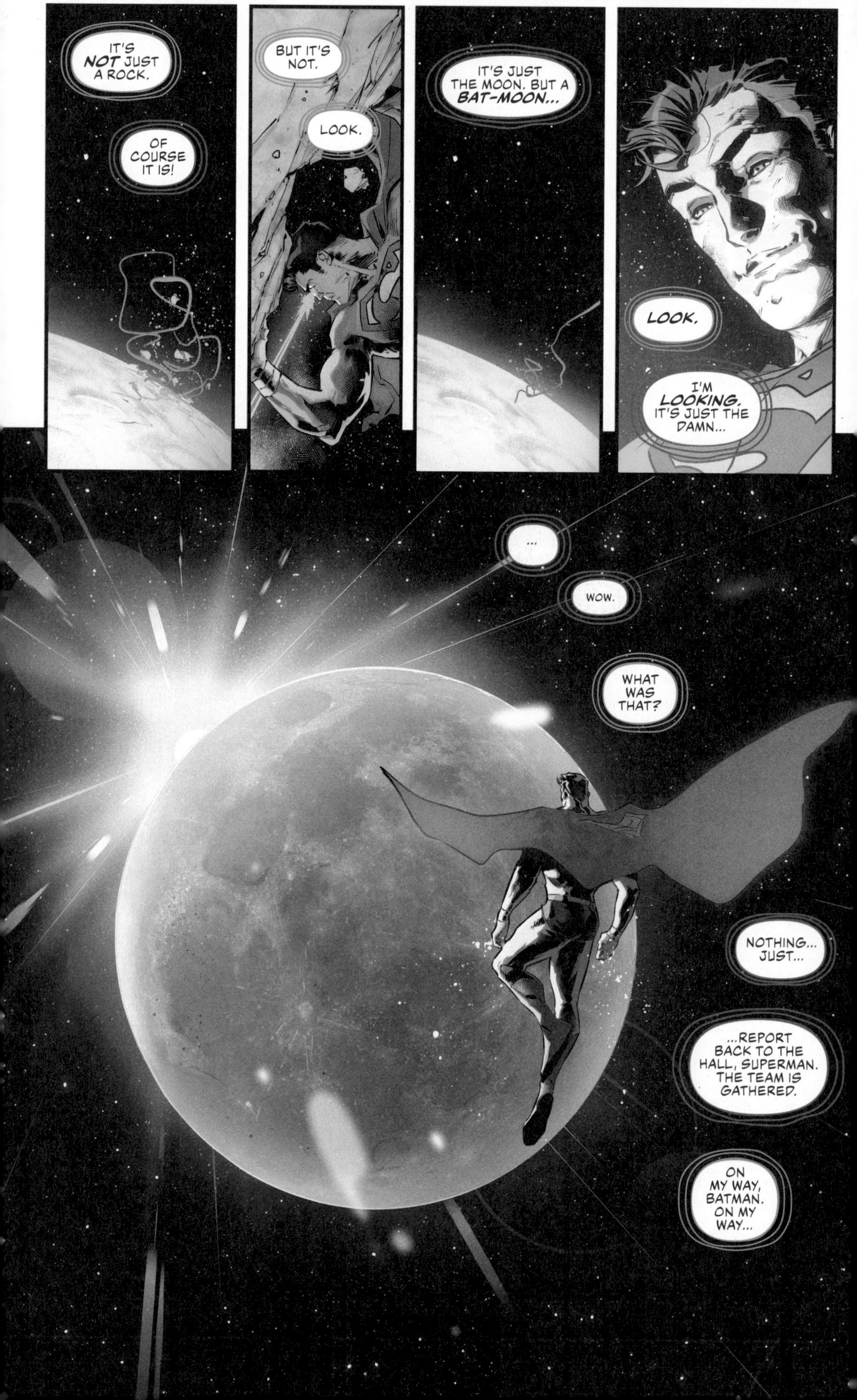
IT'S NOT JUST A ROCK.
OF COURSE IT IS!
BUT IT'S NOT.
LOOK.
IT'S JUST THE MOON. BUT A BAT-MOON...
LOOK.
I'M LOOKING. IT'S JUST THE DAMN...
...
WOW.
WHAT WAS THAT?
NOTHING... JUST...
...REPORT BACK TO THE HALL, SUPERMAN. THE TEAM IS GATHERED.
ON MY WAY, BATMAN. ON MY WAY...

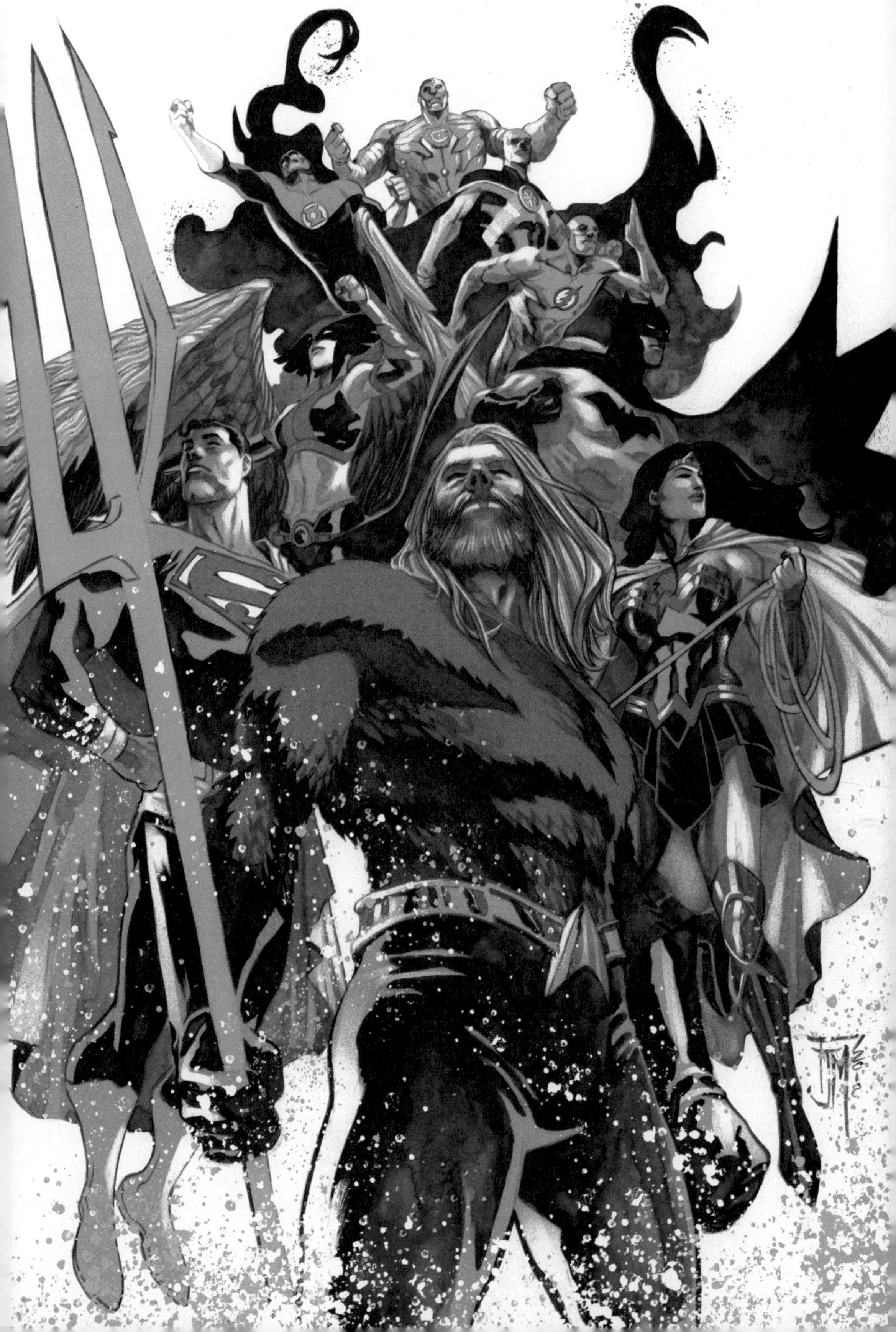

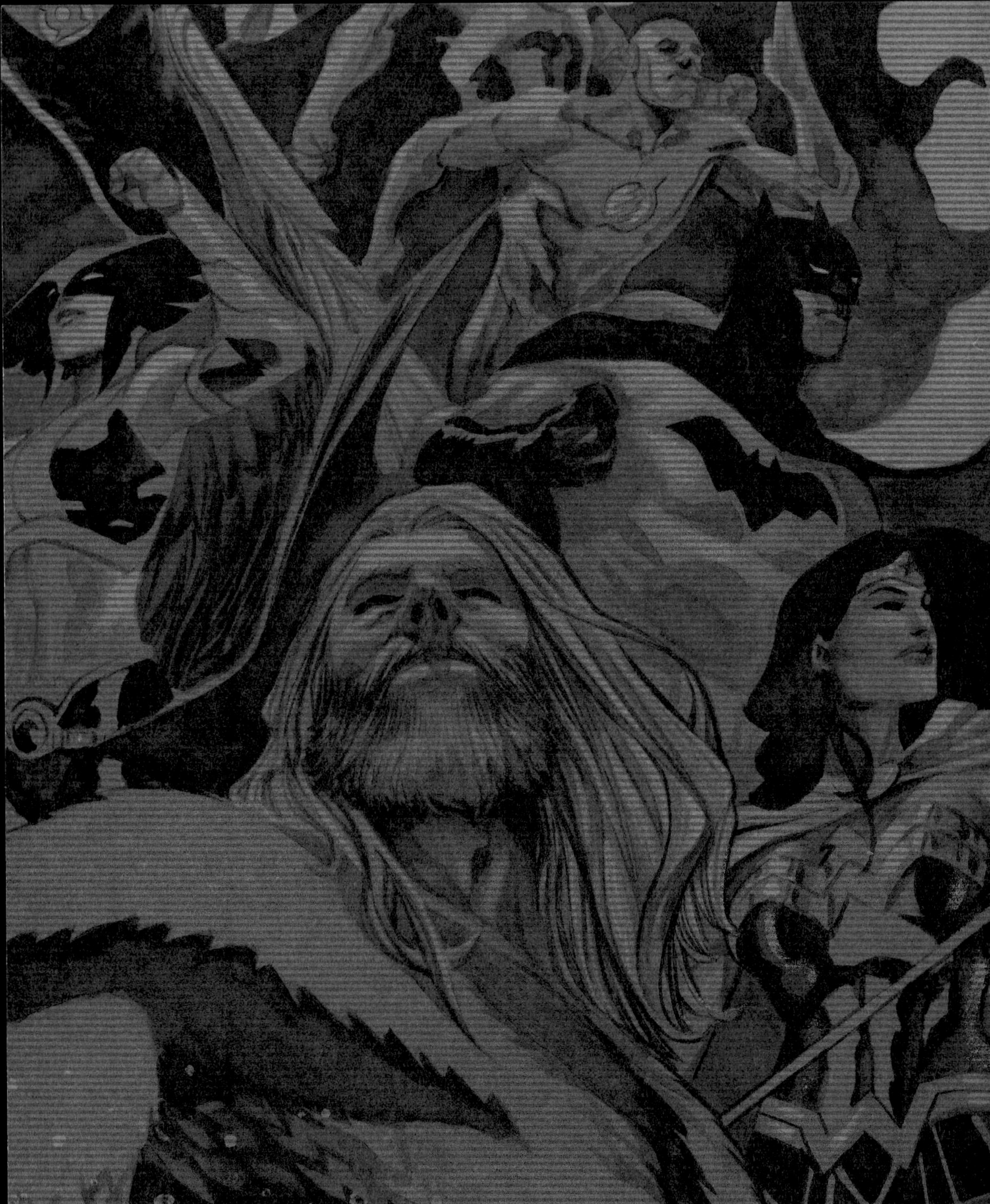

JUSTICE
LEAGUE
#10

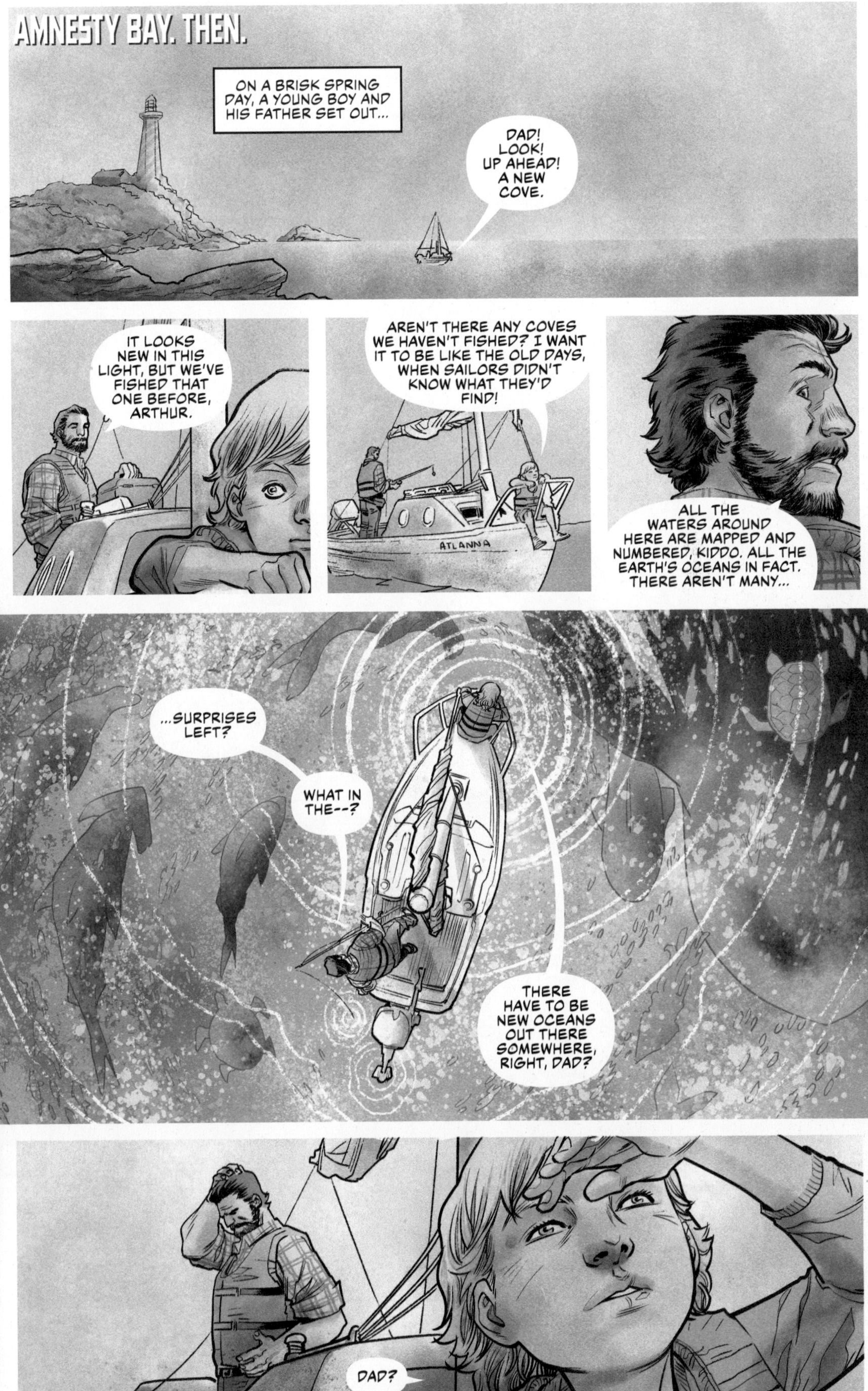
AMNESTY BAY. THEN.
ON A BRISK SPRING DAY, A YOUNG BOY AND HIS FATHER SET OUT...
DAD! LOOK! UP AHEAD! A NEW COVE.
IT LOOKS NEW IN THIS LIGHT, BUT WE'VE FISHED THAT ONE BEFORE, ARTHUR.
AREN'T THERE ANY COVES WE HAVEN'T FISHED? I WANT IT TO BE LIKE THE OLD DAYS, WHEN SAILORS DIDN'T KNOW WHAT THEY'D FIND!
ATLANNA
ALL THE WATERS AROUND HERE ARE MAPPED AND NUMBERED, KIDDO. ALL THE EARTH'S OCEANS IN FACT. THERE AREN'T MANY...
...SURPRISES LEFT?
WHAT IN THE--?
THERE HAVE TO BE NEW OCEANS OUT THERE SOMEWHERE, RIGHT, DAD?
DAD?

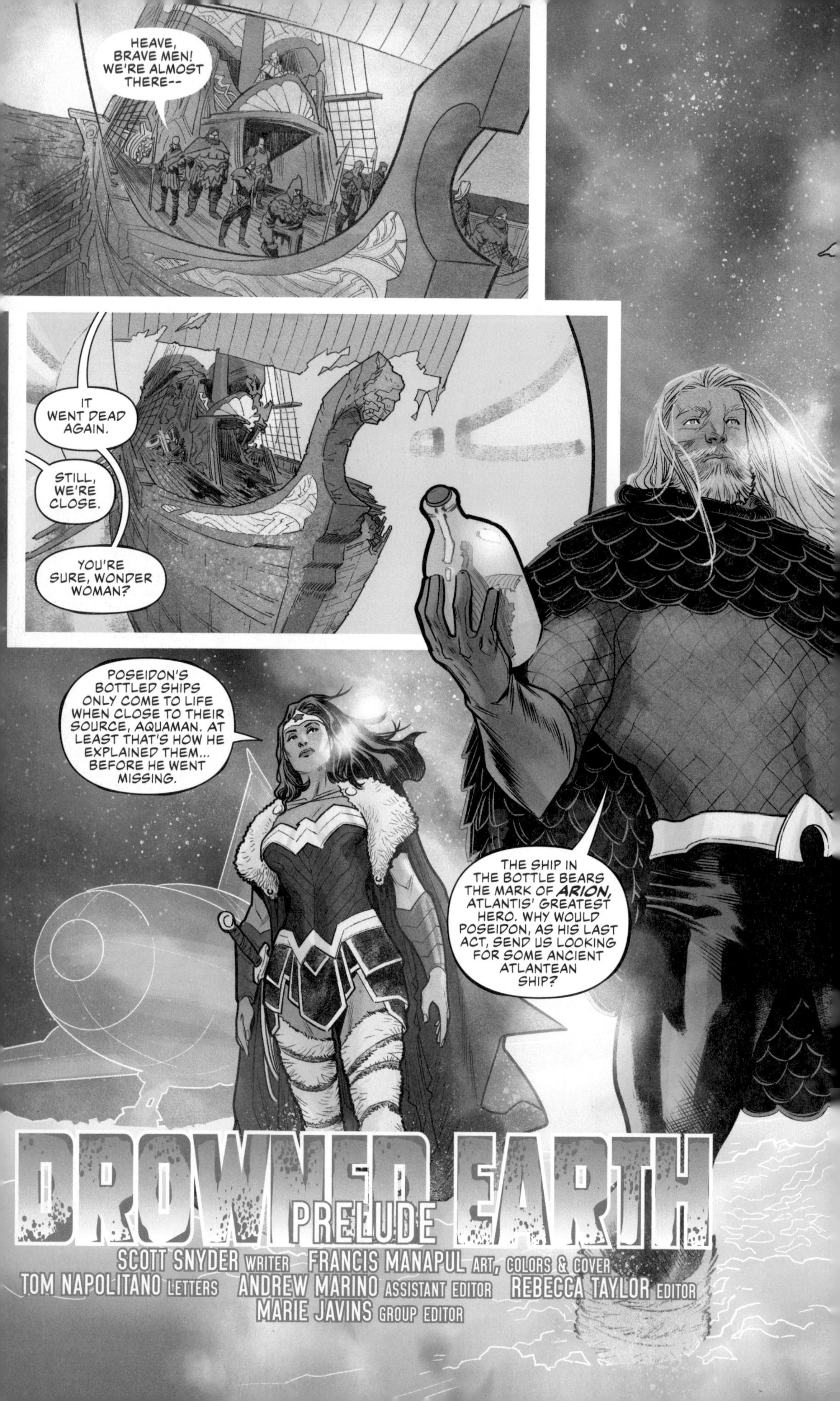
HEAVE, BRAVE MEN! WE'RE ALMOST THERE--
IT WENT DEAD AGAIN.
STILL, WE'RE CLOSE.
YOU'RE SURE, WONDER WOMAN?
POSEIDON'S BOTTLED SHIPS ONLY COME TO LIFE WHEN CLOSE TO THEIR SOURCE, AQUAMAN. AT LEAST THAT'S HOW HE EXPLAINED THEM... BEFORE HE WENT MISSING.
THE SHIP IN THE BOTTLE BEARS THE MARK OF ARION, ATLANTIS' GREATEST HERO. WHY WOULD POSEIDON, AS HIS LAST ACT, SEND US LOOKING FOR SOME ANCIENT ATLANTEAN SHIP?
DROWNED EARTH
PRELUDE
SCOTT SNYDER WRITER FRANCIS MANAPUL ART, COLORS & COVER
TOM NAPOLITANO LETTERS ANDREW MARINO ASSISTANT EDITOR REBECCA TAYLOR EDITOR
MARIE JAVINS GROUP EDITOR

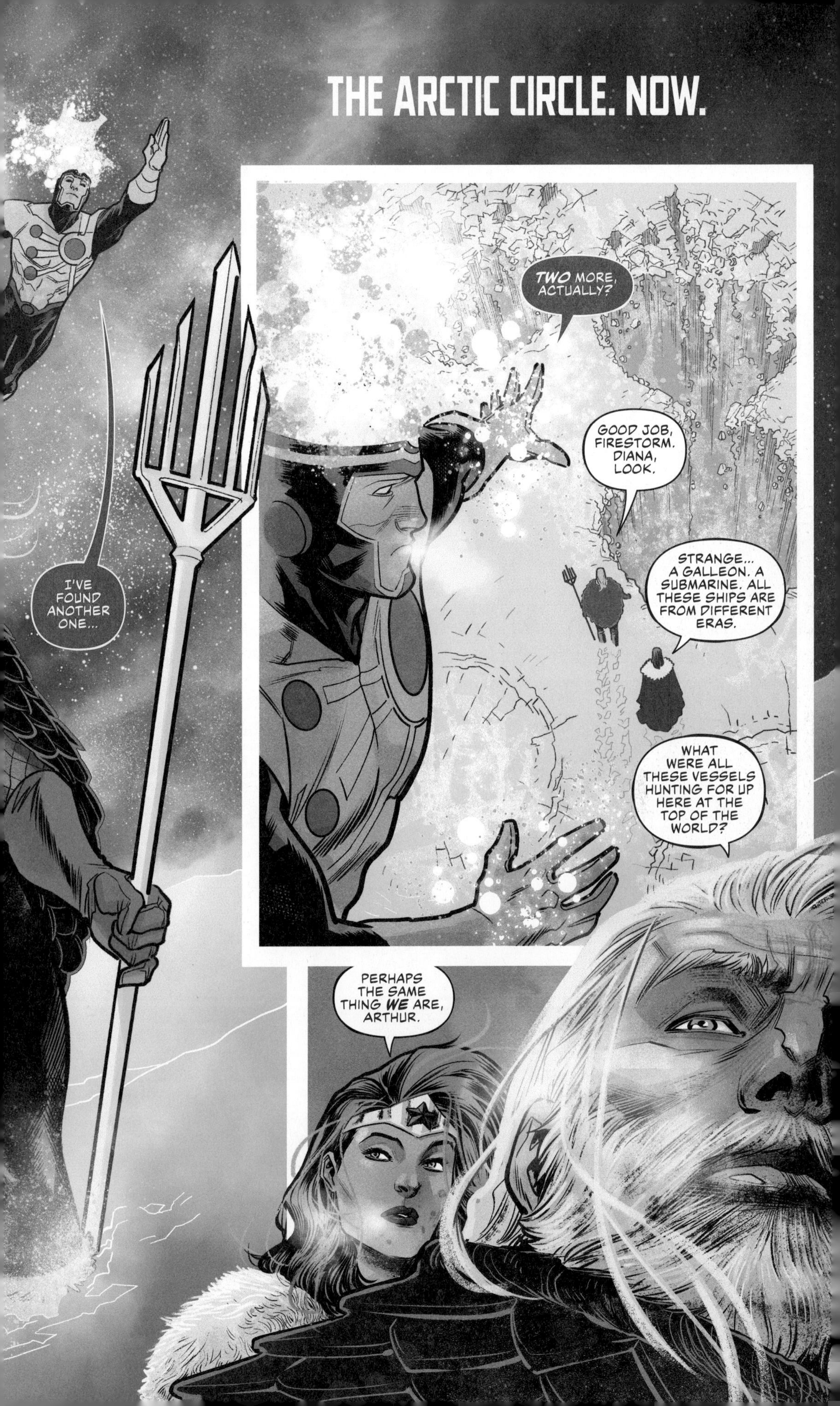
THE ARCTIC CIRCLE. NOW.
I'VE FOUND ANOTHER ONE...
TWO MORE, ACTUALLY?
GOOD JOB, FIRESTORM. DIANA, LOOK.
STRANGE... A GALLEON. A SUBMARINE. ALL THESE SHIPS ARE FROM DIFFERENT ERAS.
WHAT WERE ALL THESE VESSELS HUNTING FOR UP HERE AT THE TOP OF THE WORLD?
PERHAPS THE SAME THING WE ARE, ARTHUR.

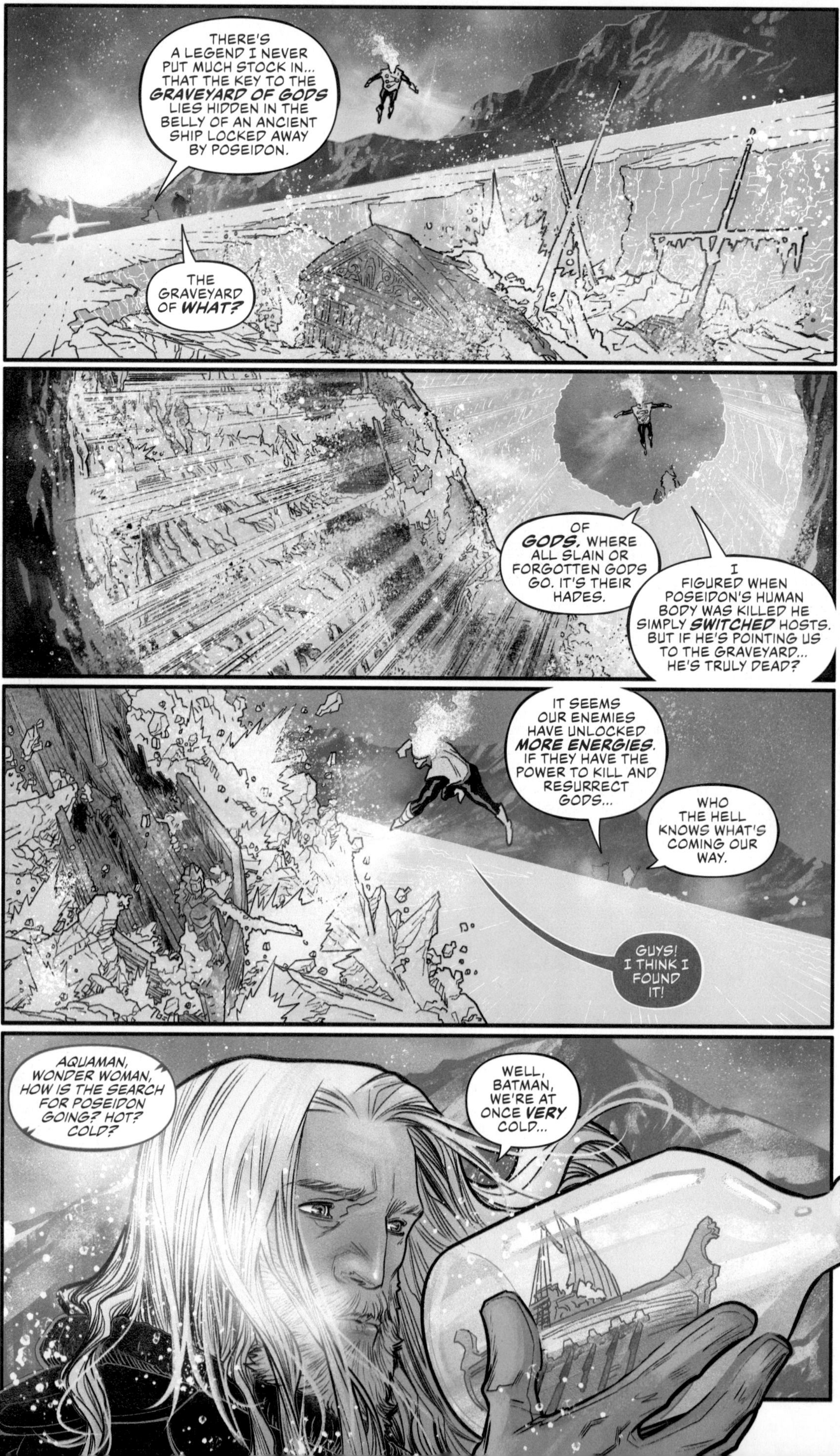
THERE'S A LEGEND I NEVER PUT MUCH STOCK IN... THAT THE KEY TO THE ***GRAVEYARD OF GODS*** LIES HIDDEN IN THE BELLY OF AN ANCIENT SHIP LOCKED AWAY BY POSEIDON.
THE GRAVEYARD OF ***WHAT?***
OF ***GODS.*** WHERE ALL SLAIN OR FORGOTTEN GODS GO. IT'S THEIR HADES.
I FIGURED WHEN POSEIDON'S HUMAN BODY WAS KILLED HE SIMPLY ***SWITCHED*** HOSTS. BUT IF HE'S POINTING US TO THE GRAVEYARD... HE'S TRULY DEAD?
IT SEEMS OUR ENEMIES HAVE UNLOCKED ***MORE ENERGIES.*** IF THEY HAVE THE POWER TO KILL AND RESURRECT GODS...
WHO THE HELL KNOWS WHAT'S COMING OUR WAY.
GUYS! I THINK I FOUND IT!
AQUAMAN, WONDER WOMAN, HOW IS THE SEARCH FOR POSEIDON GOING? HOT? COLD?
WELL, BATMAN, WE'RE AT ONCE ***VERY*** COLD...

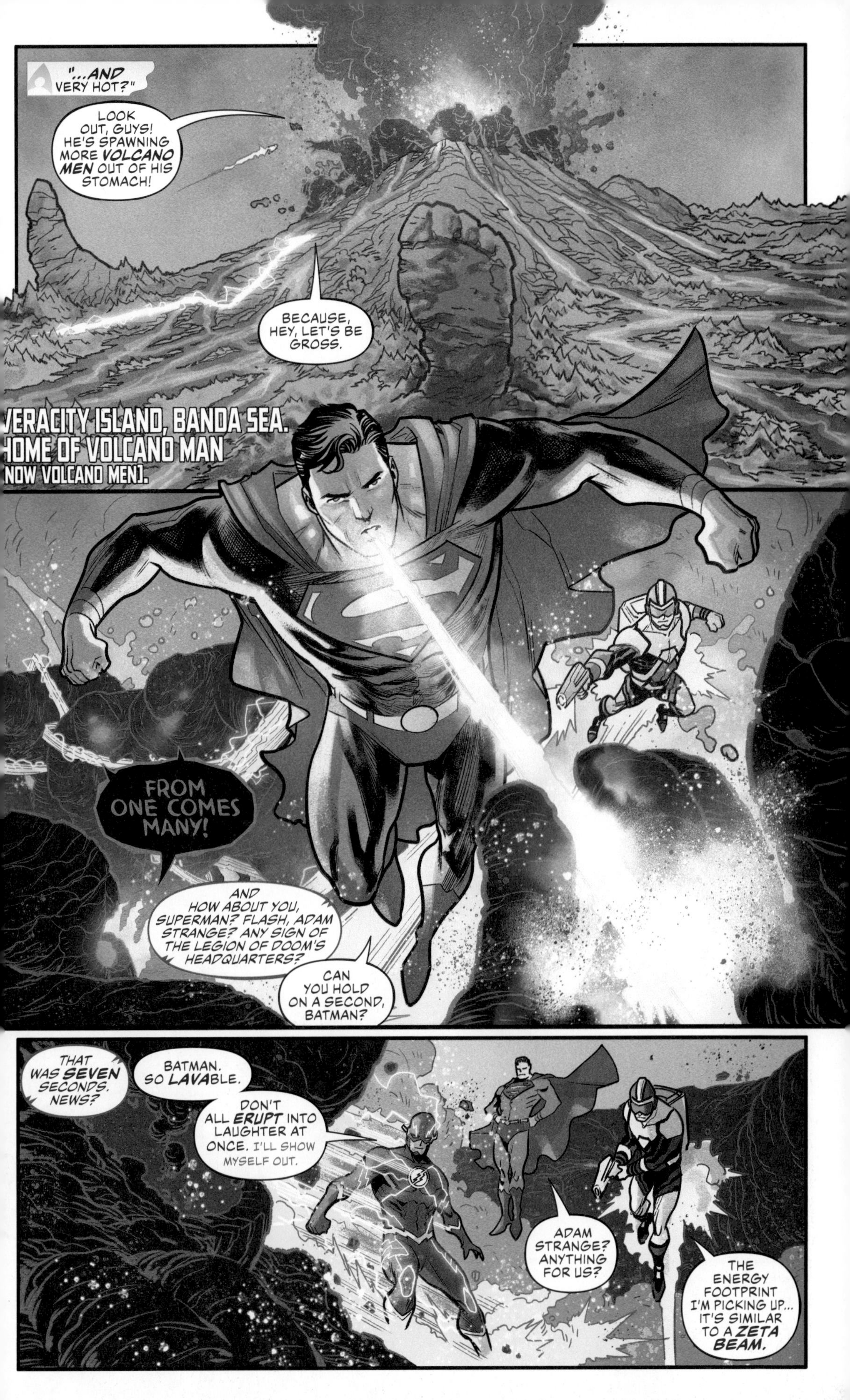
"...AND VERY HOT?"
LOOK OUT, GUYS! HE'S SPAWNING MORE VOLCANO MEN OUT OF HIS STOMACH!
BECAUSE, HEY, LET'S BE GROSS.
VERACITY ISLAND, BANDA SEA. HOME OF VOLCANO MAN (NOW VOLCANO MEN).
FROM ONE COMES MANY!
AND HOW ABOUT YOU, SUPERMAN? FLASH, ADAM STRANGE? ANY SIGN OF THE LEGION OF DOOM'S HEADQUARTERS?
CAN YOU HOLD ON A SECOND, BATMAN?
THAT WAS SEVEN SECONDS. NEWS?
BATMAN. SO LAVABLE.
DON'T ALL ERUPT INTO LAUGHTER AT ONCE. I'LL SHOW MYSELF OUT.
ADAM STRANGE? ANYTHING FOR US?
THE ENERGY FOOTPRINT I'M PICKING UP... IT'S SIMILAR TO A ZETA BEAM.

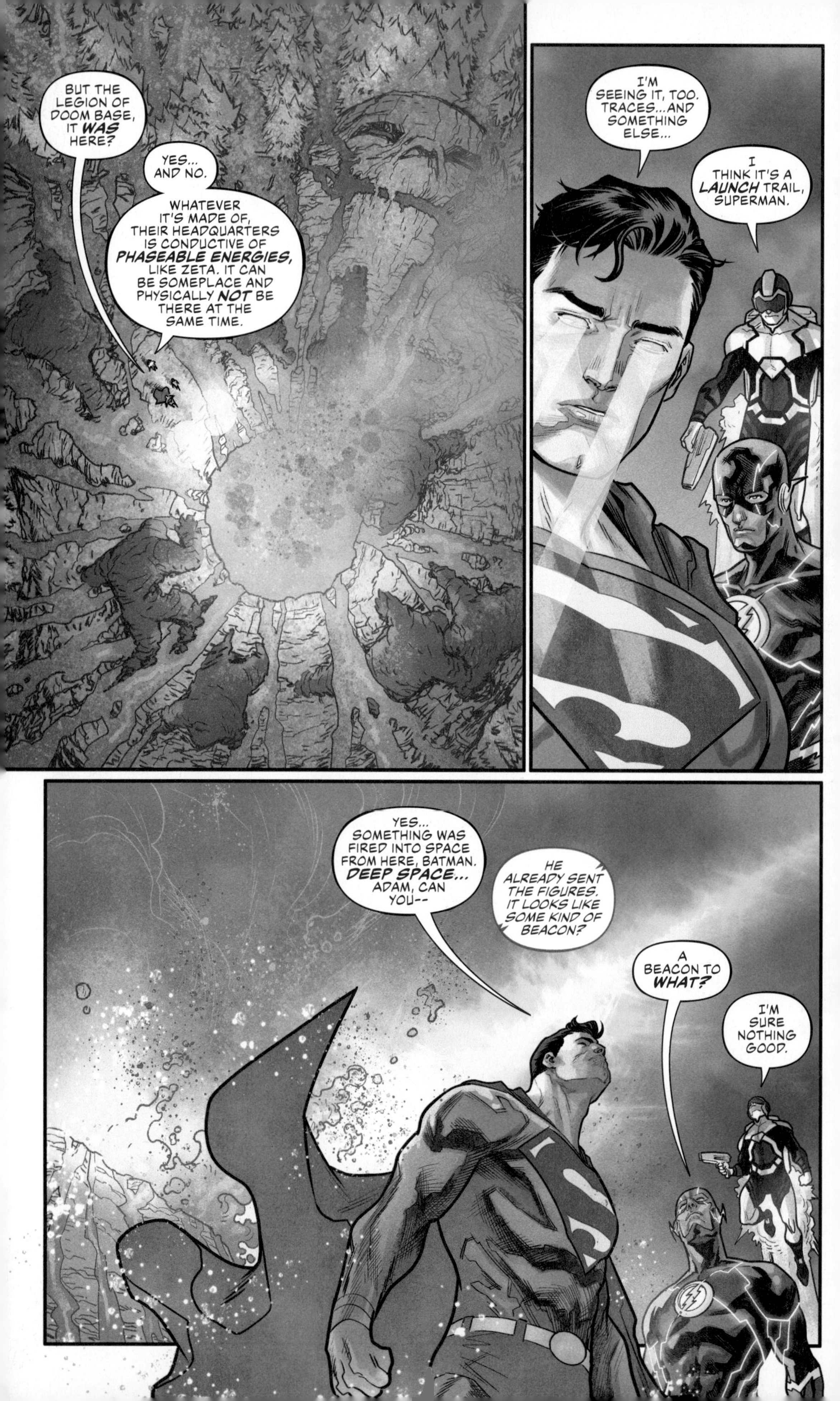
BUT THE LEGION OF DOOM BASE, IT WAS HERE?
YES... AND NO.
WHATEVER IT'S MADE OF, THEIR HEADQUARTERS IS CONDUCTIVE OF PHASEABLE ENERGIES, LIKE ZETA. IT CAN BE SOMEPLACE AND PHYSICALLY NOT BE THERE AT THE SAME TIME.
I'M SEEING IT, TOO. TRACES...AND SOMETHING ELSE...
I THINK IT'S A LAUNCH TRAIL, SUPERMAN.
YES... SOMETHING WAS FIRED INTO SPACE FROM HERE, BATMAN. DEEP SPACE... ADAM, CAN YOU--
HE ALREADY SENT THE FIGURES. IT LOOKS LIKE SOME KIND OF BEACON?
A BEACON TO WHAT?
I'M SURE NOTHING GOOD.

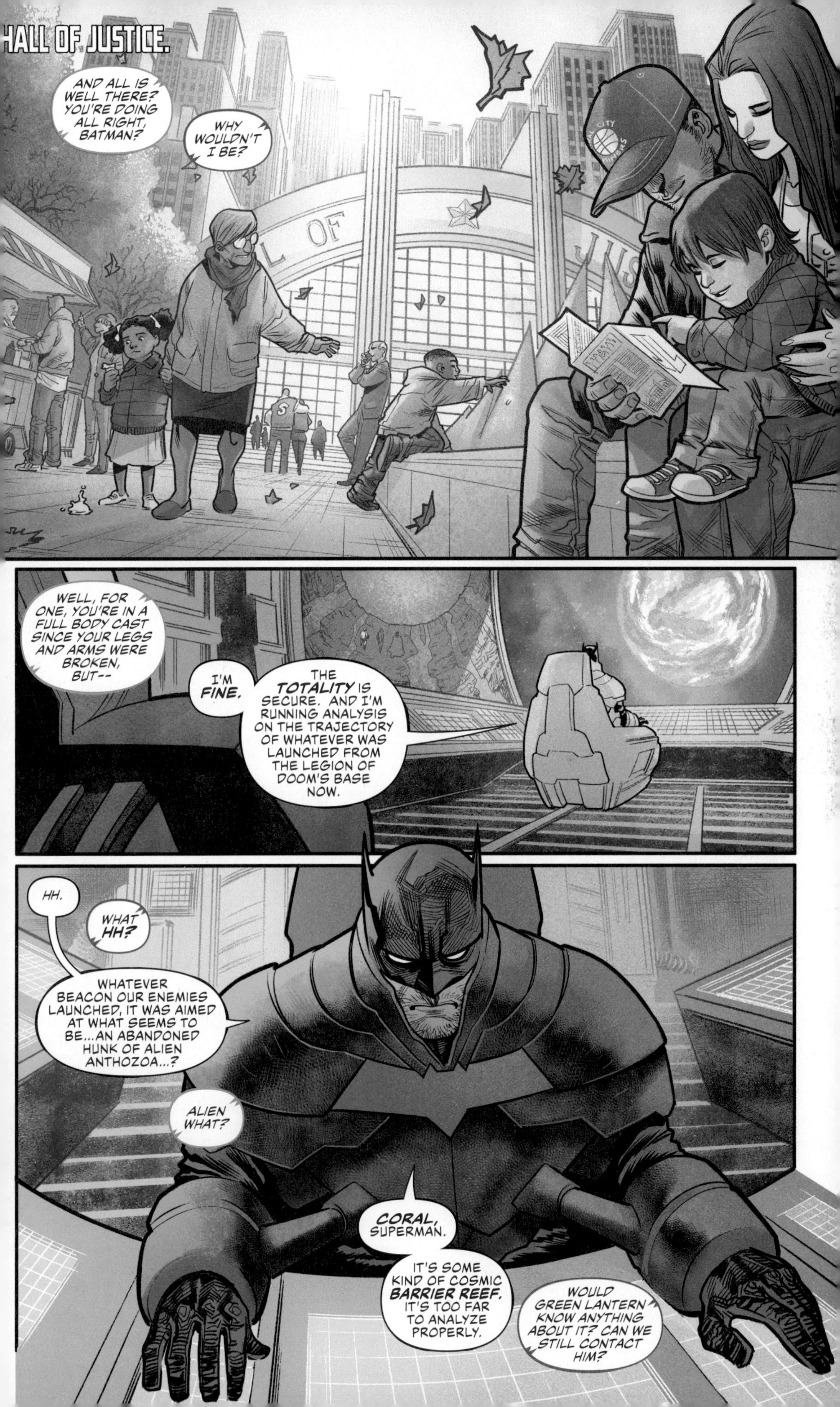

HALL OF JUSTICE.
AND ALL IS WELL THERE? YOU'RE DOING ALL RIGHT, BATMAN?
WHY WOULDN'T I BE?
WELL, FOR ONE, YOU'RE IN A FULL BODY CAST SINCE YOUR LEGS AND ARMS WERE BROKEN, BUT--
I'M FINE.
THE TOTALITY IS SECURE. AND I'M RUNNING ANALYSIS ON THE TRAJECTORY OF WHATEVER WAS LAUNCHED FROM THE LEGION OF DOOM'S BASE NOW.
HH.
WHAT HH?
WHATEVER BEACON OUR ENEMIES LAUNCHED, IT WAS AIMED AT WHAT SEEMS TO BE...AN ABANDONED HUNK OF ALIEN ANTHOZOA...?
ALIEN WHAT?
CORAL, SUPERMAN.
IT'S SOME KIND OF COSMIC BARRIER REEF. IT'S TOO FAR TO ANALYZE PROPERLY.
WOULD GREEN LANTERN KNOW ANYTHING ABOUT IT? CAN WE STILL CONTACT HIM?

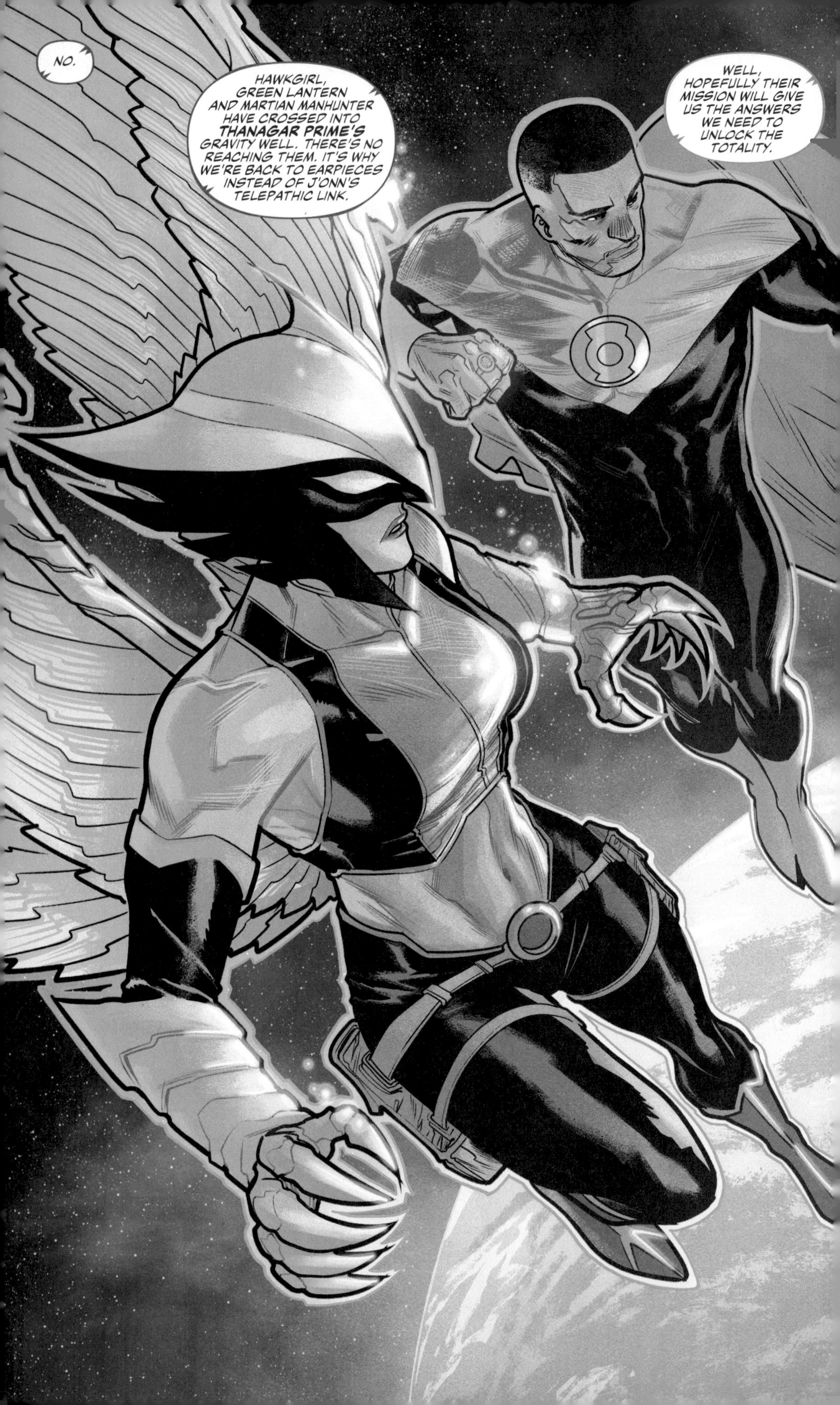
NO.
HAWKGIRL, GREEN LANTERN AND MARTIAN MANHUNTER HAVE CROSSED INTO THANAGAR PRIME'S GRAVITY WELL. THERE'S NO REACHING THEM. IT'S WHY WE'RE BACK TO EARPIECES INSTEAD OF J'ONN'S TELEPATHIC LINK.
WELL, HOPEFULLY THEIR MISSION WILL GIVE US THE ANSWERS WE NEED TO UNLOCK THE TOTALITY.

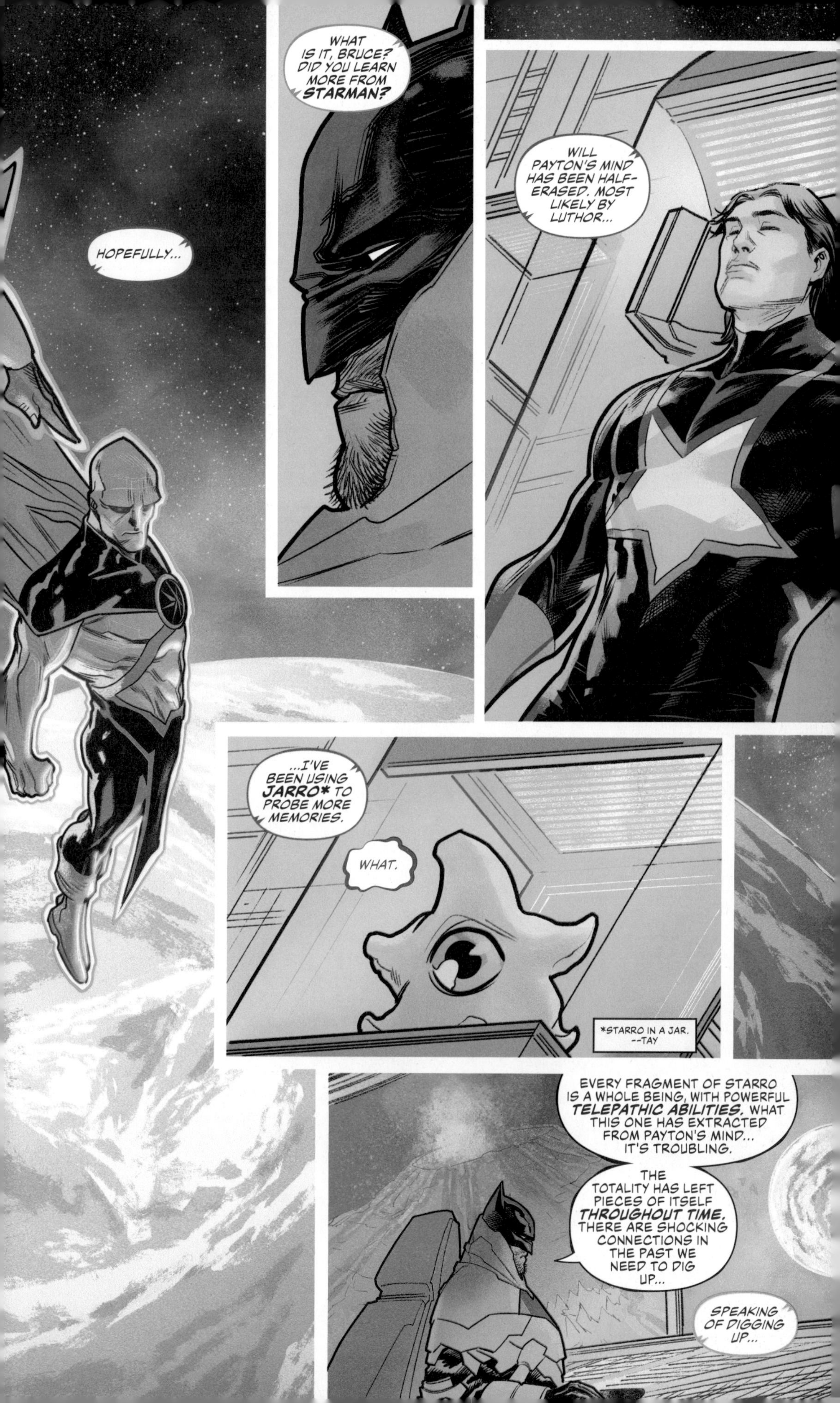
WHAT IS IT, BRUCE? DID YOU LEARN MORE FROM STARMAN?
HOPEFULLY...
WILL PAYTON'S MIND HAS BEEN HALF-ERASED. MOST LIKELY BY LUTHOR...
...I'VE BEEN USING JARRO* TO PROBE MORE MEMORIES.
WHAT.
*STARRO IN A JAR. --TAY
EVERY FRAGMENT OF STARRO IS A WHOLE BEING, WITH POWERFUL TELEPATHIC ABILITIES. WHAT THIS ONE HAS EXTRACTED FROM PAYTON'S MIND... IT'S TROUBLING.
THE TOTALITY HAS LEFT PIECES OF ITSELF THROUGHOUT TIME. THERE ARE SHOCKING CONNECTIONS IN THE PAST WE NEED TO DIG UP...
SPEAKING OF DIGGING UP...

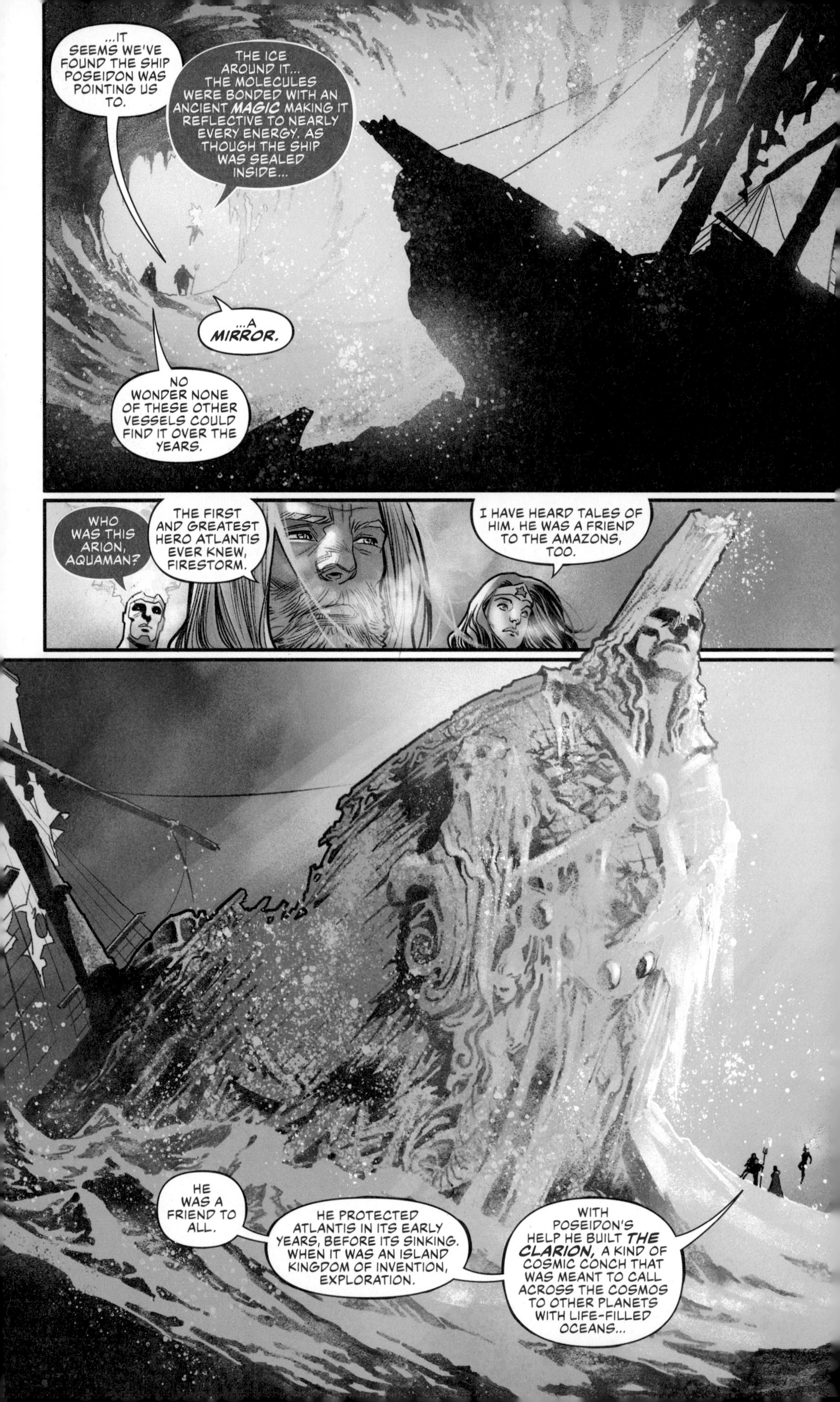
...IT SEEMS WE'VE FOUND THE SHIP POSEIDON WAS POINTING US TO.
THE ICE AROUND IT... THE MOLECULES WERE BONDED WITH AN ANCIENT MAGIC MAKING IT REFLECTIVE TO NEARLY EVERY ENERGY. AS THOUGH THE SHIP WAS SEALED INSIDE...
...A MIRROR.
NO WONDER NONE OF THESE OTHER VESSELS COULD FIND IT OVER THE YEARS.
WHO WAS THIS ARION, AQUAMAN?
THE FIRST AND GREATEST HERO ATLANTIS EVER KNEW, FIRESTORM.
I HAVE HEARD TALES OF HIM. HE WAS A FRIEND TO THE AMAZONS, TOO.
HE WAS A FRIEND TO ALL.
HE PROTECTED ATLANTIS IN ITS EARLY YEARS, BEFORE ITS SINKING. WHEN IT WAS AN ISLAND KINGDOM OF INVENTION, EXPLORATION.
WITH POSEIDON'S HELP HE BUILT THE CLARION, A KIND OF COSMIC CONCH THAT WAS MEANT TO CALL ACROSS THE COSMOS TO OTHER PLANETS WITH LIFE-FILLED OCEANS...

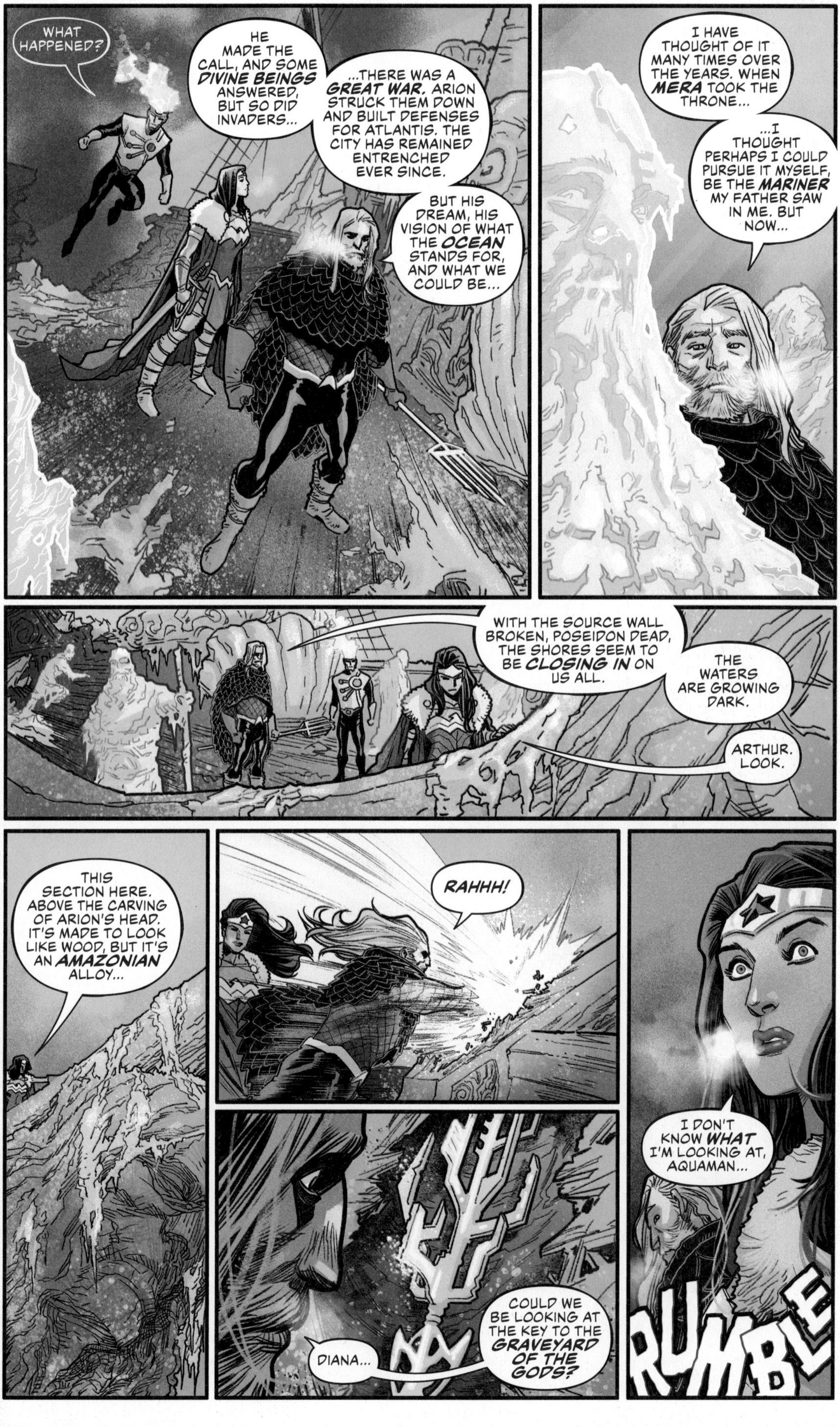
WHAT HAPPENED?
HE MADE THE CALL, AND SOME DIVINE BEINGS ANSWERED, BUT SO DID INVADERS...
...THERE WAS A GREAT WAR. ARION STRUCK THEM DOWN AND BUILT DEFENSES FOR ATLANTIS. THE CITY HAS REMAINED ENTRENCHED EVER SINCE.
BUT HIS DREAM, HIS VISION OF WHAT THE OCEAN STANDS FOR, AND WHAT WE COULD BE...
I HAVE THOUGHT OF IT MANY TIMES OVER THE YEARS. WHEN MERA TOOK THE THRONE...
...I THOUGHT PERHAPS I COULD PURSUE IT MYSELF, BE THE MARINER MY FATHER SAW IN ME. BUT NOW...
WITH THE SOURCE WALL BROKEN, POSEIDON DEAD, THE SHORES SEEM TO BE CLOSING IN ON US ALL.
THE WATERS ARE GROWING DARK.
ARTHUR. LOOK.
THIS SECTION HERE. ABOVE THE CARVING OF ARION'S HEAD. IT'S MADE TO LOOK LIKE WOOD, BUT IT'S AN AMAZONIAN ALLOY...
RAHHH!
I DON'T KNOW WHAT I'M LOOKING AT, AQUAMAN...
DIANA...
COULD WE BE LOOKING AT THE KEY TO THE GRAVEYARD OF THE GODS?
RUMBLE

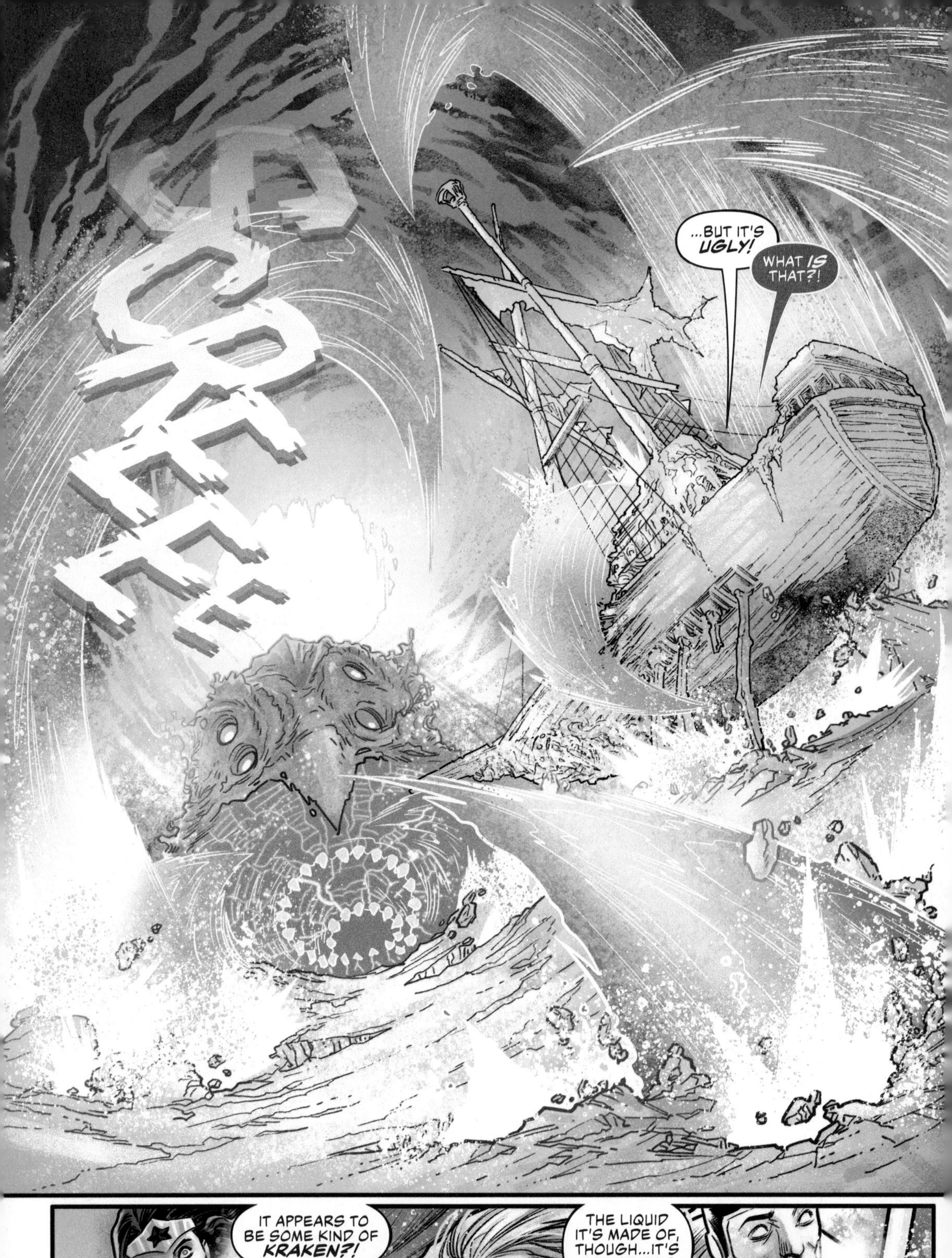

SKREEEE
...BUT IT'S UGLY!
WHAT IS THAT?!

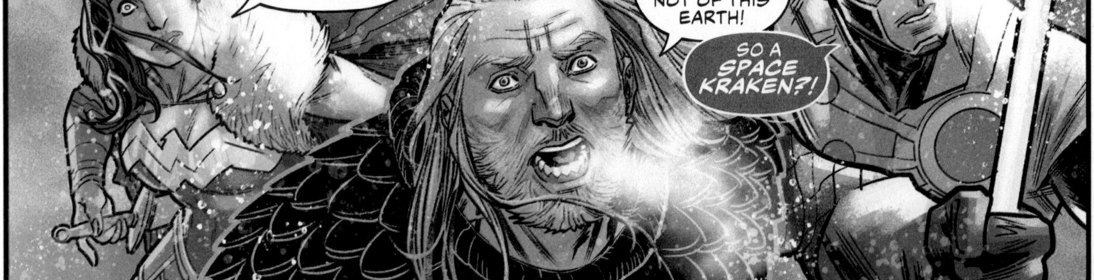

IT APPEARS TO BE SOME KIND OF KRAKEN?!
THE LIQUID IT'S MADE OF, THOUGH...IT'S NOT OF THIS EARTH!
SO A SPACE KRAKEN?!

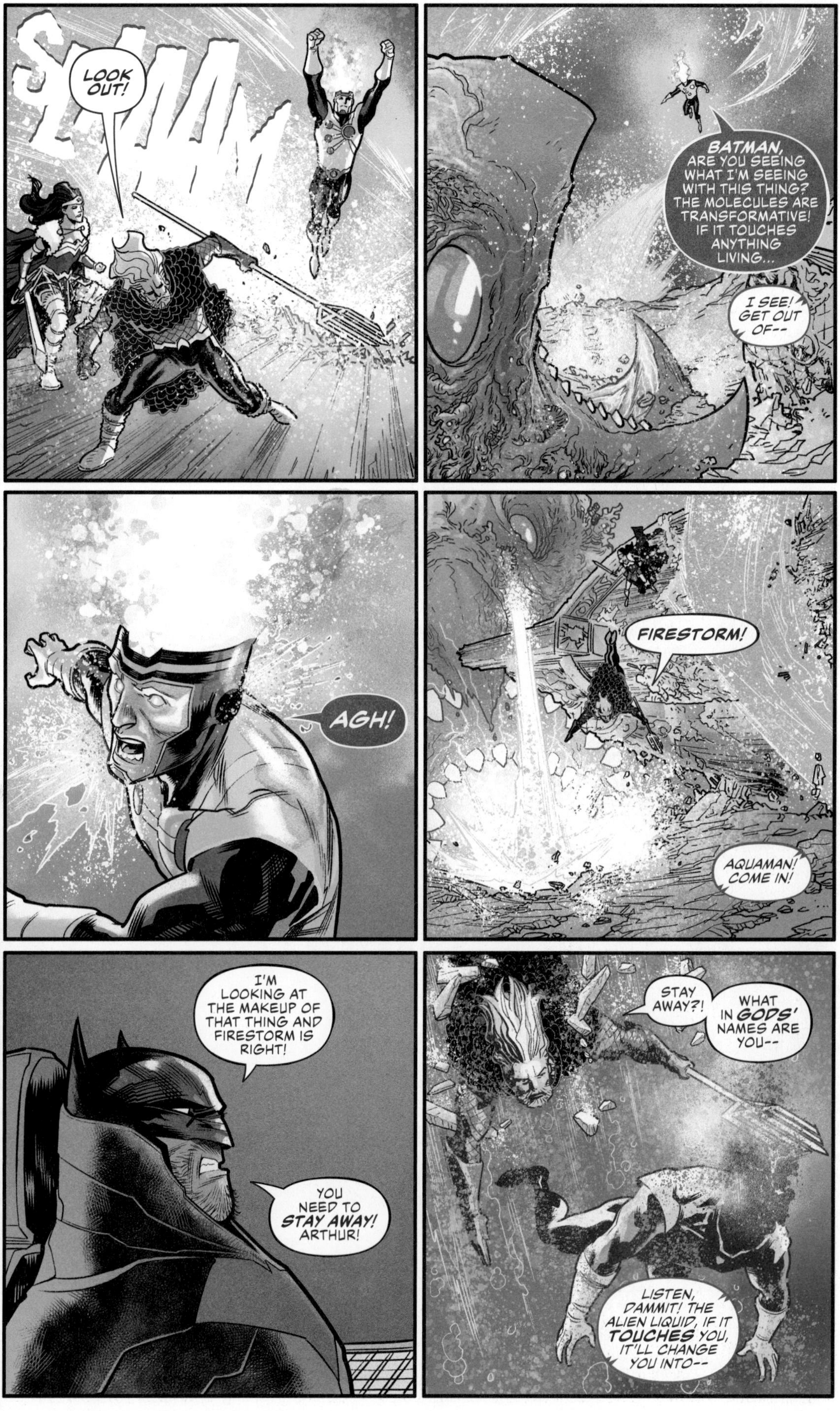
SLAM
LOOK OUT!
BATMAN, ARE YOU SEEING WHAT I'M SEEING WITH THIS THING? THE MOLECULES ARE TRANSFORMATIVE! IF IT TOUCHES ANYTHING LIVING...
I SEE! GET OUT OF--
AGH!
FIRESTORM!
AQUAMAN! COME IN!
I'M LOOKING AT THE MAKEUP OF THAT THING AND FIRESTORM IS RIGHT!
YOU NEED TO STAY AWAY! ARTHUR!
STAY AWAY?!
WHAT IN GODS' NAMES ARE YOU--
LISTEN, DAMMIT! THE ALIEN LIQUID, IF IT TOUCHES YOU, IT'LL CHANGE YOU INTO--

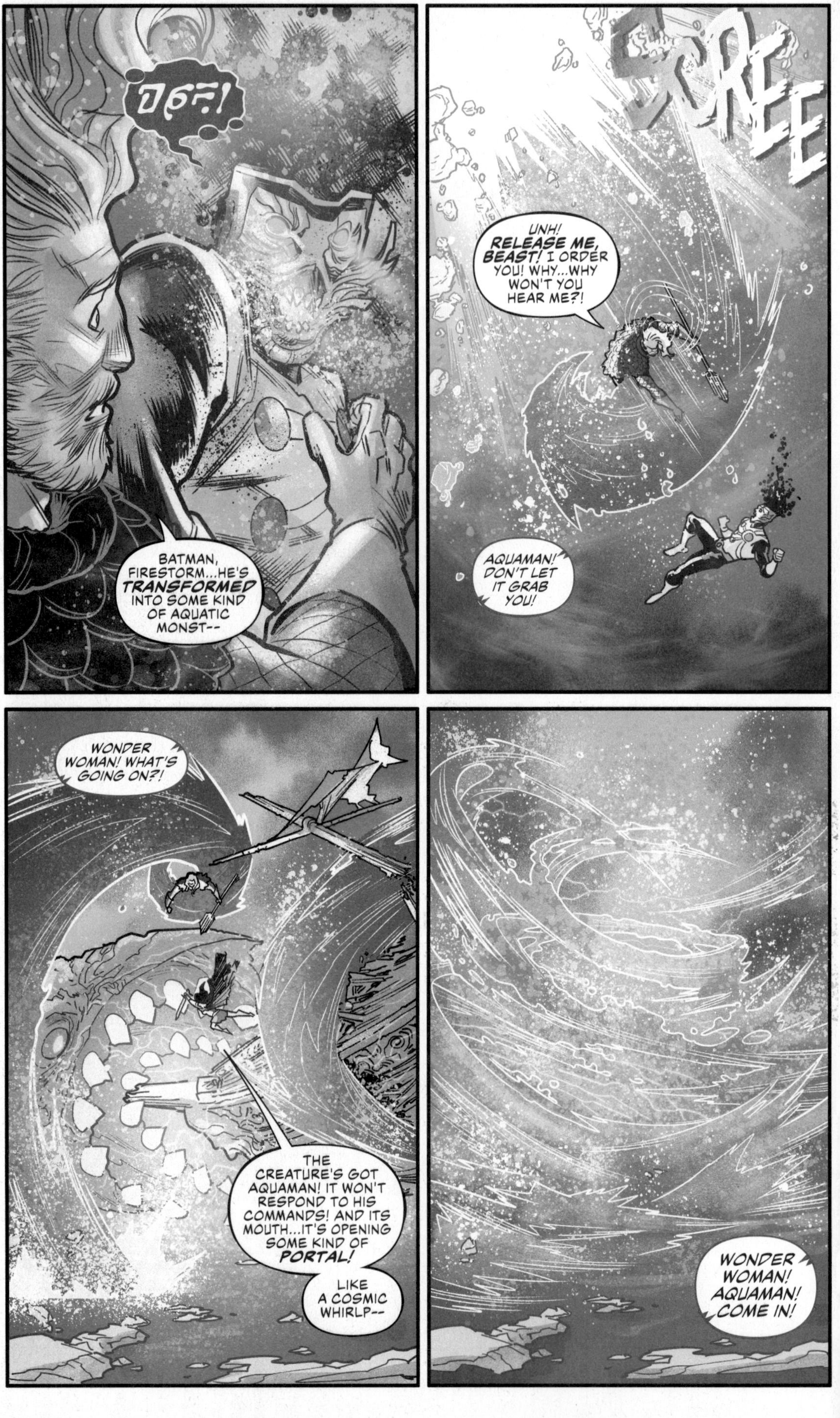
OOF!
BATMAN, FIRESTORM...HE'S TRANSFORMED INTO SOME KIND OF AQUATIC MONST--
SKREE
UNH! RELEASE ME, BEAST! I ORDER YOU! WHY...WHY WON'T YOU HEAR ME?!
AQUAMAN! DON'T LET IT GRAB YOU!
WONDER WOMAN! WHAT'S GOING ON?!
THE CREATURE'S GOT AQUAMAN! IT WON'T RESPOND TO HIS COMMANDS! AND ITS MOUTH...IT'S OPENING SOME KIND OF PORTAL!
LIKE A COSMIC WHIRLP--
WONDER WOMAN! AQUAMAN! COME IN!

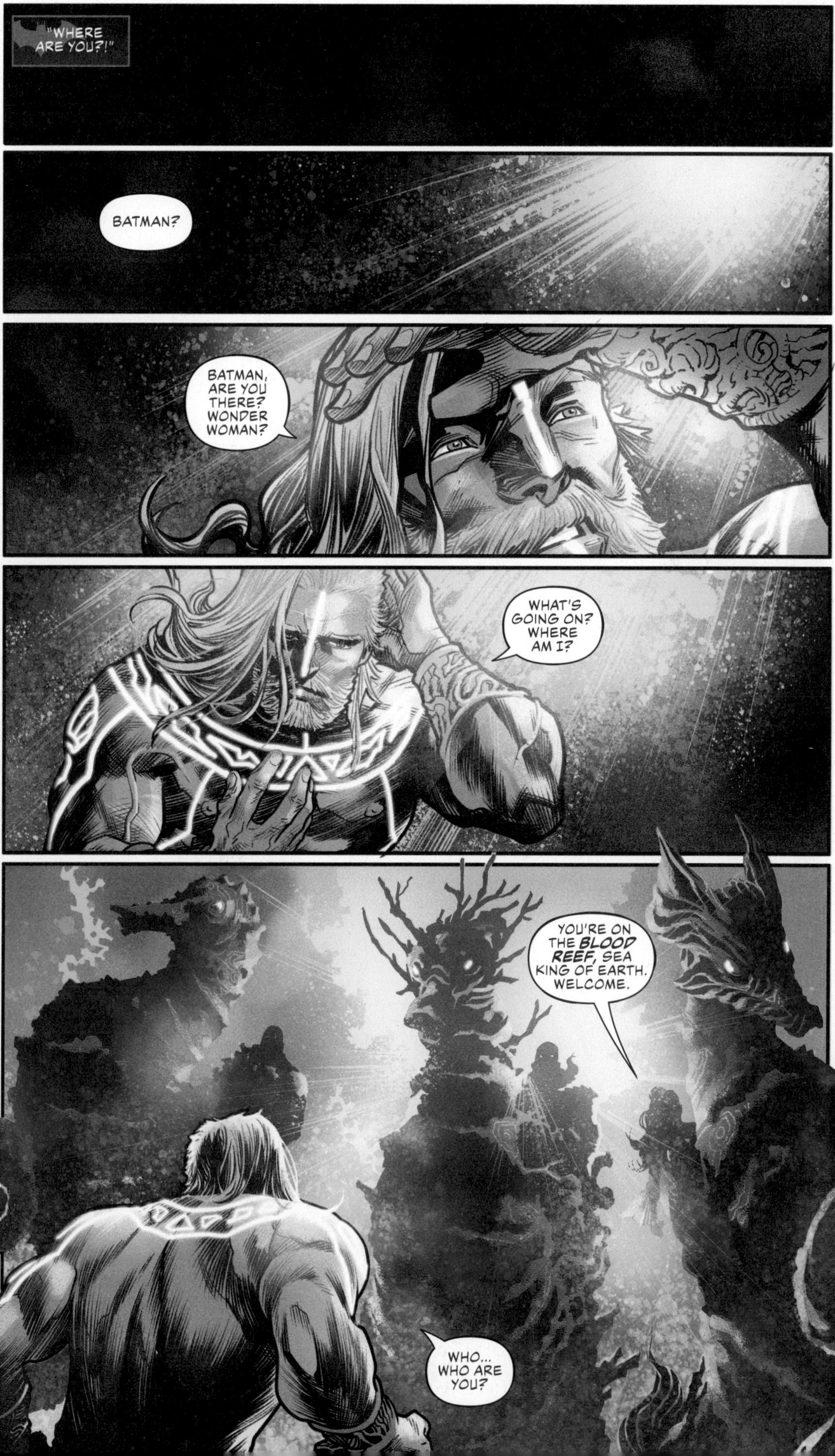
"WHERE ARE YOU?!"
BATMAN?
BATMAN, ARE YOU THERE? WONDER WOMAN?
WHAT'S GOING ON? WHERE AM I?
YOU'RE ON THE **BLOOD REEF**, SEA KING OF EARTH. WELCOME.
WHO... WHO ARE YOU?

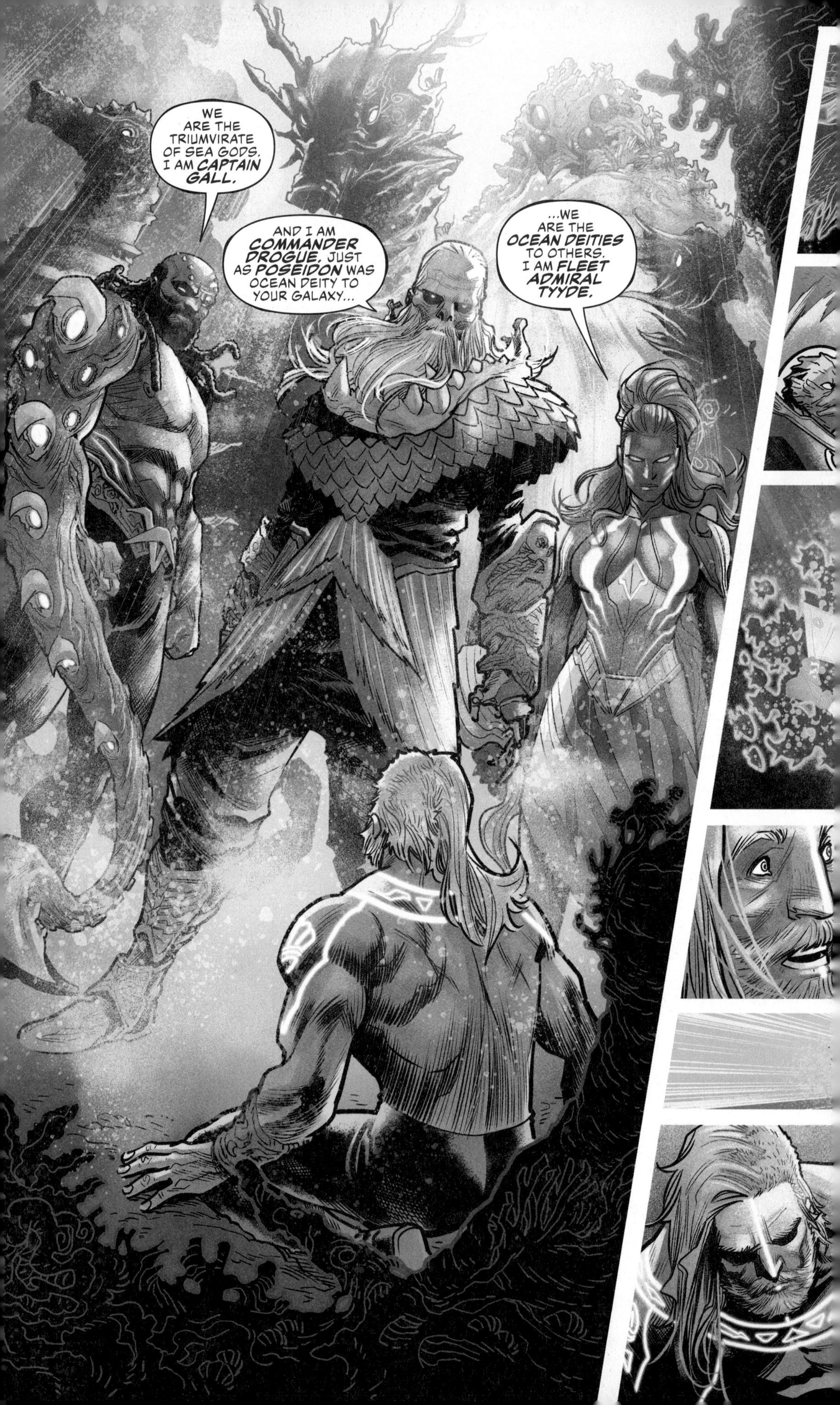

WE ARE THE TRIUMVIRATE OF SEA GODS. I AM CAPTAIN GALL.
AND I AM COMMANDER DROGUE. JUST AS POSEIDON WAS OCEAN DEITY TO YOUR GALAXY...
...WE ARE THE OCEAN DEITIES TO OTHERS. I AM FLEET ADMIRAL TYYDE.

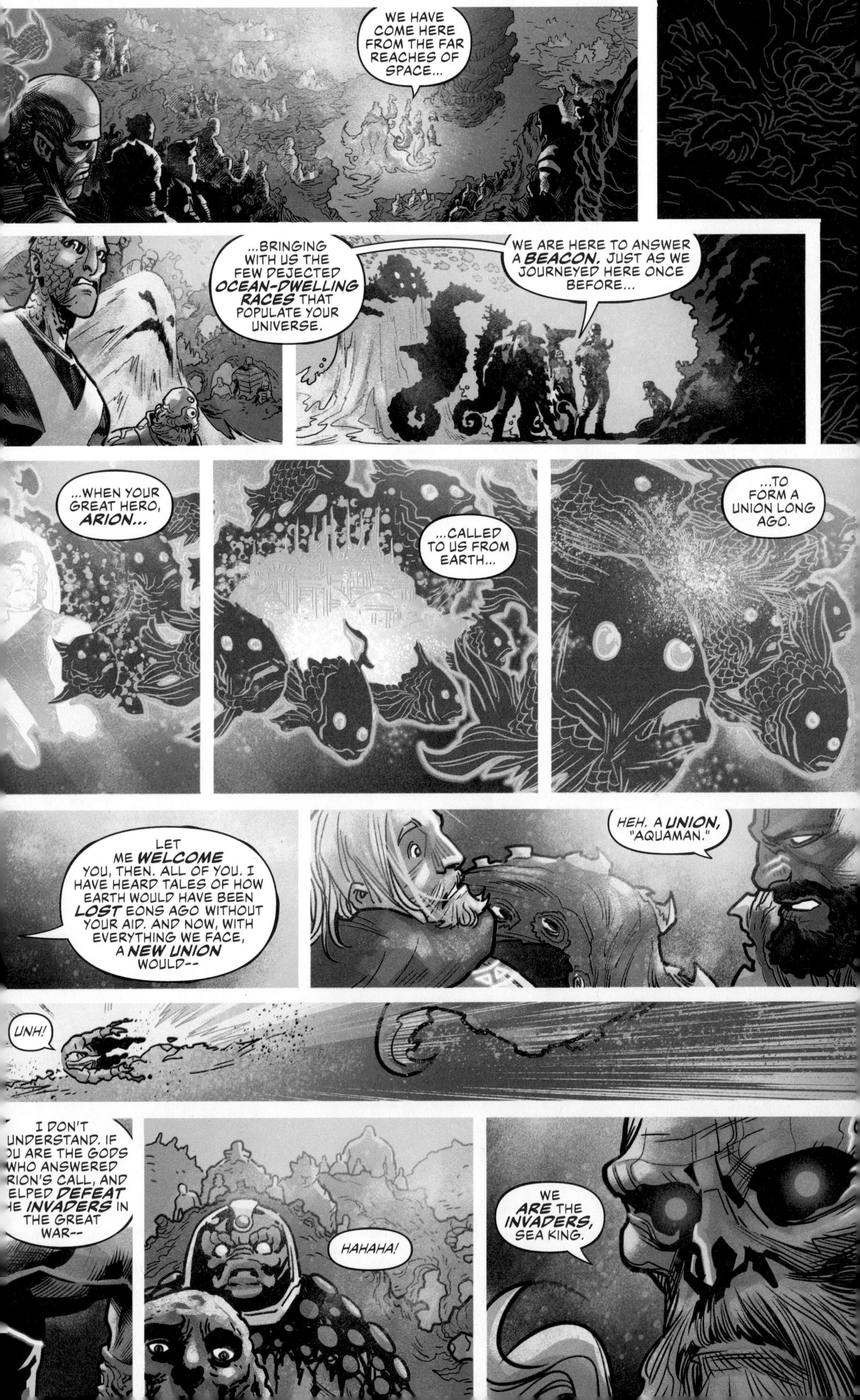

WE HAVE COME HERE FROM THE FAR REACHES OF SPACE...
...BRINGING WITH US THE FEW DEJECTED OCEAN-DWELLING RACES THAT POPULATE YOUR UNIVERSE.
WE ARE HERE TO ANSWER A BEACON. JUST AS WE JOURNEYED HERE ONCE BEFORE...
...WHEN YOUR GREAT HERO, ARION...
...CALLED TO US FROM EARTH...
...TO FORM A UNION LONG AGO.
LET ME WELCOME YOU, THEN. ALL OF YOU. I HAVE HEARD TALES OF HOW EARTH WOULD HAVE BEEN LOST EONS AGO WITHOUT YOUR AID. AND NOW, WITH EVERYTHING WE FACE, A NEW UNION WOULD--
HEH. A UNION, "AQUAMAN."
UNH!
I DON'T UNDERSTAND. IF OU ARE THE GODS WHO ANSWERED RION'S CALL, AND ELPED DEFEAT HE INVADERS IN THE GREAT WAR--
HAHAHA!
WE ARE THE INVADERS, SEA KING.

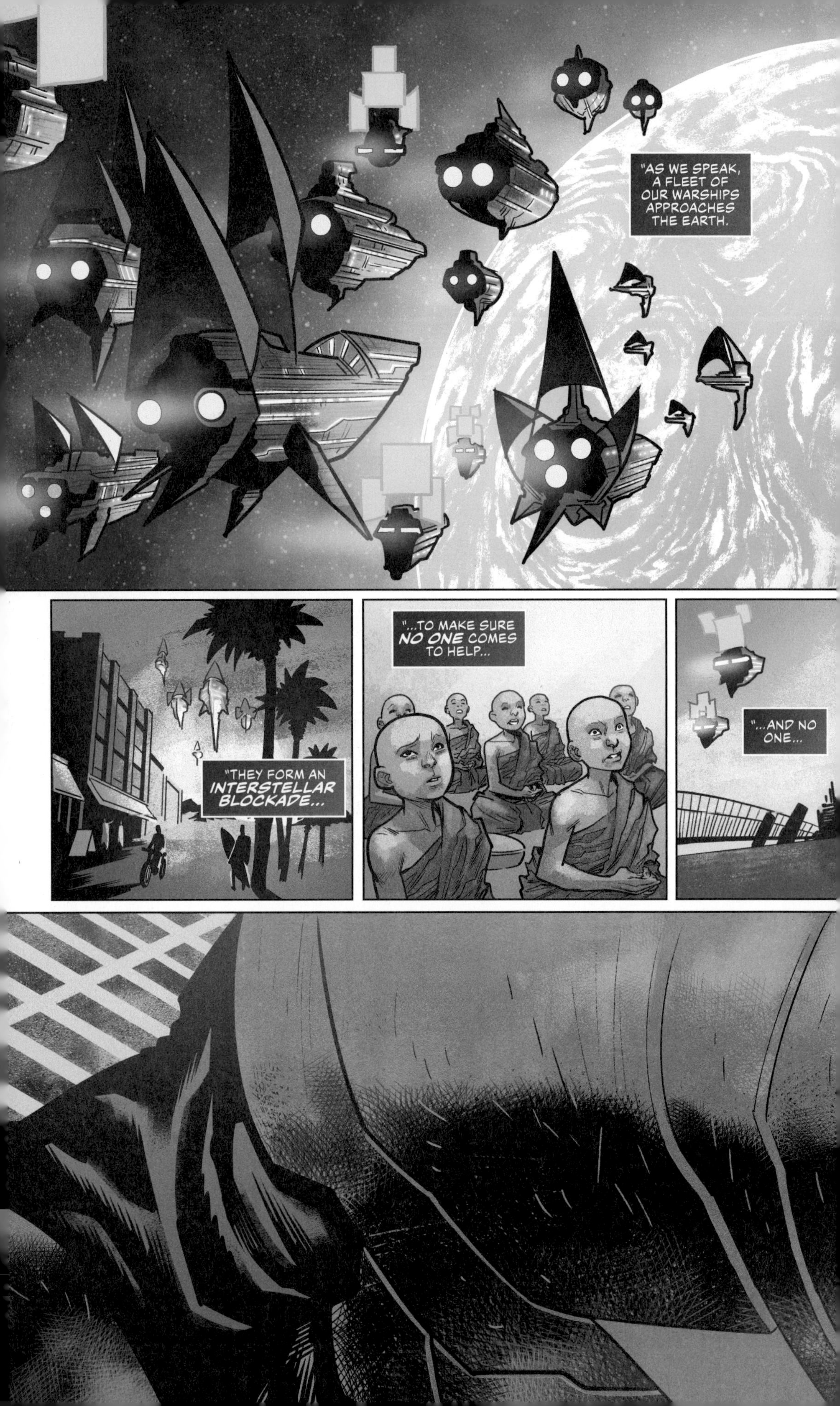
"AS WE SPEAK, A FLEET OF OUR WARSHIPS APPROACHES THE EARTH.
"THEY FORM AN *INTERSTELLAR BLOCKADE*...
"...TO MAKE SURE **NO ONE** COMES TO HELP...
"...AND NO ONE...

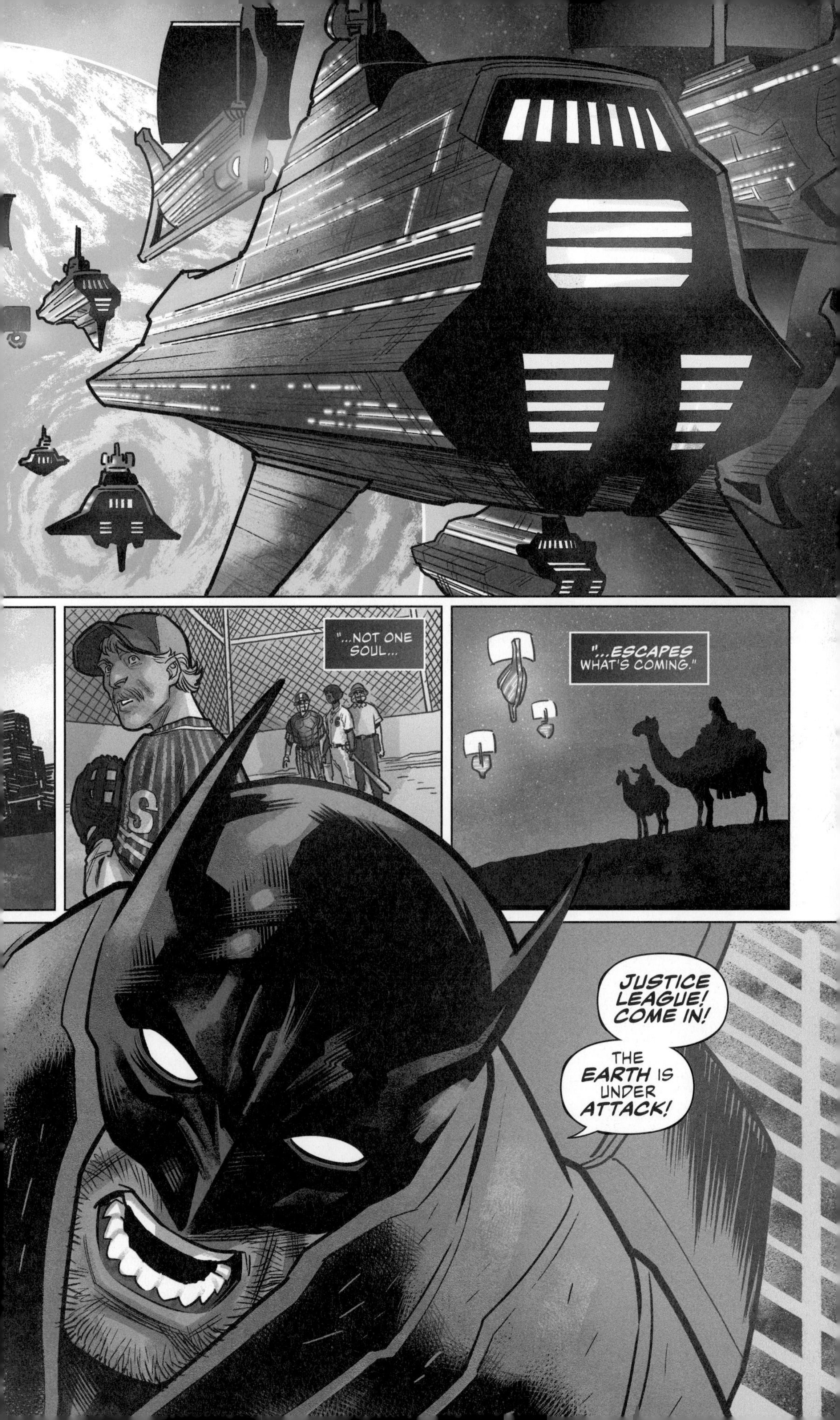
"...NOT ONE SOUL...
"...ESCAPES WHAT'S COMING."
JUSTICE LEAGUE! COME IN!
THE EARTH IS UNDER ATTACK!

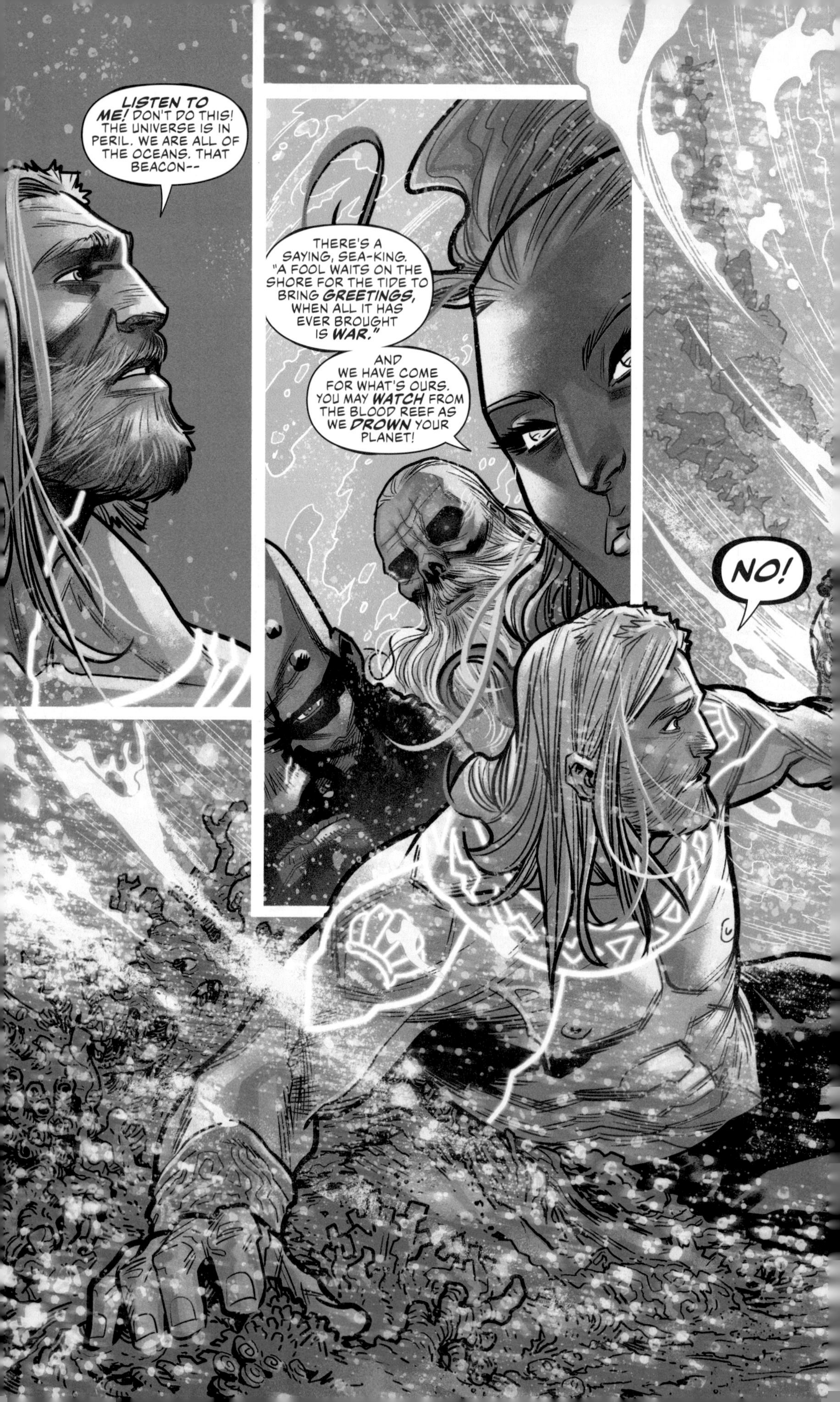
LISTEN TO ME! DON'T DO THIS! THE UNIVERSE IS IN PERIL. WE ARE ALL OF THE OCEANS. THAT BEACON--
THERE'S A SAYING, SEA-KING. "A FOOL WAITS ON THE SHORE FOR THE TIDE TO BRING GREETINGS, WHEN ALL IT HAS EVER BROUGHT IS WAR."
AND WE HAVE COME FOR WHAT'S OURS. YOU MAY WATCH FROM THE BLOOD REEF AS WE DROWN YOUR PLANET!
NO!

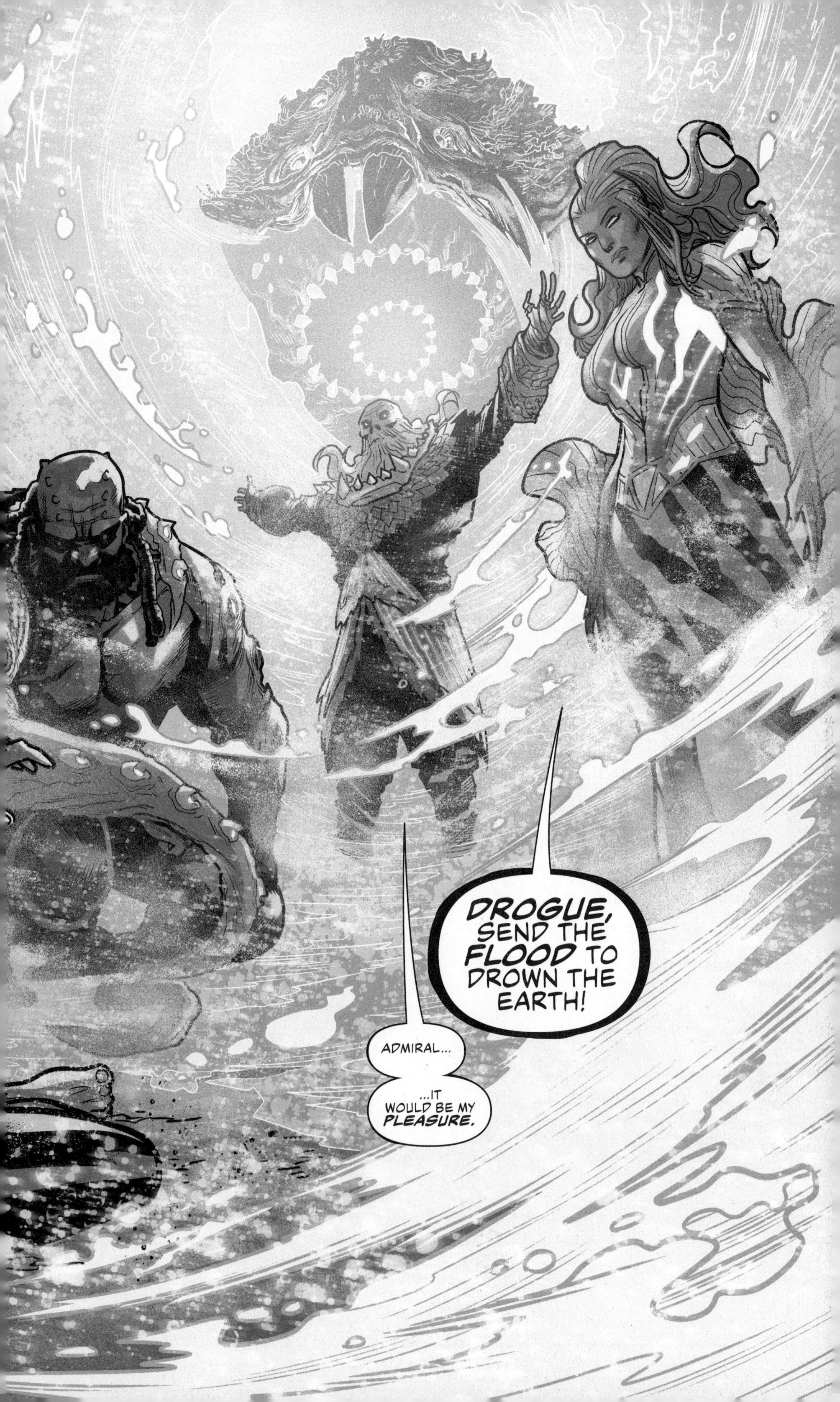
DROGUE, SEND THE FLOOD TO DROWN THE EARTH!
ADMIRAL...
...IT WOULD BE MY PLEASURE.

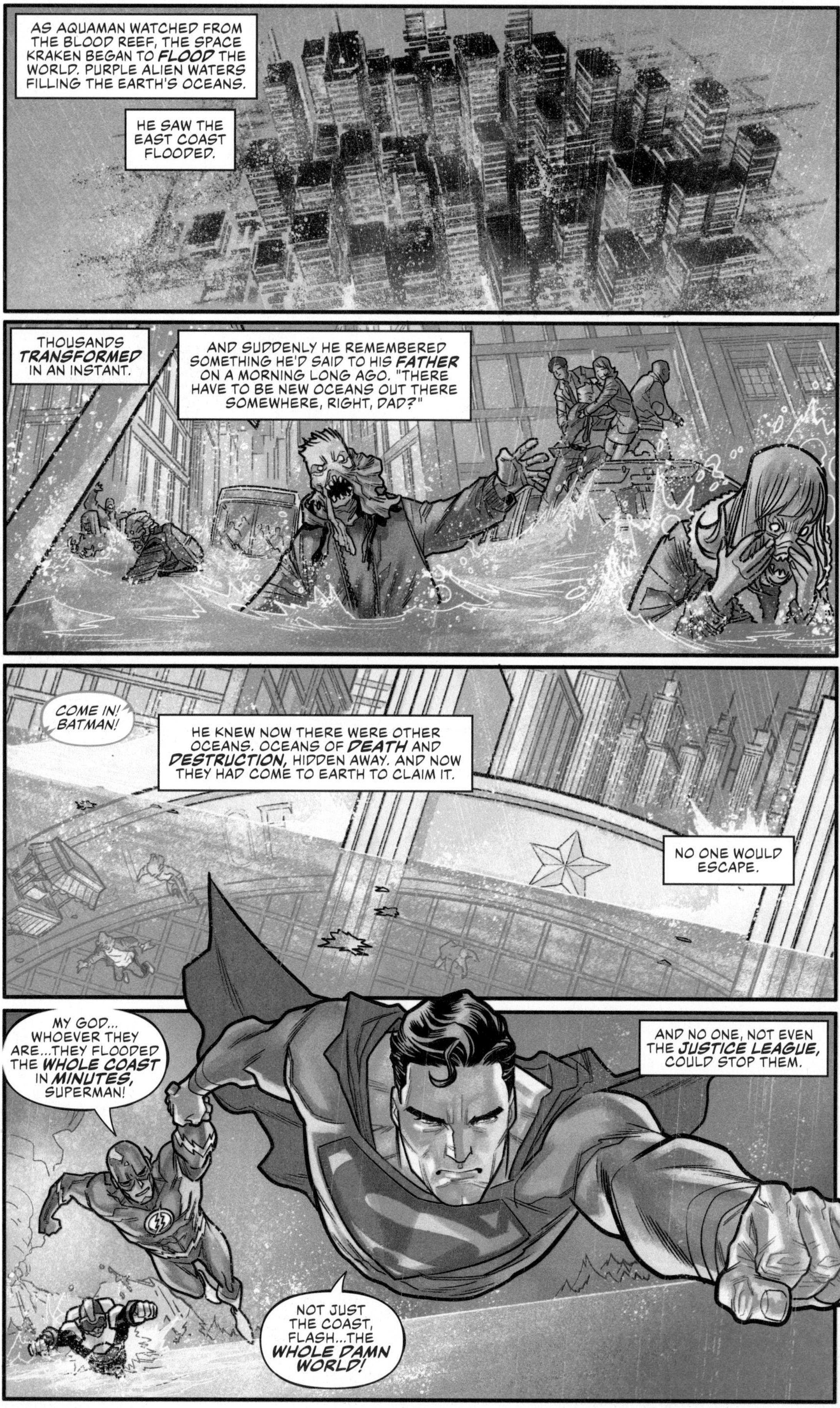

AS AQUAMAN WATCHED FROM THE BLOOD REEF, THE SPACE KRAKEN BEGAN TO *FLOOD* THE WORLD. PURPLE ALIEN WATERS FILLING THE EARTH'S OCEANS.
HE SAW THE EAST COAST FLOODED.
THOUSANDS *TRANSFORMED* IN AN INSTANT.
AND SUDDENLY HE REMEMBERED SOMETHING HE'D SAID TO HIS *FATHER* ON A MORNING LONG AGO. "THERE HAVE TO BE NEW OCEANS OUT THERE SOMEWHERE, RIGHT, DAD?"
COME IN! BATMAN!
HE KNEW NOW THERE WERE OTHER OCEANS. OCEANS OF *DEATH* AND *DESTRUCTION,* HIDDEN AWAY. AND NOW THEY HAD COME TO EARTH TO CLAIM IT.
NO ONE WOULD ESCAPE.
MY GOD... WHOEVER THEY ARE...THEY FLOODED THE *WHOLE COAST* IN *MINUTES,* SUPERMAN!
AND NO ONE, NOT EVEN THE *JUSTICE LEAGUE,* COULD STOP THEM.
NOT JUST THE COAST, FLASH...THE *WHOLE DAMN WORLD!*

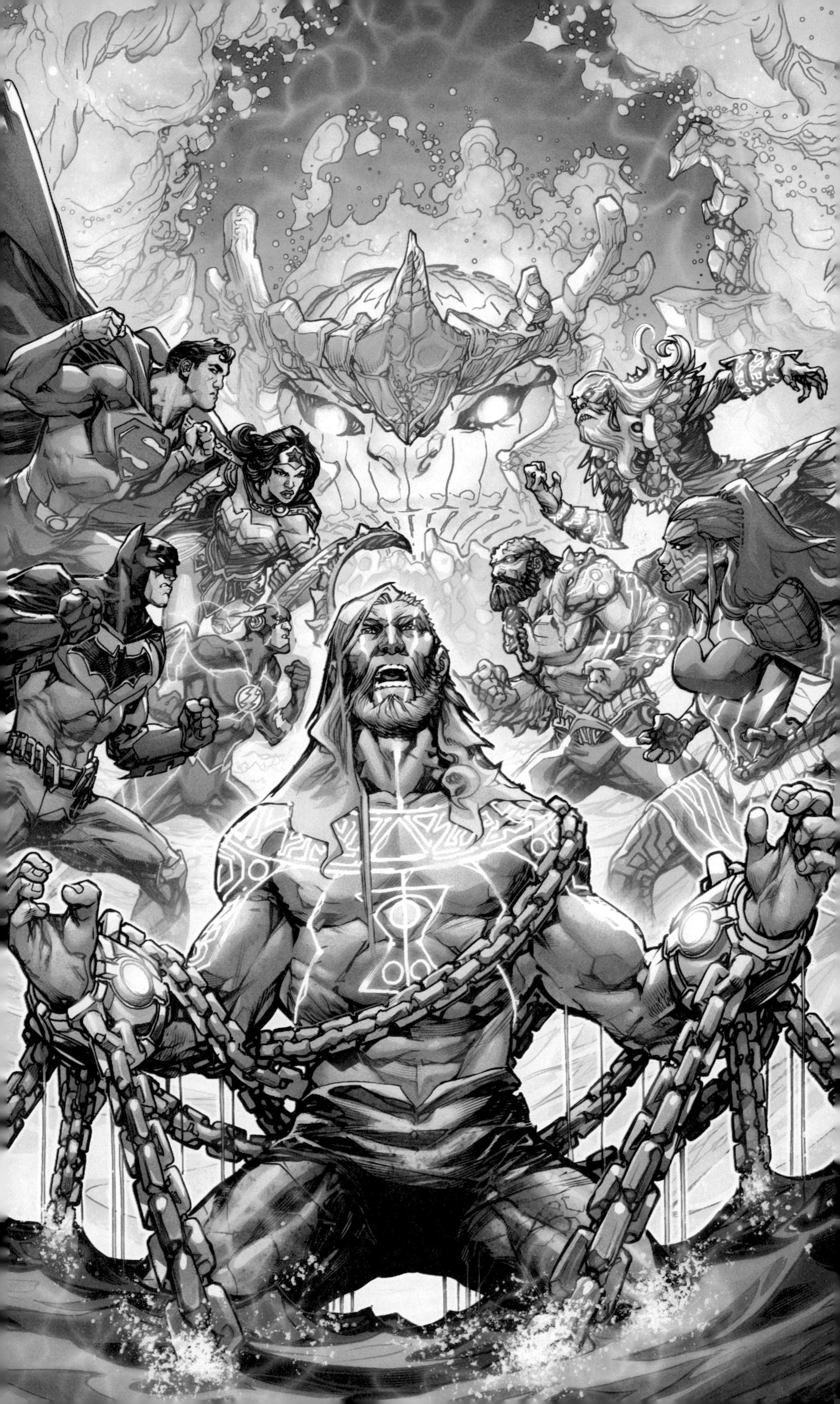

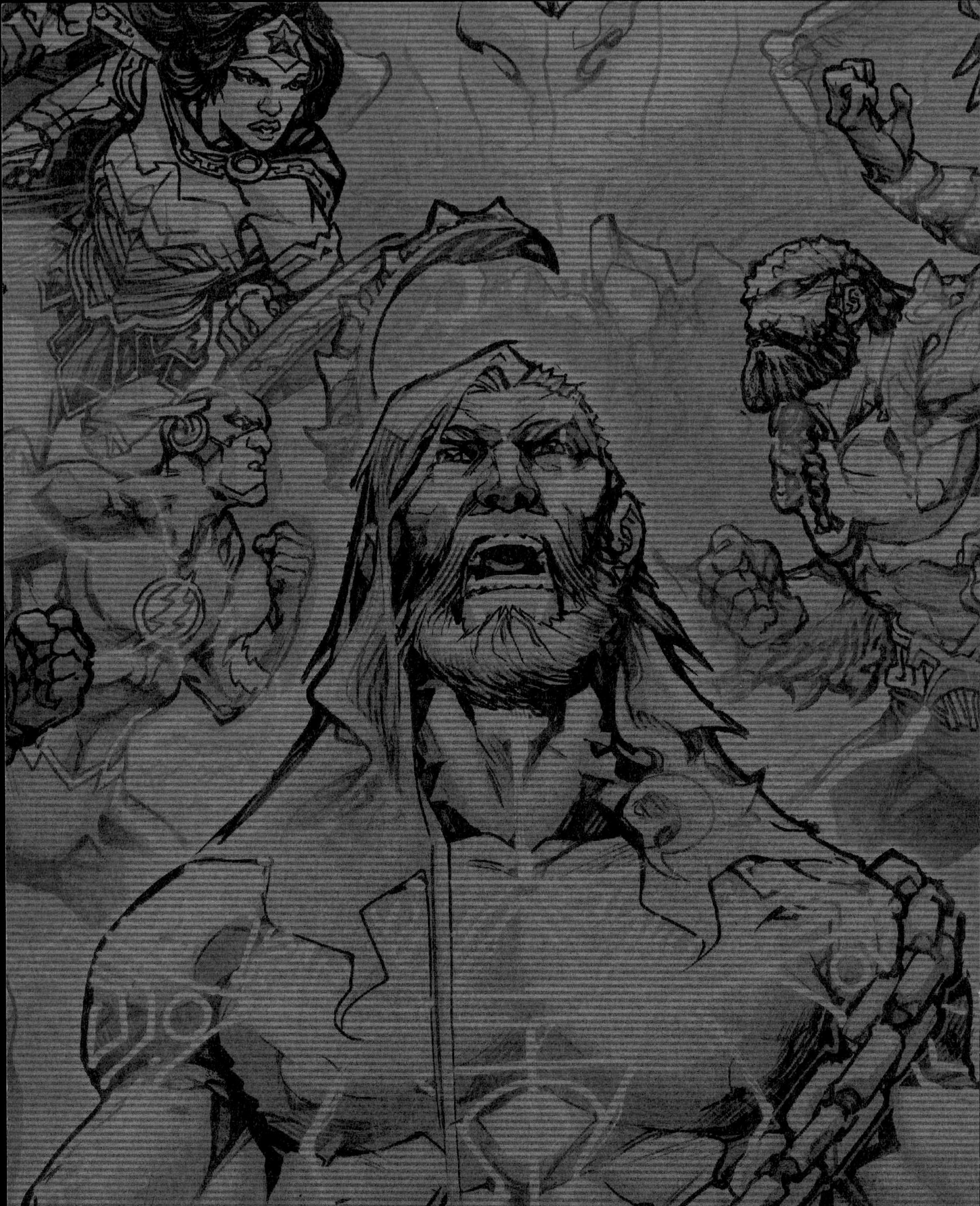

JUSTICE
LEAGUE/AQUAMAN
SPECIAL #1

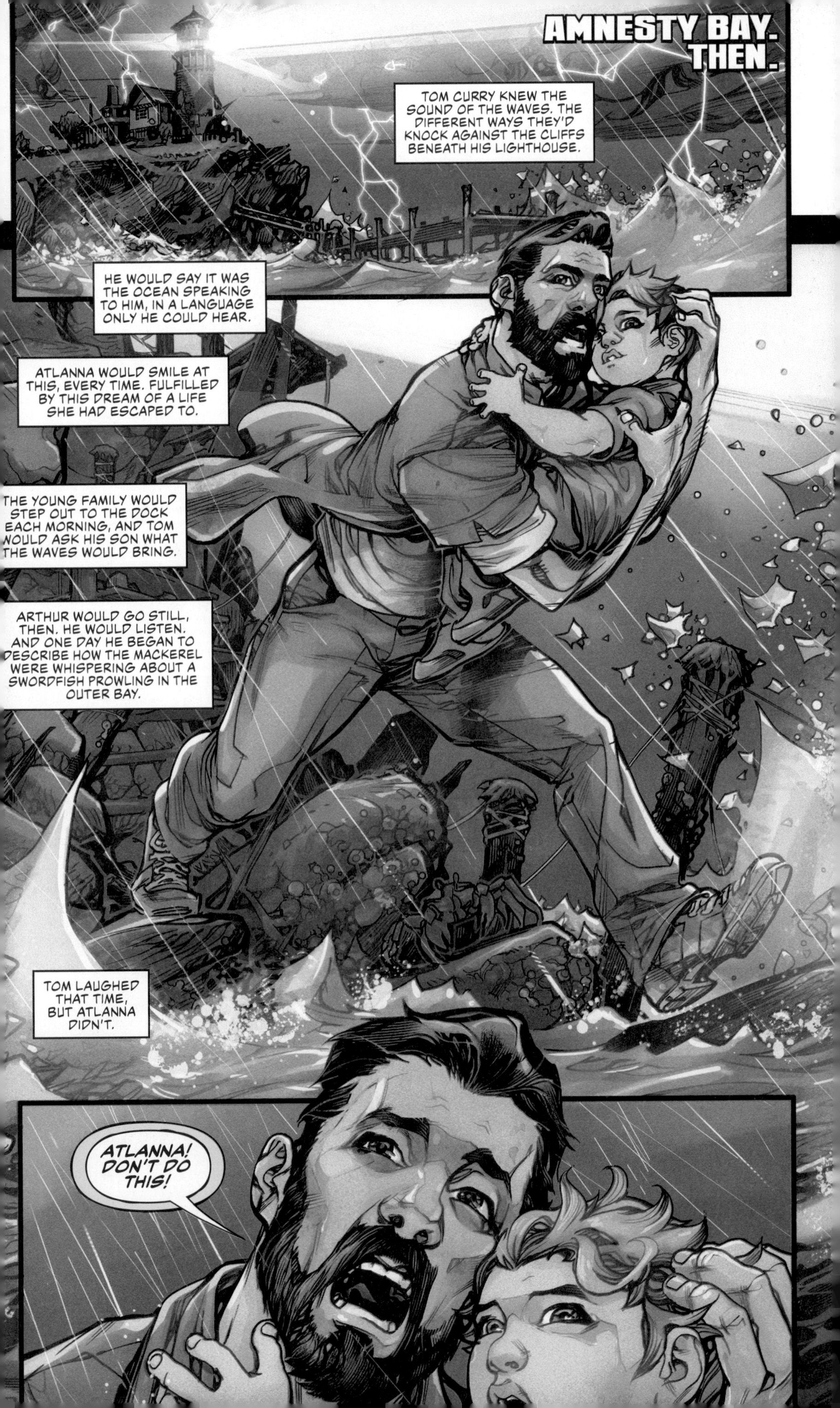
AMNESTY BAY. THEN.
TOM CURRY KNEW THE SOUND OF THE WAVES. THE DIFFERENT WAYS THEY'D KNOCK AGAINST THE CLIFFS BENEATH HIS LIGHTHOUSE.
HE WOULD SAY IT WAS THE OCEAN SPEAKING TO HIM, IN A LANGUAGE ONLY HE COULD HEAR.
ATLANNA WOULD SMILE AT THIS, EVERY TIME. FULFILLED BY THIS DREAM OF A LIFE SHE HAD ESCAPED TO.
THE YOUNG FAMILY WOULD STEP OUT TO THE DOCK EACH MORNING, AND TOM WOULD ASK HIS SON WHAT THE WAVES WOULD BRING.
ARTHUR WOULD GO STILL, THEN. HE WOULD LISTEN. AND ONE DAY HE BEGAN TO DESCRIBE HOW THE MACKEREL WERE WHISPERING ABOUT A SWORDFISH PROWLING IN THE OUTER BAY.
TOM LAUGHED THAT TIME, BUT ATLANNA DIDN'T.
ATLANNA! DON'T DO THIS!

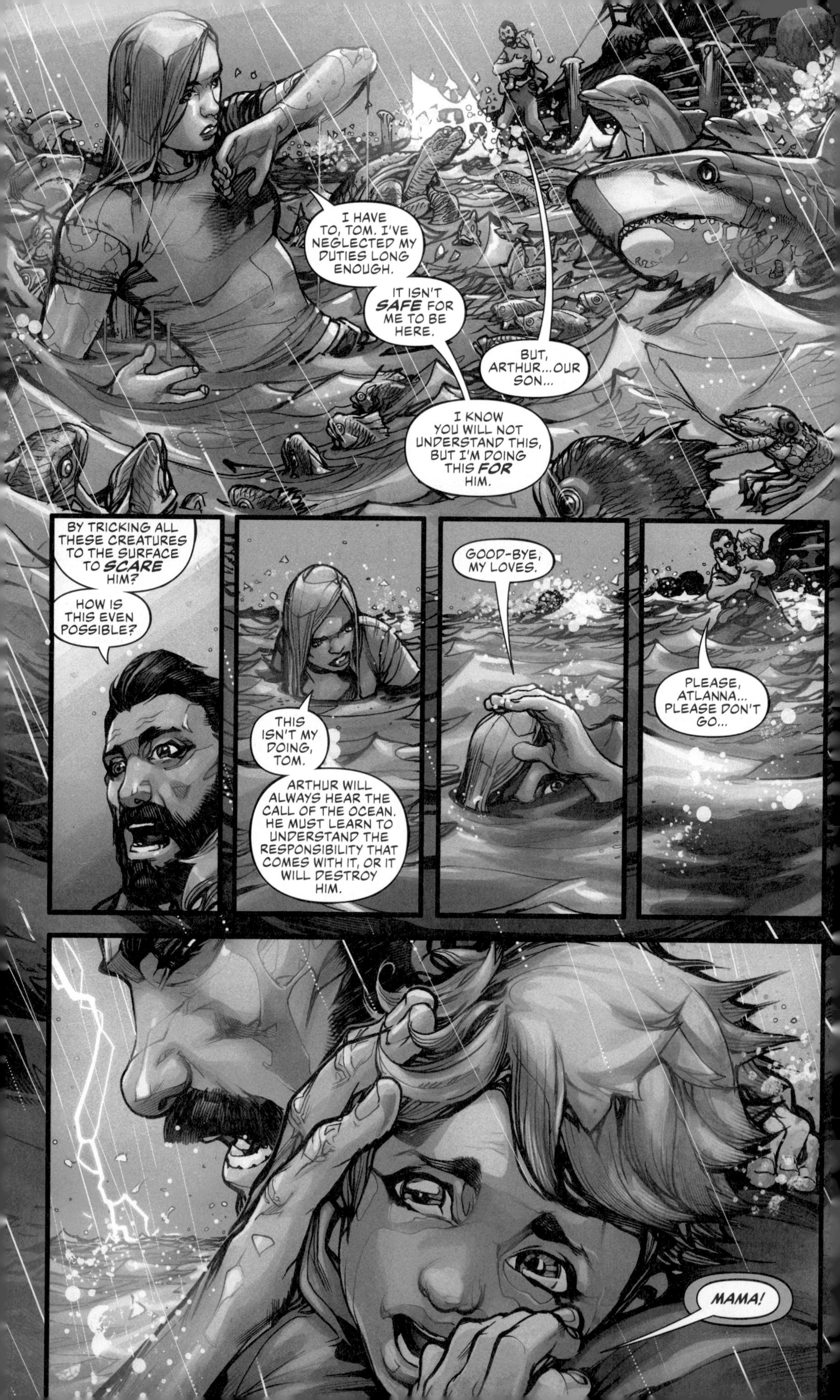
I HAVE TO, TOM. I'VE NEGLECTED MY DUTIES LONG ENOUGH.
IT ISN'T *SAFE* FOR ME TO BE HERE.
BUT, ARTHUR...OUR SON...
I KNOW YOU WILL NOT UNDERSTAND THIS, BUT I'M DOING THIS *FOR* HIM.
BY TRICKING ALL THESE CREATURES TO THE SURFACE TO *SCARE* HIM?
HOW IS THIS EVEN POSSIBLE?
THIS ISN'T MY DOING, TOM.
ARTHUR WILL ALWAYS HEAR THE CALL OF THE OCEAN. HE MUST LEARN TO UNDERSTAND THE RESPONSIBILITY THAT COMES WITH IT, OR IT WILL DESTROY HIM.
GOOD-BYE, MY LOVES.
PLEASE, ATLANNA... PLEASE DON'T GO...
MAMA!

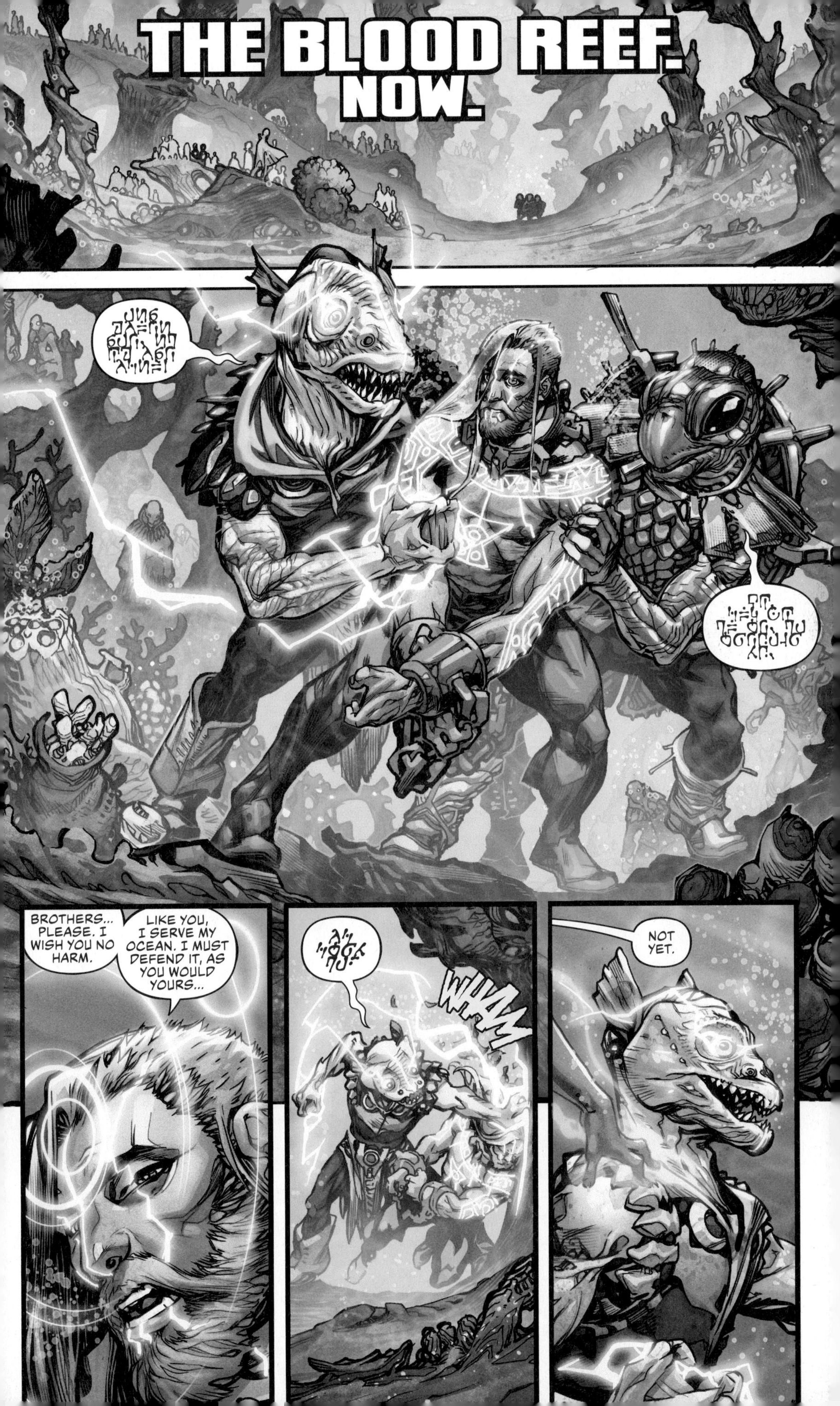
THE BLOOD REEF.
NOW.
BROTHERS... PLEASE. I WISH YOU NO HARM.
LIKE YOU, I SERVE MY OCEAN. I MUST DEFEND IT, AS YOU WOULD YOURS...
WHAM
NOT YET.

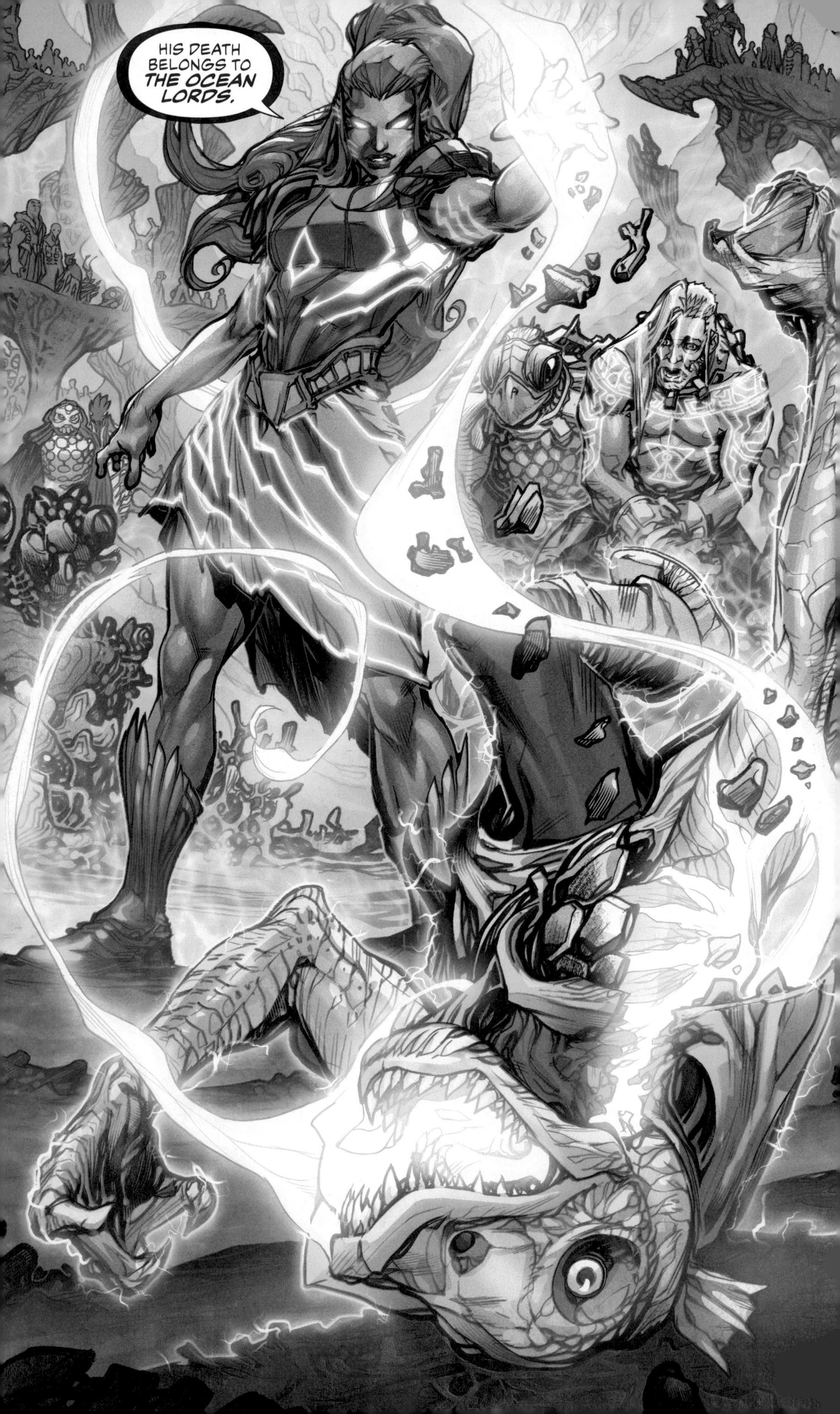

HIS DEATH BELONGS TO *THE OCEAN LORDS.*

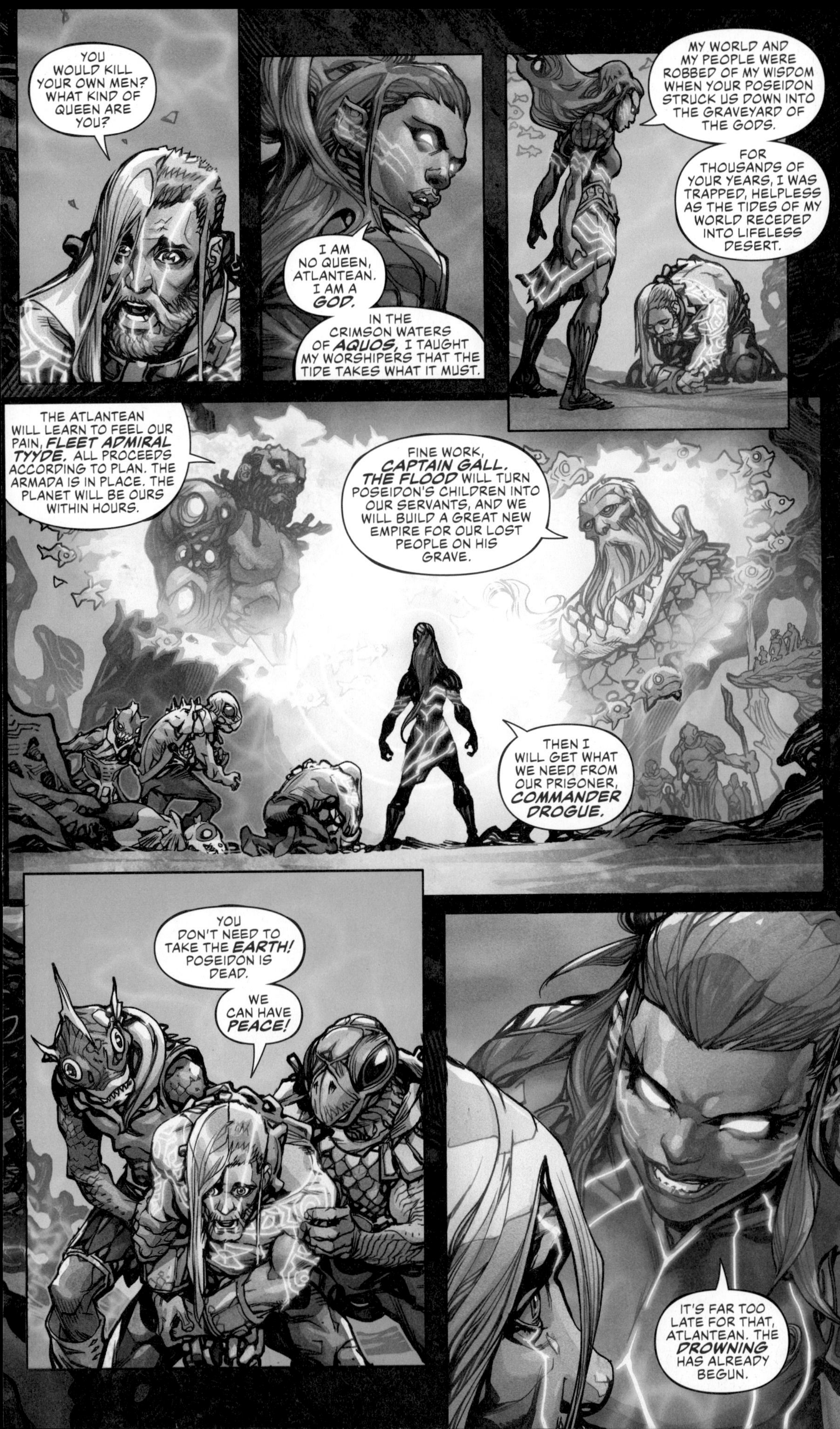

YOU WOULD KILL YOUR OWN MEN? WHAT KIND OF QUEEN ARE YOU?
I AM NO QUEEN, ATLANTEAN. I AM A GOD.
IN THE CRIMSON WATERS OF AQUOS, I TAUGHT MY WORSHIPERS THAT THE TIDE TAKES WHAT IT MUST.
MY WORLD AND MY PEOPLE WERE ROBBED OF MY WISDOM WHEN YOUR POSEIDON STRUCK US DOWN INTO THE GRAVEYARD OF THE GODS.
FOR THOUSANDS OF YOUR YEARS, I WAS TRAPPED, HELPLESS AS THE TIDES OF MY WORLD RECEDED INTO LIFELESS DESERT.
THE ATLANTEAN WILL LEARN TO FEEL OUR PAIN, FLEET ADMIRAL TYYDE. ALL PROCEEDS ACCORDING TO PLAN. THE ARMADA IS IN PLACE. THE PLANET WILL BE OURS WITHIN HOURS.
FINE WORK, CAPTAIN GALL. THE FLOOD WILL TURN POSEIDON'S CHILDREN INTO OUR SERVANTS, AND WE WILL BUILD A GREAT NEW EMPIRE FOR OUR LOST PEOPLE ON HIS GRAVE.
THEN I WILL GET WHAT WE NEED FROM OUR PRISONER, COMMANDER DROGUE.
YOU DON'T NEED TO TAKE THE EARTH! POSEIDON IS DEAD.
WE CAN HAVE PEACE!
IT'S FAR TOO LATE FOR THAT, ATLANTEAN. THE DROWNING HAS ALREADY BEGUN.

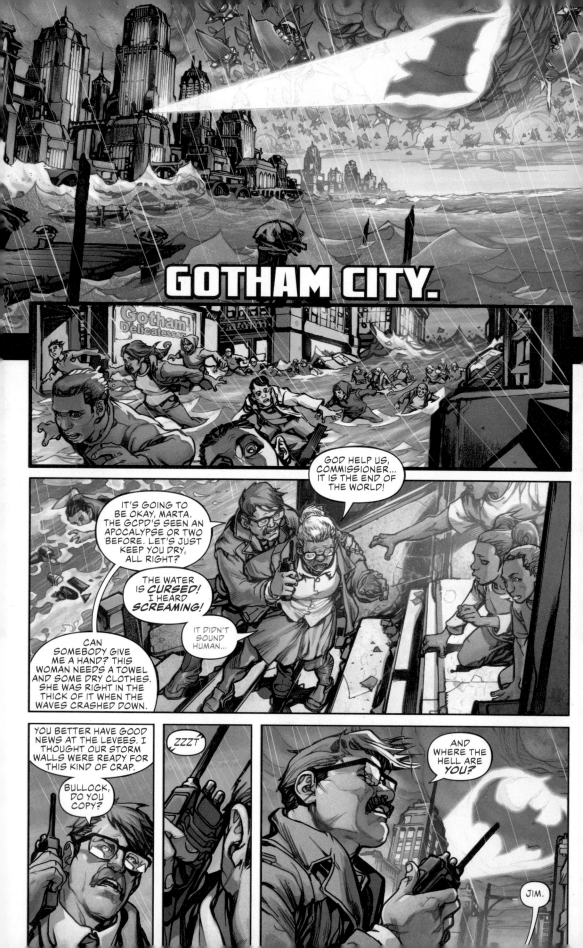

GOTHAM CITY.

GOD HELP US, COMMISSIONER... IT IS THE END OF THE WORLD!

IT'S GOING TO BE OKAY, MARTA. THE GCPD'S SEEN AN APOCALYPSE OR TWO BEFORE. LET'S JUST KEEP YOU DRY, ALL RIGHT?

THE WATER IS *CURSED!* I HEARD *SCREAMING!*

IT DIDN'T SOUND HUMAN...

CAN SOMEBODY GIVE ME A HAND? THIS WOMAN NEEDS A TOWEL AND SOME DRY CLOTHES. SHE WAS RIGHT IN THE THICK OF IT WHEN THE WAVES CRASHED DOWN.

YOU BETTER HAVE GOOD NEWS AT THE LEVEES. I THOUGHT OUR STORM WALLS WERE READY FOR THIS KIND OF CRAP.

BULLOCK, DO YOU COPY?

ZZZT

AND WHERE THE HELL ARE *YOU?*

JIM.

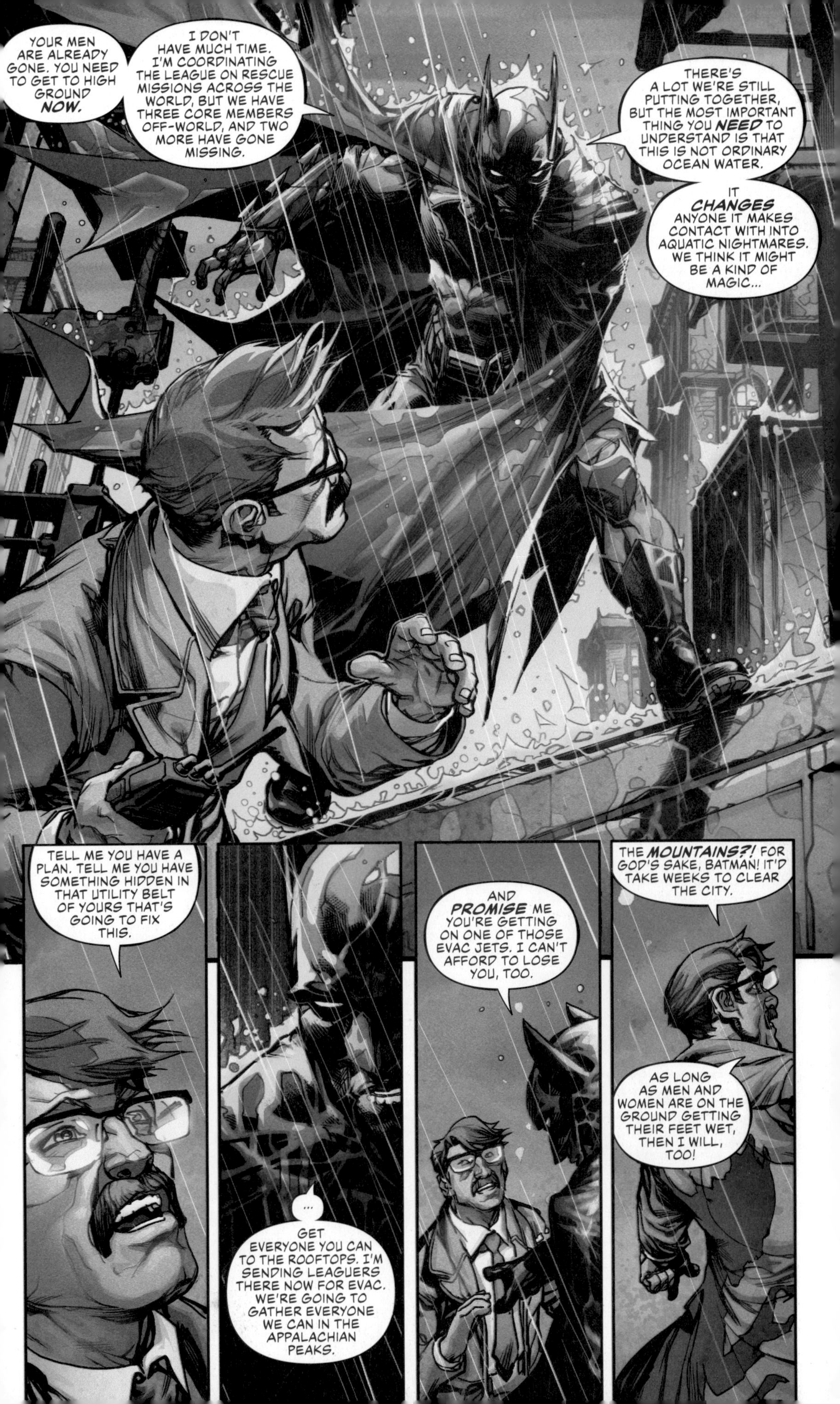
YOUR MEN ARE ALREADY GONE. YOU NEED TO GET TO HIGH GROUND NOW.
I DON'T HAVE MUCH TIME. I'M COORDINATING THE LEAGUE ON RESCUE MISSIONS ACROSS THE WORLD, BUT WE HAVE THREE CORE MEMBERS OFF-WORLD, AND TWO MORE HAVE GONE MISSING.
THERE'S A LOT WE'RE STILL PUTTING TOGETHER, BUT THE MOST IMPORTANT THING YOU NEED TO UNDERSTAND IS THAT THIS IS NOT ORDINARY OCEAN WATER.
IT CHANGES ANYONE IT MAKES CONTACT WITH INTO AQUATIC NIGHTMARES. WE THINK IT MIGHT BE A KIND OF MAGIC...
TELL ME YOU HAVE A PLAN. TELL ME YOU HAVE SOMETHING HIDDEN IN THAT UTILITY BELT OF YOURS THAT'S GOING TO FIX THIS.
...
GET EVERYONE YOU CAN TO THE ROOFTOPS. I'M SENDING LEAGUERS THERE NOW FOR EVAC. WE'RE GOING TO GATHER EVERYONE WE CAN IN THE APPALACHIAN PEAKS.
AND PROMISE ME YOU'RE GETTING ON ONE OF THOSE EVAC JETS. I CAN'T AFFORD TO LOSE YOU, TOO.
THE MOUNTAINS?! FOR GOD'S SAKE, BATMAN! IT'D TAKE WEEKS TO CLEAR THE CITY.
AS LONG AS MEN AND WOMEN ARE ON THE GROUND GETTING THEIR FEET WET, THEN I WILL, TOO!

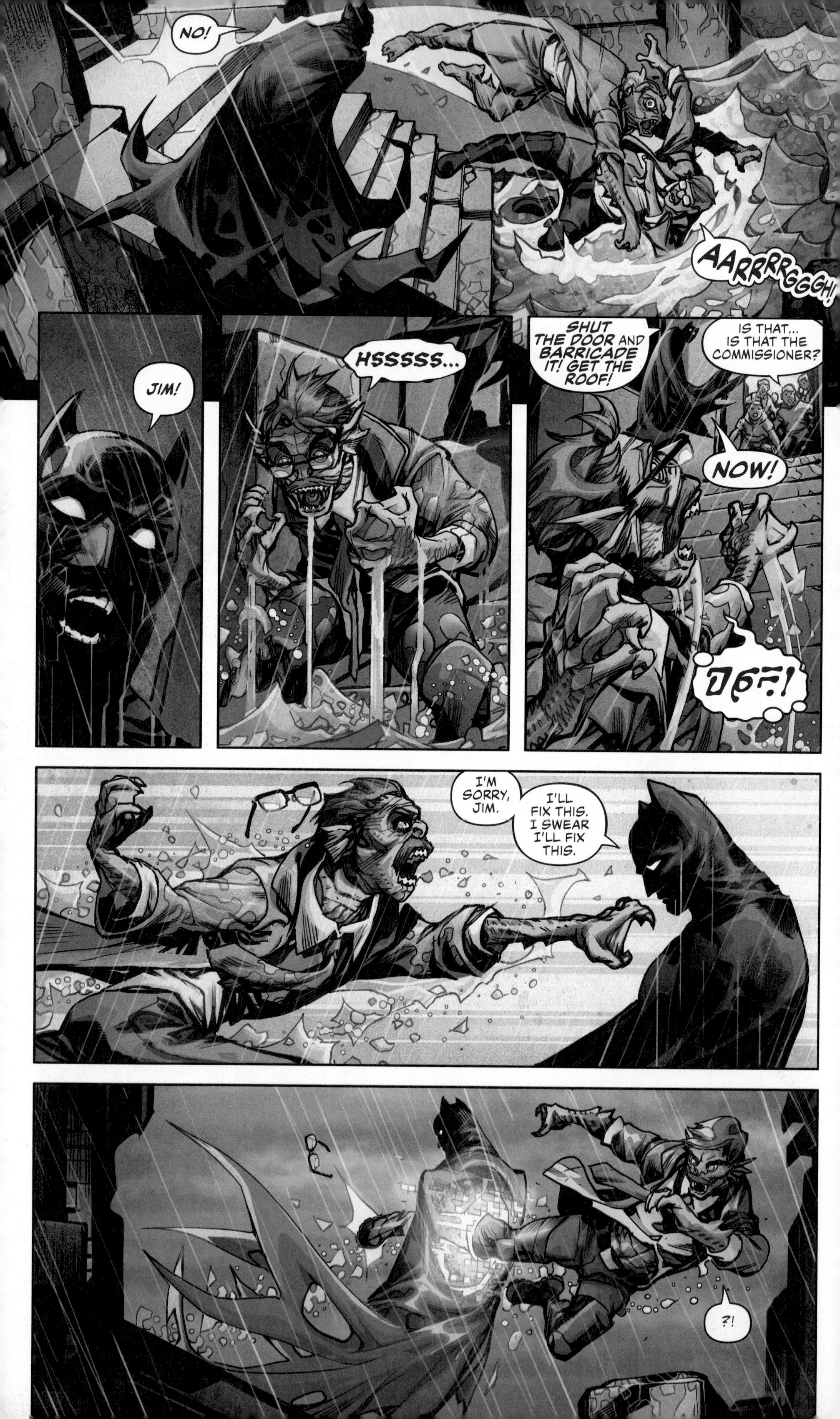
NO!
AARRRRGGGH!
JIM!
HSSSSS...
SHUT THE DOOR AND BARRICADE IT! GET THE ROOF!
IS THAT... IS THAT THE COMMISSIONER?
NOW!
OOF!
I'M SORRY, JIM.
I'LL FIX THIS. I SWEAR I'LL FIX THIS.
?!

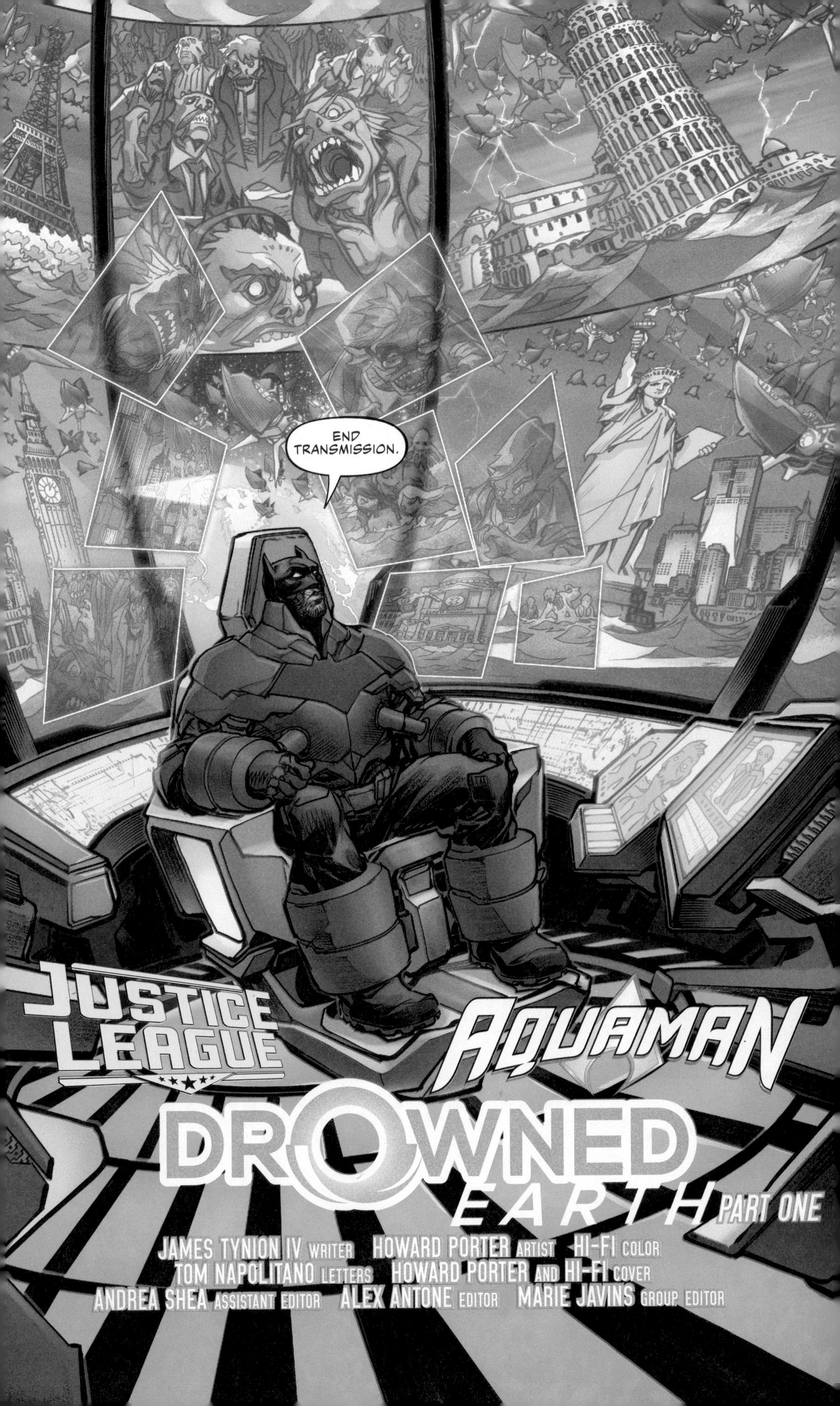
END TRANSMISSION.
JUSTICE LEAGUE
AQUAMAN
DROWNED EARTH PART ONE
JAMES TYNION IV WRITER HOWARD PORTER ARTIST HI-FI COLOR
TOM NAPOLITANO LETTERS HOWARD PORTER AND HI-FI COVER
ANDREA SHEA ASSISTANT EDITOR ALEX ANTONE EDITOR MARIE JAVINS GROUP EDITOR

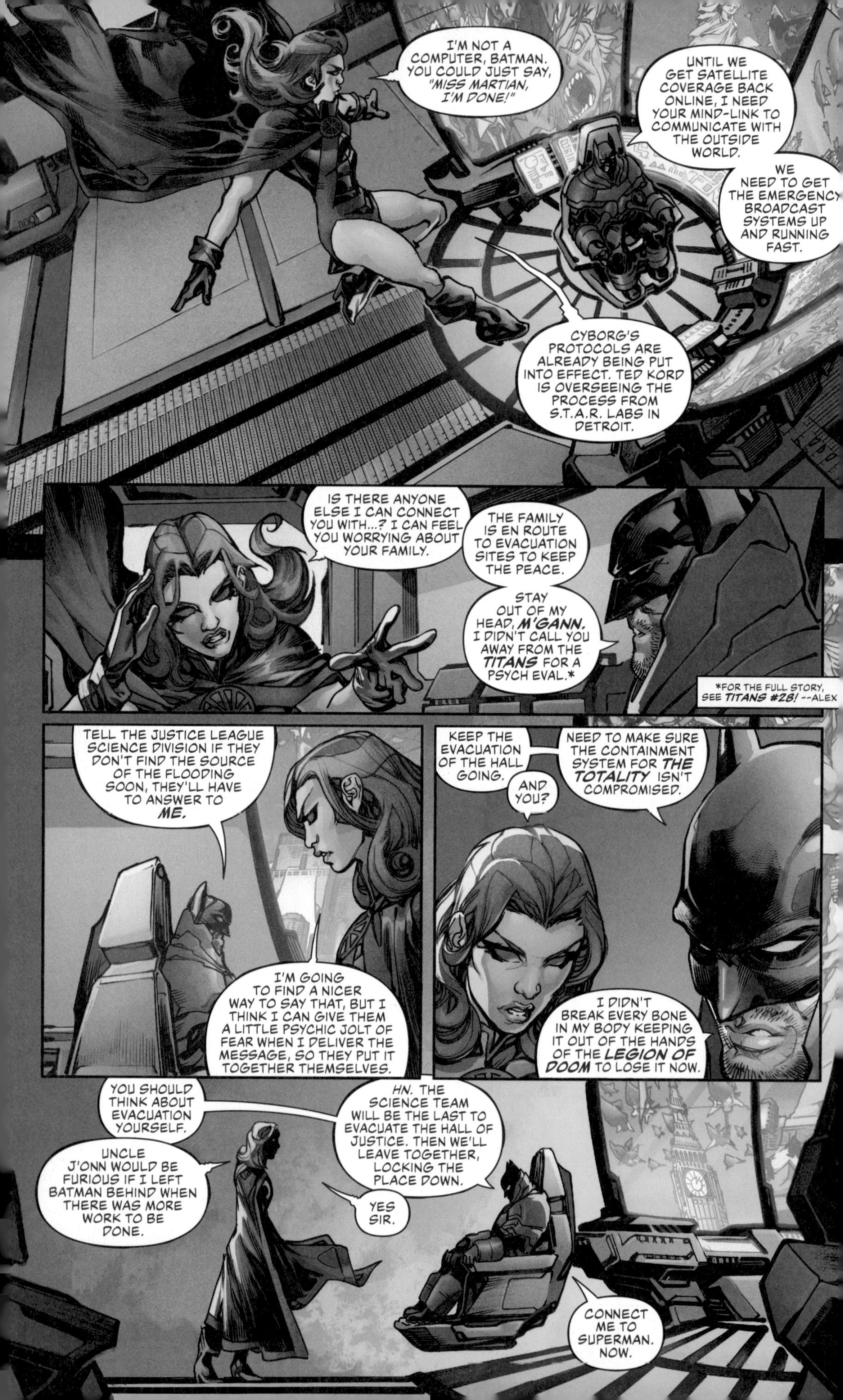

I'M NOT A COMPUTER, BATMAN. YOU COULD JUST SAY, "MISS MARTIAN, I'M DONE!"
UNTIL WE GET SATELLITE COVERAGE BACK ONLINE, I NEED YOUR MIND-LINK TO COMMUNICATE WITH THE OUTSIDE WORLD.
WE NEED TO GET THE EMERGENCY BROADCAST SYSTEMS UP AND RUNNING FAST.
CYBORG'S PROTOCOLS ARE ALREADY BEING PUT INTO EFFECT. TED KORD IS OVERSEEING THE PROCESS FROM S.T.A.R. LABS IN DETROIT.
IS THERE ANYONE ELSE I CAN CONNECT YOU WITH...? I CAN FEEL YOU WORRYING ABOUT YOUR FAMILY.
THE FAMILY IS EN ROUTE TO EVACUATION SITES TO KEEP THE PEACE.
STAY OUT OF MY HEAD, M'GANN. I DIDN'T CALL YOU AWAY FROM THE TITANS FOR A PSYCH EVAL.*
*FOR THE FULL STORY, SEE TITANS #28! --ALEX
TELL THE JUSTICE LEAGUE SCIENCE DIVISION IF THEY DON'T FIND THE SOURCE OF THE FLOODING SOON, THEY'LL HAVE TO ANSWER TO ME.
I'M GOING TO FIND A NICER WAY TO SAY THAT, BUT I THINK I CAN GIVE THEM A LITTLE PSYCHIC JOLT OF FEAR WHEN I DELIVER THE MESSAGE, SO THEY PUT IT TOGETHER THEMSELVES.
KEEP THE EVACUATION OF THE HALL GOING.
AND YOU?
NEED TO MAKE SURE THE CONTAINMENT SYSTEM FOR THE TOTALITY ISN'T COMPROMISED.
I DIDN'T BREAK EVERY BONE IN MY BODY KEEPING IT OUT OF THE HANDS OF THE LEGION OF DOOM TO LOSE IT NOW.
YOU SHOULD THINK ABOUT EVACUATION YOURSELF.
HN. THE SCIENCE TEAM WILL BE THE LAST TO EVACUATE THE HALL OF JUSTICE. THEN WE'LL LEAVE TOGETHER, LOCKING THE PLACE DOWN.
UNCLE J'ONN WOULD BE FURIOUS IF I LEFT BATMAN BEHIND WHEN THERE WAS MORE WORK TO BE DONE.
YES SIR.
CONNECT ME TO SUPERMAN. NOW.

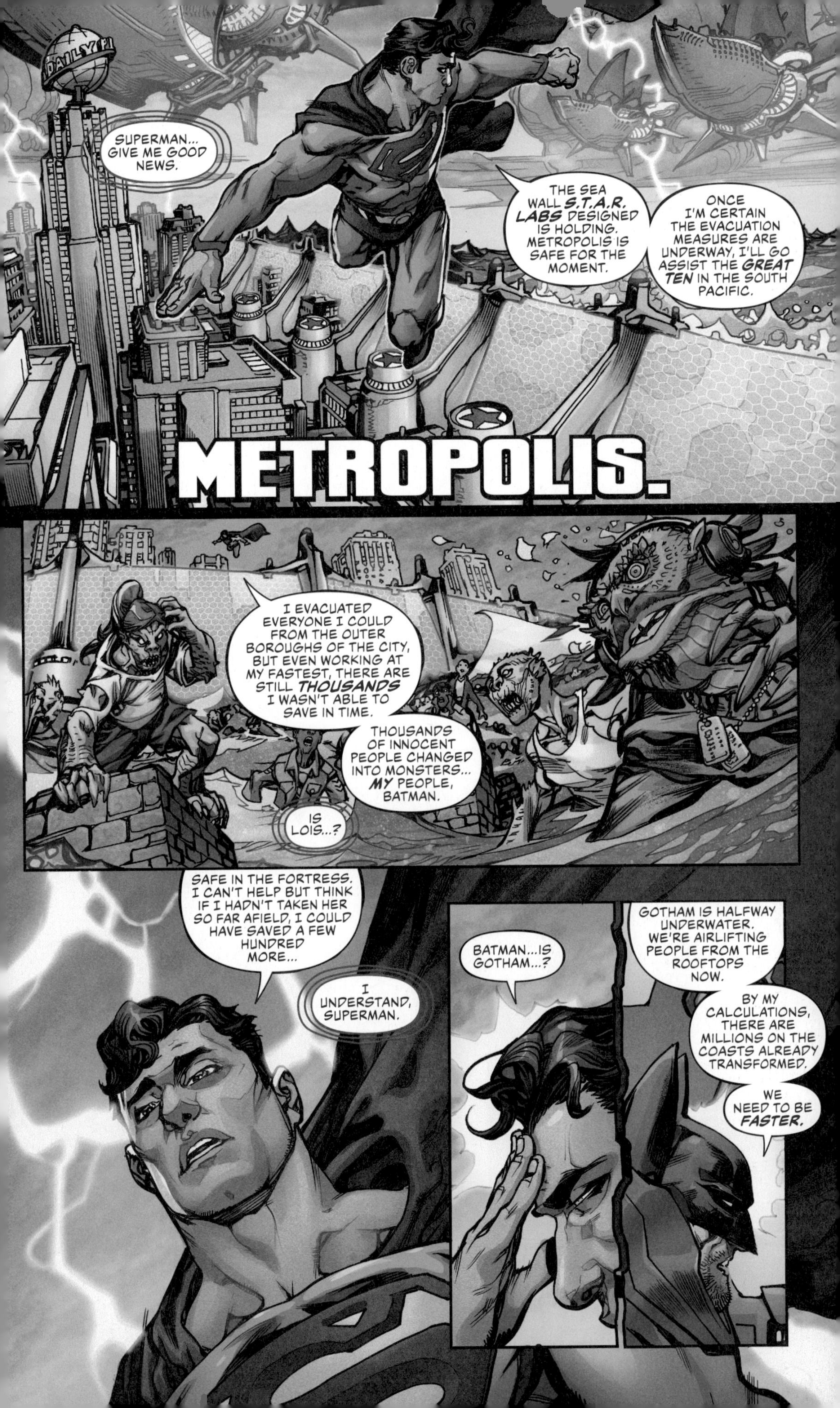

SUPERMAN... GIVE ME GOOD NEWS.
THE SEA WALL S.T.A.R. LABS DESIGNED IS HOLDING. METROPOLIS IS SAFE FOR THE MOMENT.
ONCE I'M CERTAIN THE EVACUATION MEASURES ARE UNDERWAY, I'LL GO ASSIST THE GREAT TEN IN THE SOUTH PACIFIC.
METROPOLIS.
I EVACUATED EVERYONE I COULD FROM THE OUTER BOROUGHS OF THE CITY, BUT EVEN WORKING AT MY FASTEST, THERE ARE STILL THOUSANDS I WASN'T ABLE TO SAVE IN TIME.
THOUSANDS OF INNOCENT PEOPLE CHANGED INTO MONSTERS... MY PEOPLE, BATMAN.
IS LOIS...?
SAFE IN THE FORTRESS. I CAN'T HELP BUT THINK IF I HADN'T TAKEN HER SO FAR AFIELD, I COULD HAVE SAVED A FEW HUNDRED MORE...
I UNDERSTAND, SUPERMAN.
BATMAN...IS GOTHAM...?
GOTHAM IS HALFWAY UNDERWATER. WE'RE AIRLIFTING PEOPLE FROM THE ROOFTOPS NOW.
BY MY CALCULATIONS, THERE ARE MILLIONS ON THE COASTS ALREADY TRANSFORMED.
WE NEED TO BE FASTER.

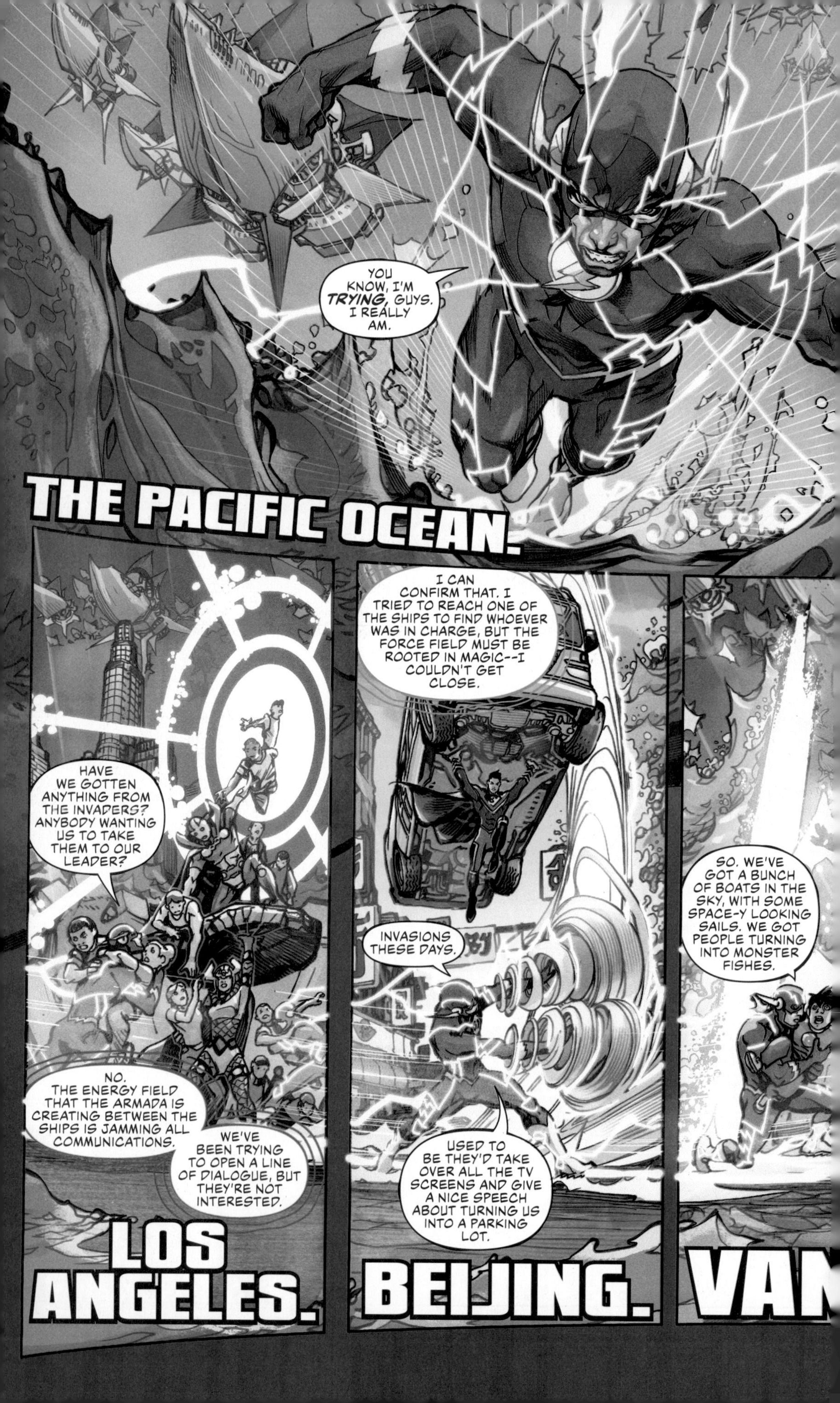

YOU KNOW, I'M *TRYING*, GUYS. I REALLY AM.
THE PACIFIC OCEAN.
HAVE WE GOTTEN ANYTHING FROM THE INVADERS? ANYBODY WANTING US TO TAKE THEM TO OUR LEADER?
NO. THE ENERGY FIELD THAT THE ARMADA IS CREATING BETWEEN THE SHIPS IS JAMMING ALL COMMUNICATIONS.
WE'VE BEEN TRYING TO OPEN A LINE OF DIALOGUE, BUT THEY'RE NOT INTERESTED.
LOS ANGELES.
I CAN CONFIRM THAT. I TRIED TO REACH ONE OF THE SHIPS TO FIND WHOEVER WAS IN CHARGE, BUT THE FORCE FIELD MUST BE ROOTED IN MAGIC--I COULDN'T GET CLOSE.
INVASIONS THESE DAYS.
USED TO BE THEY'D TAKE OVER ALL THE TV SCREENS AND GIVE A NICE SPEECH ABOUT TURNING US INTO A PARKING LOT.
BEIJING.
SO. WE'VE GOT A BUNCH OF BOATS IN THE SKY, WITH SOME SPACE-Y LOOKING SAILS. WE GOT PEOPLE TURNING INTO MONSTER FISHES.
VAN

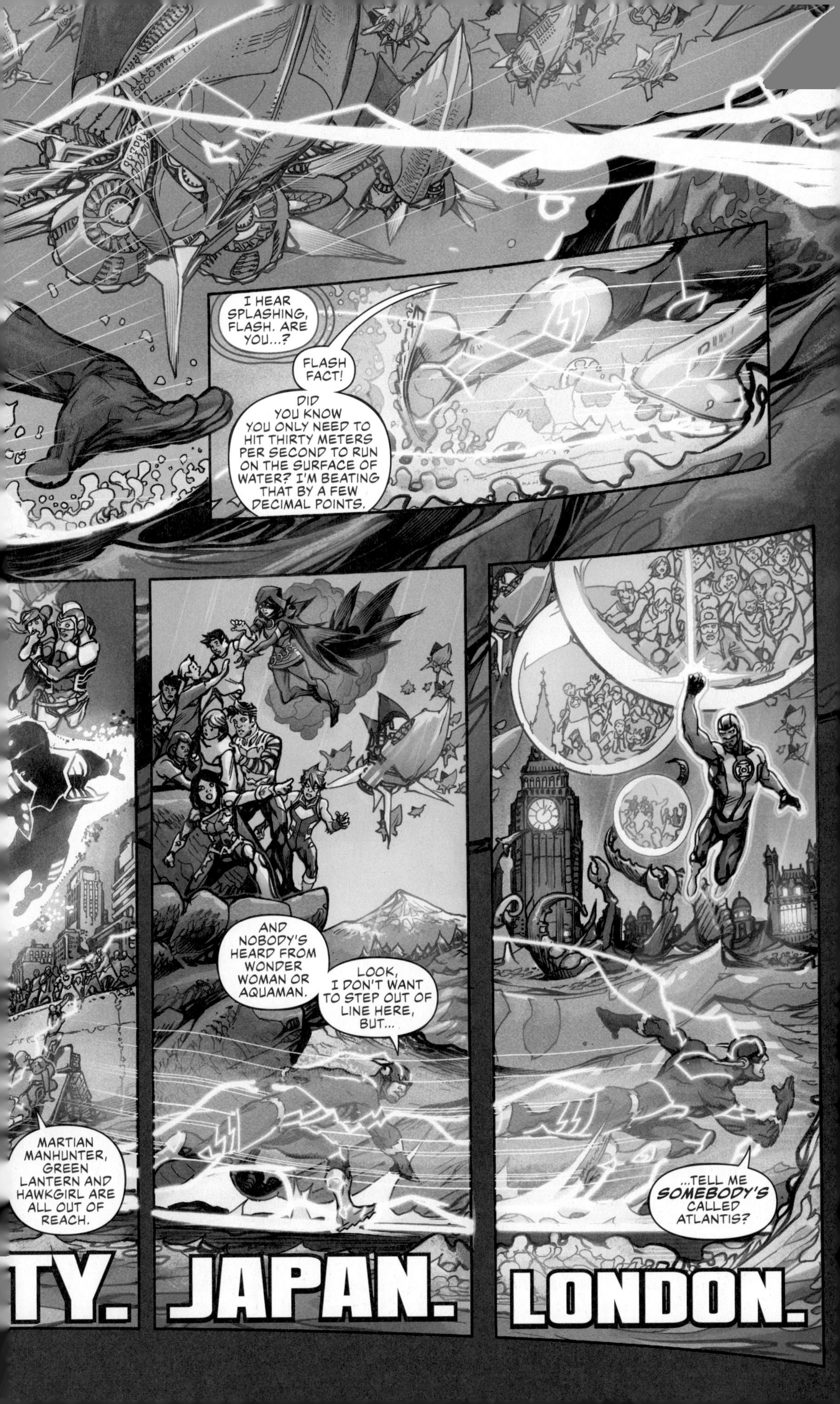
I HEAR SPLASHING, FLASH. ARE YOU...?
FLASH FACT!
DID YOU KNOW YOU ONLY NEED TO HIT THIRTY METERS PER SECOND TO RUN ON THE SURFACE OF WATER? I'M BEATING THAT BY A FEW DECIMAL POINTS.
MARTIAN MANHUNTER, GREEN LANTERN AND HAWKGIRL ARE ALL OUT OF REACH.
TY.
AND NOBODY'S HEARD FROM WONDER WOMAN OR AQUAMAN.
LOOK, I DON'T WANT TO STEP OUT OF LINE HERE, BUT...
JAPAN.
...TELL ME SOMEBODY'S CALLED ATLANTIS?
LONDON.

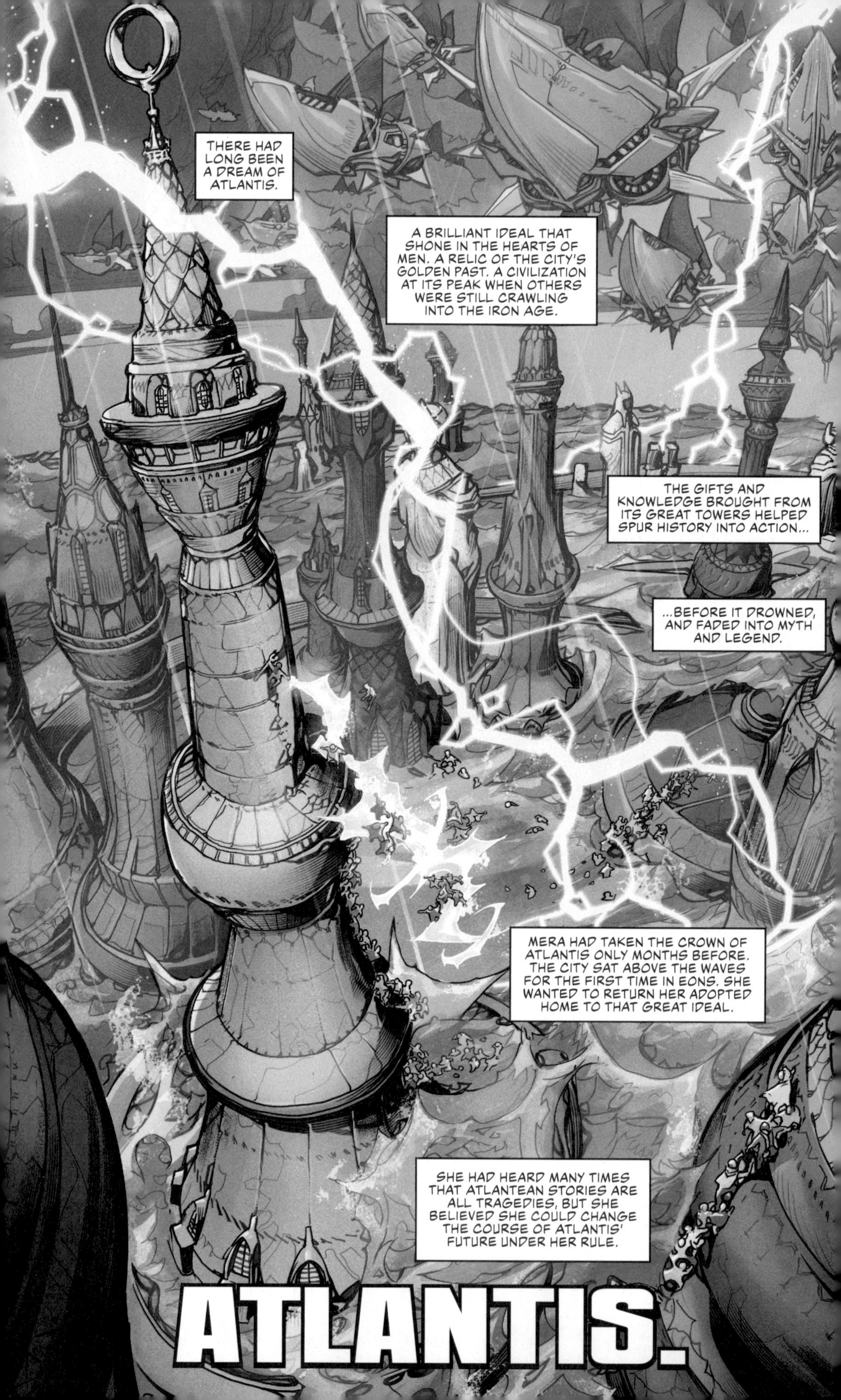
THERE HAD LONG BEEN A DREAM OF ATLANTIS.
A BRILLIANT IDEAL THAT SHONE IN THE HEARTS OF MEN. A RELIC OF THE CITY'S GOLDEN PAST. A CIVILIZATION AT ITS PEAK WHEN OTHERS WERE STILL CRAWLING INTO THE IRON AGE.
THE GIFTS AND KNOWLEDGE BROUGHT FROM ITS GREAT TOWERS HELPED SPUR HISTORY INTO ACTION...
...BEFORE IT DROWNED, AND FADED INTO MYTH AND LEGEND.
MERA HAD TAKEN THE CROWN OF ATLANTIS ONLY MONTHS BEFORE. THE CITY SAT ABOVE THE WAVES FOR THE FIRST TIME IN EONS. SHE WANTED TO RETURN HER ADOPTED HOME TO THAT GREAT IDEAL.
SHE HAD HEARD MANY TIMES THAT ATLANTEAN STORIES ARE ALL TRAGEDIES, BUT SHE BELIEVED SHE COULD CHANGE THE COURSE OF ATLANTIS' FUTURE UNDER HER RULE.
ATLANTIS.

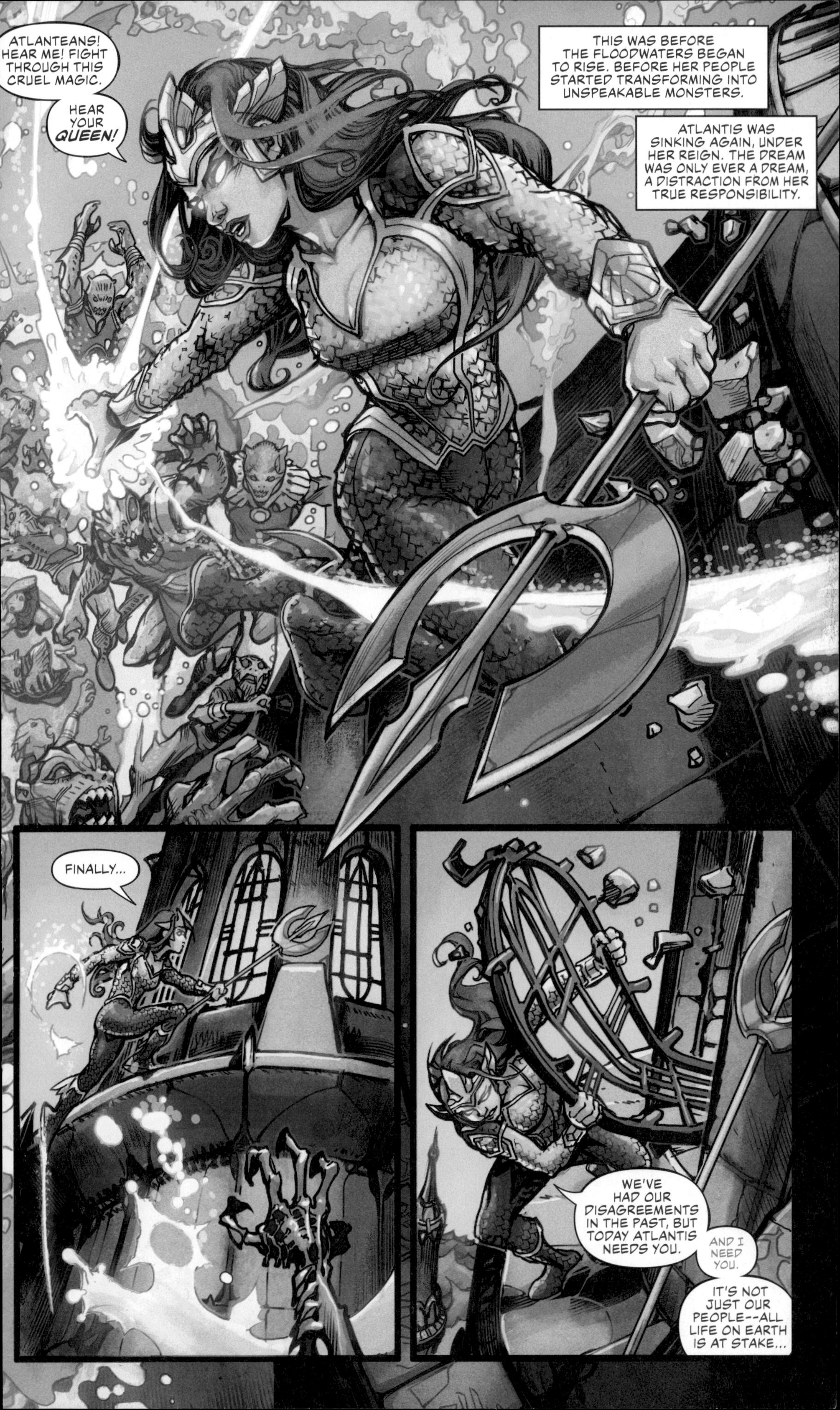
ATLANTEANS! HEAR ME! FIGHT THROUGH THIS CRUEL MAGIC.
HEAR YOUR *QUEEN!*
THIS WAS BEFORE THE FLOODWATERS BEGAN TO RISE. BEFORE HER PEOPLE STARTED TRANSFORMING INTO UNSPEAKABLE MONSTERS.
ATLANTIS WAS SINKING AGAIN, UNDER HER REIGN. THE DREAM WAS ONLY EVER A DREAM, A DISTRACTION FROM HER TRUE RESPONSIBILITY.
FINALLY...
WE'VE HAD OUR DISAGREEMENTS IN THE PAST, BUT TODAY ATLANTIS NEEDS YOU.
AND I NEED YOU.
IT'S NOT JUST OUR PEOPLE--ALL LIFE ON EARTH IS AT STAKE...

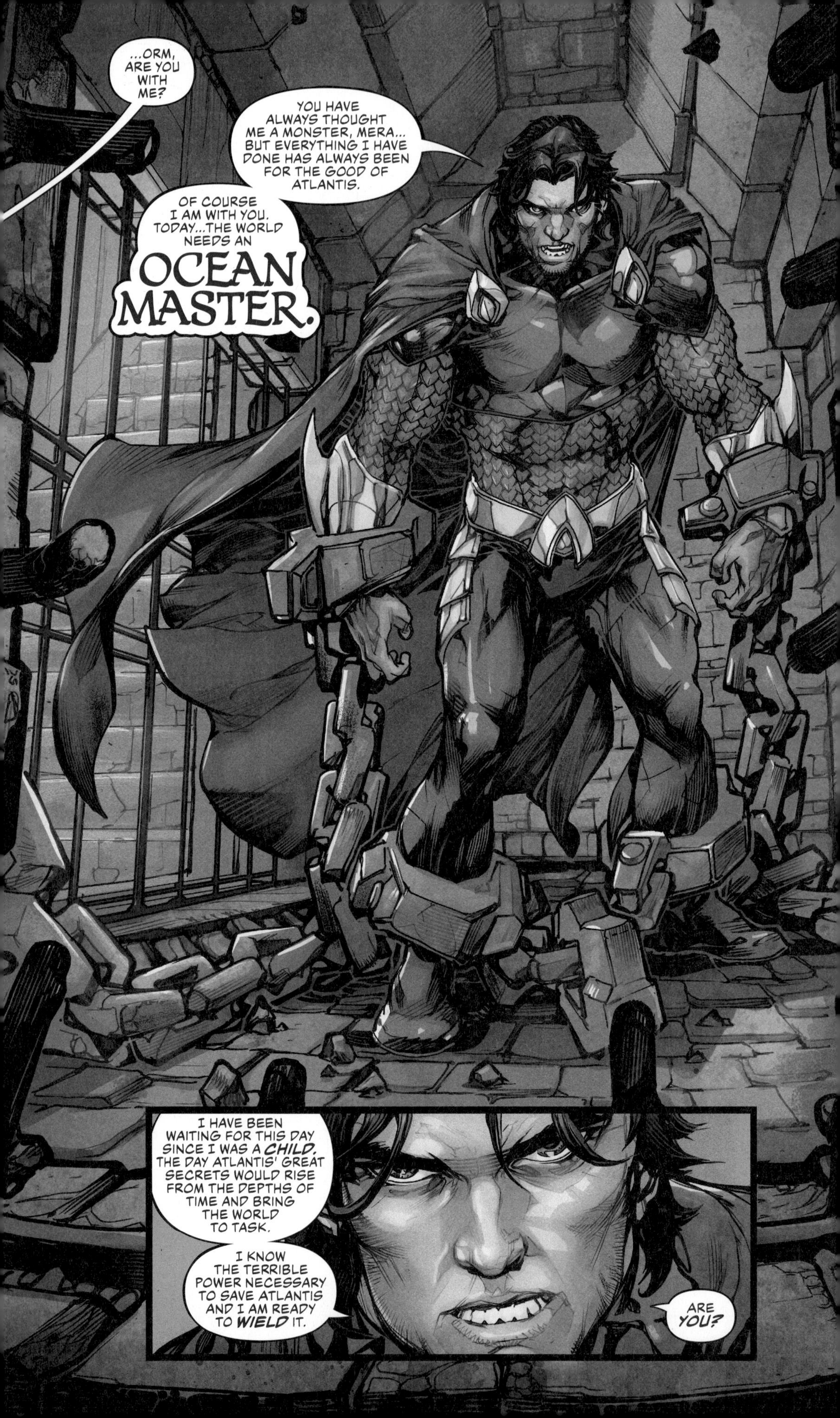
...ORM, ARE YOU WITH ME?
YOU HAVE ALWAYS THOUGHT ME A MONSTER, MERA... BUT EVERYTHING I HAVE DONE HAS ALWAYS BEEN FOR THE GOOD OF ATLANTIS.
OF COURSE I AM WITH YOU. TODAY...THE WORLD NEEDS AN
OCEAN MASTER.
I HAVE BEEN WAITING FOR THIS DAY SINCE I WAS A CHILD. THE DAY ATLANTIS' GREAT SECRETS WOULD RISE FROM THE DEPTHS OF TIME AND BRING THE WORLD TO TASK.
I KNOW THE TERRIBLE POWER NECESSARY TO SAVE ATLANTIS AND I AM READY TO WIELD IT.
ARE YOU?

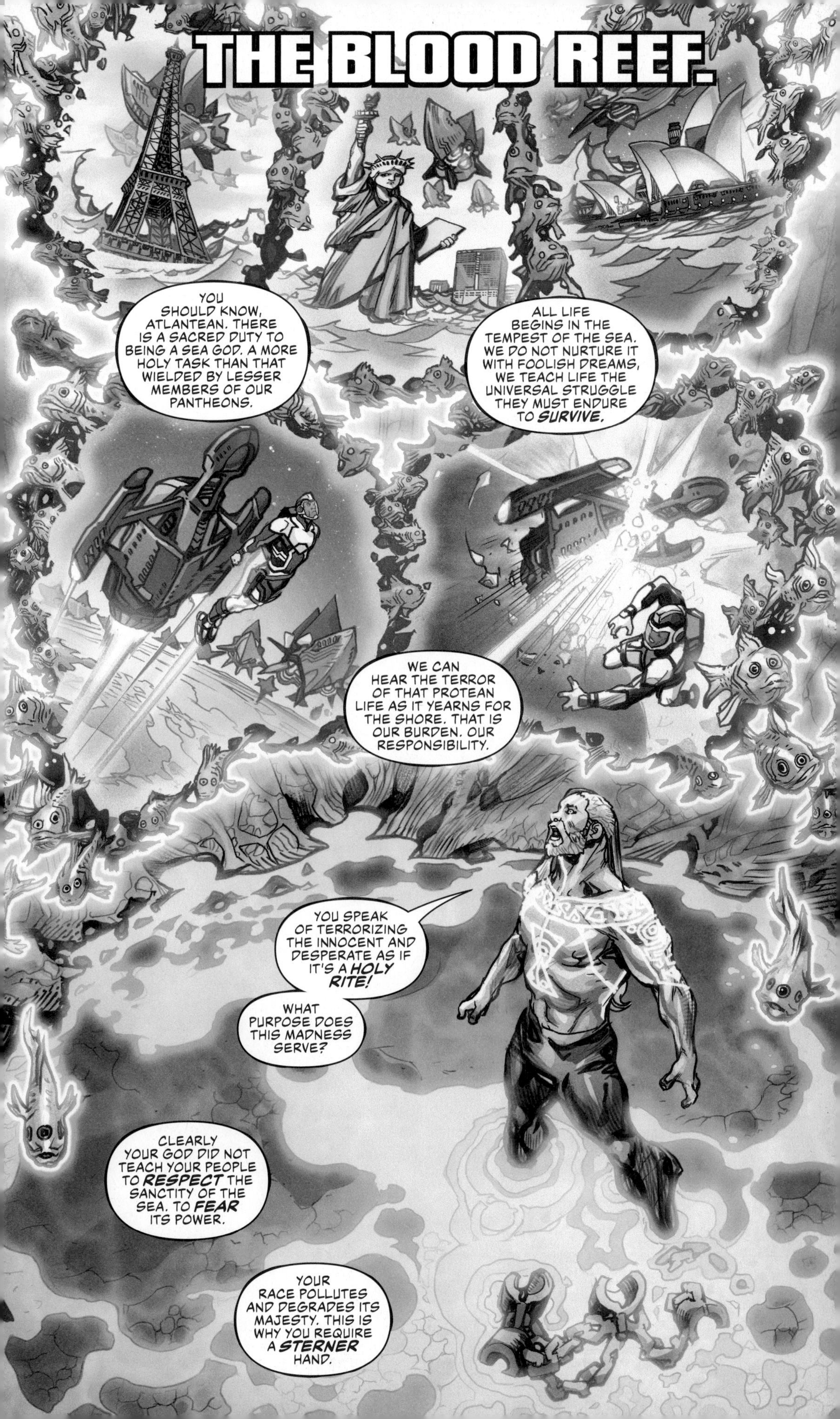
THE BLOOD REEF.
YOU SHOULD KNOW, ATLANTEAN. THERE IS A SACRED DUTY TO BEING A SEA GOD. A MORE HOLY TASK THAN THAT WIELDED BY LESSER MEMBERS OF OUR PANTHEONS.
ALL LIFE BEGINS IN THE TEMPEST OF THE SEA. WE DO NOT NURTURE IT WITH FOOLISH DREAMS, WE TEACH LIFE THE UNIVERSAL STRUGGLE THEY MUST ENDURE TO SURVIVE.
WE CAN HEAR THE TERROR OF THAT PROTEAN LIFE AS IT YEARNS FOR THE SHORE. THAT IS OUR BURDEN. OUR RESPONSIBILITY.
YOU SPEAK OF TERRORIZING THE INNOCENT AND DESPERATE AS IF IT'S A HOLY RITE!
WHAT PURPOSE DOES THIS MADNESS SERVE?
CLEARLY YOUR GOD DID NOT TEACH YOUR PEOPLE TO RESPECT THE SANCTITY OF THE SEA. TO FEAR ITS POWER.
YOUR RACE POLLUTES AND DEGRADES ITS MAJESTY. THIS IS WHY YOU REQUIRE A STERNER HAND.

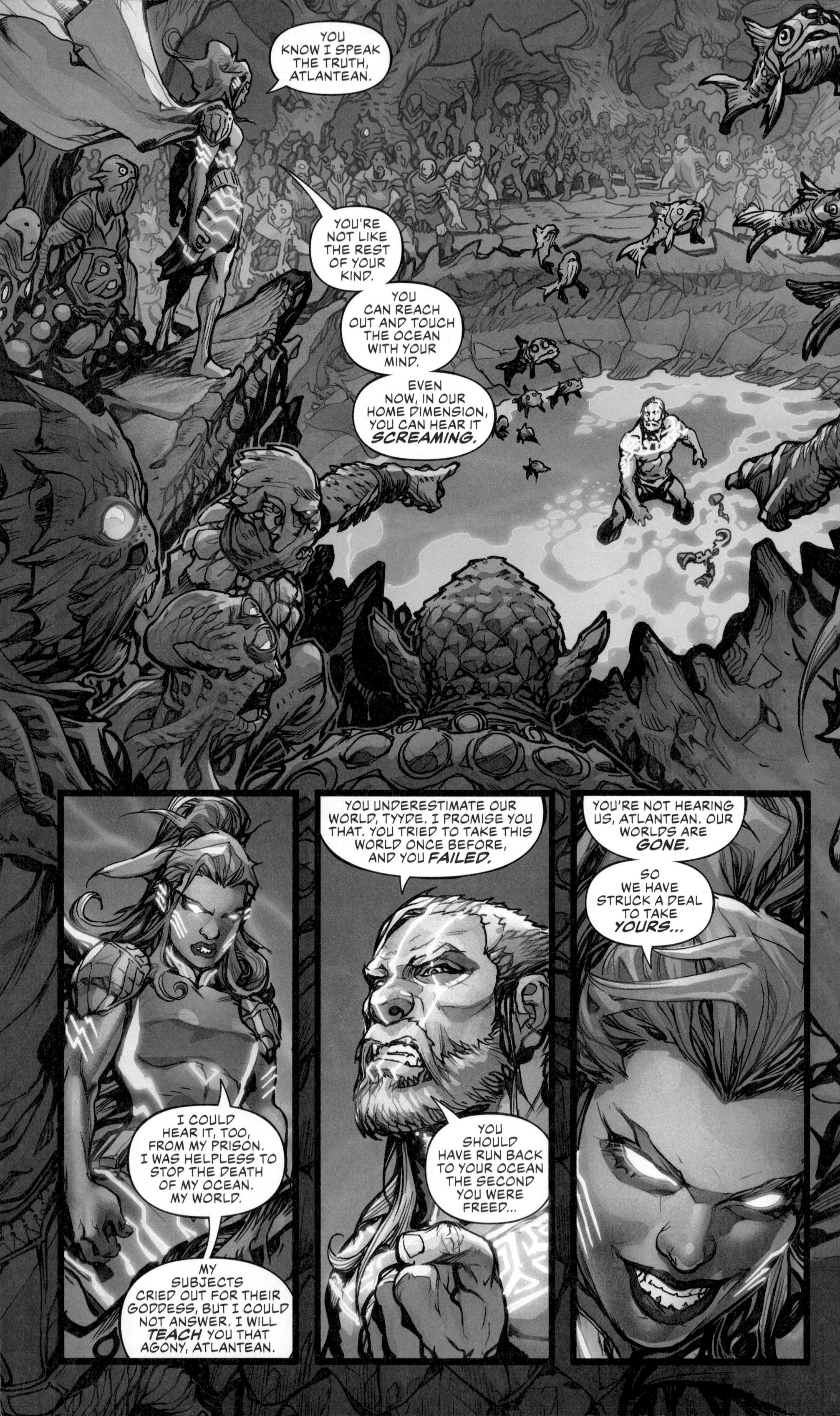
YOU KNOW I SPEAK THE TRUTH, ATLANTEAN.
YOU'RE NOT LIKE THE REST OF YOUR KIND.
YOU CAN REACH OUT AND TOUCH THE OCEAN WITH YOUR MIND.
EVEN NOW, IN OUR HOME DIMENSION, YOU CAN HEAR IT SCREAMING.
I COULD HEAR IT, TOO, FROM MY PRISON. I WAS HELPLESS TO STOP THE DEATH OF MY OCEAN. MY WORLD.
MY SUBJECTS CRIED OUT FOR THEIR GODDESS, BUT I COULD NOT ANSWER. I WILL TEACH YOU THAT AGONY, ATLANTEAN.
YOU UNDERESTIMATE OUR WORLD, TYYDE. I PROMISE YOU THAT. YOU TRIED TO TAKE THIS WORLD ONCE BEFORE, AND YOU FAILED.
YOU SHOULD HAVE RUN BACK TO YOUR OCEAN THE SECOND YOU WERE FREED...
YOU'RE NOT HEARING US, ATLANTEAN. OUR WORLDS ARE GONE.
SO WE HAVE STRUCK A DEAL TO TAKE YOURS...

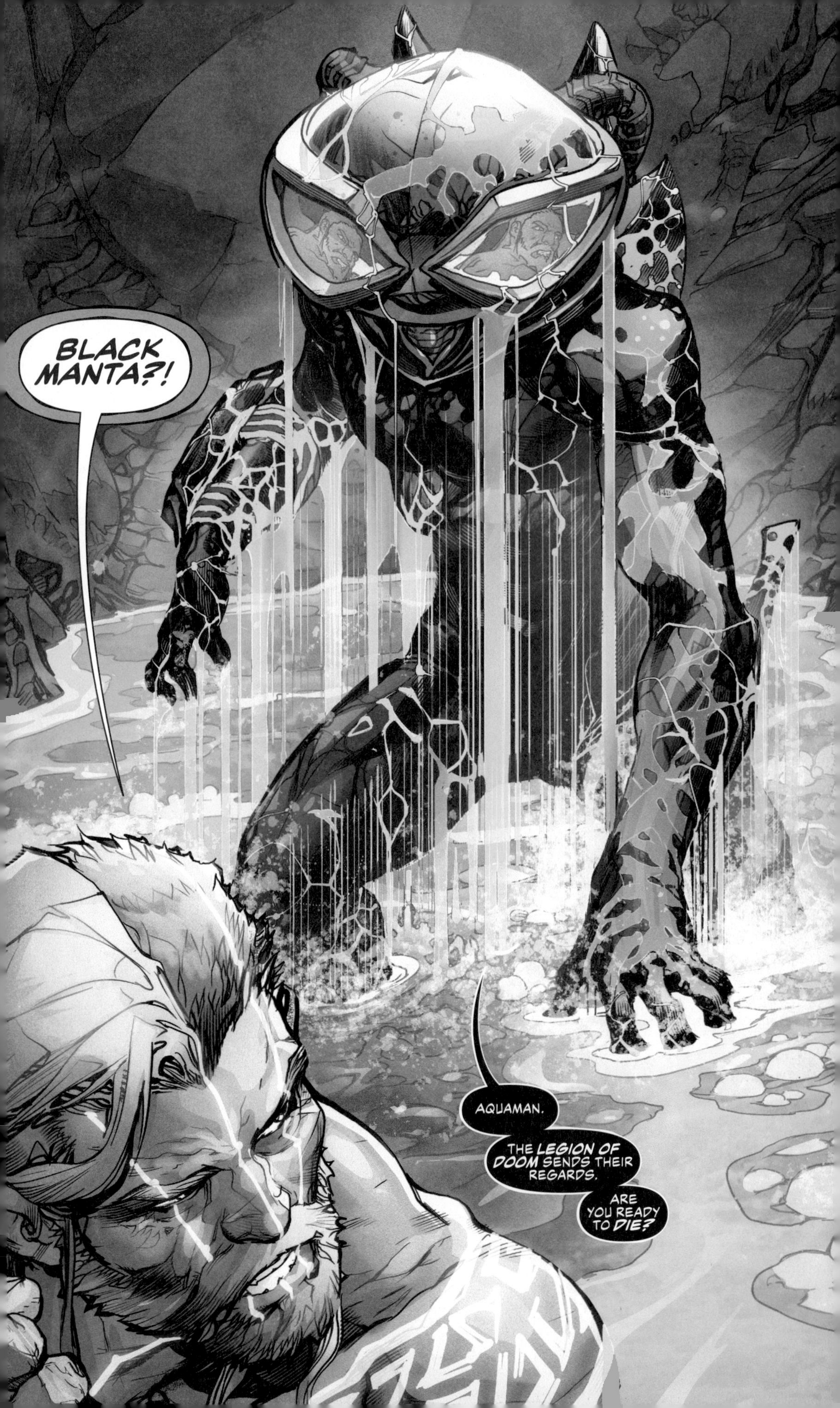
BLACK MANTA?!
AQUAMAN.
THE LEGION OF DOOM SENDS THEIR REGARDS.
ARE YOU READY TO DIE?

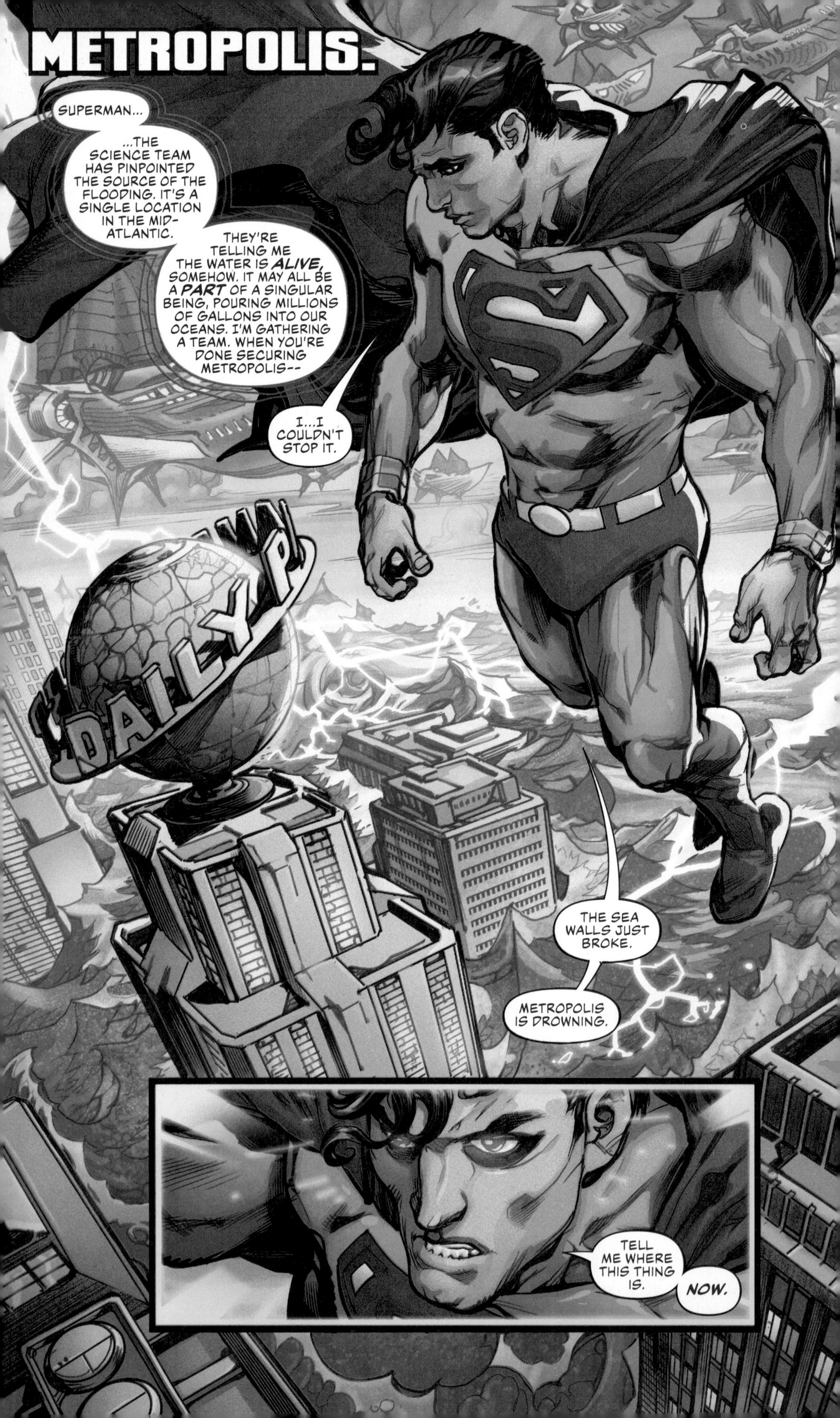
METROPOLIS.
SUPERMAN...
...THE SCIENCE TEAM HAS PINPOINTED THE SOURCE OF THE FLOODING. IT'S A SINGLE LOCATION IN THE MID-ATLANTIC.
THEY'RE TELLING ME THE WATER IS ALIVE, SOMEHOW. IT MAY ALL BE A PART OF A SINGULAR BEING, POURING MILLIONS OF GALLONS INTO OUR OCEANS. I'M GATHERING A TEAM. WHEN YOU'RE DONE SECURING METROPOLIS--
I...I COULDN'T STOP IT.
THE SEA WALLS JUST BROKE.
METROPOLIS IS DROWNING.
TELL ME WHERE THIS THING IS.
NOW.

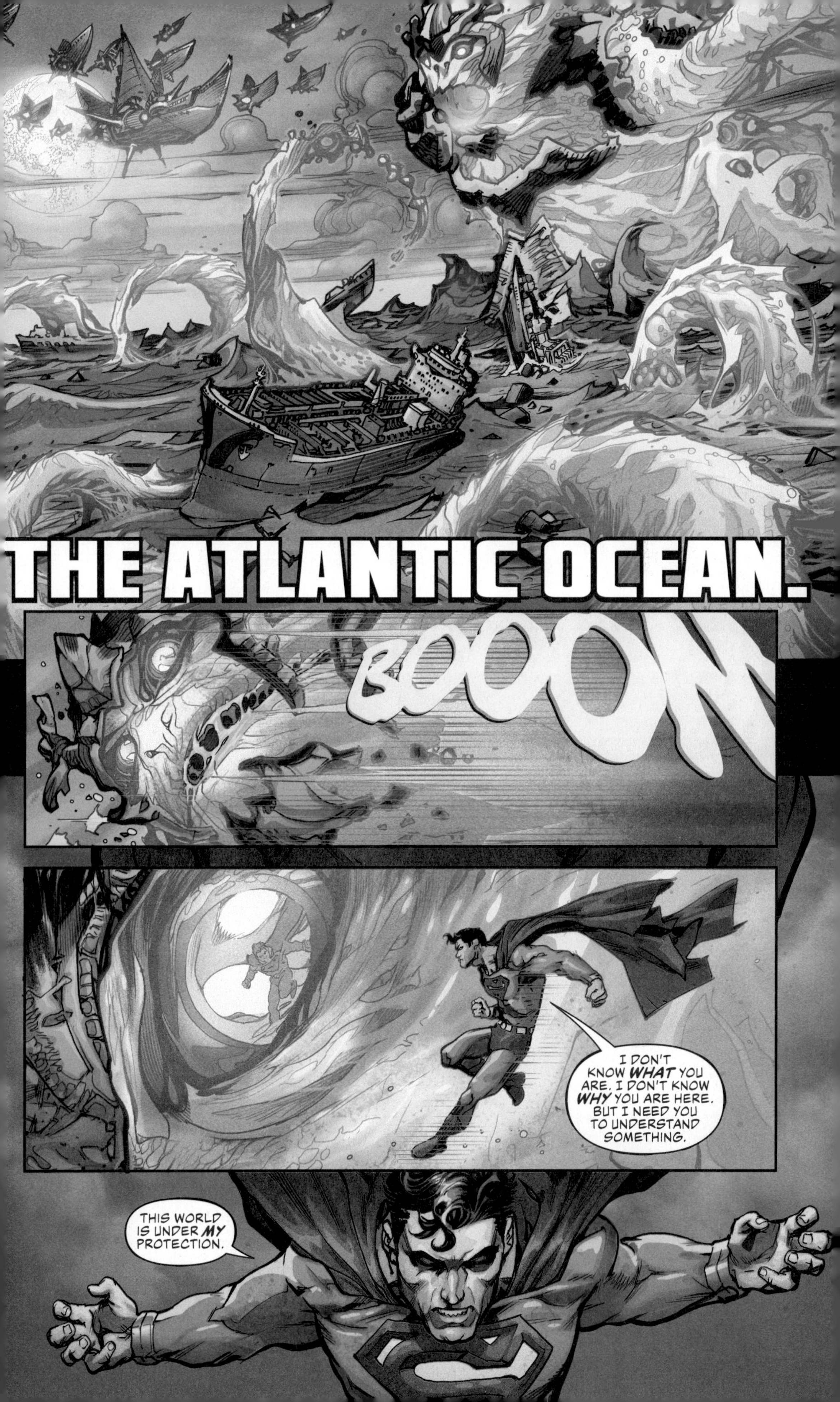
THE ATLANTIC OCEAN.
BOOOM
I DON'T KNOW WHAT YOU ARE. I DON'T KNOW WHY YOU ARE HERE. BUT I NEED YOU TO UNDERSTAND SOMETHING.
THIS WORLD IS UNDER MY PROTECTION.

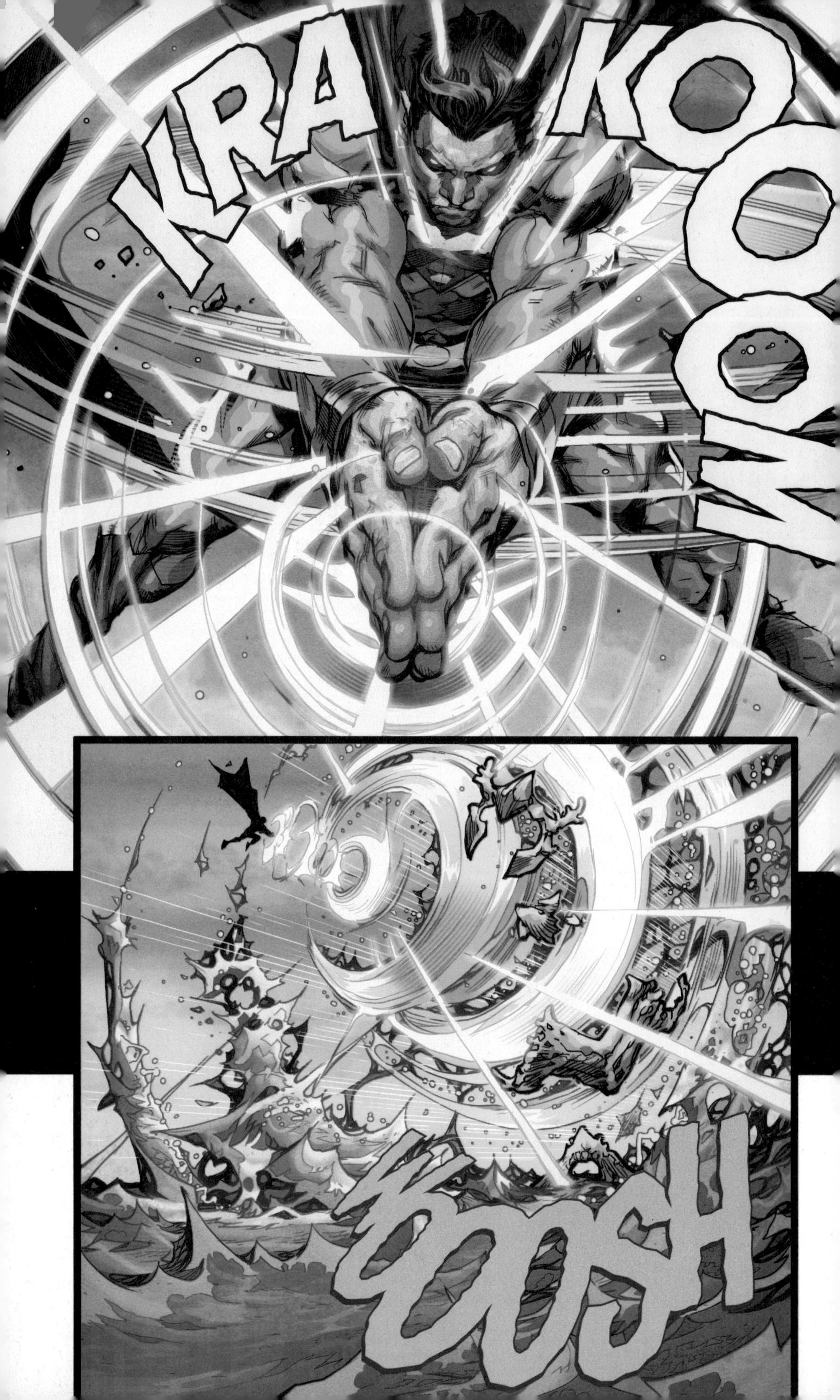
KRA KOOOM
WOOSH

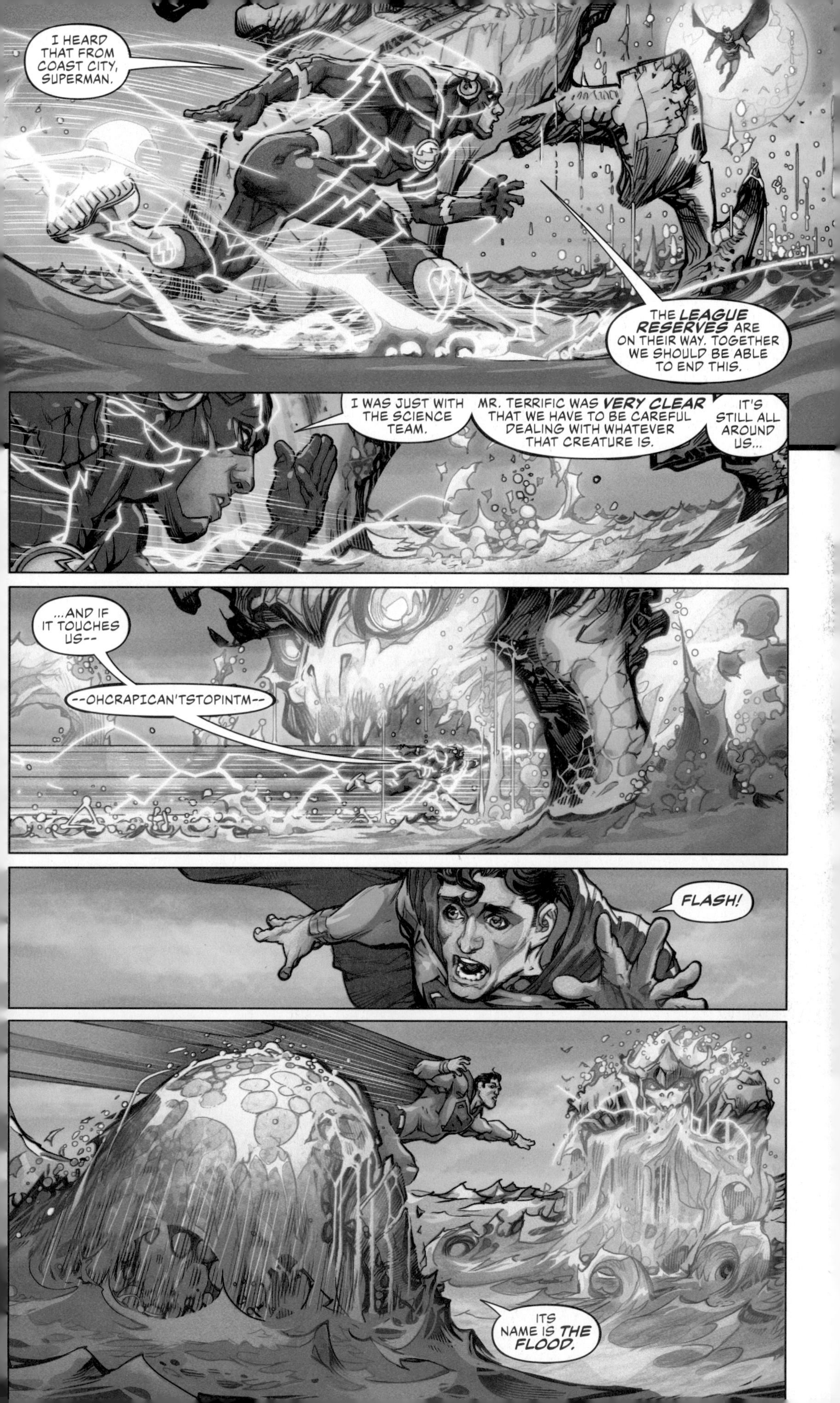
I HEARD THAT FROM COAST CITY, SUPERMAN.
THE LEAGUE RESERVES ARE ON THEIR WAY. TOGETHER WE SHOULD BE ABLE TO END THIS.
I WAS JUST WITH THE SCIENCE TEAM.
MR. TERRIFIC WAS VERY CLEAR THAT WE HAVE TO BE CAREFUL DEALING WITH WHATEVER THAT CREATURE IS.
IT'S STILL ALL AROUND US...
...AND IF IT TOUCHES US--
--OHCRAPICAN'TSTOPINTM--
FLASH!
ITS NAME IS THE FLOOD.

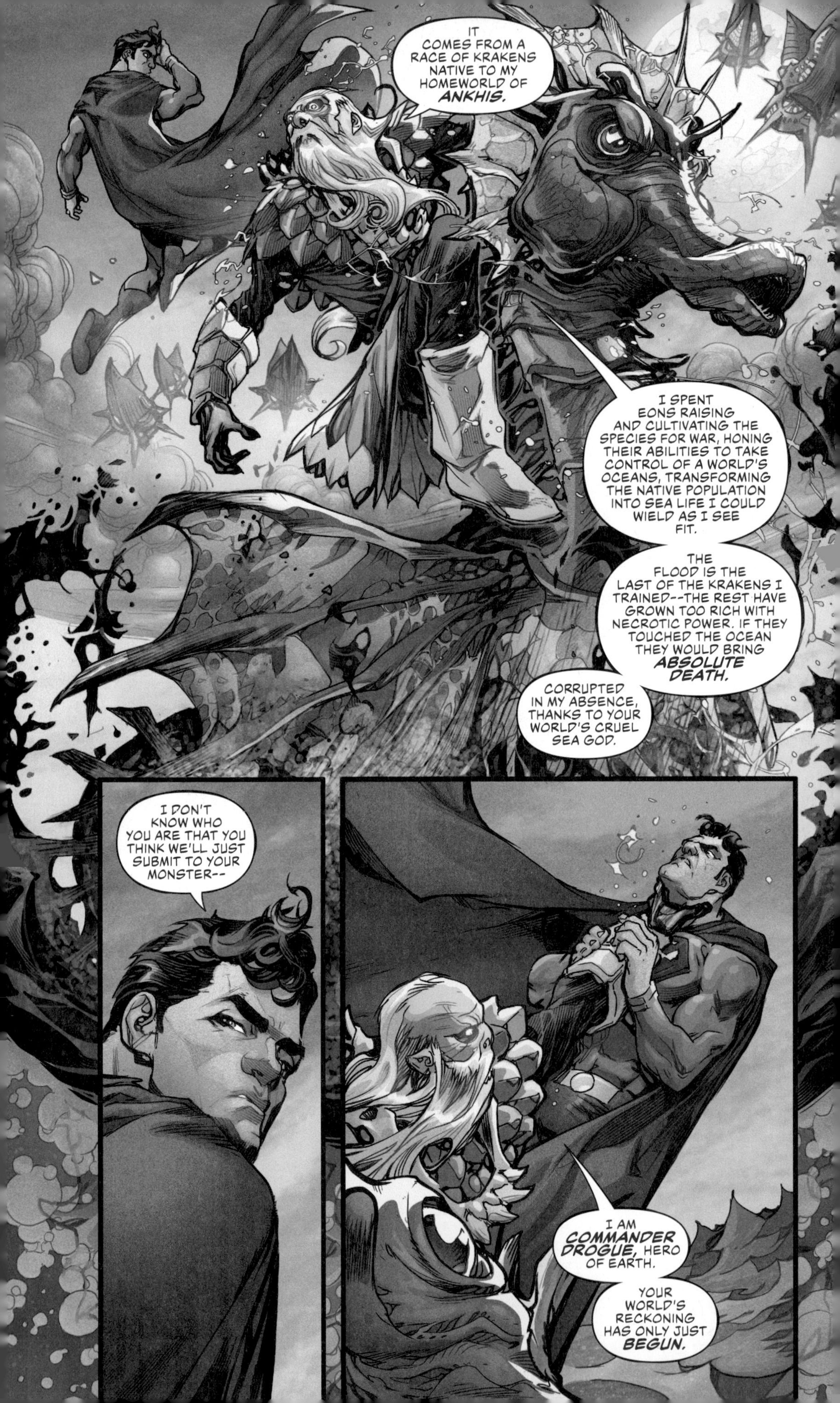

IT COMES FROM A RACE OF KRAKENS NATIVE TO MY HOMEWORLD OF ANKHIS.
I SPENT EONS RAISING AND CULTIVATING THE SPECIES FOR WAR, HONING THEIR ABILITIES TO TAKE CONTROL OF A WORLD'S OCEANS, TRANSFORMING THE NATIVE POPULATION INTO SEA LIFE I COULD WIELD AS I SEE FIT.
THE FLOOD IS THE LAST OF THE KRAKENS I TRAINED--THE REST HAVE GROWN TOO RICH WITH NECROTIC POWER. IF THEY TOUCHED THE OCEAN THEY WOULD BRING ABSOLUTE DEATH.
CORRUPTED IN MY ABSENCE, THANKS TO YOUR WORLD'S CRUEL SEA GOD.
I DON'T KNOW WHO YOU ARE THAT YOU THINK WE'LL JUST SUBMIT TO YOUR MONSTER--
I AM COMMANDER DROGUE, HERO OF EARTH.
YOUR WORLD'S RECKONING HAS ONLY JUST BEGUN.

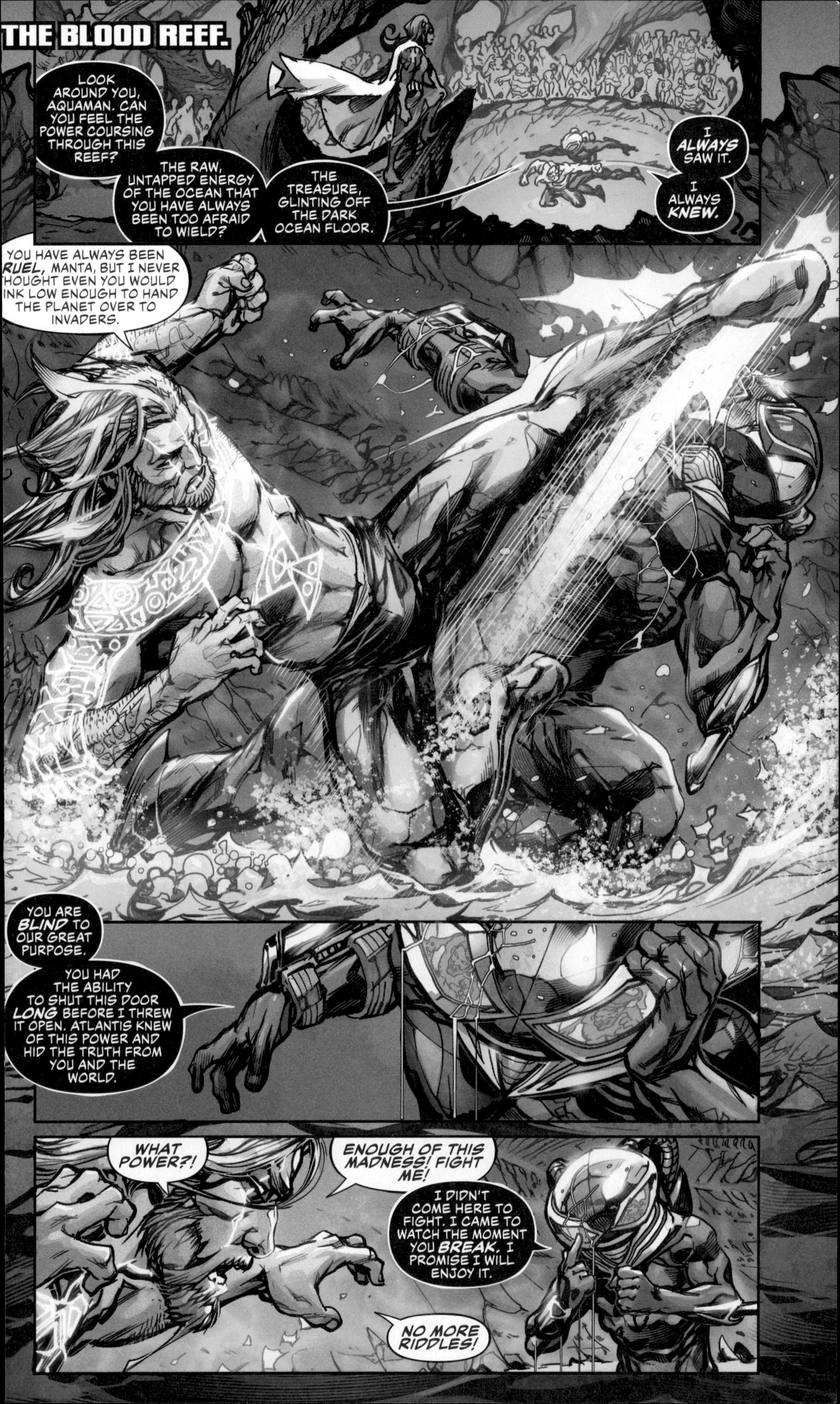
THE BLOOD REEF.
LOOK AROUND YOU, AQUAMAN. CAN YOU FEEL THE POWER COURSING THROUGH THIS REEF?
THE RAW, UNTAPPED ENERGY OF THE OCEAN THAT YOU HAVE ALWAYS BEEN TOO AFRAID TO WIELD?
THE TREASURE, GLINTING OFF THE DARK OCEAN FLOOR.
I ALWAYS SAW IT.
I ALWAYS KNEW.
YOU HAVE ALWAYS BEEN RUEL, MANTA, BUT I NEVER HOUGHT EVEN YOU WOULD INK LOW ENOUGH TO HAND THE PLANET OVER TO INVADERS.
YOU ARE BLIND TO OUR GREAT PURPOSE.
YOU HAD THE ABILITY TO SHUT THIS DOOR LONG BEFORE I THREW IT OPEN. ATLANTIS KNEW OF THIS POWER AND HID THE TRUTH FROM YOU AND THE WORLD.
WHAT POWER?!
ENOUGH OF THIS MADNESS! FIGHT ME!
I DIDN'T COME HERE TO FIGHT. I CAME TO WATCH THE MOMENT YOU BREAK. I PROMISE I WILL ENJOY IT.
NO MORE RIDDLES!

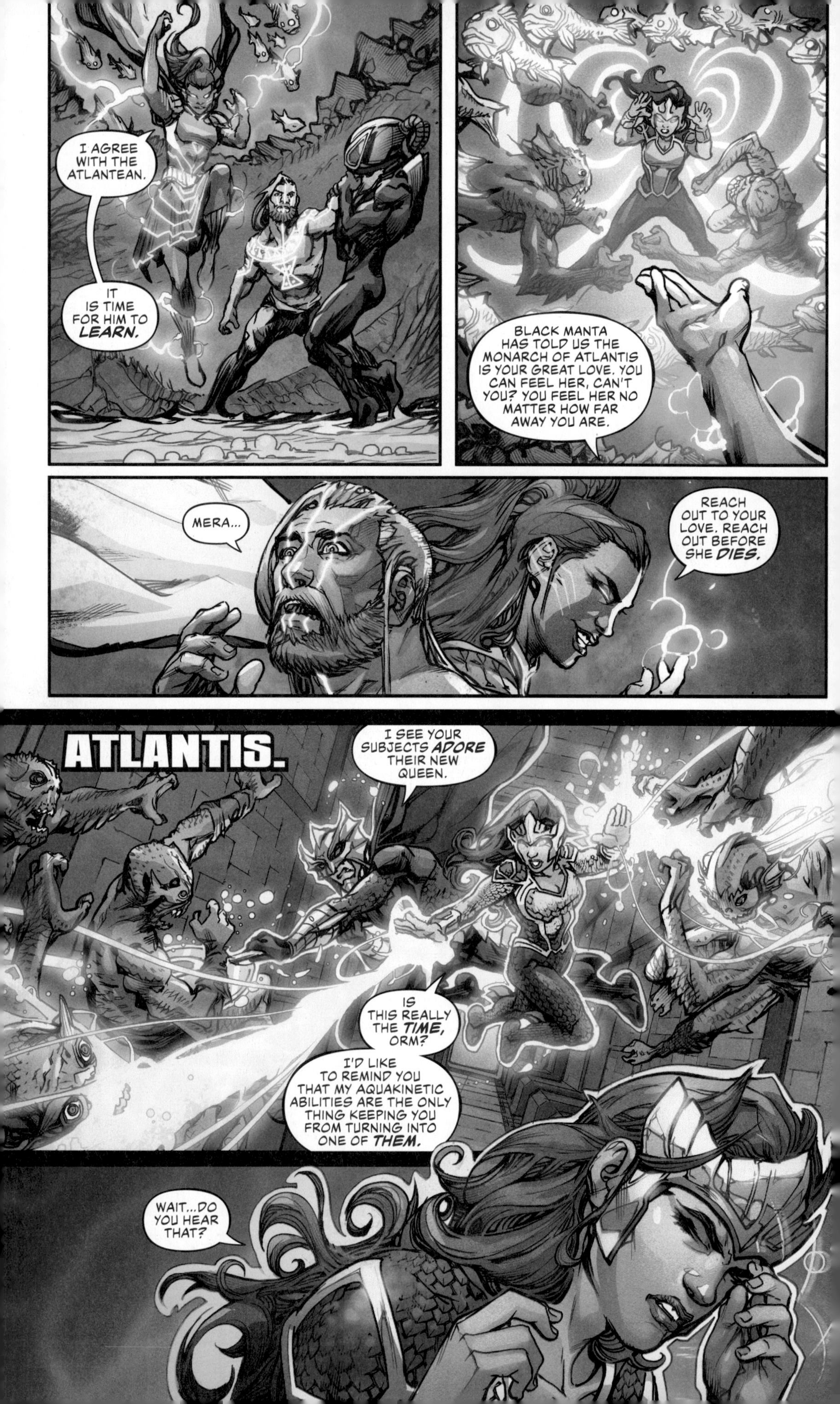
I AGREE WITH THE ATLANTEAN.
IT IS TIME FOR HIM TO LEARN.
BLACK MANTA HAS TOLD US THE MONARCH OF ATLANTIS IS YOUR GREAT LOVE. YOU CAN FEEL HER, CAN'T YOU? YOU FEEL HER NO MATTER HOW FAR AWAY YOU ARE.
MERA...
REACH OUT TO YOUR LOVE. REACH OUT BEFORE SHE DIES.
ATLANTIS.
I SEE YOUR SUBJECTS ADORE THEIR NEW QUEEN.
IS THIS REALLY THE TIME, ORM?
I'D LIKE TO REMIND YOU THAT MY AQUAKINETIC ABILITIES ARE THE ONLY THING KEEPING YOU FROM TURNING INTO ONE OF THEM.
WAIT...DO YOU HEAR THAT?

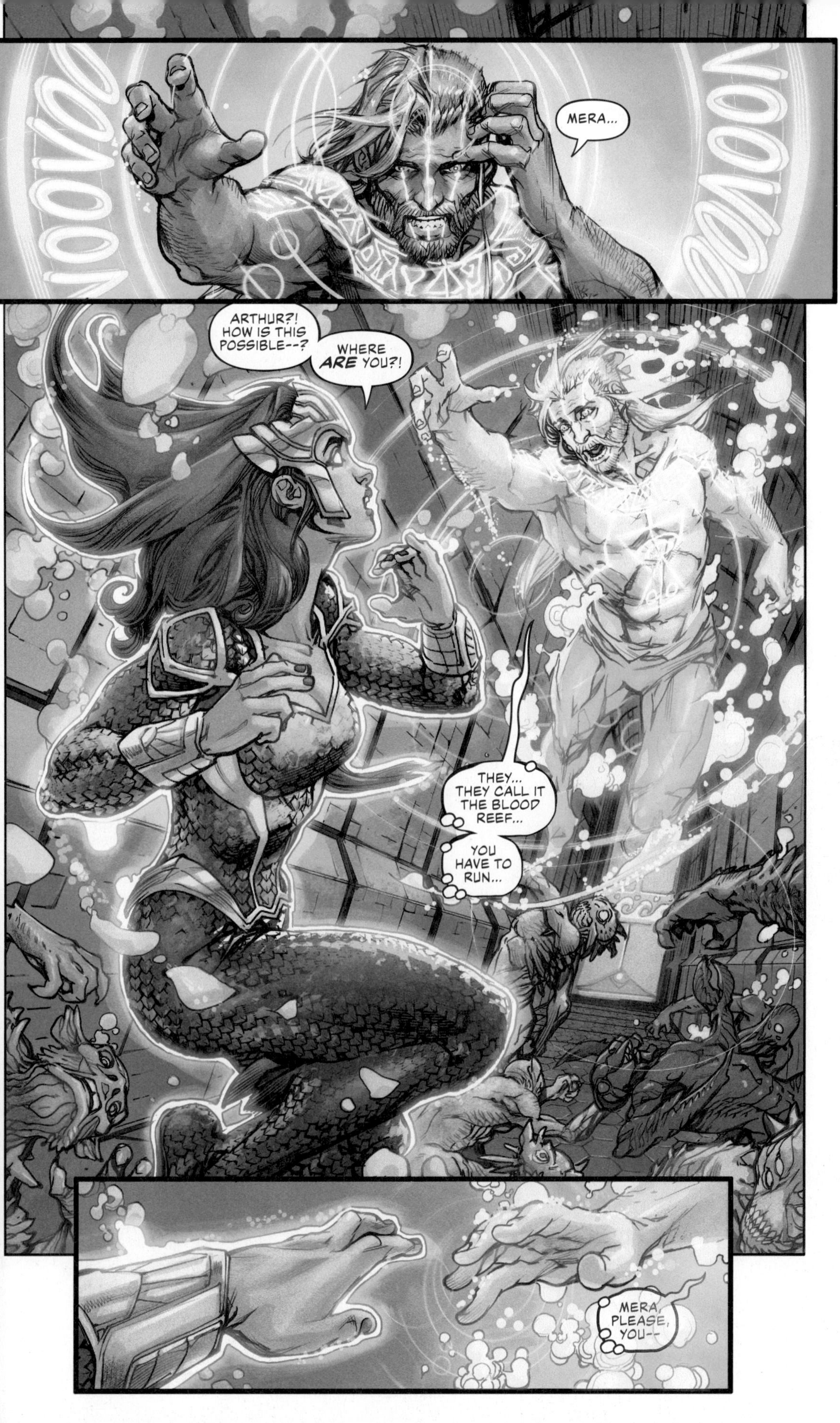

MERA...
ARTHUR?! HOW IS THIS POSSIBLE--?
WHERE ARE YOU?!
THEY... THEY CALL IT THE BLOOD REEF...
YOU HAVE TO RUN...
MERA, PLEASE, YOU--

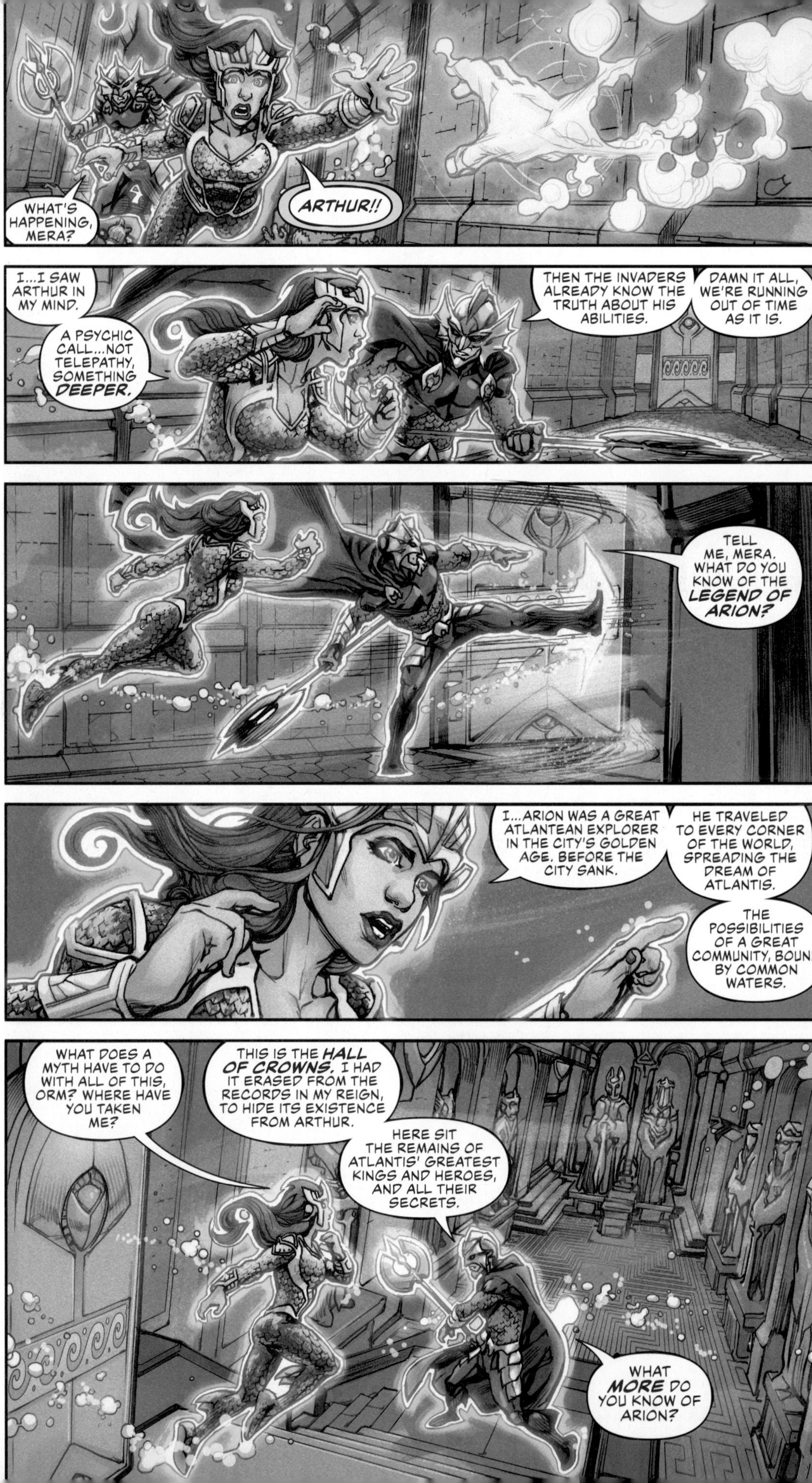
WHAT'S HAPPENING, MERA?
ARTHUR!!
I...I SAW ARTHUR IN MY MIND.
A PSYCHIC CALL...NOT TELEPATHY, SOMETHING DEEPER.
THEN THE INVADERS ALREADY KNOW THE TRUTH ABOUT HIS ABILITIES.
DAMN IT ALL, WE'RE RUNNING OUT OF TIME AS IT IS.
TELL ME, MERA. WHAT DO YOU KNOW OF THE LEGEND OF ARION?
I...ARION WAS A GREAT ATLANTEAN EXPLORER IN THE CITY'S GOLDEN AGE. BEFORE THE CITY SANK.
HE TRAVELED TO EVERY CORNER OF THE WORLD, SPREADING THE DREAM OF ATLANTIS.
THE POSSIBILITIES OF A GREAT COMMUNITY, BOUND BY COMMON WATERS.
WHAT DOES A MYTH HAVE TO DO WITH ALL OF THIS, ORM? WHERE HAVE YOU TAKEN ME?
THIS IS THE HALL OF CROWNS. I HAD IT ERASED FROM THE RECORDS IN MY REIGN, TO HIDE ITS EXISTENCE FROM ARTHUR.
HERE SIT THE REMAINS OF ATLANTIS' GREATEST KINGS AND HEROES, AND ALL THEIR SECRETS.
WHAT MORE DO YOU KNOW OF ARION?

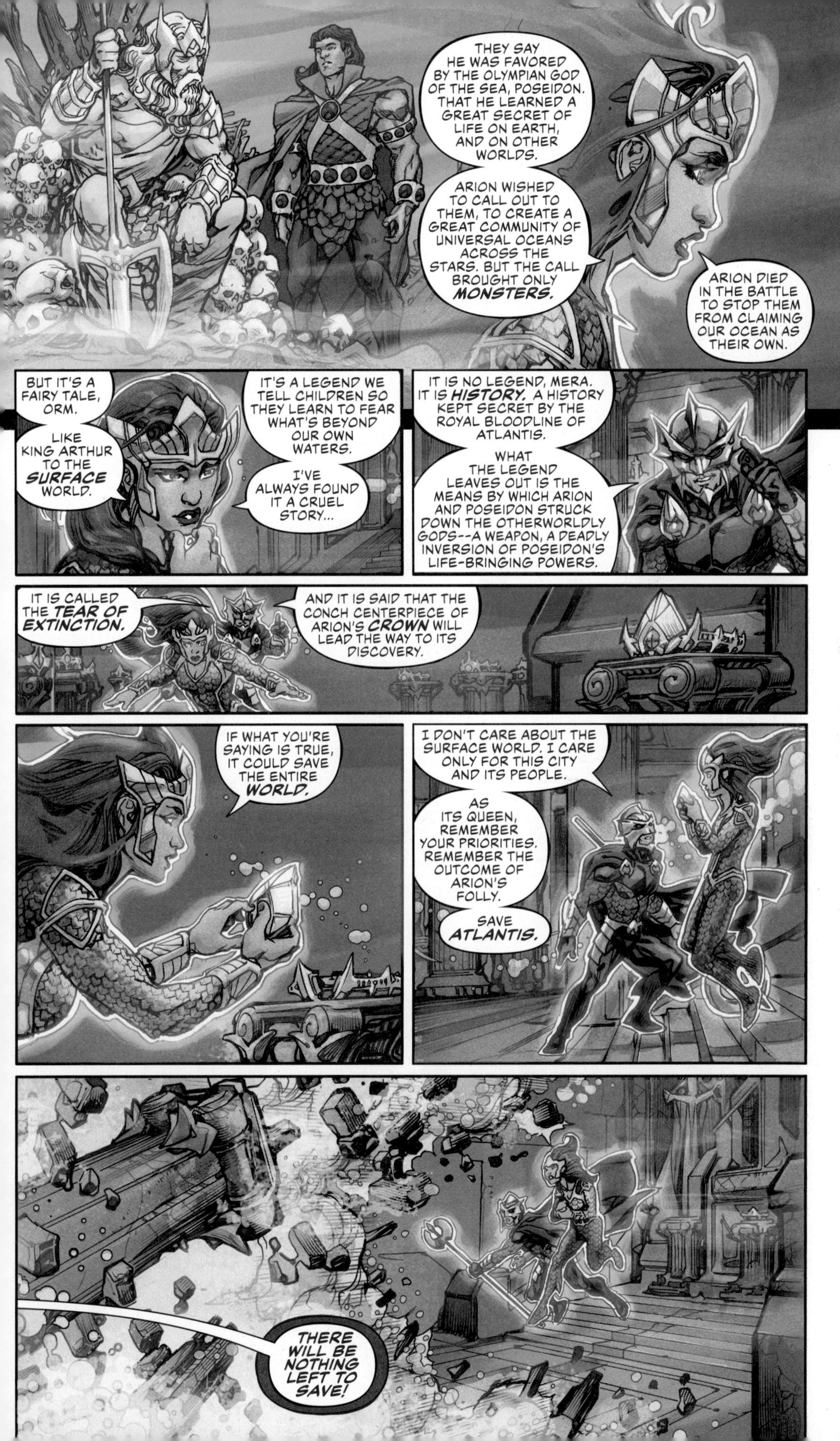
THEY SAY HE WAS FAVORED BY THE OLYMPIAN GOD OF THE SEA, POSEIDON. THAT HE LEARNED A GREAT SECRET OF LIFE ON EARTH, AND ON OTHER WORLDS.
ARION WISHED TO CALL OUT TO THEM, TO CREATE A GREAT COMMUNITY OF UNIVERSAL OCEANS ACROSS THE STARS. BUT THE CALL BROUGHT ONLY *MONSTERS.*
ARION DIED IN THE BATTLE TO STOP THEM FROM CLAIMING OUR OCEAN AS THEIR OWN.
BUT IT'S A FAIRY TALE, ORM.
LIKE KING ARTHUR TO THE *SURFACE* WORLD.
IT'S A LEGEND WE TELL CHILDREN SO THEY LEARN TO FEAR WHAT'S BEYOND OUR OWN WATERS.
I'VE ALWAYS FOUND IT A CRUEL STORY...
IT IS NO LEGEND, MERA. IT IS *HISTORY.* A HISTORY KEPT SECRET BY THE ROYAL BLOODLINE OF ATLANTIS.
WHAT THE LEGEND LEAVES OUT IS THE MEANS BY WHICH ARION AND POSEIDON STRUCK DOWN THE OTHERWORLDLY GODS--A WEAPON, A DEADLY INVERSION OF POSEIDON'S LIFE-BRINGING POWERS.
IT IS CALLED THE *TEAR OF EXTINCTION.*
AND IT IS SAID THAT THE CONCH CENTERPIECE OF ARION'S *CROWN* WILL LEAD THE WAY TO ITS DISCOVERY.
IF WHAT YOU'RE SAYING IS TRUE, IT COULD SAVE THE ENTIRE *WORLD.*
I DON'T CARE ABOUT THE SURFACE WORLD. I CARE ONLY FOR THIS CITY AND ITS PEOPLE.
AS ITS QUEEN, REMEMBER YOUR PRIORITIES. REMEMBER THE OUTCOME OF ARION'S FOLLY.
SAVE *ATLANTIS.*
THERE WILL BE NOTHING LEFT TO SAVE!

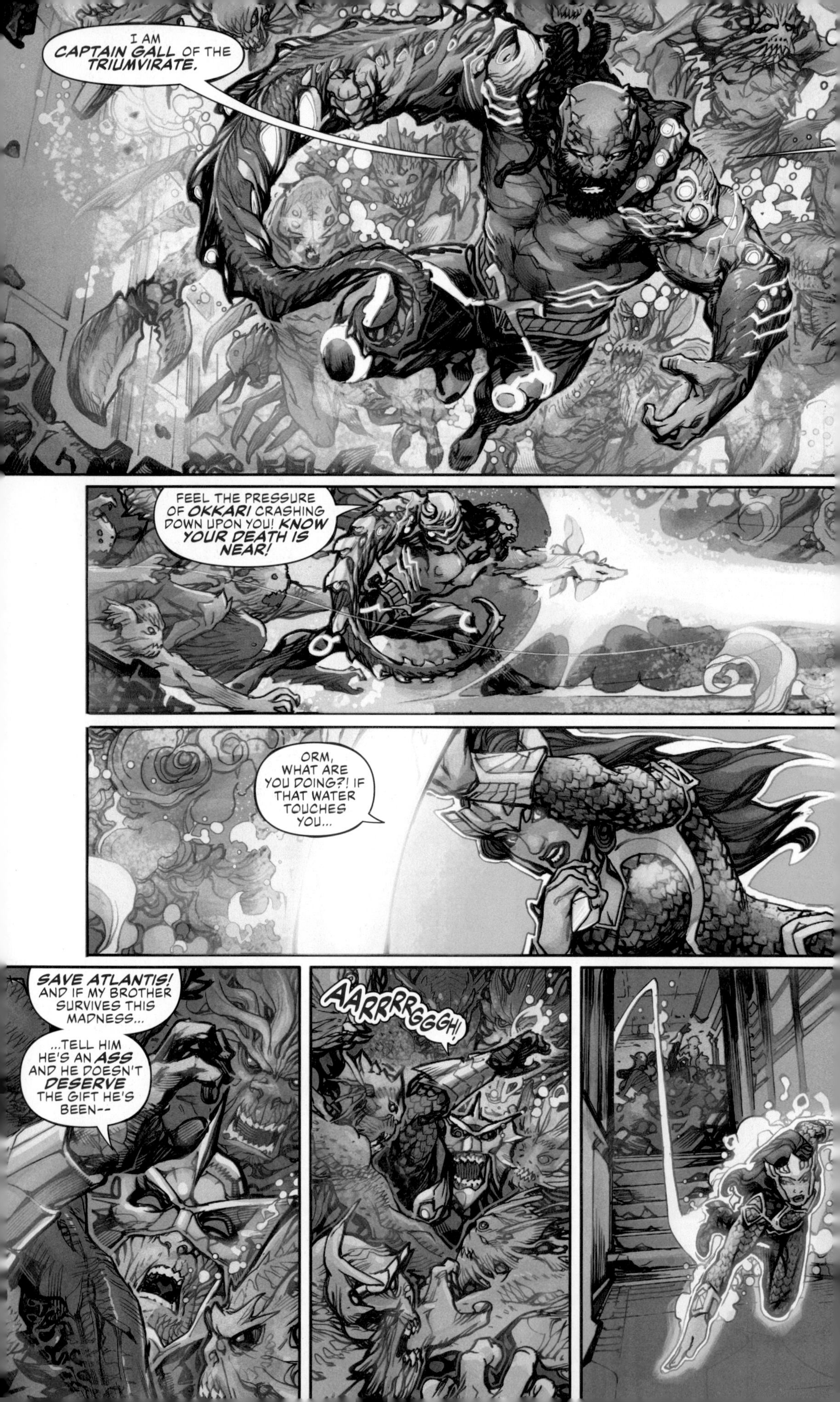
I AM CAPTAIN GALL OF THE TRIUMVIRATE.
FEEL THE PRESSURE OF OKKARI CRASHING DOWN UPON YOU! KNOW YOUR DEATH IS NEAR!
ORM, WHAT ARE YOU DOING?! IF THAT WATER TOUCHES YOU...
SAVE ATLANTIS! AND IF MY BROTHER SURVIVES THIS MADNESS...
...TELL HIM HE'S AN ASS AND HE DOESN'T DESERVE THE GIFT HE'S BEEN--
AARRRRGGGH!

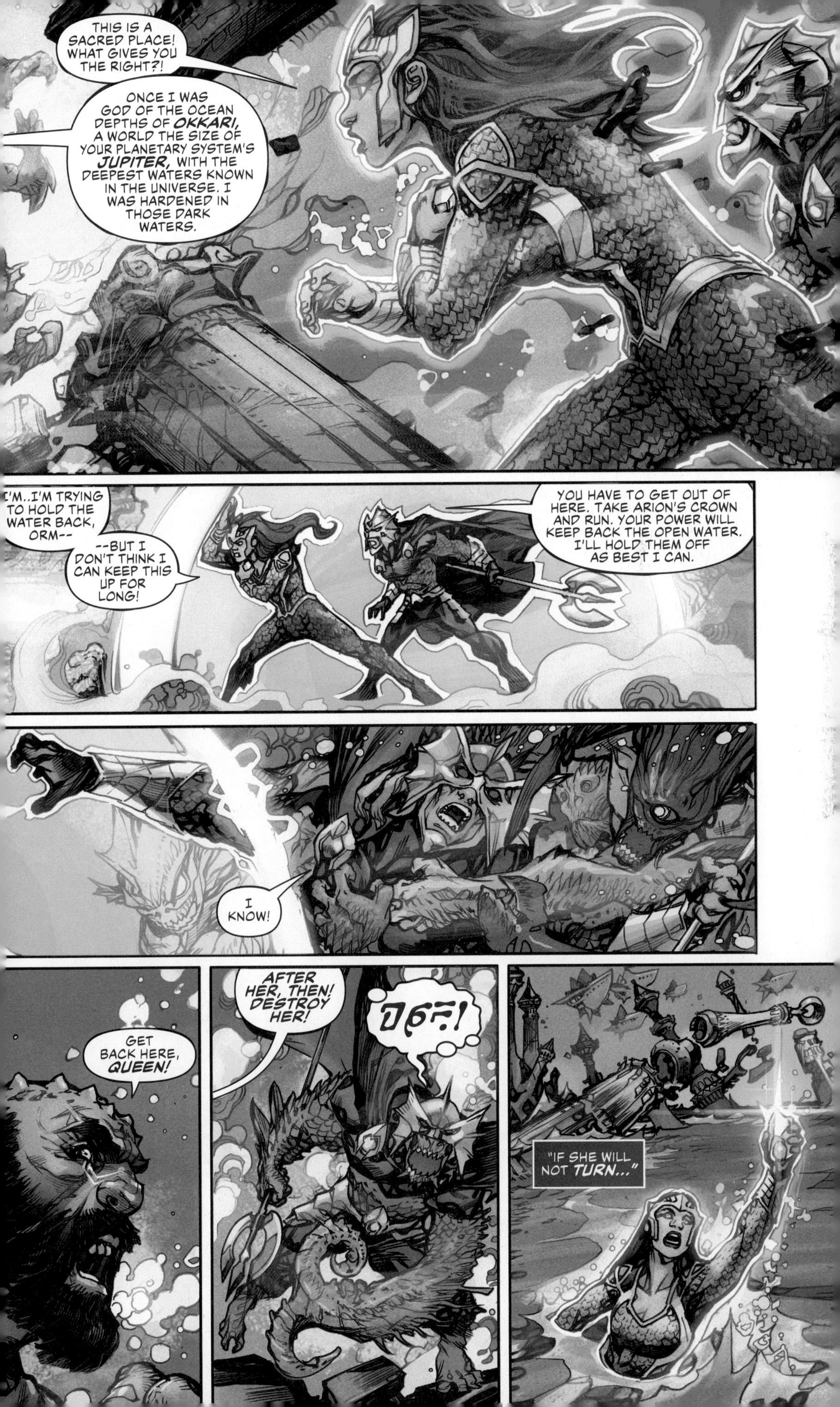
THIS IS A SACRED PLACE! WHAT GIVES YOU THE RIGHT?!
ONCE I WAS GOD OF THE OCEAN DEPTHS OF OKKARI, A WORLD THE SIZE OF YOUR PLANETARY SYSTEM'S JUPITER, WITH THE DEEPEST WATERS KNOWN IN THE UNIVERSE. I WAS HARDENED IN THOSE DARK WATERS.
I'M..I'M TRYING TO HOLD THE WATER BACK, ORM--
--BUT I DON'T THINK I CAN KEEP THIS UP FOR LONG!
YOU HAVE TO GET OUT OF HERE. TAKE ARION'S CROWN AND RUN. YOUR POWER WILL KEEP BACK THE OPEN WATER. I'LL HOLD THEM OFF AS BEST I CAN.
I KNOW!
GET BACK HERE, QUEEN!
AFTER HER, THEN! DESTROY HER!
OOF!
"IF SHE WILL NOT TURN..."

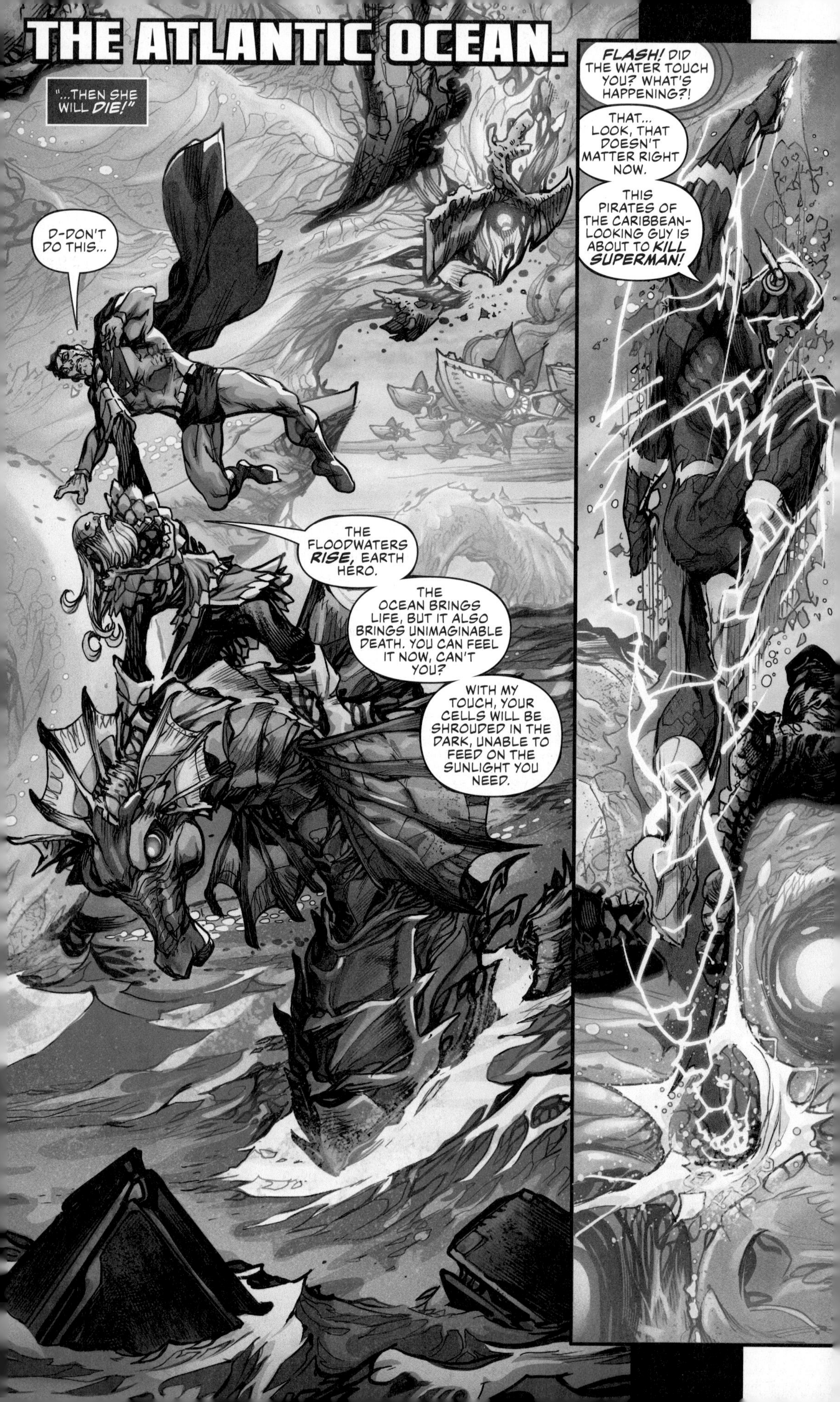
THE ATLANTIC OCEAN.
"...THEN SHE WILL DIE!"
D-DON'T DO THIS...
THE FLOODWATERS RISE, EARTH HERO.
THE OCEAN BRINGS LIFE, BUT IT ALSO BRINGS UNIMAGINABLE DEATH. YOU CAN FEEL IT NOW, CAN'T YOU?
WITH MY TOUCH, YOUR CELLS WILL BE SHROUDED IN THE DARK, UNABLE TO FEED ON THE SUNLIGHT YOU NEED.
FLASH! DID THE WATER TOUCH YOU? WHAT'S HAPPENING?!
THAT... LOOK, THAT DOESN'T MATTER RIGHT NOW.
THIS PIRATES OF THE CARIBBEAN-LOOKING GUY IS ABOUT TO KILL SUPERMAN!

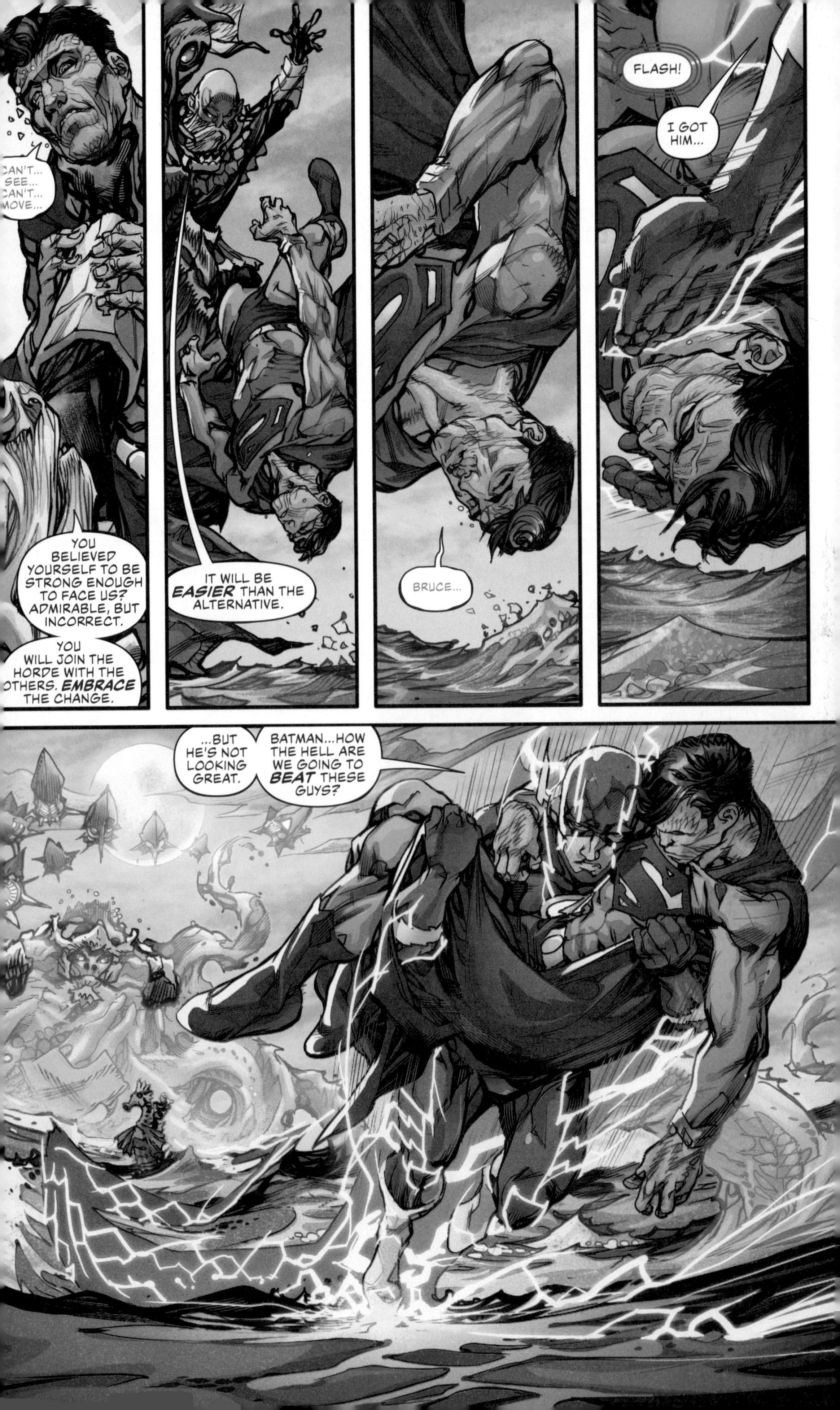
CAN'T... SEE... CAN'T... MOVE...
YOU BELIEVED YOURSELF TO BE STRONG ENOUGH TO FACE US? ADMIRABLE, BUT INCORRECT.
YOU WILL JOIN THE HORDE WITH THE OTHERS. EMBRACE THE CHANGE.
IT WILL BE EASIER THAN THE ALTERNATIVE.
BRUCE...
FLASH!
I GOT HIM...
...BUT HE'S NOT LOOKING GREAT.
BATMAN...HOW THE HELL ARE WE GOING TO BEAT THESE GUYS?

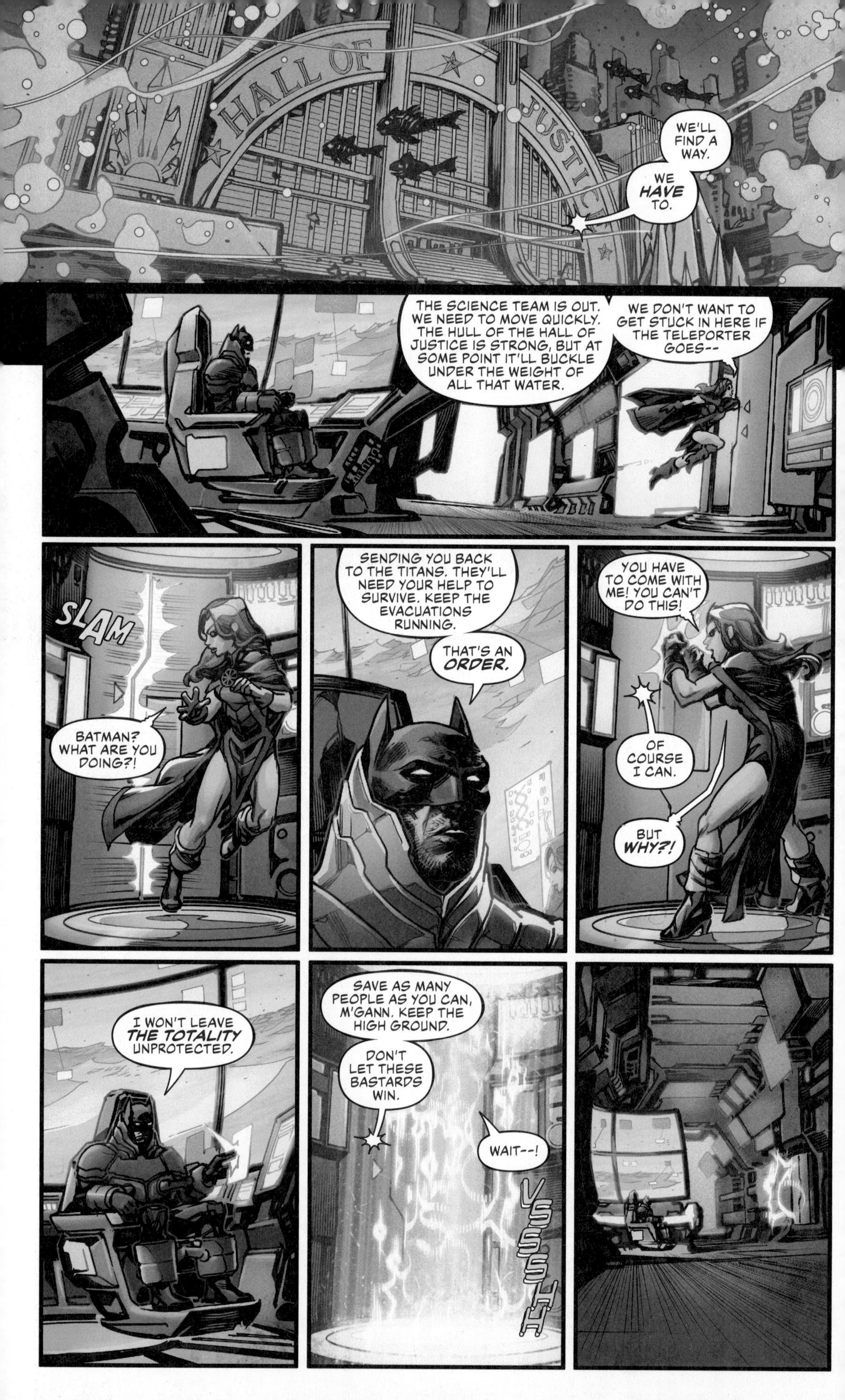
HALL OF JUSTICE
WE'LL FIND A WAY.
WE HAVE TO.
THE SCIENCE TEAM IS OUT. WE NEED TO MOVE QUICKLY. THE HULL OF THE HALL OF JUSTICE IS STRONG, BUT AT SOME POINT IT'LL BUCKLE UNDER THE WEIGHT OF ALL THAT WATER.
WE DON'T WANT TO GET STUCK IN HERE IF THE TELEPORTER GOES--
SLAM
BATMAN? WHAT ARE YOU DOING?!
SENDING YOU BACK TO THE TITANS. THEY'LL NEED YOUR HELP TO SURVIVE. KEEP THE EVACUATIONS RUNNING.
THAT'S AN ORDER.
YOU HAVE TO COME WITH ME! YOU CAN'T DO THIS!
OF COURSE I CAN.
BUT WHY?!
I WON'T LEAVE THE TOTALITY UNPROTECTED.
SAVE AS MANY PEOPLE AS YOU CAN, M'GANN. KEEP THE HIGH GROUND.
DON'T LET THESE BASTARDS WIN.
WAIT--!
VSSSHH

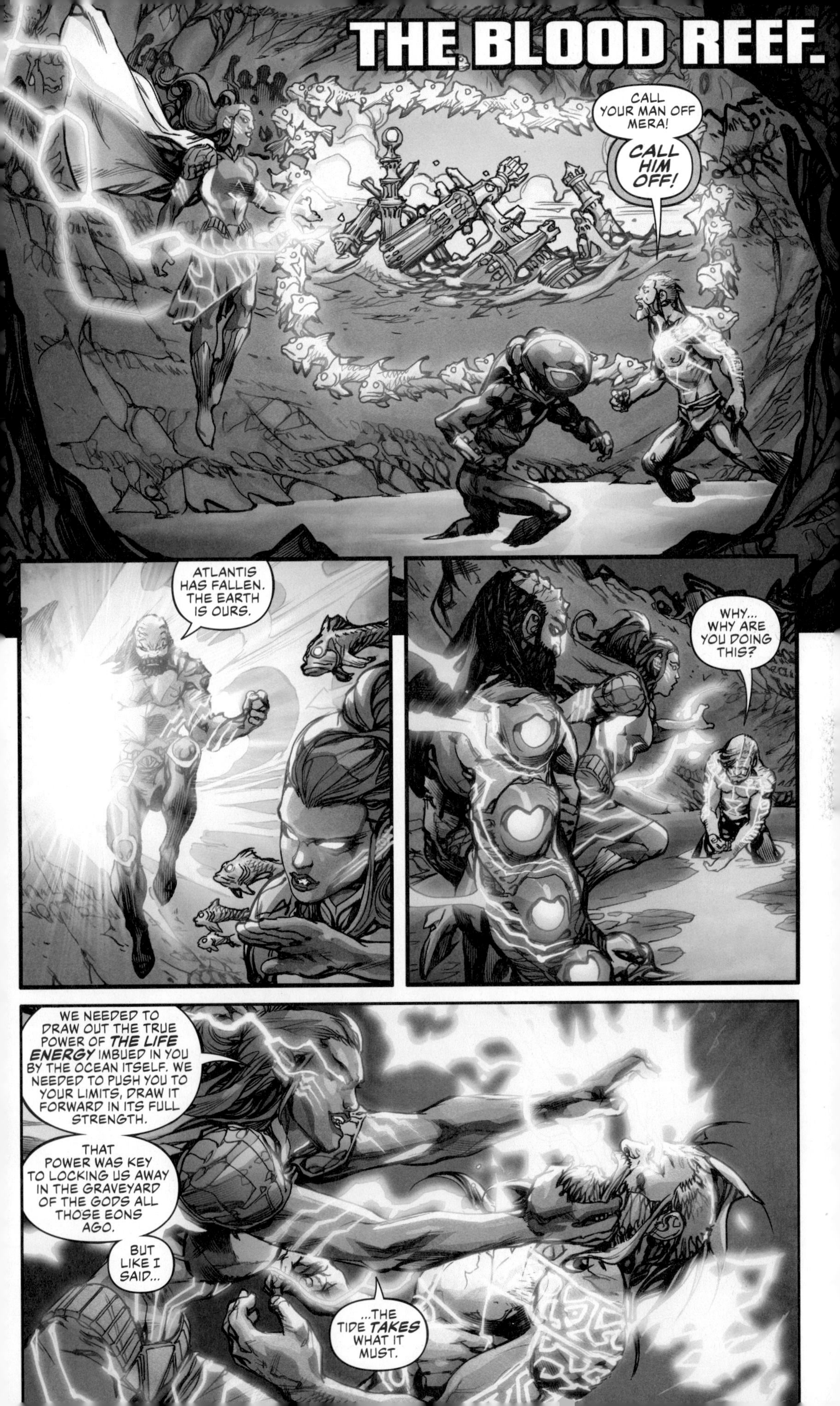
THE BLOOD REEF.
CALL YOUR MAN OFF MERA!
CALL HIM OFF!
ATLANTIS HAS FALLEN. THE EARTH IS OURS.
WHY... WHY ARE YOU DOING THIS?
WE NEEDED TO DRAW OUT THE TRUE POWER OF THE LIFE ENERGY IMBUED IN YOU BY THE OCEAN ITSELF. WE NEEDED TO PUSH YOU TO YOUR LIMITS, DRAW IT FORWARD IN ITS FULL STRENGTH.
THAT POWER WAS KEY TO LOCKING US AWAY IN THE GRAVEYARD OF THE GODS ALL THOSE EONS AGO.
BUT LIKE I SAID...
...THE TIDE TAKES WHAT IT MUST.

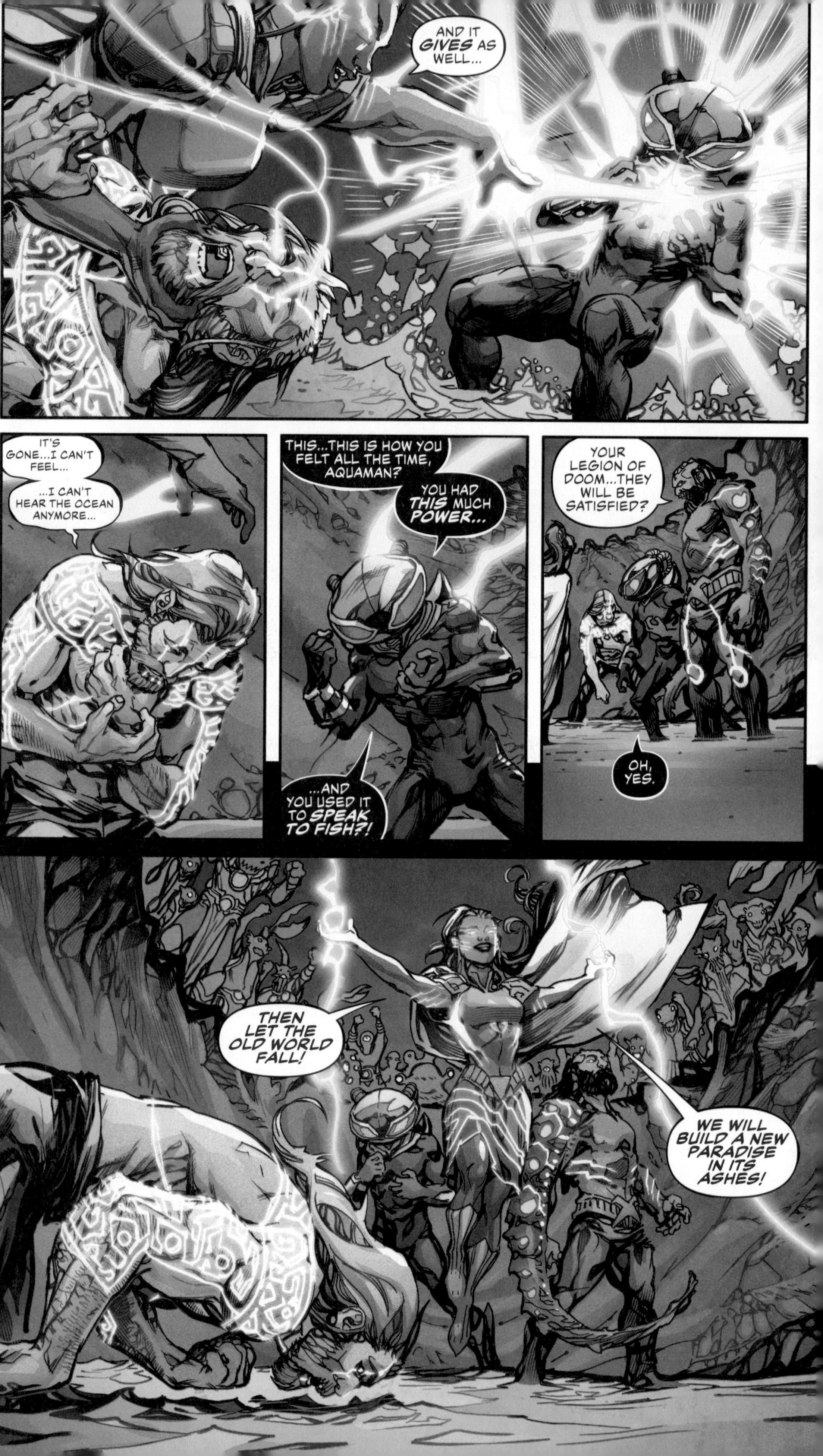

AND IT GIVES AS WELL...
IT'S GONE...I CAN'T FEEL...
...I CAN'T HEAR THE OCEAN ANYMORE...
THIS...THIS IS HOW YOU FELT ALL THE TIME, AQUAMAN?
YOU HAD THIS MUCH POWER...
...AND YOU USED IT TO SPEAK TO FISH?!
YOUR LEGION OF DOOM...THEY WILL BE SATISFIED?
OH, YES.
THEN LET THE OLD WORLD FALL!
WE WILL BUILD A NEW PARADISE IN ITS ASHES!

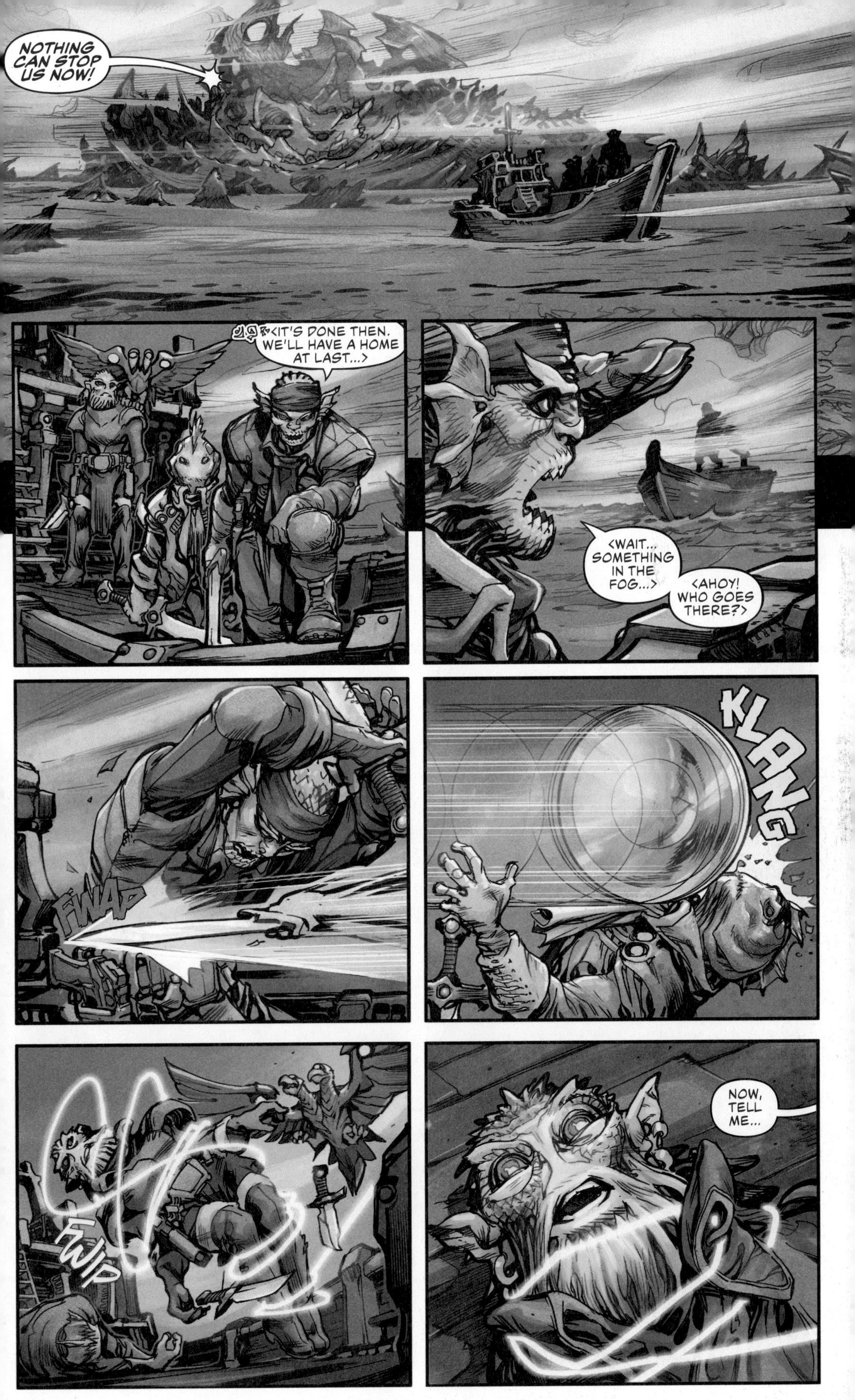
NOTHING CAN STOP US NOW!
<IT'S DONE THEN. WE'LL HAVE A HOME AT LAST...>
<WAIT... SOMETHING IN THE FOG...>
<AHOY! WHO GOES THERE?>
FWAP
KLANG
FWIP
NOW, TELL ME...

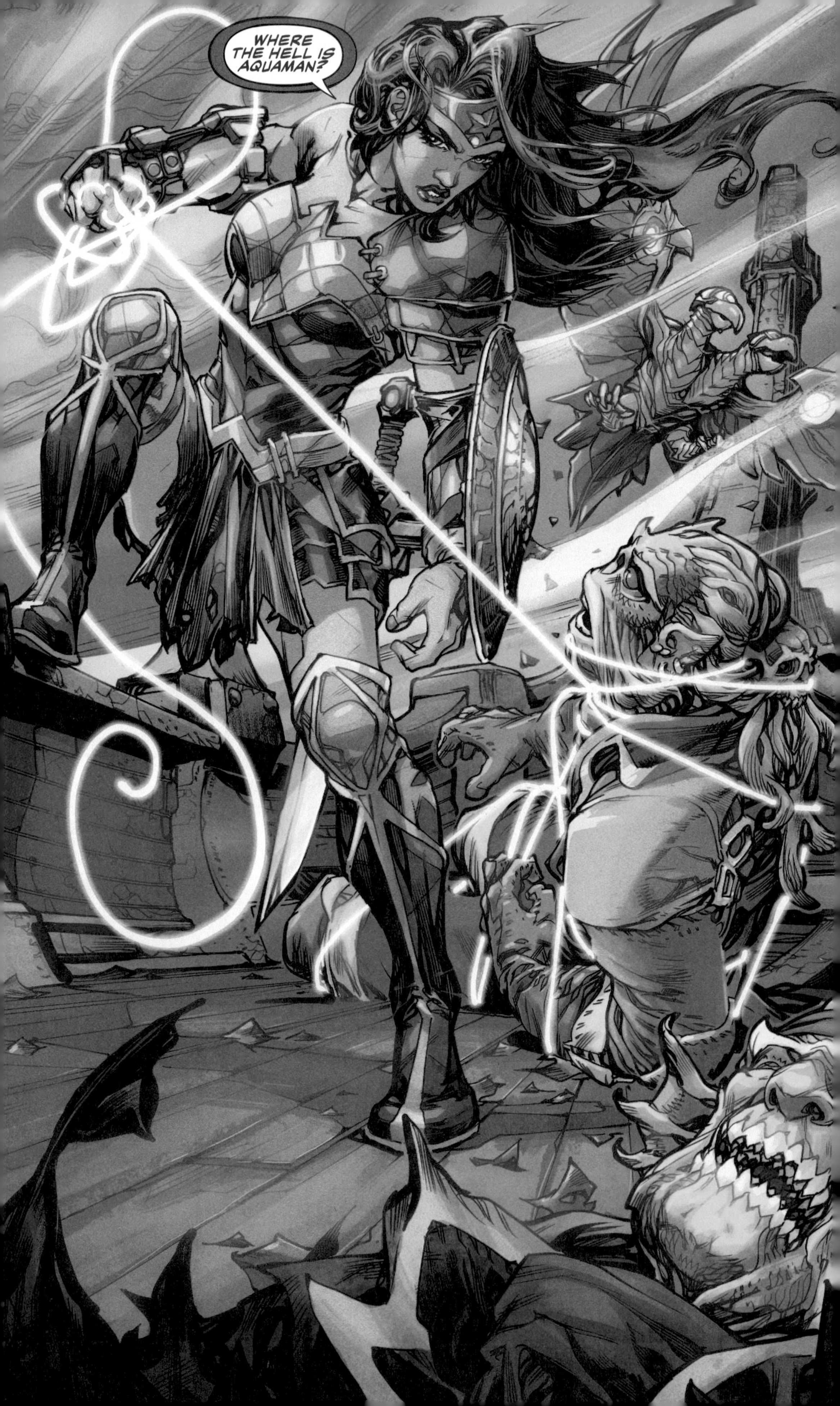
WHERE THE HELL IS AQUAMAN?

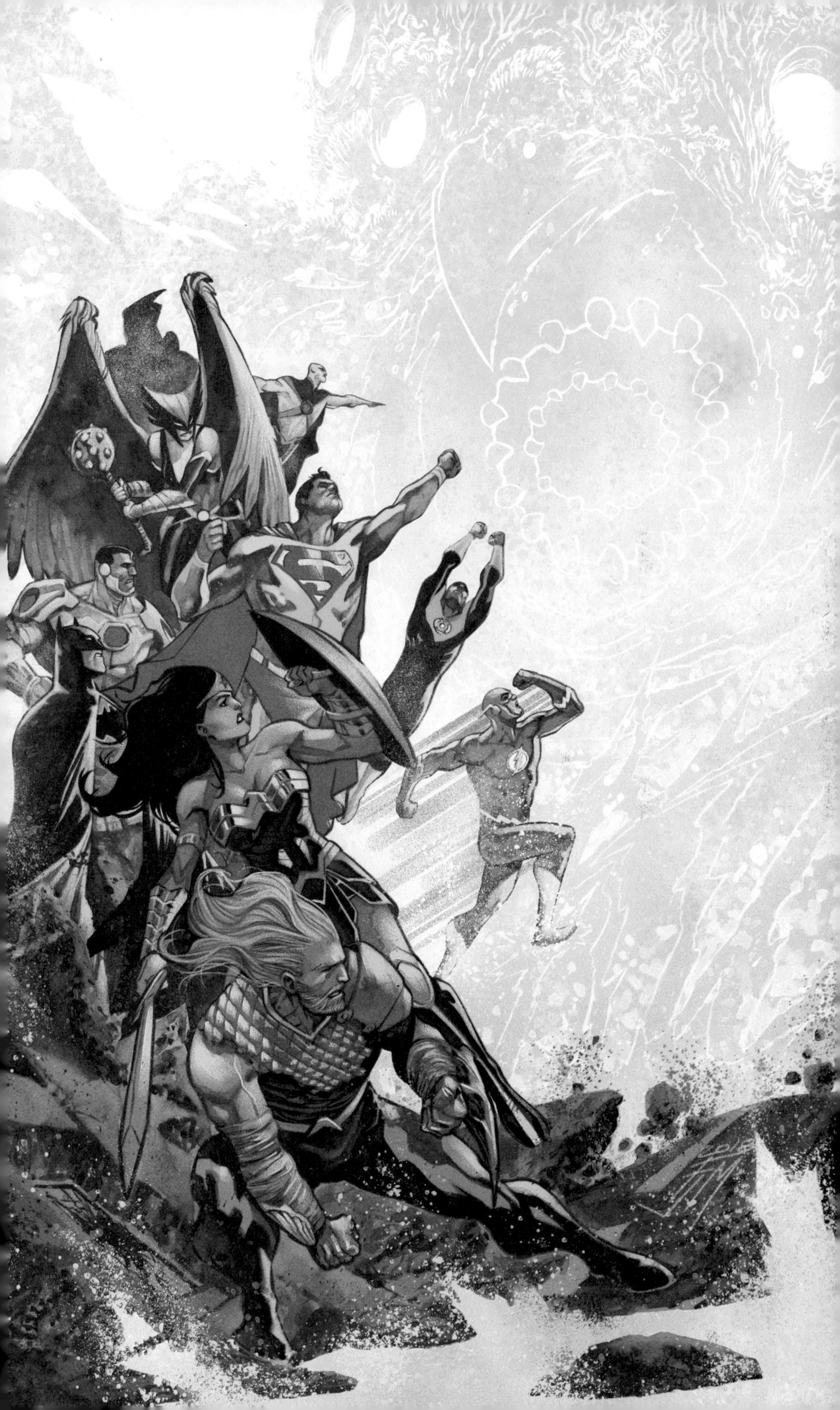

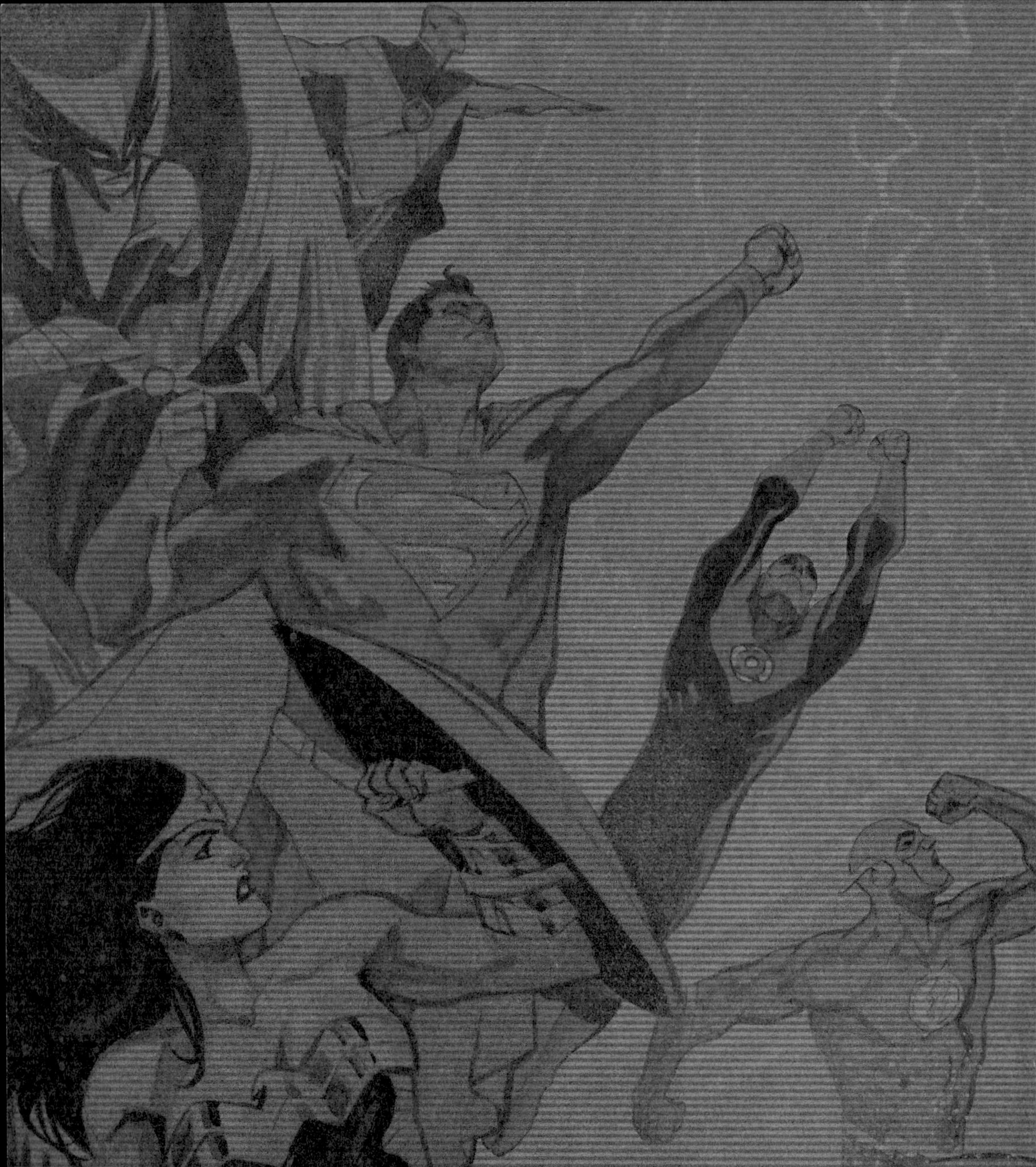

JUSTICE LEAGUE
#11

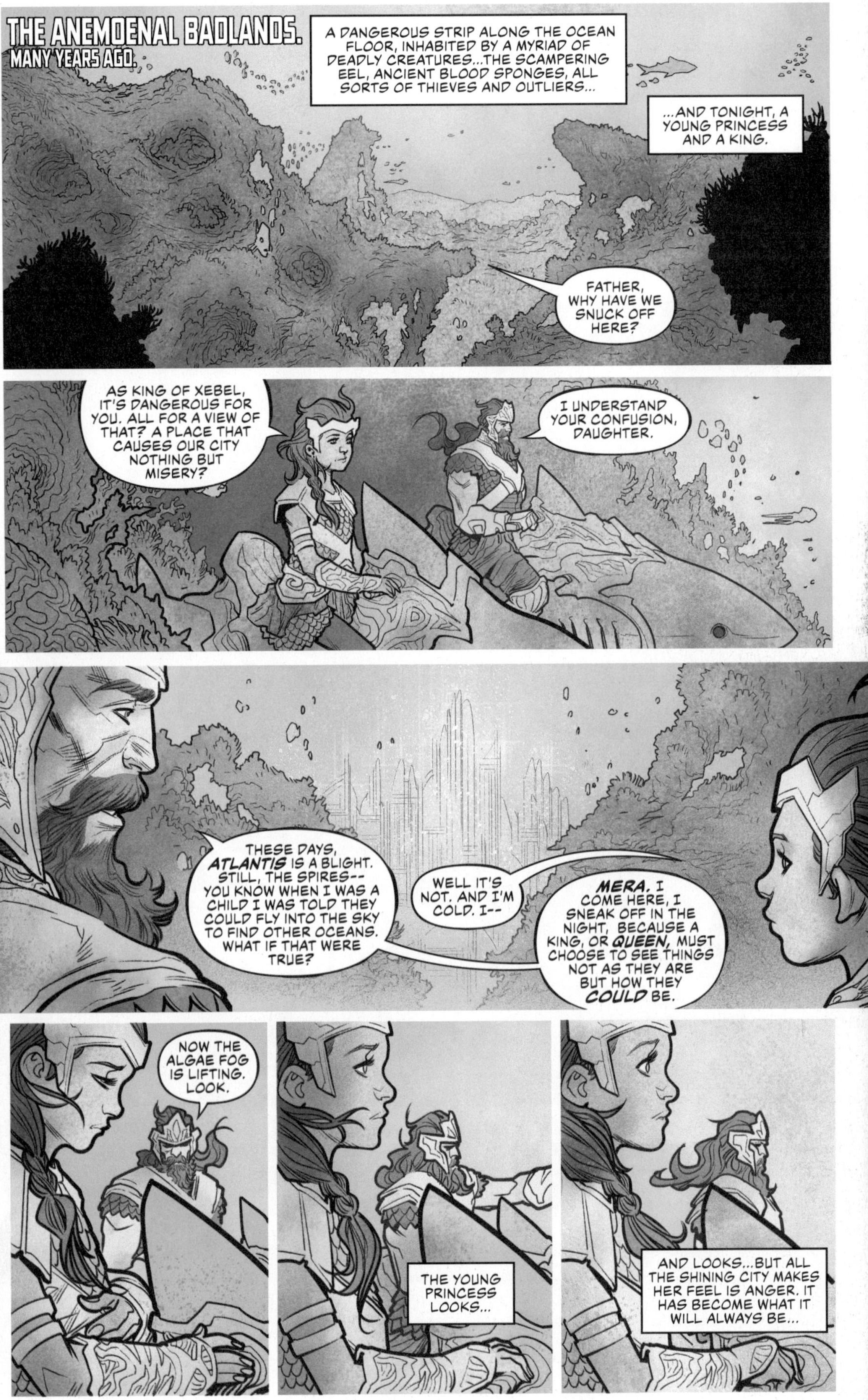
THE ANEMOENAL BADLANDS.
MANY YEARS AGO.
A DANGEROUS STRIP ALONG THE OCEAN FLOOR, INHABITED BY A MYRIAD OF DEADLY CREATURES...THE SCAMPERING EEL, ANCIENT BLOOD SPONGES, ALL SORTS OF THIEVES AND OUTLIERS...
...AND TONIGHT, A YOUNG PRINCESS AND A KING.
FATHER, WHY HAVE WE SNUCK OFF HERE?
AS KING OF XEBEL, IT'S DANGEROUS FOR YOU. ALL FOR A VIEW OF THAT? A PLACE THAT CAUSES OUR CITY NOTHING BUT MISERY?
I UNDERSTAND YOUR CONFUSION, DAUGHTER.
THESE DAYS, ATLANTIS IS A BLIGHT. STILL, THE SPIRES-- YOU KNOW WHEN I WAS A CHILD I WAS TOLD THEY COULD FLY INTO THE SKY TO FIND OTHER OCEANS. WHAT IF THAT WERE TRUE?
WELL IT'S NOT. AND I'M COLD. I--
MERA. I COME HERE, I SNEAK OFF IN THE NIGHT, BECAUSE A KING, OR QUEEN, MUST CHOOSE TO SEE THINGS NOT AS THEY ARE BUT HOW THEY COULD BE.
NOW THE ALGAE FOG IS LIFTING. LOOK.
THE YOUNG PRINCESS LOOKS...
AND LOOKS...BUT ALL THE SHINING CITY MAKES HER FEEL IS ANGER. IT HAS BECOME WHAT IT WILL ALWAYS BE...

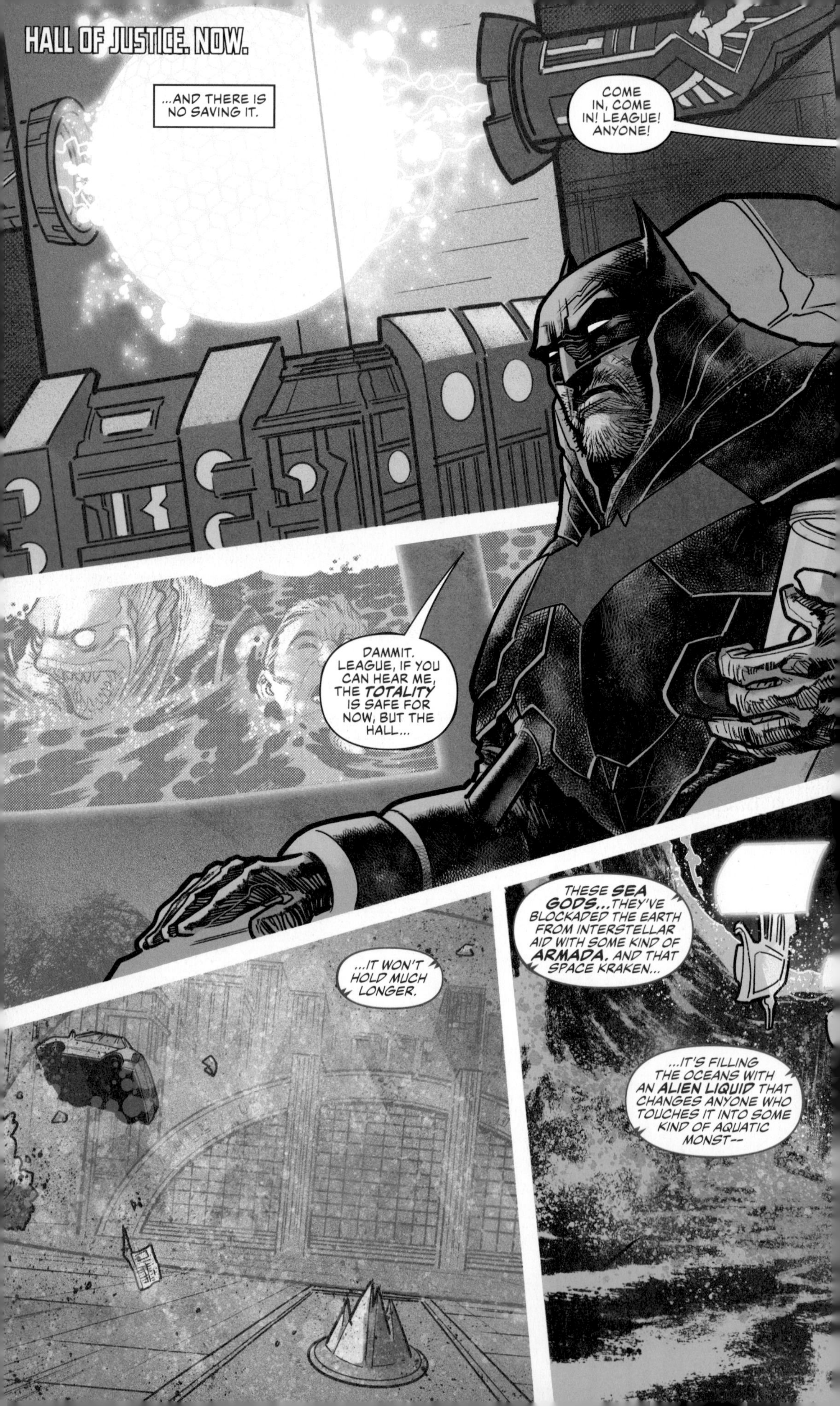
HALL OF JUSTICE. NOW.
...AND THERE IS NO SAVING IT.
COME IN, COME IN! LEAGUE! ANYONE!
DAMMIT. LEAGUE, IF YOU CAN HEAR ME, THE TOTALITY IS SAFE FOR NOW, BUT THE HALL...
...IT WON'T HOLD MUCH LONGER.
THESE SEA GODS...THEY'VE BLOCKADED THE EARTH FROM INTERSTELLAR AID WITH SOME KIND OF ARMADA. AND THAT SPACE KRAKEN...
...IT'S FILLING THE OCEANS WITH AN ALIEN LIQUID THAT CHANGES ANYONE WHO TOUCHES IT INTO SOME KIND OF AQUATIC MONST--

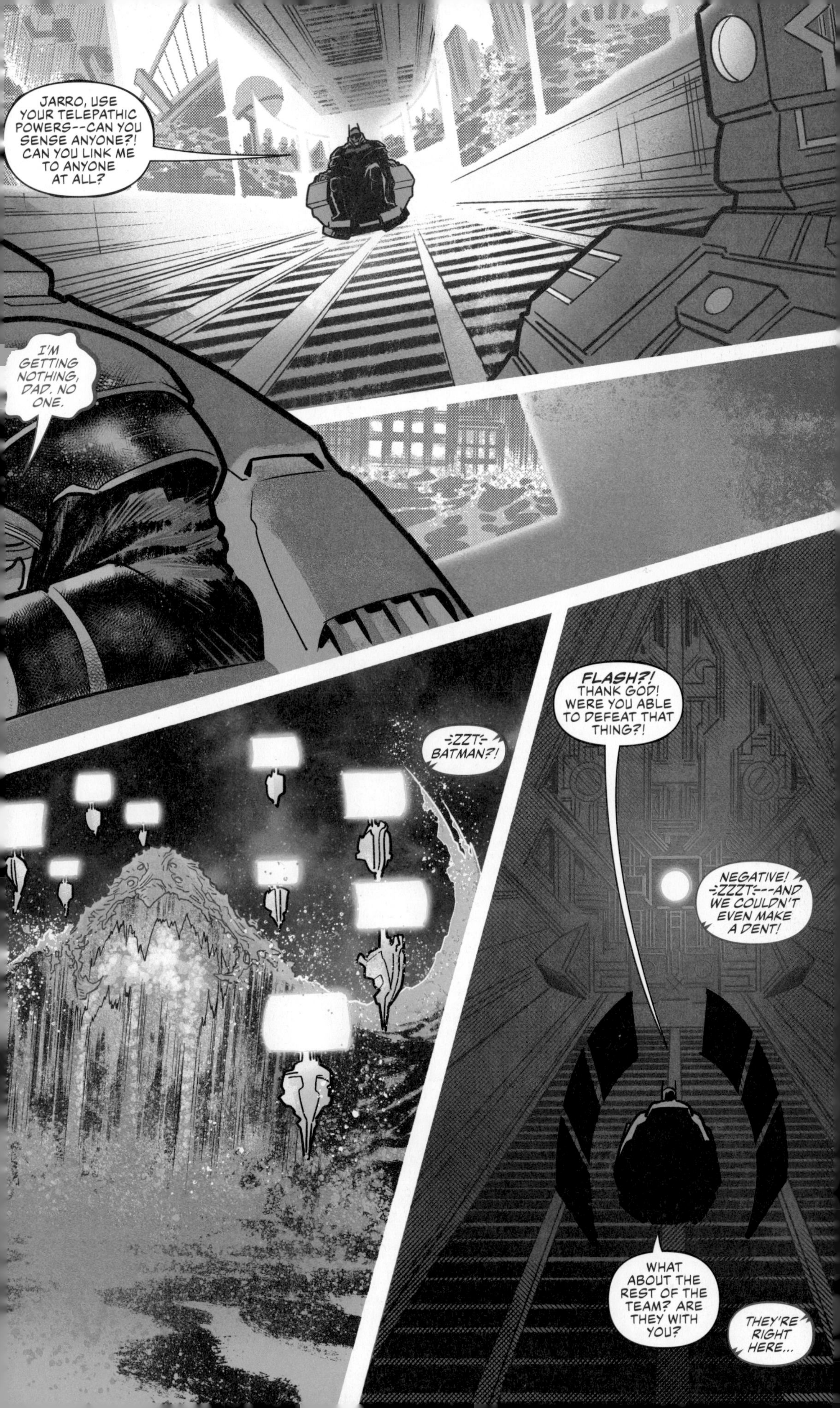

JARRO, USE YOUR TELEPATHIC POWERS--CAN YOU SENSE ANYONE?! CAN YOU LINK ME TO ANYONE AT ALL?
I'M GETTING NOTHING, DAD. NO ONE.
-ZZZT- BATMAN?!
FLASH?! THANK GOD! WERE YOU ABLE TO DEFEAT THAT THING?!
NEGATIVE! -ZZZT- --AND WE COULDN'T EVEN MAKE A DENT!
WHAT ABOUT THE REST OF THE TEAM? ARE THEY WITH YOU?
THEY'RE RIGHT HERE...

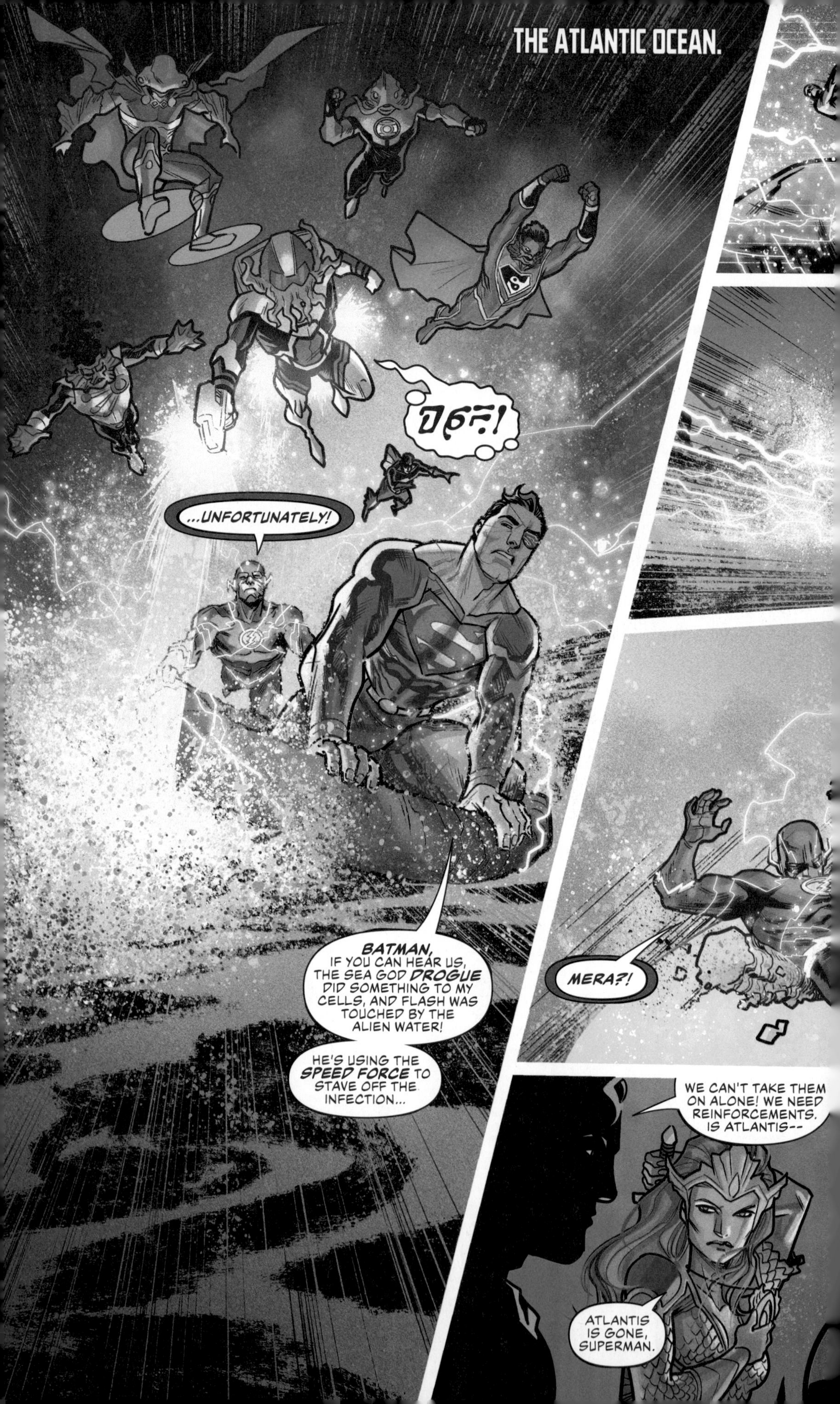
THE ATLANTIC OCEAN.
OOF?!
...UNFORTUNATELY!
BATMAN, IF YOU CAN HEAR US, THE SEA GOD DROGUE DID SOMETHING TO MY CELLS, AND FLASH WAS TOUCHED BY THE ALIEN WATER!
HE'S USING THE SPEED FORCE TO STAVE OFF THE INFECTION...
MERA?!
WE CAN'T TAKE THEM ON ALONE! WE NEED REINFORCEMENTS. IS ATLANTIS--
ATLANTIS IS GONE, SUPERMAN.

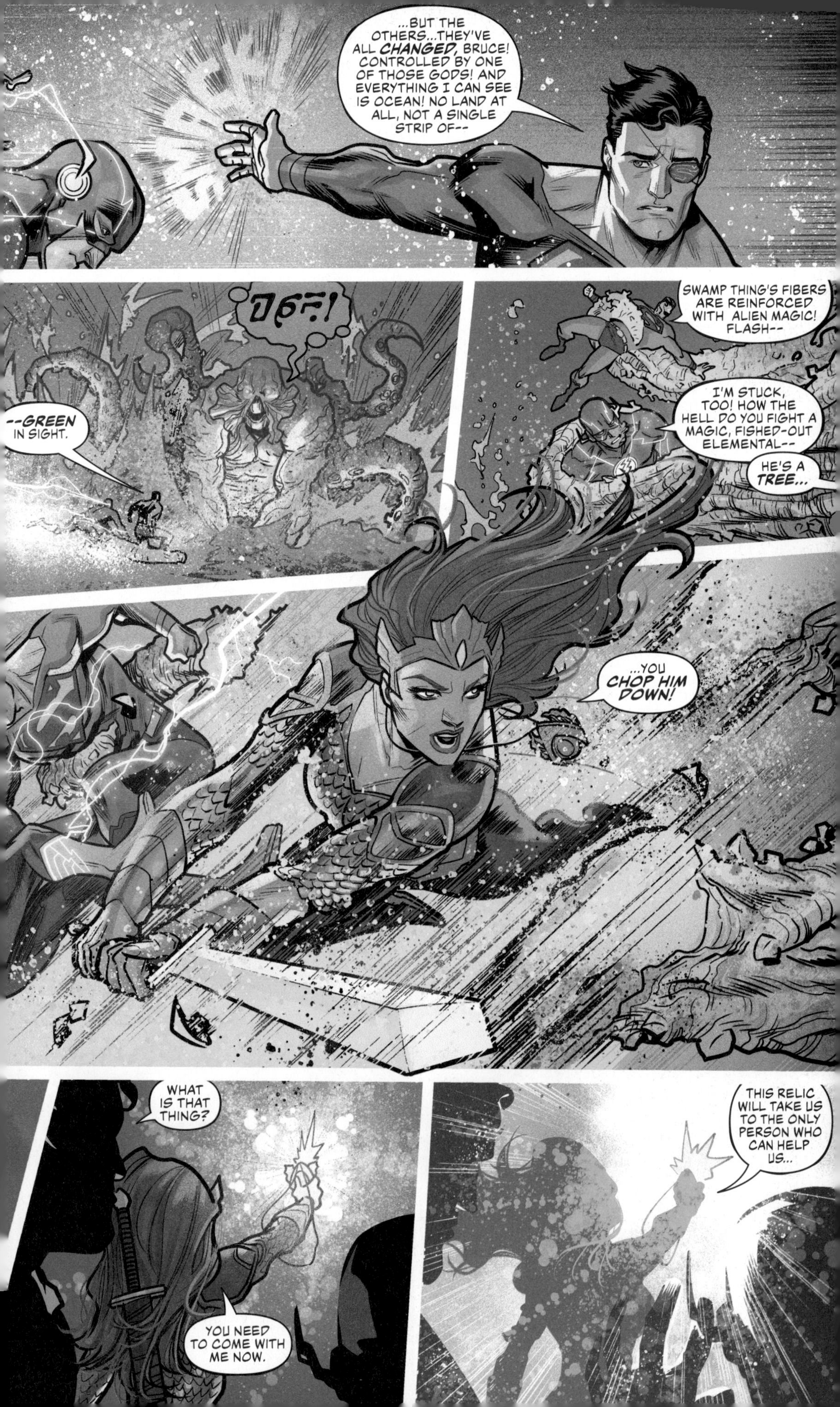
...BUT THE OTHERS...THEY'VE ALL CHANGED, BRUCE! CONTROLLED BY ONE OF THOSE GODS! AND EVERYTHING I CAN SEE IS OCEAN! NO LAND AT ALL, NOT A SINGLE STRIP OF--
OOF!
--GREEN IN SIGHT.
SWAMP THING'S FIBERS ARE REINFORCED WITH ALIEN MAGIC! FLASH--
I'M STUCK, TOO! HOW THE HELL DO YOU FIGHT A MAGIC, FISHED-OUT ELEMENTAL--
HE'S A TREE...
...YOU CHOP HIM DOWN!
WHAT IS THAT THING?
YOU NEED TO COME WITH ME NOW.
THIS RELIC WILL TAKE US TO THE ONLY PERSON WHO CAN HELP US...

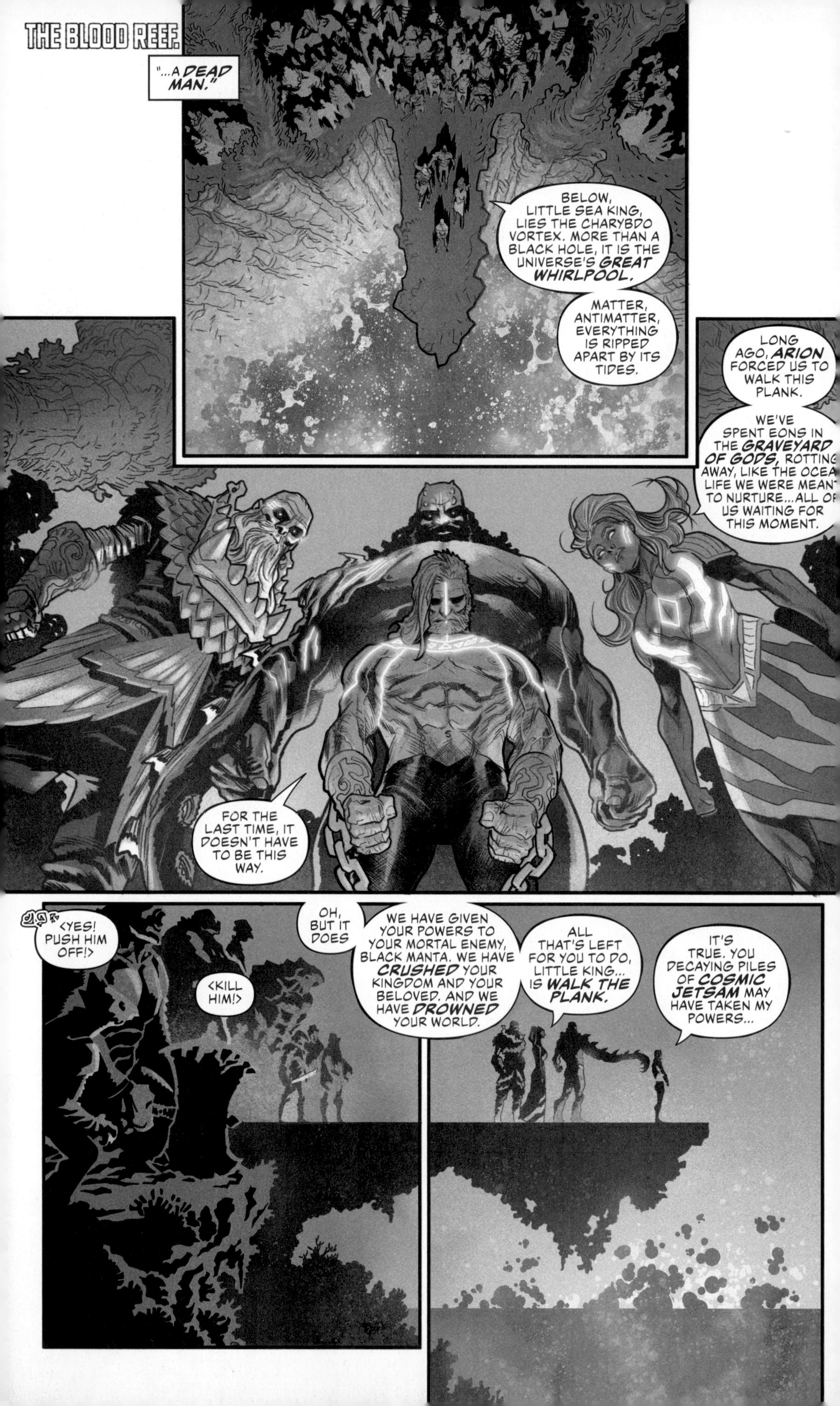

THE BLOOD REEF.
"...A DEAD MAN."
BELOW, LITTLE SEA KING, LIES THE CHARYBDO VORTEX. MORE THAN A BLACK HOLE, IT IS THE UNIVERSE'S GREAT WHIRLPOOL.
MATTER, ANTIMATTER, EVERYTHING IS RIPPED APART BY ITS TIDES.
LONG AGO, ARION FORCED US TO WALK THIS PLANK.
WE'VE SPENT EONS IN THE GRAVEYARD OF GODS, ROTTING AWAY, LIKE THE OCEA LIFE WE WERE MEANT TO NURTURE...ALL OF US WAITING FOR THIS MOMENT.
FOR THE LAST TIME, IT DOESN'T HAVE TO BE THIS WAY.
<YES! PUSH HIM OFF!>
<KILL HIM!>
OH, BUT IT DOES
WE HAVE GIVEN YOUR POWERS TO YOUR MORTAL ENEMY, BLACK MANTA. WE HAVE CRUSHED YOUR KINGDOM AND YOUR BELOVED. AND WE HAVE DROWNED YOUR WORLD.
ALL THAT'S LEFT FOR YOU TO DO, LITTLE KING... IS WALK THE PLANK.
IT'S TRUE. YOU DECAYING PILES OF COSMIC JETSAM MAY HAVE TAKEN MY POWERS...

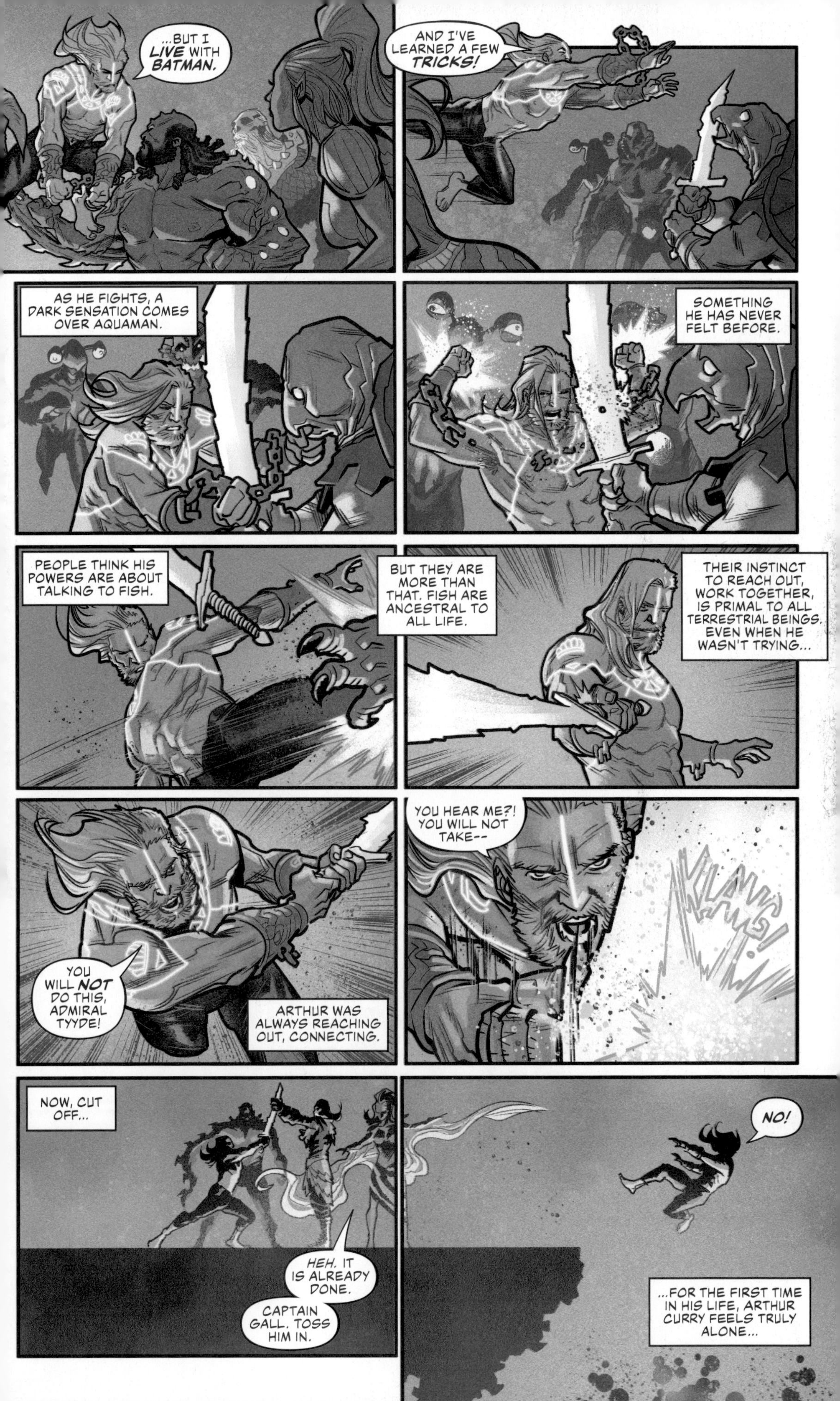
...BUT I LIVE WITH BATMAN.
AND I'VE LEARNED A FEW TRICKS!
AS HE FIGHTS, A DARK SENSATION COMES OVER AQUAMAN.
SOMETHING HE HAS NEVER FELT BEFORE.
PEOPLE THINK HIS POWERS ARE ABOUT TALKING TO FISH.
BUT THEY ARE MORE THAN THAT. FISH ARE ANCESTRAL TO ALL LIFE.
THEIR INSTINCT TO REACH OUT, WORK TOGETHER, IS PRIMAL TO ALL TERRESTRIAL BEINGS. EVEN WHEN HE WASN'T TRYING...
YOU WILL NOT DO THIS, ADMIRAL TYYDE!
ARTHUR WAS ALWAYS REACHING OUT, CONNECTING.
YOU HEAR ME?! YOU WILL NOT TAKE--
NOW, CUT OFF...
HEH. IT IS ALREADY DONE.
CAPTAIN GALL. TOSS HIM IN.
NO!
...FOR THE FIRST TIME IN HIS LIFE, ARTHUR CURRY FEELS TRULY ALONE...

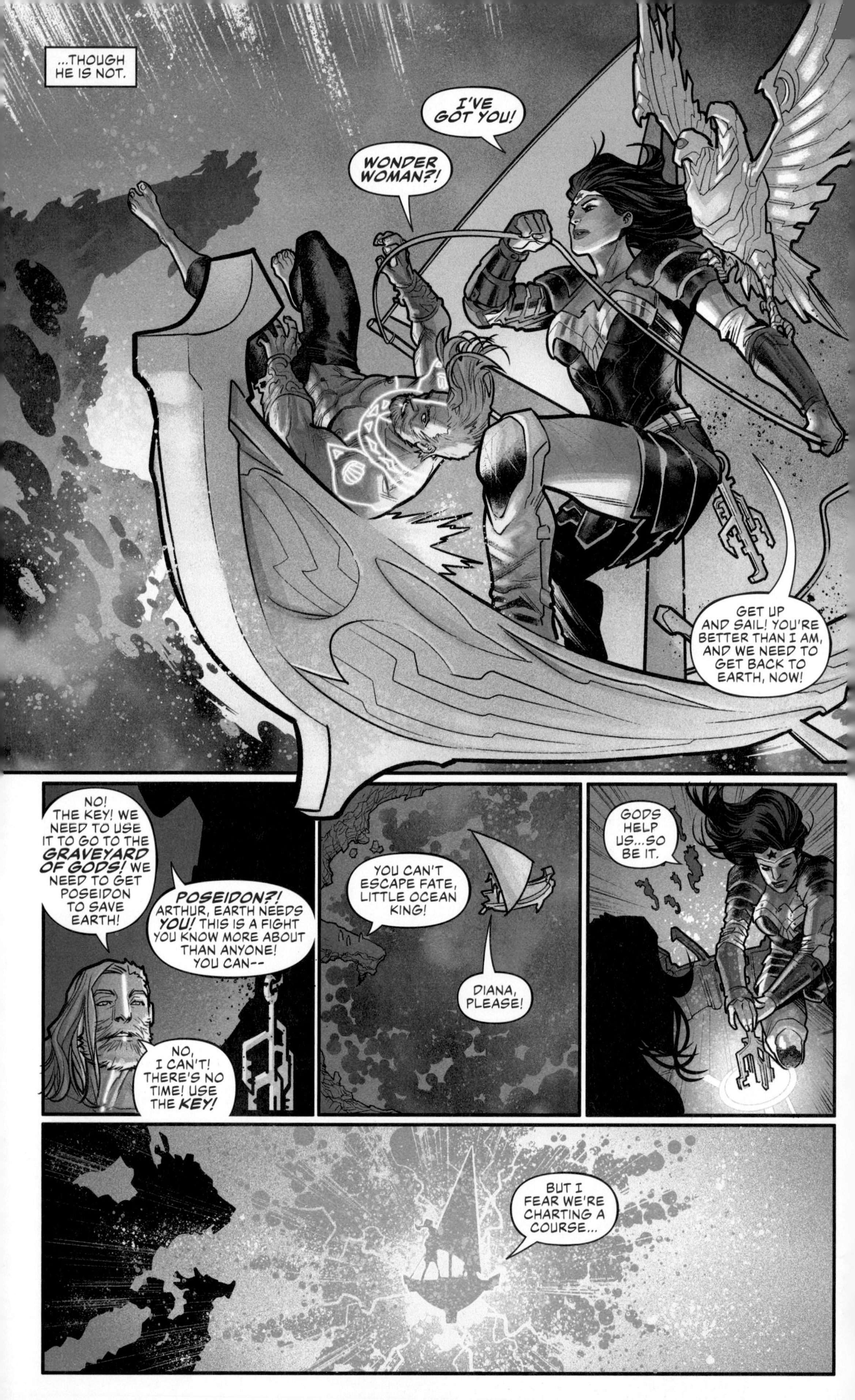
...THOUGH HE IS NOT.
WONDER WOMAN?!
I'VE GOT YOU!
GET UP AND SAIL! YOU'RE BETTER THAN I AM, AND WE NEED TO GET BACK TO EARTH, NOW!
NO! THE KEY! WE NEED TO USE IT TO GO TO THE GRAVEYARD OF GODS! WE NEED TO GET POSEIDON TO SAVE EARTH!
POSEIDON?! ARTHUR, EARTH NEEDS YOU! THIS IS A FIGHT YOU KNOW MORE ABOUT THAN ANYONE! YOU CAN--
NO, I CAN'T! THERE'S NO TIME! USE THE KEY!
YOU CAN'T ESCAPE FATE, LITTLE OCEAN KING!
DIANA, PLEASE!
GODS HELP US...SO BE IT.
BUT I FEAR WE'RE CHARTING A COURSE...

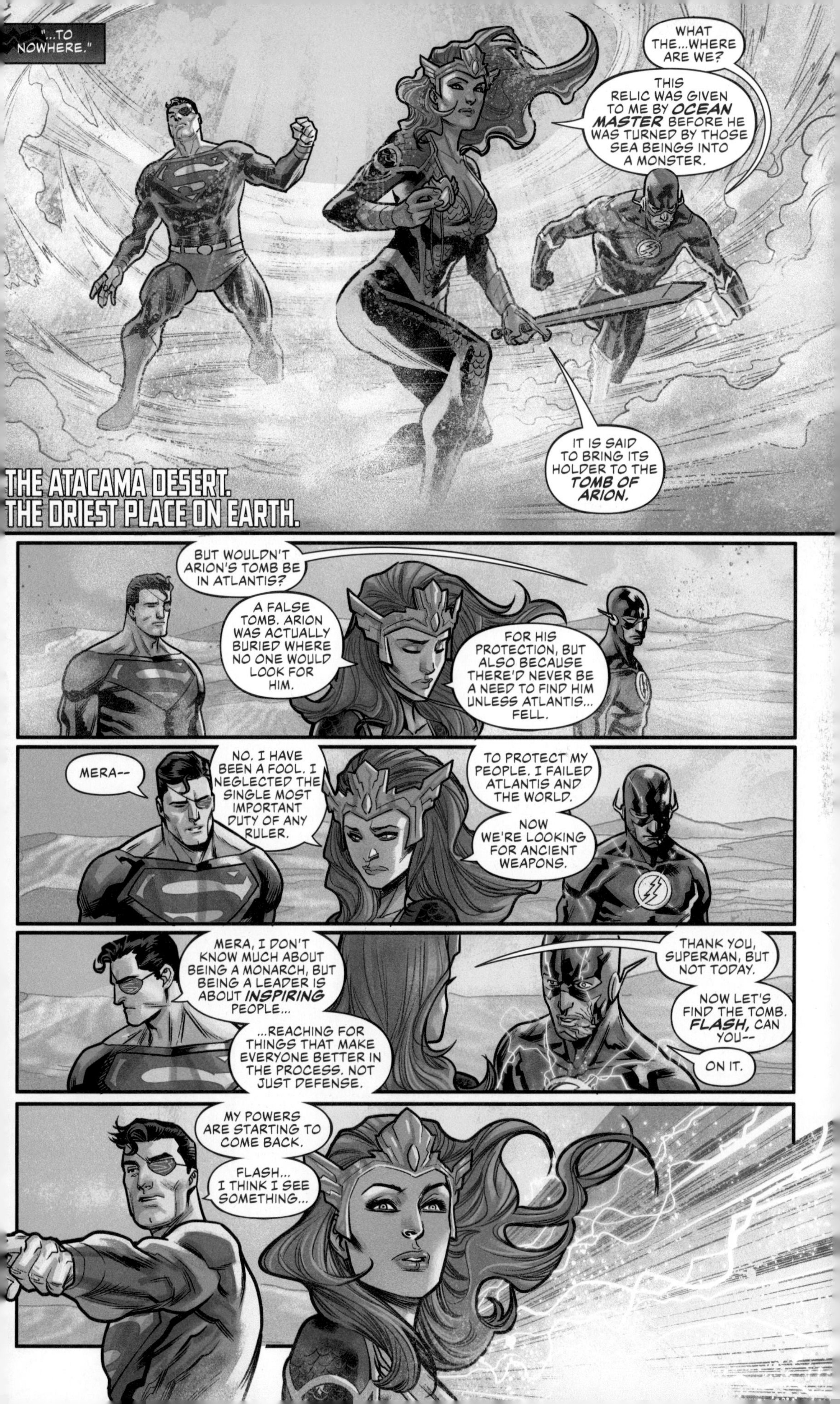

"...TO NOWHERE."
WHAT THE...WHERE ARE WE?
THIS RELIC WAS GIVEN TO ME BY OCEAN MASTER BEFORE HE WAS TURNED BY THOSE SEA BEINGS INTO A MONSTER.
IT IS SAID TO BRING ITS HOLDER TO THE TOMB OF ARION.
THE ATACAMA DESERT. THE DRIEST PLACE ON EARTH.
BUT WOULDN'T ARION'S TOMB BE IN ATLANTIS?
A FALSE TOMB. ARION WAS ACTUALLY BURIED WHERE NO ONE WOULD LOOK FOR HIM.
FOR HIS PROTECTION, BUT ALSO BECAUSE THERE'D NEVER BE A NEED TO FIND HIM UNLESS ATLANTIS... FELL.
MERA--
NO. I HAVE BEEN A FOOL. I NEGLECTED THE SINGLE MOST IMPORTANT DUTY OF ANY RULER.
TO PROTECT MY PEOPLE. I FAILED ATLANTIS AND THE WORLD.
NOW WE'RE LOOKING FOR ANCIENT WEAPONS.
MERA, I DON'T KNOW MUCH ABOUT BEING A MONARCH, BUT BEING A LEADER IS ABOUT INSPIRING PEOPLE...
...REACHING FOR THINGS THAT MAKE EVERYONE BETTER IN THE PROCESS. NOT JUST DEFENSE.
THANK YOU, SUPERMAN, BUT NOT TODAY.
NOW LET'S FIND THE TOMB. FLASH, CAN YOU--
ON IT.
MY POWERS ARE STARTING TO COME BACK.
FLASH... I THINK I SEE SOMETHING...

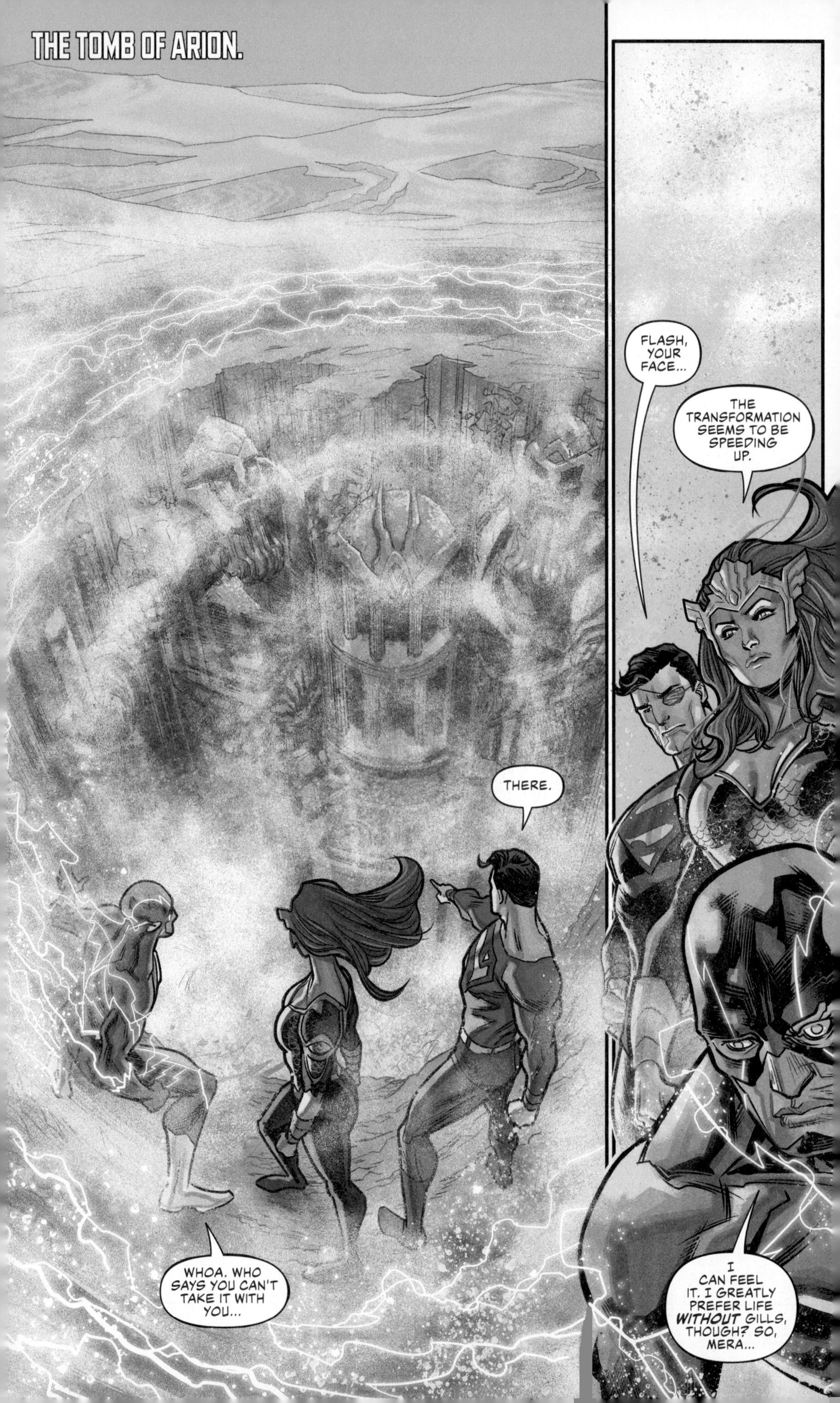
THE TOMB OF ARION.
THERE.
WHOA. WHO SAYS YOU CAN'T TAKE IT WITH YOU...
FLASH, YOUR FACE...
THE TRANSFORMATION SEEMS TO BE SPEEDING UP.
I CAN FEEL IT. I GREATLY PREFER LIFE WITHOUT GILLS, THOUGH? SO, MERA...

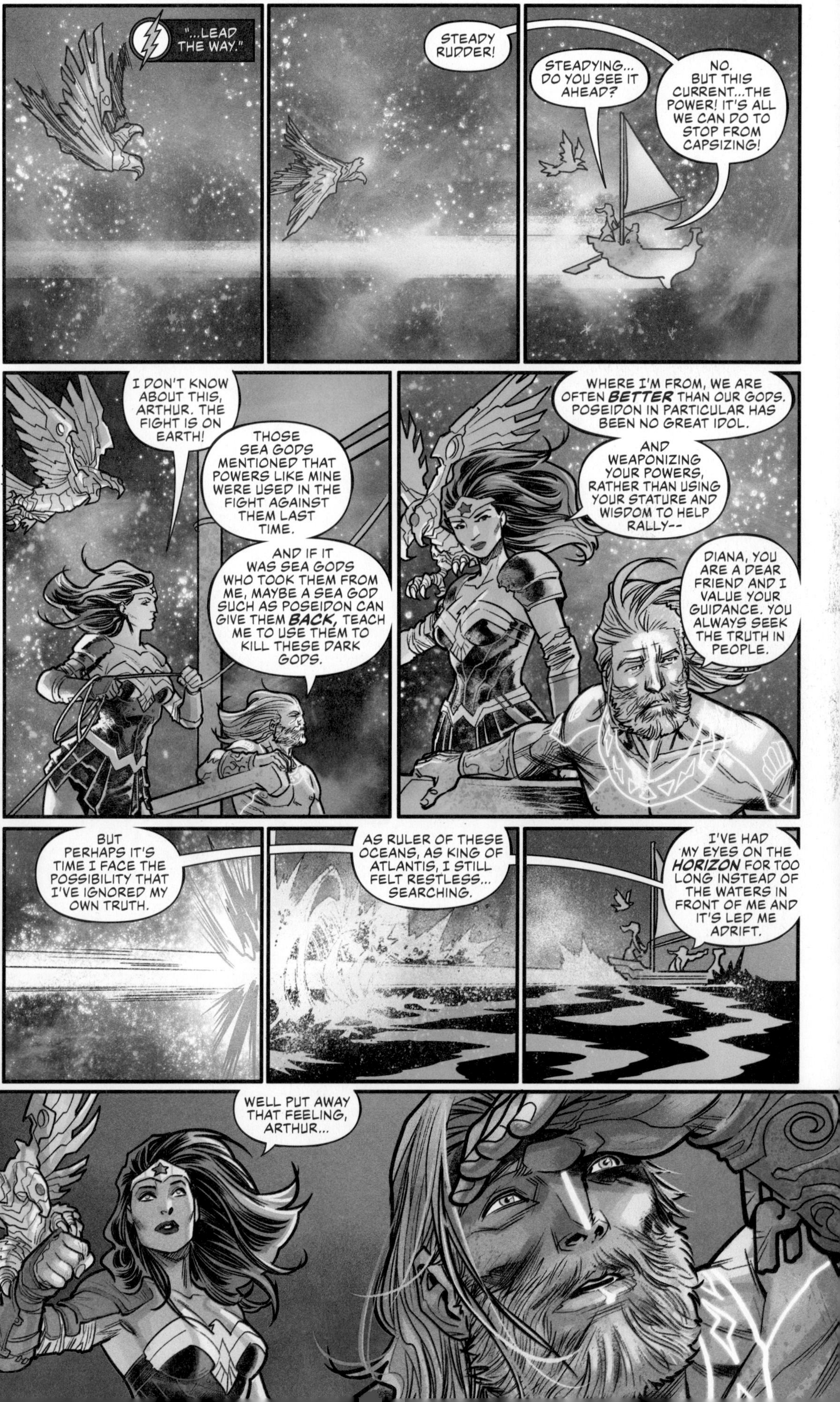
"...LEAD THE WAY."
STEADY RUDDER!
STEADYING... DO YOU SEE IT AHEAD?
NO. BUT THIS CURRENT...THE POWER! IT'S ALL WE CAN DO TO STOP FROM CAPSIZING!
I DON'T KNOW ABOUT THIS, ARTHUR. THE FIGHT IS ON EARTH!
THOSE SEA GODS MENTIONED THAT POWERS LIKE MINE WERE USED IN THE FIGHT AGAINST THEM LAST TIME.
AND IF IT WAS SEA GODS WHO TOOK THEM FROM ME, MAYBE A SEA GOD SUCH AS POSEIDON CAN GIVE THEM BACK, TEACH ME TO USE THEM TO KILL THESE DARK GODS.
WHERE I'M FROM, WE ARE OFTEN BETTER THAN OUR GODS. POSEIDON IN PARTICULAR HAS BEEN NO GREAT IDOL.
AND WEAPONIZING YOUR POWERS, RATHER THAN USING YOUR STATURE AND WISDOM TO HELP RALLY--
DIANA, YOU ARE A DEAR FRIEND AND I VALUE YOUR GUIDANCE. YOU ALWAYS SEEK THE TRUTH IN PEOPLE.
BUT PERHAPS IT'S TIME I FACE THE POSSIBILITY THAT I'VE IGNORED MY OWN TRUTH.
AS RULER OF THESE OCEANS, AS KING OF ATLANTIS, I STILL FELT RESTLESS... SEARCHING.
I'VE HAD MY EYES ON THE HORIZON FOR TOO LONG INSTEAD OF THE WATERS IN FRONT OF ME AND IT'S LED ME ADRIFT.
WELL PUT AWAY THAT FEELING, ARTHUR...

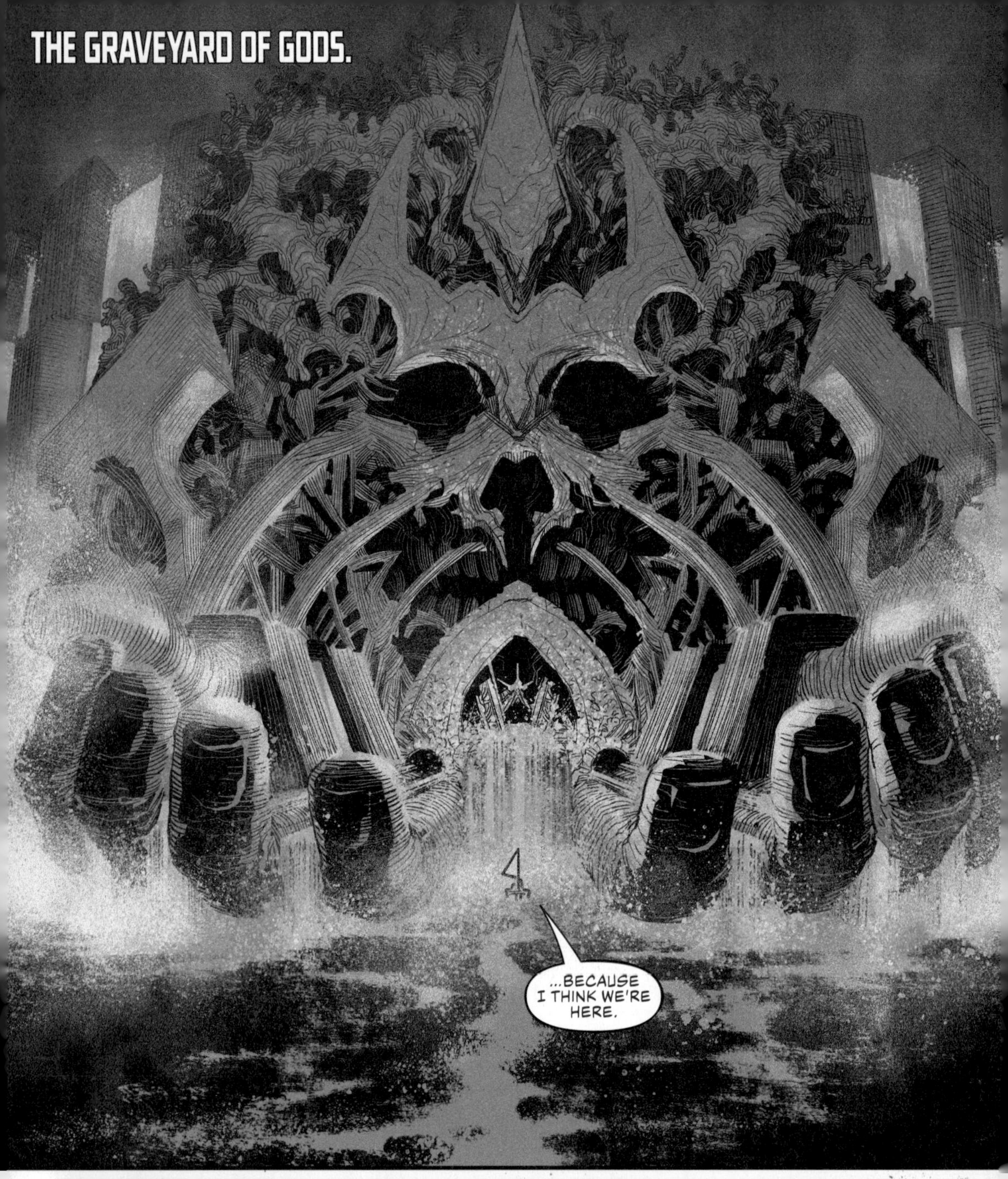
THE GRAVEYARD OF GODS.
...BECAUSE I THINK WE'RE HERE.

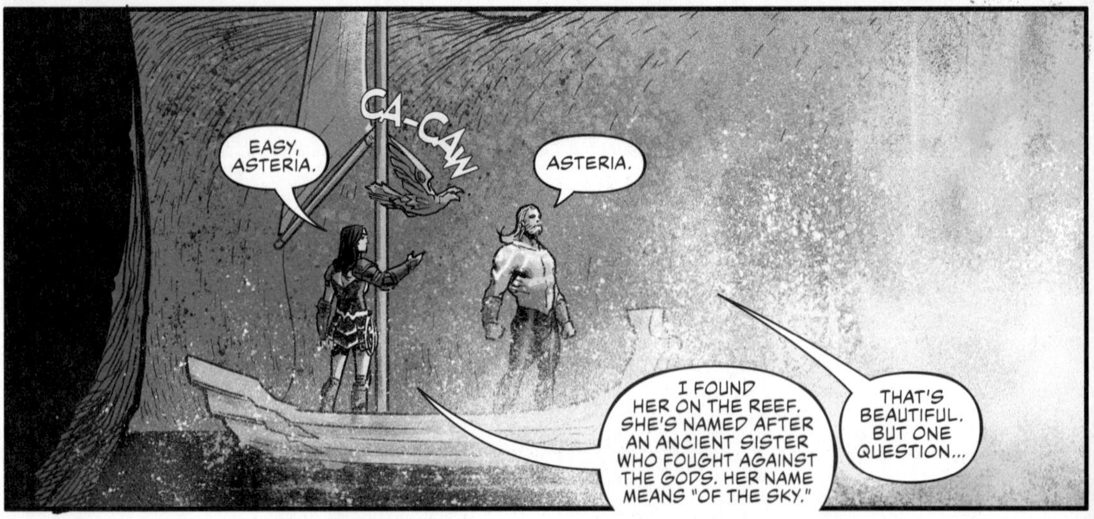
CA-CAW
EASY, ASTERIA.
ASTERIA.
I FOUND HER ON THE REEF. SHE'S NAMED AFTER AN ANCIENT SISTER WHO FOUGHT AGAINST THE GODS. HER NAME MEANS "OF THE SKY."
THAT'S BEAUTIFUL. BUT ONE QUESTION...

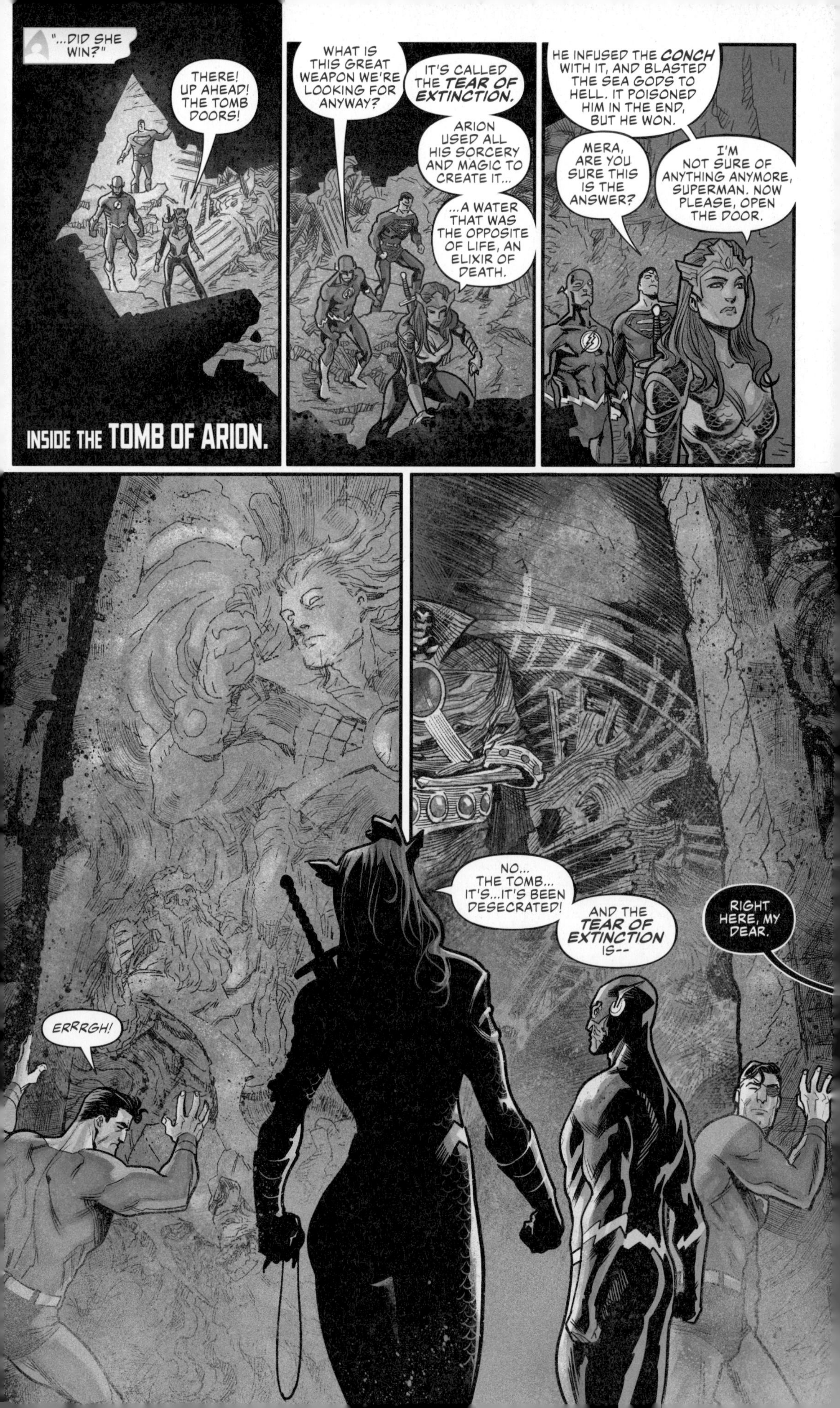
"...DID SHE WIN?"
THERE! UP AHEAD! THE TOMB DOORS!
INSIDE THE TOMB OF ARION.
WHAT IS THIS GREAT WEAPON WE'RE LOOKING FOR ANYWAY?
IT'S CALLED THE TEAR OF EXTINCTION.
ARION USED ALL HIS SORCERY AND MAGIC TO CREATE IT...
...A WATER THAT WAS THE OPPOSITE OF LIFE, AN ELIXIR OF DEATH.
HE INFUSED THE CONCH WITH IT, AND BLASTED THE SEA GODS TO HELL. IT POISONED HIM IN THE END, BUT HE WON.
MERA, ARE YOU SURE THIS IS THE ANSWER?
I'M NOT SURE OF ANYTHING ANYMORE, SUPERMAN. NOW PLEASE, OPEN THE DOOR.
ERRRGH!
NO... THE TOMB... IT'S...IT'S BEEN DESECRATED!
AND THE TEAR OF EXTINCTION IS--
RIGHT HERE, MY DEAR.

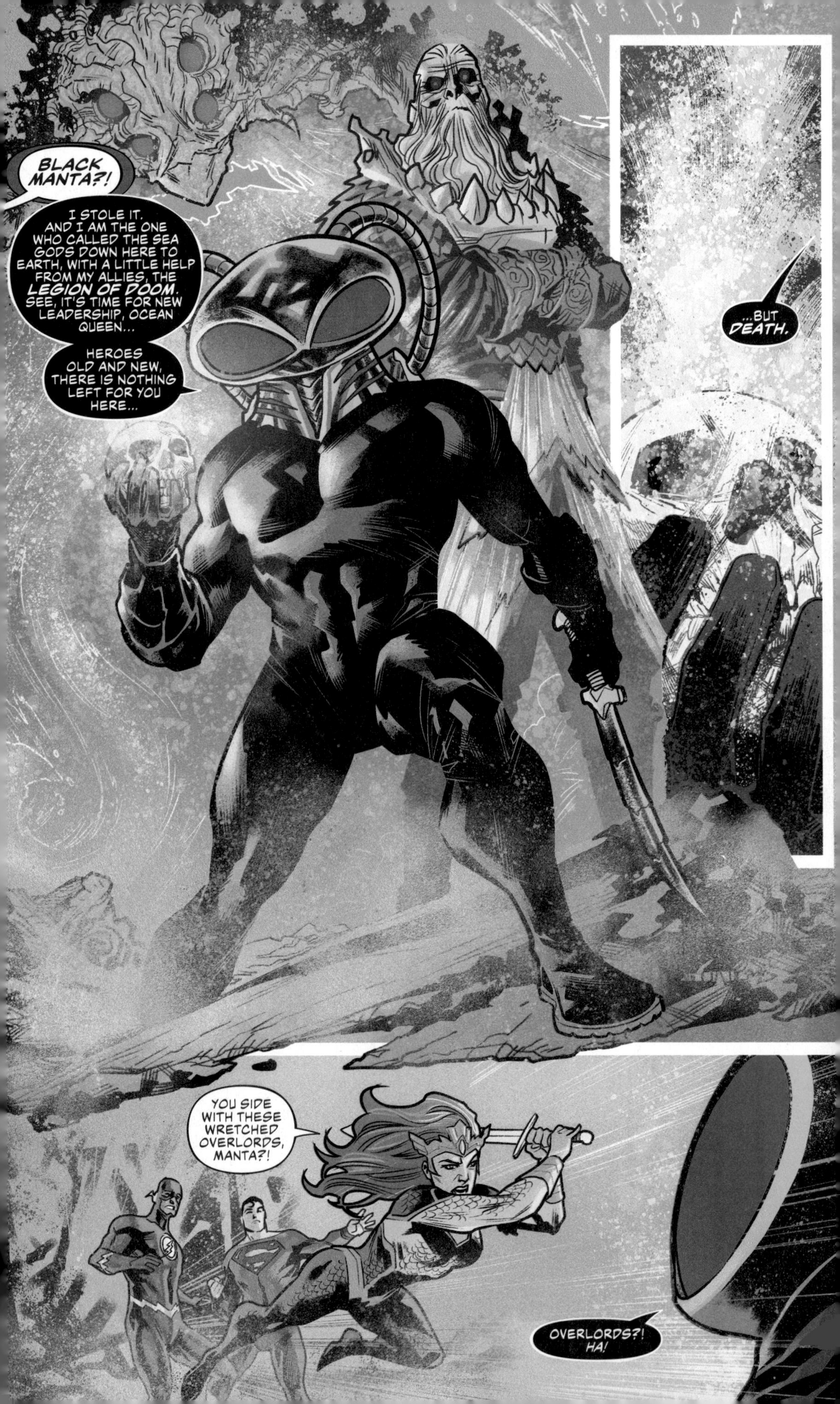
BLACK MANTA?!
I STOLE IT. AND I AM THE ONE WHO CALLED THE SEA GODS DOWN HERE TO EARTH, WITH A LITTLE HELP FROM MY ALLIES, THE LEGION OF DOOM. SEE, IT'S TIME FOR NEW LEADERSHIP, OCEAN QUEEN...
HEROES OLD AND NEW, THERE IS NOTHING LEFT FOR YOU HERE...
...BUT DEATH.
YOU SIDE WITH THESE WRETCHED OVERLORDS, MANTA?!
OVERLORDS?! HA!

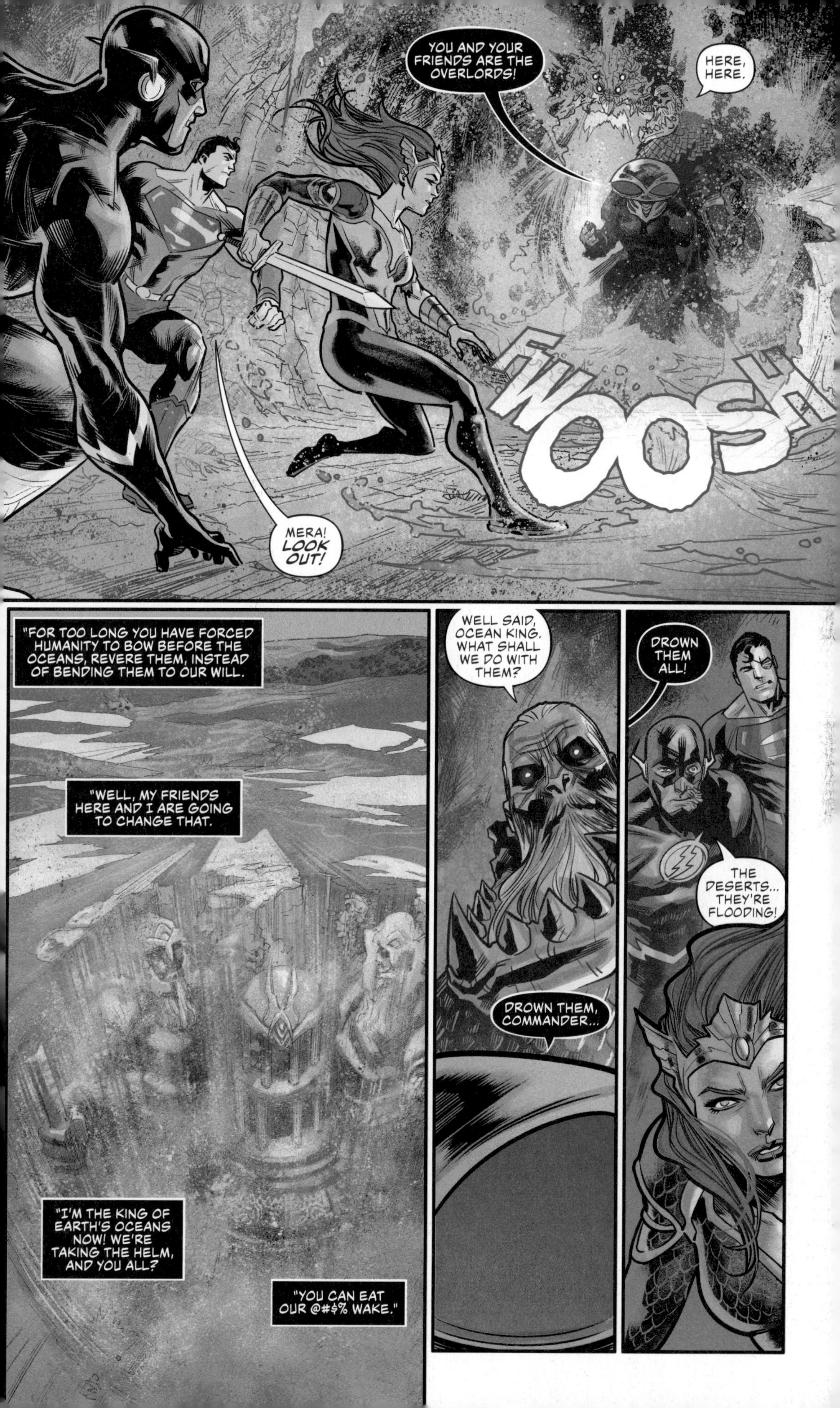

YOU AND YOUR FRIENDS ARE THE OVERLORDS!
HERE, HERE.
WOOSH
MERA! LOOK OUT!
"FOR TOO LONG YOU HAVE FORCED HUMANITY TO BOW BEFORE THE OCEANS, REVERE THEM, INSTEAD OF BENDING THEM TO OUR WILL.
"WELL, MY FRIENDS HERE AND I ARE GOING TO CHANGE THAT.
"I'M THE KING OF EARTH'S OCEANS NOW! WE'RE TAKING THE HELM, AND YOU ALL?
"YOU CAN EAT OUR @#$% WAKE."
WELL SAID, OCEAN KING. WHAT SHALL WE DO WITH THEM?
DROWN THEM, COMMANDER...
DROWN THEM ALL!
THE DESERTS... THEY'RE FLOODING!

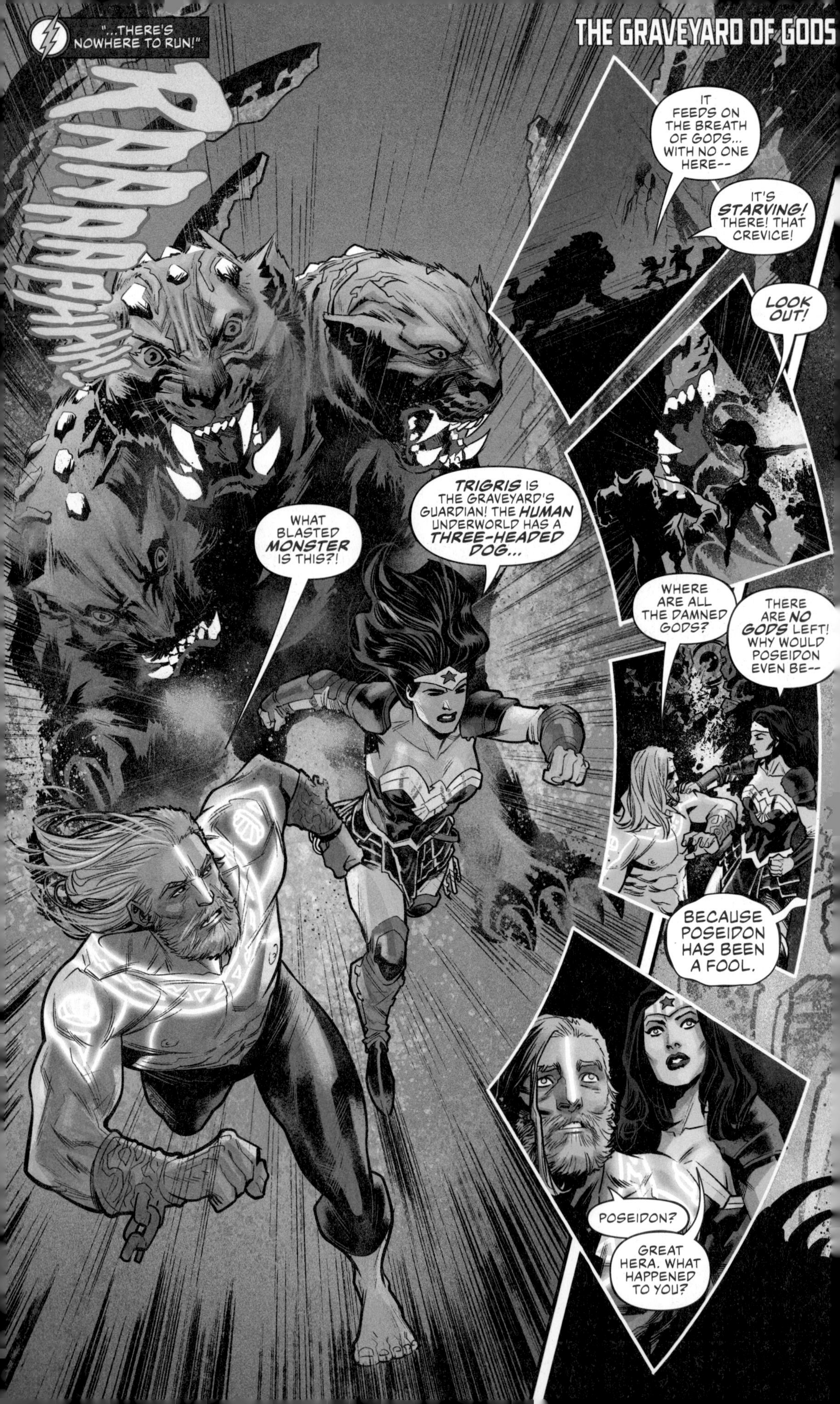
"...THERE'S NOWHERE TO RUN!"
THE GRAVEYARD OF GODS
RRAAAAAAHH!
IT FEEDS ON THE BREATH OF GODS... WITH NO ONE HERE--
IT'S STARVING! THERE! THAT CREVICE!
LOOK OUT!
WHAT BLASTED MONSTER IS THIS?!
TRIGRIS IS THE GRAVEYARD'S GUARDIAN! THE HUMAN UNDERWORLD HAS A THREE-HEADED DOG...
WHERE ARE ALL THE DAMNED GODS?
THERE ARE NO GODS LEFT! WHY WOULD POSEIDON EVEN BE--
BECAUSE POSEIDON HAS BEEN A FOOL.
POSEIDON?
GREAT HERA. WHAT HAPPENED TO YOU?

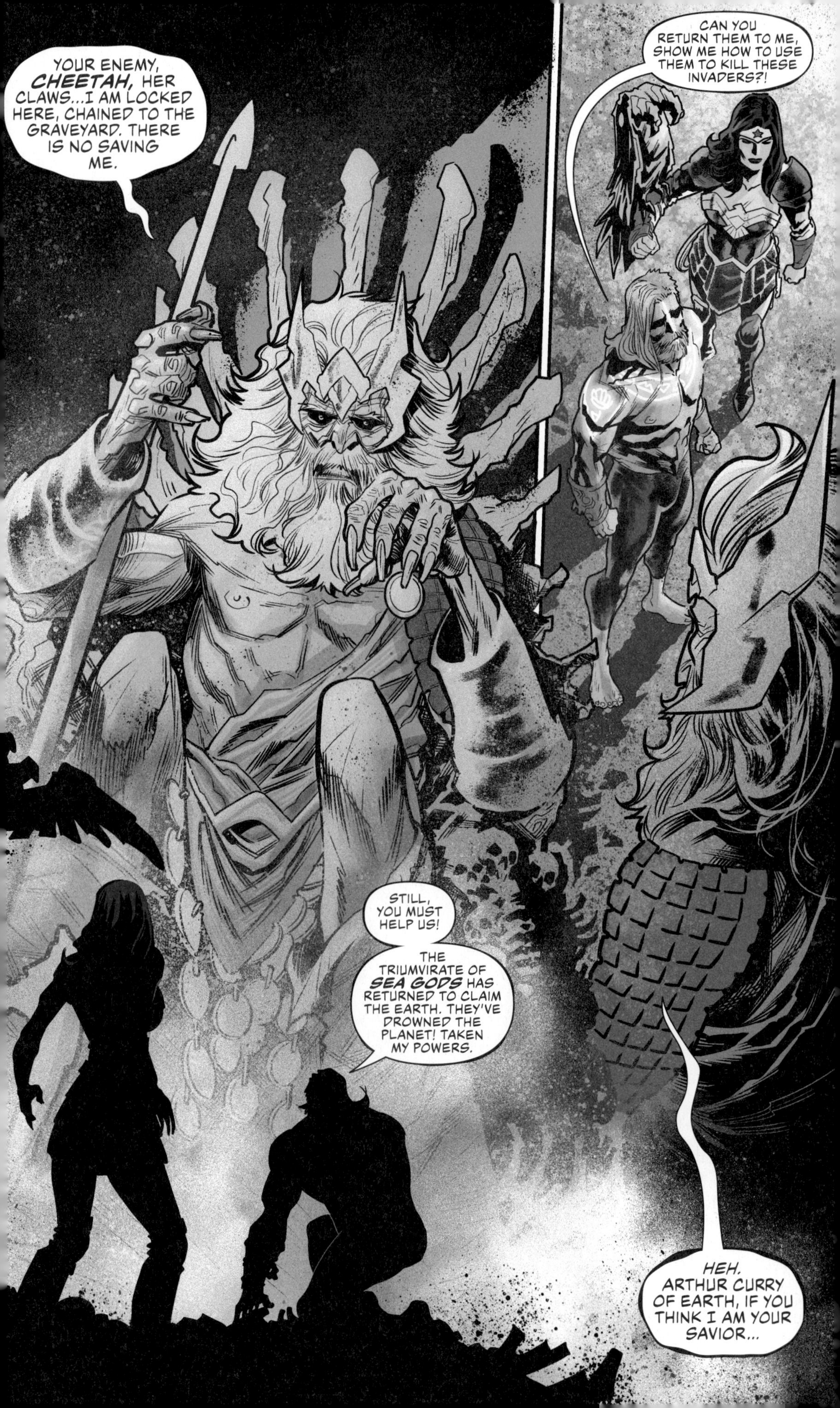

YOUR ENEMY, **CHEETAH,** HER CLAWS...I AM LOCKED HERE, CHAINED TO THE GRAVEYARD. THERE IS NO SAVING ME.
CAN YOU RETURN THEM TO ME, SHOW ME HOW TO USE THEM TO KILL THESE INVADERS?!
STILL, YOU MUST HELP US!
THE TRIUMVIRATE OF ***SEA GODS*** HAS RETURNED TO CLAIM THE EARTH. THEY'VE DROWNED THE PLANET! TAKEN MY POWERS.
HEH. ARTHUR CURRY OF EARTH, IF YOU THINK I AM YOUR SAVIOR...

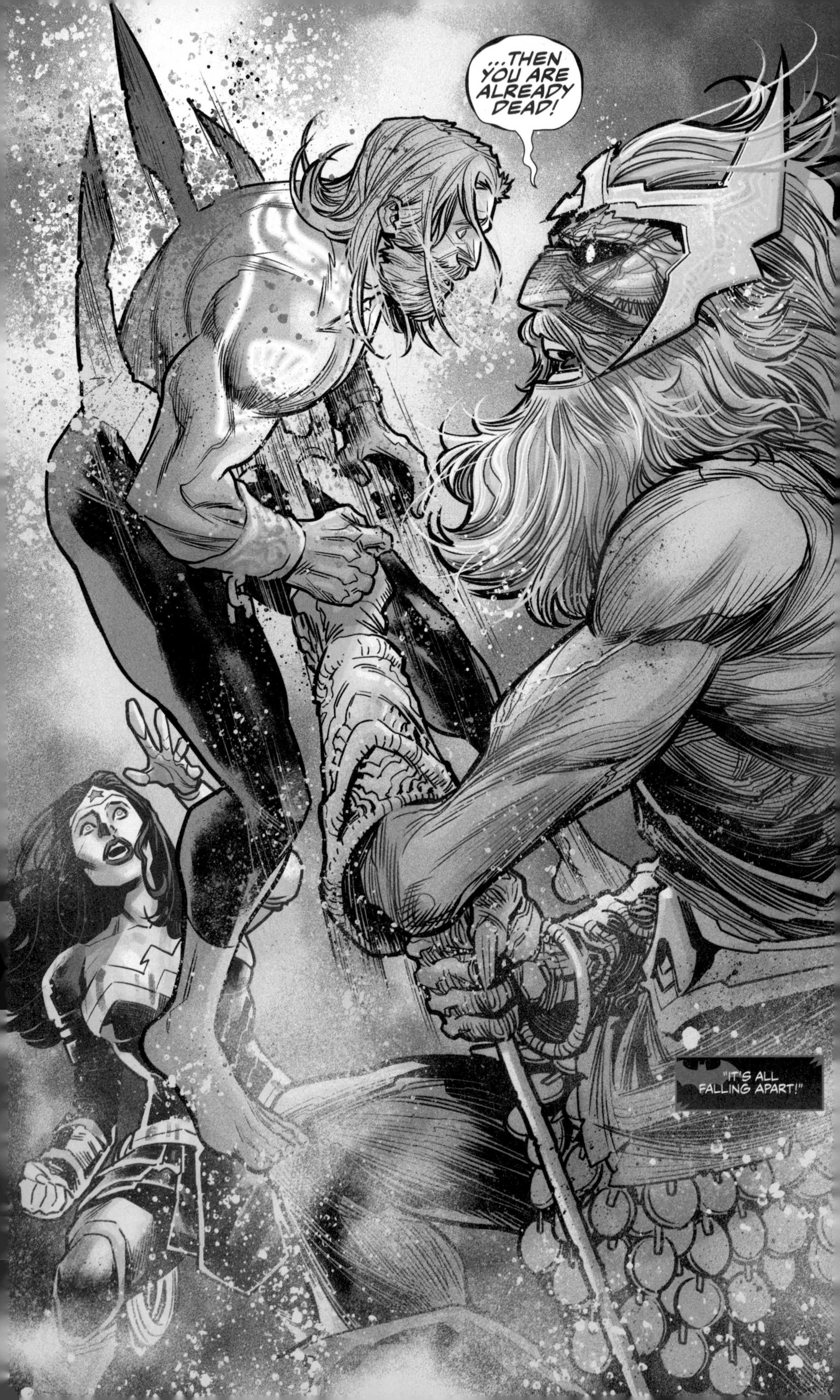
...THEN YOU ARE ALREADY DEAD!
"IT'S ALL FALLING APART!"

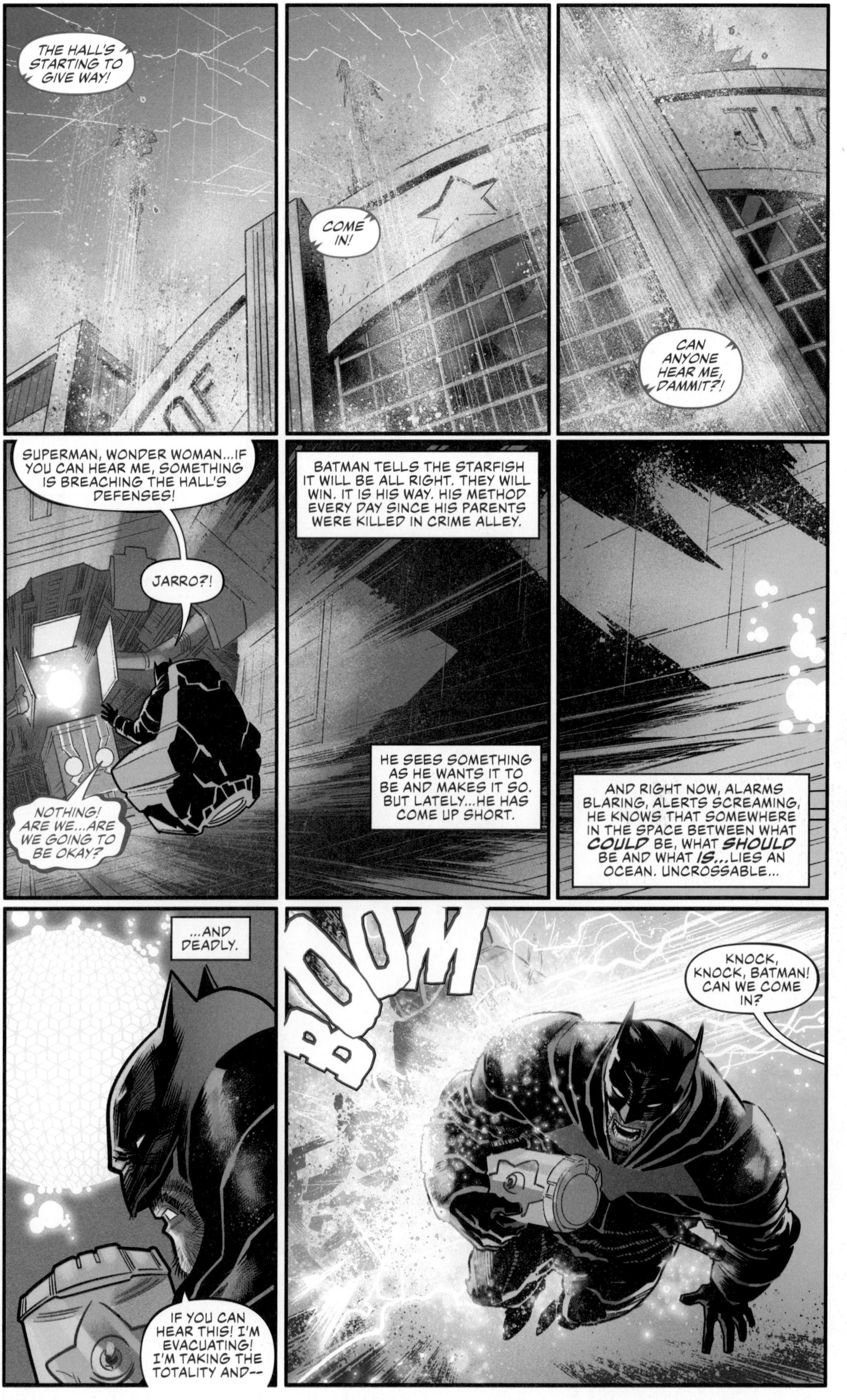

THE HALL'S STARTING TO GIVE WAY!
COME IN!
CAN ANYONE HEAR ME, DAMMIT?!
SUPERMAN, WONDER WOMAN...IF YOU CAN HEAR ME, SOMETHING IS BREACHING THE HALL'S DEFENSES!
JARRO?!
NOTHING! ARE WE...ARE WE GOING TO BE OKAY?
BATMAN TELLS THE STARFISH IT WILL BE ALL RIGHT. THEY WILL WIN. IT IS HIS WAY. HIS METHOD EVERY DAY SINCE HIS PARENTS WERE KILLED IN CRIME ALLEY.
HE SEES SOMETHING AS HE WANTS IT TO BE AND MAKES IT SO. BUT LATELY...HE HAS COME UP SHORT.
AND RIGHT NOW, ALARMS BLARING, ALERTS SCREAMING, HE KNOWS THAT SOMEWHERE IN THE SPACE BETWEEN WHAT COULD BE, WHAT SHOULD BE AND WHAT IS...LIES AN OCEAN. UNCROSSABLE...
...AND DEADLY.
IF YOU CAN HEAR THIS! I'M EVACUATING! I'M TAKING THE TOTALITY AND--
BOOM
KNOCK, KNOCK, BATMAN! CAN WE COME IN?

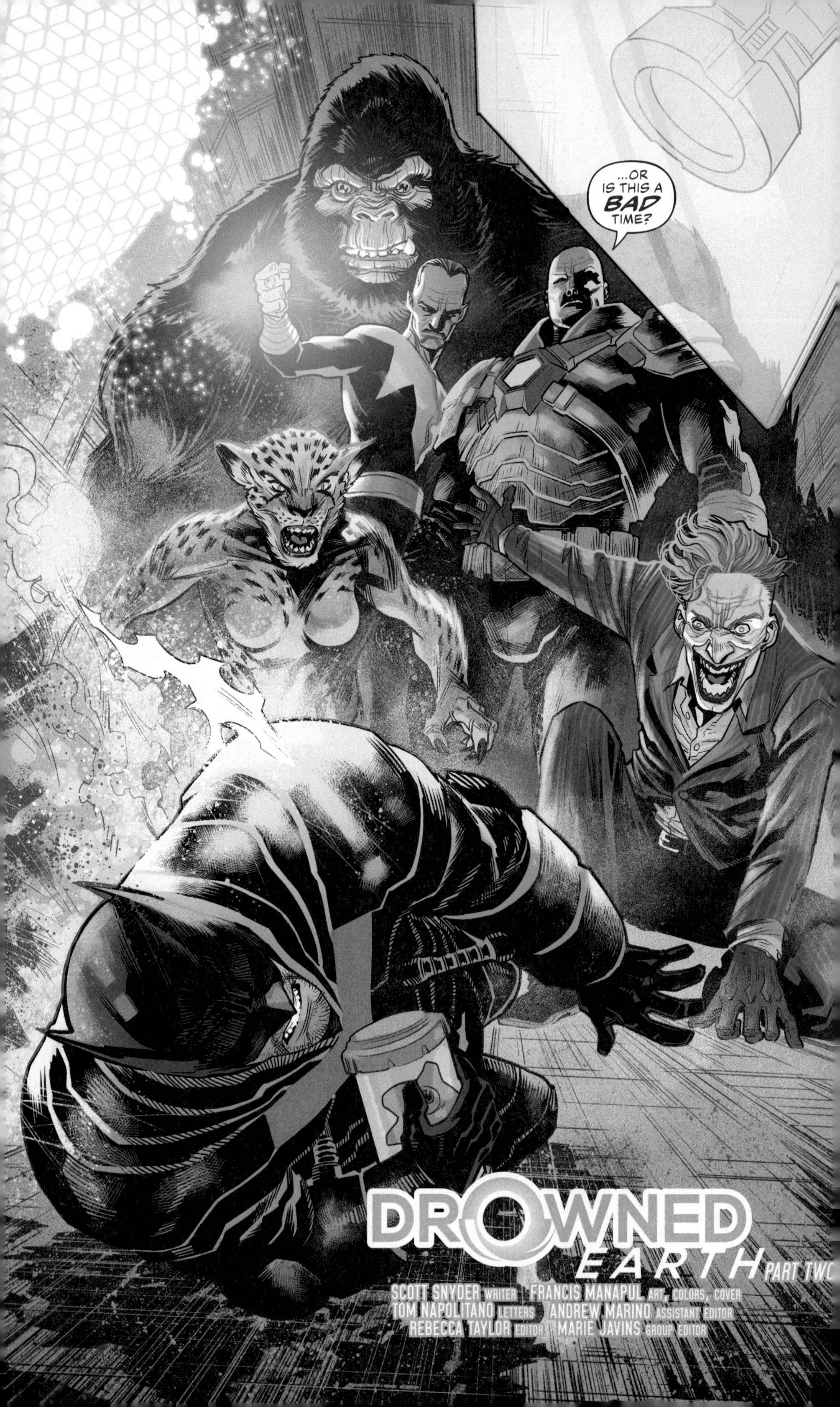

...OR IS THIS A BAD TIME?
DROWNED EARTH PART TWO
SCOTT SNYDER WRITER FRANCIS MANAPUL ART, COLORS, COVER
TOM NAPOLITANO LETTERS ANDREW MARINO ASSISTANT EDITOR
REBECCA TAYLOR EDITOR MARIE JAVINS GROUP EDITOR

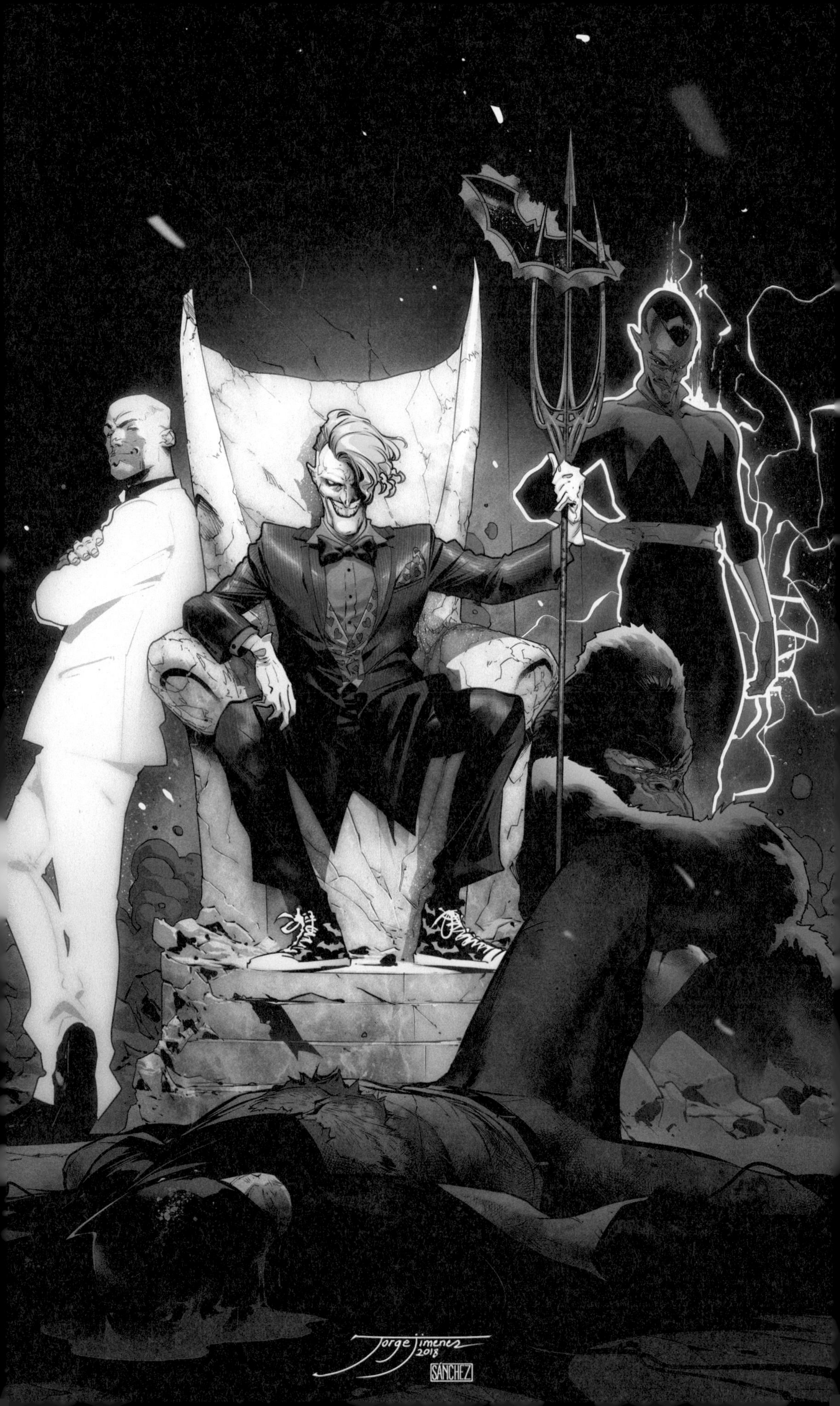
Jorge Jimenez 2018
SÁNCHEZ

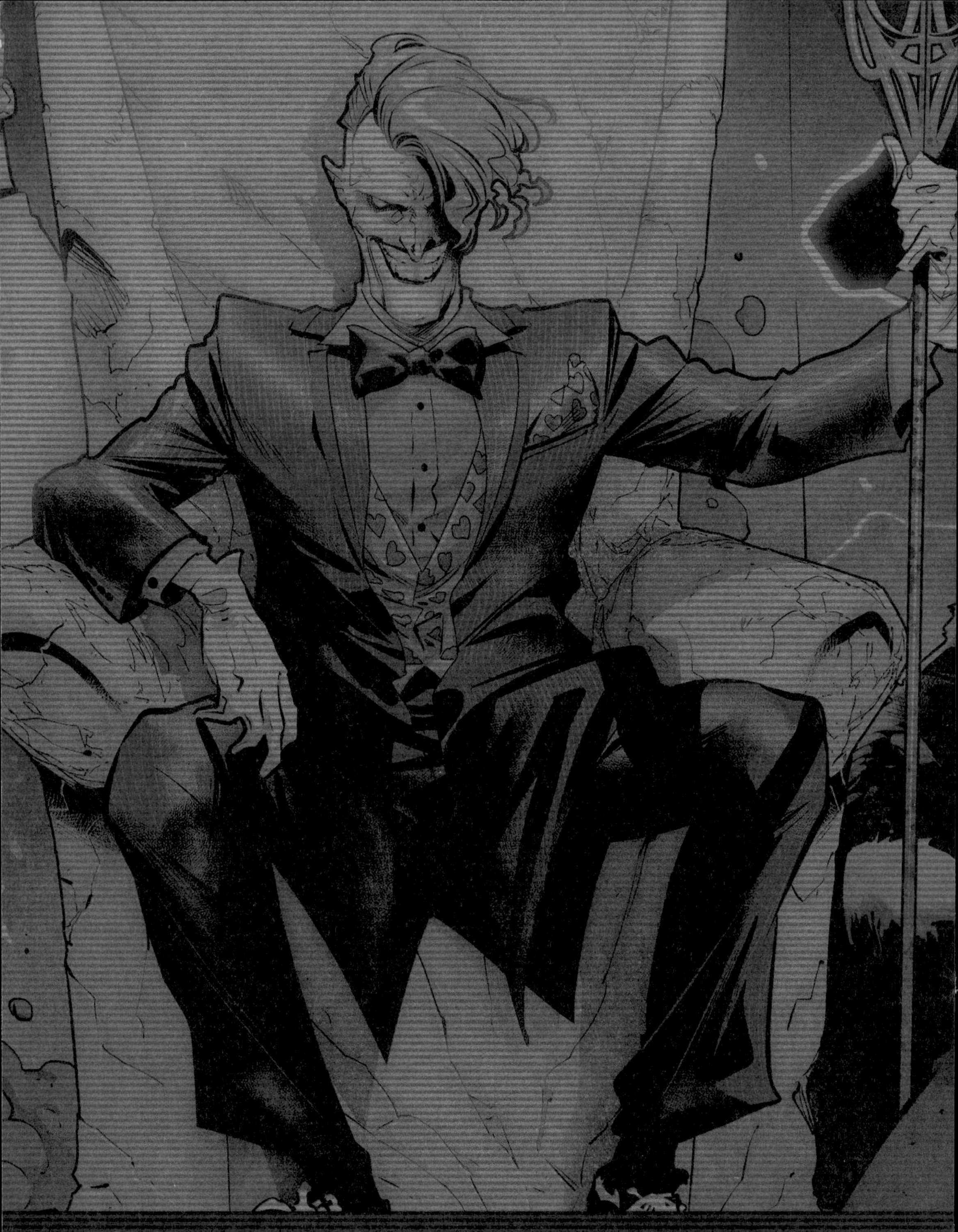

JUSTICE
LEAGUE

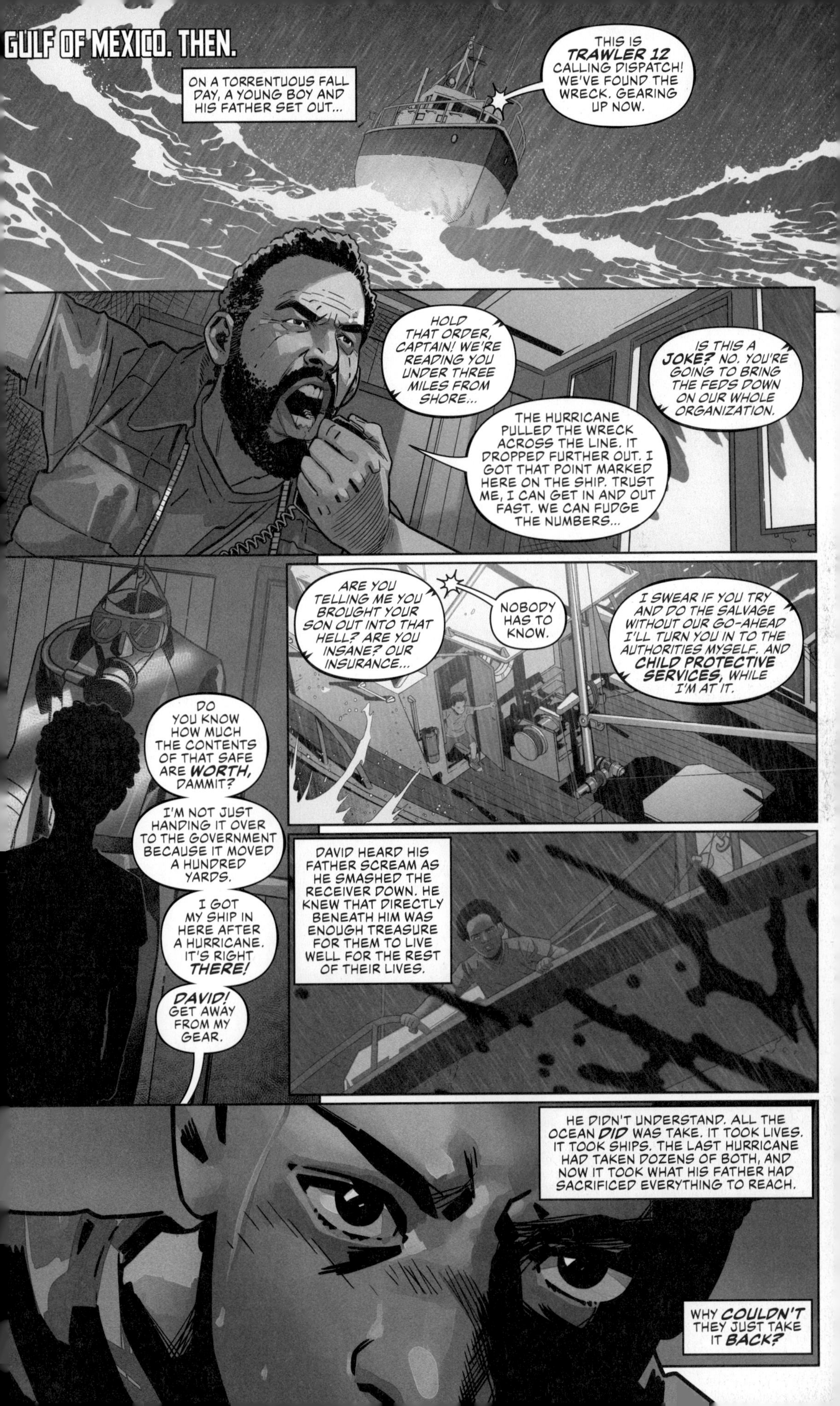

GULF OF MEXICO. THEN.
ON A TORRENTUOUS FALL DAY, A YOUNG BOY AND HIS FATHER SET OUT...
THIS IS TRAWLER 12 CALLING DISPATCH! WE'VE FOUND THE WRECK. GEARING UP NOW.
HOLD THAT ORDER, CAPTAIN! WE'RE READING YOU UNDER THREE MILES FROM SHORE...
THE HURRICANE PULLED THE WRECK ACROSS THE LINE. IT DROPPED FURTHER OUT. I GOT THAT POINT MARKED HERE ON THE SHIP. TRUST ME, I CAN GET IN AND OUT FAST. WE CAN FUDGE THE NUMBERS...
IS THIS A JOKE? NO. YOU'RE GOING TO BRING THE FEDS DOWN ON OUR WHOLE ORGANIZATION.
ARE YOU TELLING ME YOU BROUGHT YOUR SON OUT INTO THAT HELL? ARE YOU INSANE? OUR INSURANCE...
NOBODY HAS TO KNOW.
I SWEAR IF YOU TRY AND DO THE SALVAGE WITHOUT OUR GO-AHEAD I'LL TURN YOU IN TO THE AUTHORITIES MYSELF. AND CHILD PROTECTIVE SERVICES, WHILE I'M AT IT.
DO YOU KNOW HOW MUCH THE CONTENTS OF THAT SAFE ARE WORTH, DAMMIT?
I'M NOT JUST HANDING IT OVER TO THE GOVERNMENT BECAUSE IT MOVED A HUNDRED YARDS.
I GOT MY SHIP IN HERE AFTER A HURRICANE. IT'S RIGHT THERE!
DAVID! GET AWAY FROM MY GEAR.
DAVID HEARD HIS FATHER SCREAM AS HE SMASHED THE RECEIVER DOWN. HE KNEW THAT DIRECTLY BENEATH HIM WAS ENOUGH TREASURE FOR THEM TO LIVE WELL FOR THE REST OF THEIR LIVES.
HE DIDN'T UNDERSTAND. ALL THE OCEAN DID WAS TAKE. IT TOOK LIVES. IT TOOK SHIPS. THE LAST HURRICANE HAD TAKEN DOZENS OF BOTH, AND NOW IT TOOK WHAT HIS FATHER HAD SACRIFICED EVERYTHING TO REACH.
WHY COULDN'T THEY JUST TAKE IT BACK?

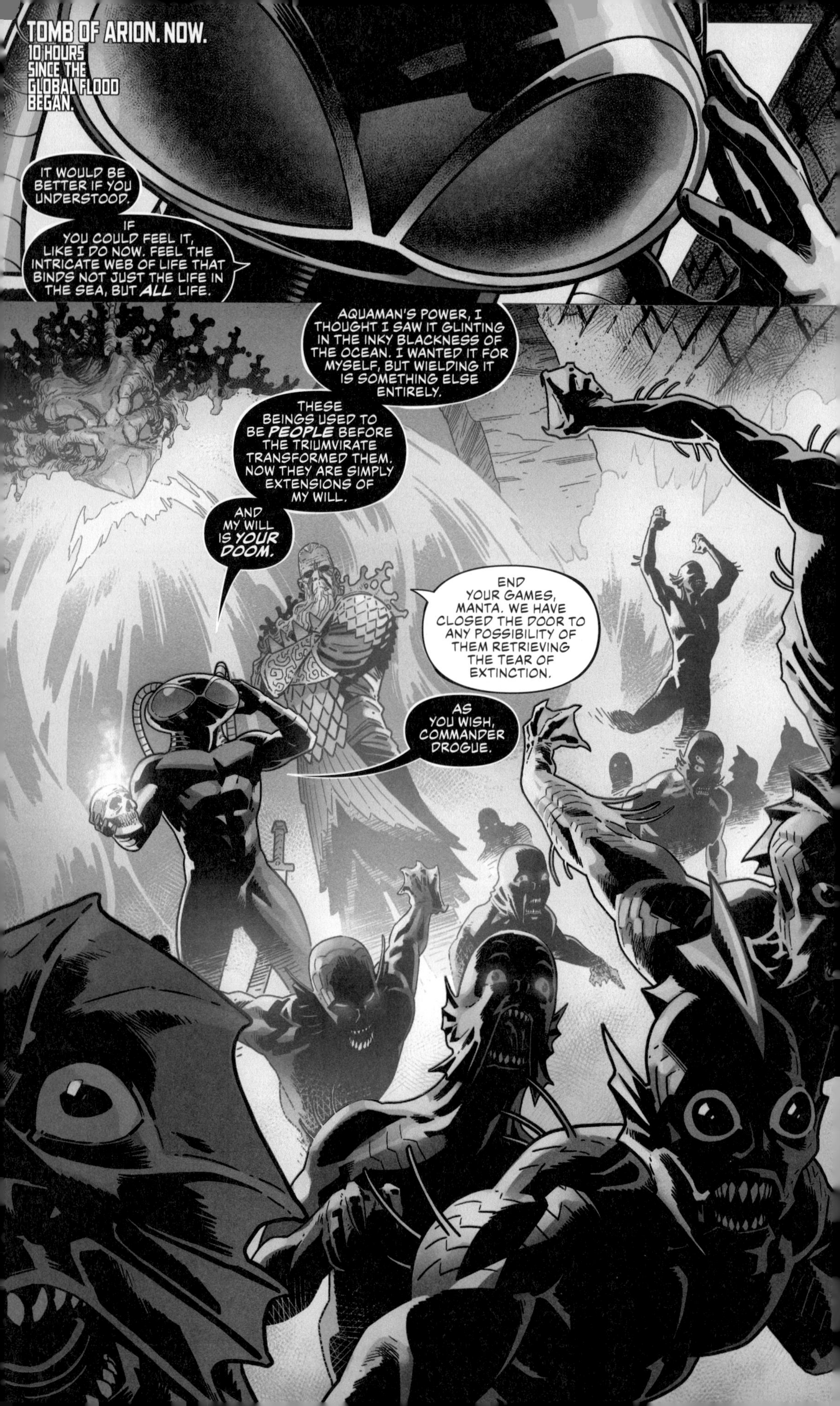
TOMB OF ARION. NOW.
10 HOURS SINCE THE GLOBAL FLOOD BEGAN.
IT WOULD BE BETTER IF YOU UNDERSTOOD.
IF YOU COULD FEEL IT, LIKE I DO NOW. FEEL THE INTRICATE WEB OF LIFE THAT BINDS NOT JUST THE LIFE IN THE SEA, BUT ALL LIFE.
AQUAMAN'S POWER, I THOUGHT I SAW IT GLINTING IN THE INKY BLACKNESS OF THE OCEAN. I WANTED IT FOR MYSELF, BUT WIELDING IT IS SOMETHING ELSE ENTIRELY.
THESE BEINGS USED TO BE PEOPLE BEFORE THE TRIUMVIRATE TRANSFORMED THEM. NOW THEY ARE SIMPLY EXTENSIONS OF MY WILL.
AND MY WILL IS YOUR DOOM.
END YOUR GAMES, MANTA. WE HAVE CLOSED THE DOOR TO ANY POSSIBILITY OF THEM RETRIEVING THE TEAR OF EXTINCTION.
AS YOU WISH, COMMANDER DROGUE.

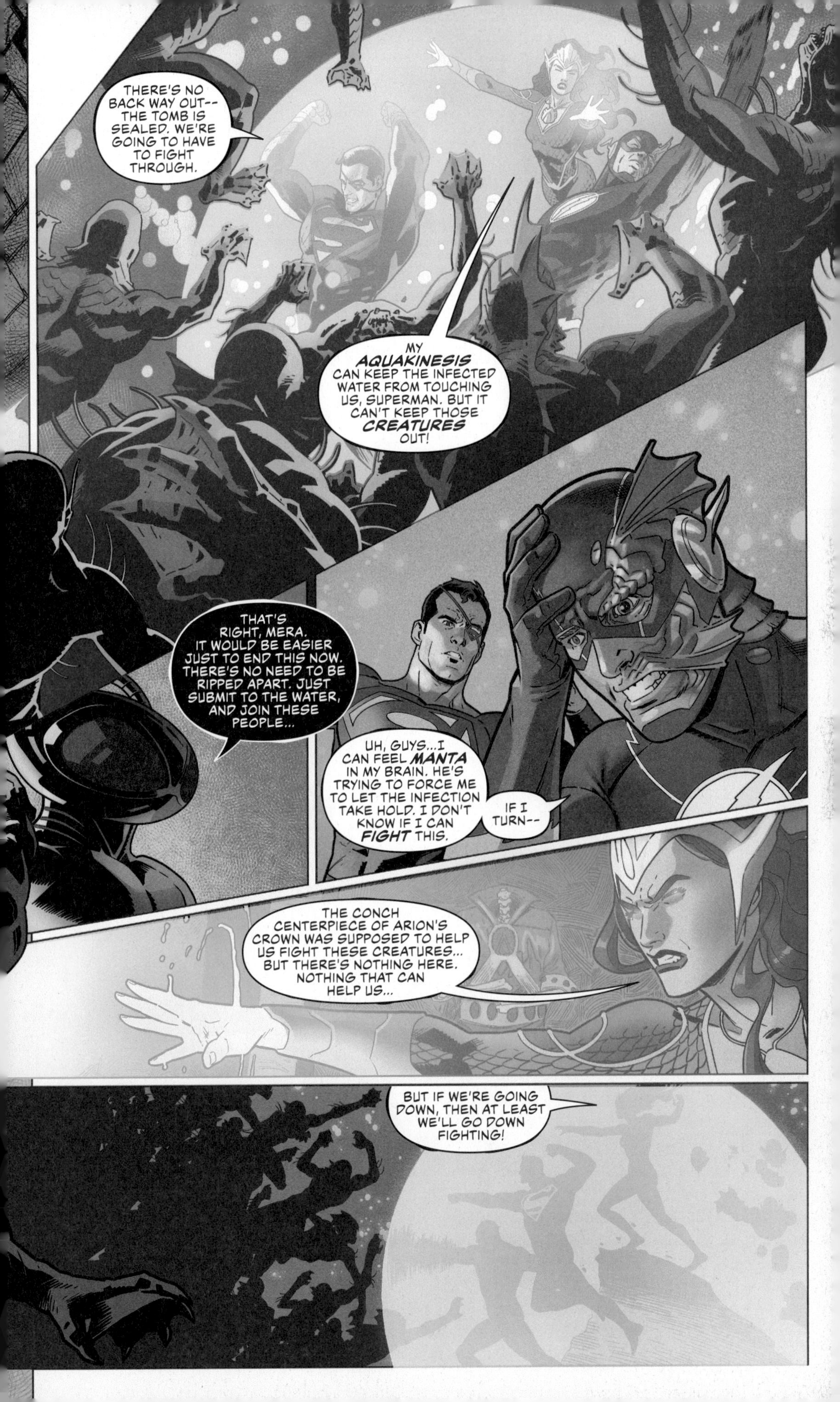
THERE'S NO BACK WAY OUT-- THE TOMB IS SEALED. WE'RE GOING TO HAVE TO FIGHT THROUGH.
MY AQUAKINESIS CAN KEEP THE INFECTED WATER FROM TOUCHING US, SUPERMAN. BUT IT CAN'T KEEP THOSE CREATURES OUT!
THAT'S RIGHT, MERA. IT WOULD BE EASIER JUST TO END THIS NOW. THERE'S NO NEED TO BE RIPPED APART. JUST SUBMIT TO THE WATER, AND JOIN THESE PEOPLE...
UH, GUYS...I CAN FEEL MANTA IN MY BRAIN. HE'S TRYING TO FORCE ME TO LET THE INFECTION TAKE HOLD. I DON'T KNOW IF I CAN FIGHT THIS.
IF I TURN--
THE CONCH CENTERPIECE OF ARION'S CROWN WAS SUPPOSED TO HELP US FIGHT THESE CREATURES... BUT THERE'S NOTHING HERE. NOTHING THAT CAN HELP US...
BUT IF WE'RE GOING DOWN, THEN AT LEAST WE'LL GO DOWN FIGHTING!

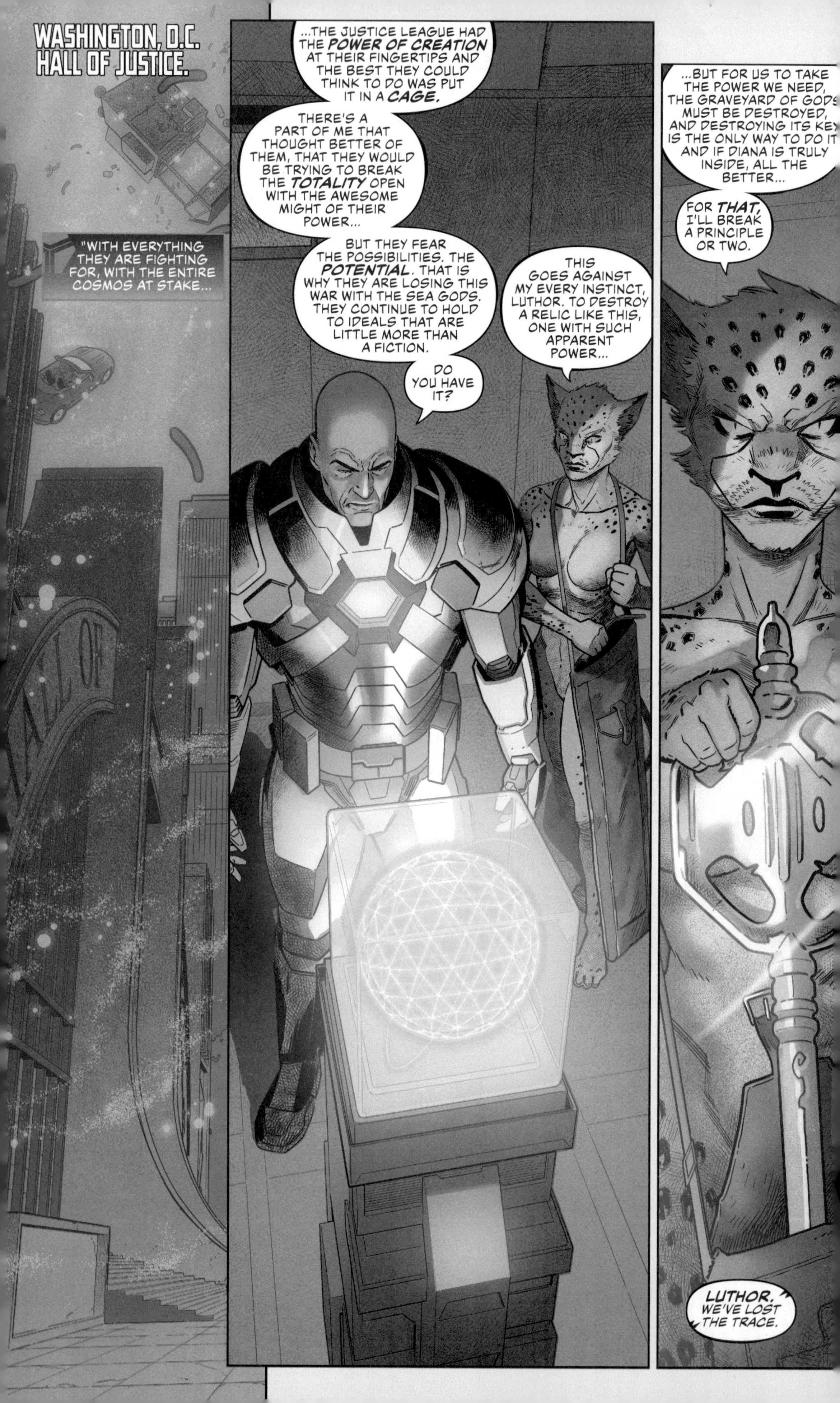
WASHINGTON, D.C. HALL OF JUSTICE.
"WITH EVERYTHING THEY ARE FIGHTING FOR, WITH THE ENTIRE COSMOS AT STAKE...
...THE JUSTICE LEAGUE HAD THE POWER OF CREATION AT THEIR FINGERTIPS AND THE BEST THEY COULD THINK TO DO WAS PUT IT IN A CAGE.
THERE'S A PART OF ME THAT THOUGHT BETTER OF THEM, THAT THEY WOULD BE TRYING TO BREAK THE TOTALITY OPEN WITH THE AWESOME MIGHT OF THEIR POWER...
BUT THEY FEAR THE POSSIBILITIES. THE POTENTIAL. THAT IS WHY THEY ARE LOSING THIS WAR WITH THE SEA GODS. THEY CONTINUE TO HOLD TO IDEALS THAT ARE LITTLE MORE THAN A FICTION.
DO YOU HAVE IT?
THIS GOES AGAINST MY EVERY INSTINCT, LUTHOR. TO DESTROY A RELIC LIKE THIS, ONE WITH SUCH APPARENT POWER...
...BUT FOR US TO TAKE THE POWER WE NEED, THE GRAVEYARD OF GODS MUST BE DESTROYED, AND DESTROYING ITS KEY IS THE ONLY WAY TO DO IT. AND IF DIANA IS TRULY INSIDE, ALL THE BETTER...
FOR THAT, I'LL BREAK A PRINCIPLE OR TWO.
LUTHOR. WE'VE LOST THE TRACE.

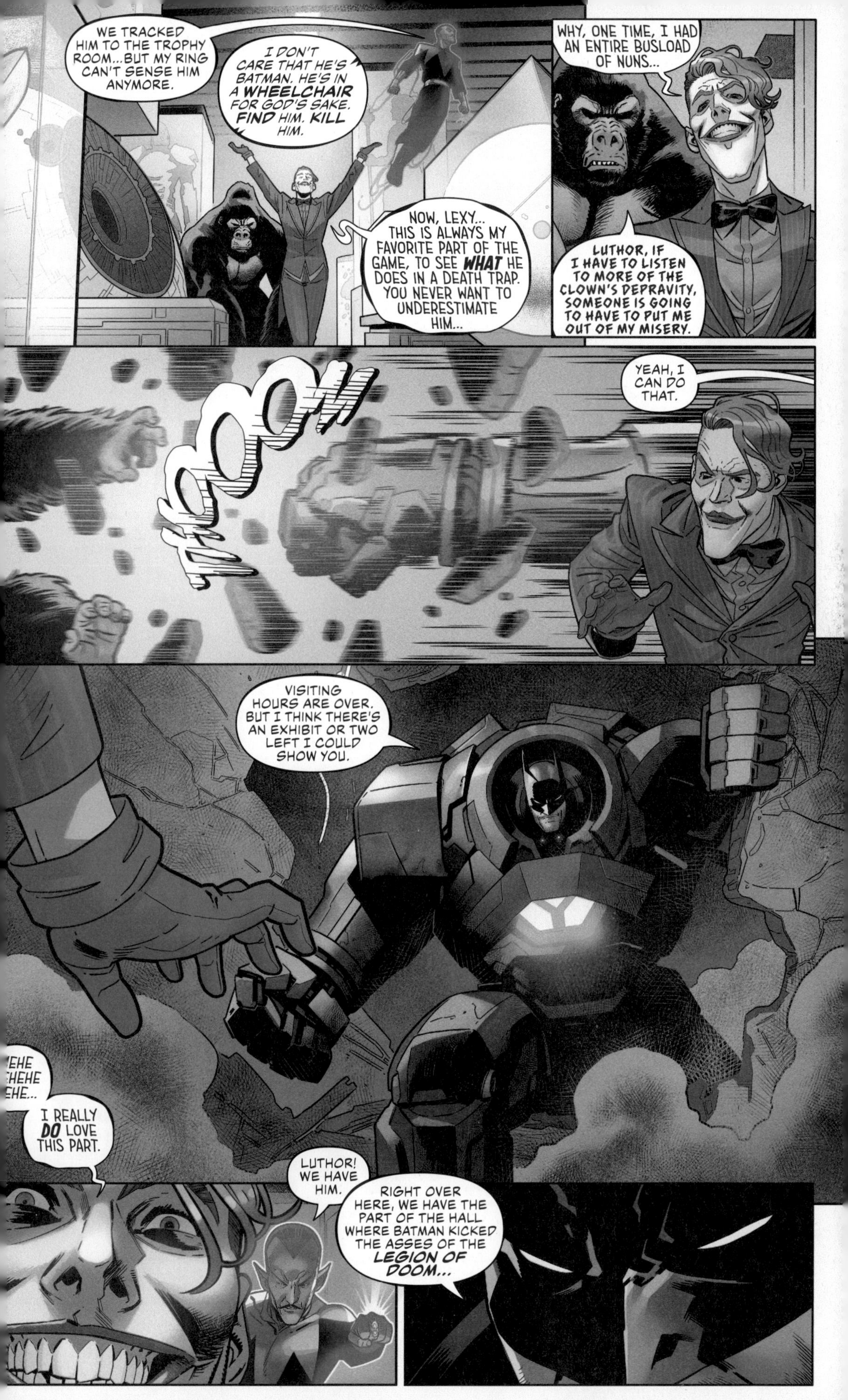
WE TRACKED HIM TO THE TROPHY ROOM...BUT MY RING CAN'T SENSE HIM ANYMORE.
I DON'T CARE THAT HE'S BATMAN. HE'S IN A WHEELCHAIR FOR GOD'S SAKE. FIND HIM. KILL HIM.
NOW, LEXY... THIS IS ALWAYS MY FAVORITE PART OF THE GAME, TO SEE WHAT HE DOES IN A DEATH TRAP. YOU NEVER WANT TO UNDERESTIMATE HIM...
WHY, ONE TIME, I HAD AN ENTIRE BUSLOAD OF NUNS...
LUTHOR, IF I HAVE TO LISTEN TO MORE OF THE CLOWN'S DEPRAVITY, SOMEONE IS GOING TO HAVE TO PUT ME OUT OF MY MISERY.
THOOOM
YEAH, I CAN DO THAT.
VISITING HOURS ARE OVER. BUT I THINK THERE'S AN EXHIBIT OR TWO LEFT I COULD SHOW YOU.
HEHE HEHE HEHE...
I REALLY DO LOVE THIS PART.
LUTHOR! WE HAVE HIM.
RIGHT OVER HERE, WE HAVE THE PART OF THE HALL WHERE BATMAN KICKED THE ASSES OF THE LEGION OF DOOM...

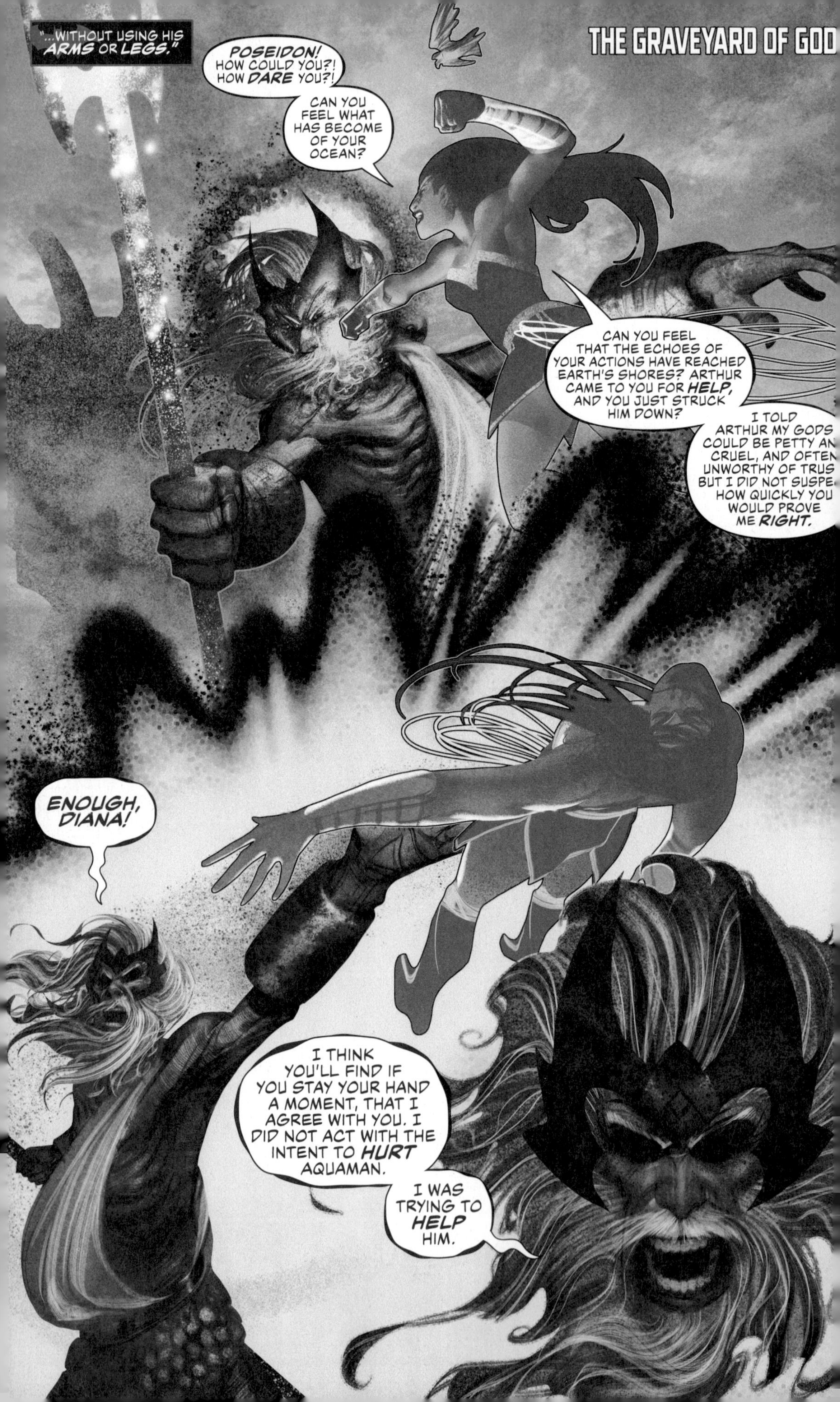

"...WITHOUT USING HIS ARMS OR LEGS."
THE GRAVEYARD OF GOD
POSEIDON! HOW COULD YOU?! HOW DARE YOU?!
CAN YOU FEEL WHAT HAS BECOME OF YOUR OCEAN?
CAN YOU FEEL THAT THE ECHOES OF YOUR ACTIONS HAVE REACHED EARTH'S SHORES? ARTHUR CAME TO YOU FOR HELP, AND YOU JUST STRUCK HIM DOWN?
I TOLD ARTHUR MY GODS COULD BE PETTY AN CRUEL, AND OFTEN UNWORTHY OF TRUS BUT I DID NOT SUSPE HOW QUICKLY YOU WOULD PROVE ME RIGHT.
ENOUGH, DIANA!
I THINK YOU'LL FIND IF YOU STAY YOUR HAND A MOMENT, THAT I AGREE WITH YOU. I DID NOT ACT WITH THE INTENT TO HURT AQUAMAN.
I WAS TRYING TO HELP HIM.

IF *PAIN* IS HELP IN THIS TWISTED REALM, THEN LET ME *RETURN THE FAVOR!*

BE GLAD I DID NOT BRING A TRIDENT OF MY OWN...

THE EARTH IS DROWNED AT THE HANDS OF THREE POWERFUL OCEAN LORDS, ALIEN SEA GODS YOU CAST DOWN INTO THIS VERY GRAVEYARD EONS AGO.

DROGUE. TYYDE. GALL. YES. I REMEMBER THEM...

YOU ONCE STOOD SIDE BY SIDE WITH A GREAT HERO OF ATLANTIS AND FOUGHT BACK THE HORROR OF THEIR FIRST ASSAULT ON EARTH. WE NEED A WAY TO COMBAT THEM.

≈SIGH≈

THERE IS NOT MUCH TIME. THE DAMNED CHEETAH WOMAN WHO TRAPPED ME HERE IS GOING TO DESTROY THIS ENTIRE REALM IN MOMENTS. I CAN FEEL HER PLAN COMING TO FRUITION.

I WISHED TO ENHANCE YOU WITH THE RAW POWER OF THE LIFE FORCE USING MY TRIDENT. BUT THE GODS STRIPPED YOU OF YOUR POWER AND CONNECTION TO IT, GIVING IT TO THE TRAITOR, MANTA.

THAT POWER IS THE *KEY.* IT IS WHAT SPURS THEIR RAGE. IT IS WHAT BROUGHT THEM TO OUR WORLD IN THE FIRST PLACE...BUT NOT AS ENEMIES. YOU MUST UNDERSTAND...

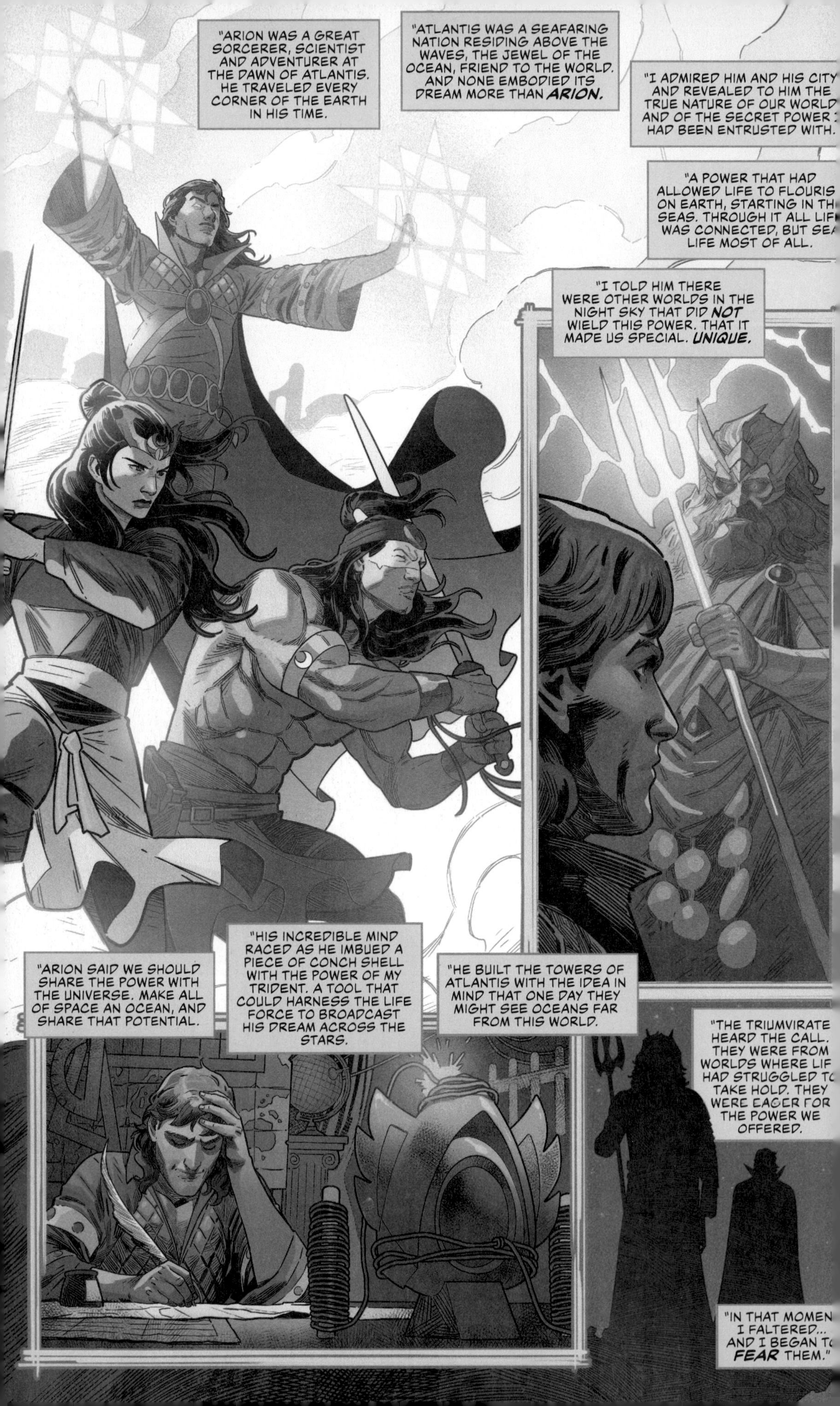
"ARION WAS A GREAT SORCERER, SCIENTIST AND ADVENTURER AT THE DAWN OF ATLANTIS. HE TRAVELED EVERY CORNER OF THE EARTH IN HIS TIME.
"ATLANTIS WAS A SEAFARING NATION RESIDING ABOVE THE WAVES, THE JEWEL OF THE OCEAN, FRIEND TO THE WORLD. AND NONE EMBODIED ITS DREAM MORE THAN ARION.
"I ADMIRED HIM AND HIS CITY AND REVEALED TO HIM THE TRUE NATURE OF OUR WORLD AND OF THE SECRET POWER HAD BEEN ENTRUSTED WITH.
"A POWER THAT HAD ALLOWED LIFE TO FLOURIS ON EARTH, STARTING IN TH SEAS. THROUGH IT ALL LIF WAS CONNECTED, BUT SEA LIFE MOST OF ALL.
"I TOLD HIM THERE WERE OTHER WORLDS IN THE NIGHT SKY THAT DID NOT WIELD THIS POWER. THAT IT MADE US SPECIAL. UNIQUE.
"ARION SAID WE SHOULD SHARE THE POWER WITH THE UNIVERSE. MAKE ALL OF SPACE AN OCEAN, AND SHARE THAT POTENTIAL.
"HIS INCREDIBLE MIND RACED AS HE IMBUED A PIECE OF CONCH SHELL WITH THE POWER OF MY TRIDENT. A TOOL THAT COULD HARNESS THE LIFE FORCE TO BROADCAST HIS DREAM ACROSS THE STARS.
"HE BUILT THE TOWERS OF ATLANTIS WITH THE IDEA IN MIND THAT ONE DAY THEY MIGHT SEE OCEANS FAR FROM THIS WORLD.
"THE TRIUMVIRATE HEARD THE CALL. THEY WERE FROM WORLDS WHERE LIF HAD STRUGGLED TO TAKE HOLD. THEY WERE EAGER FOR THE POWER WE OFFERED.
"IN THAT MOMEN I FALTERED... AND I BEGAN TO FEAR THEM."

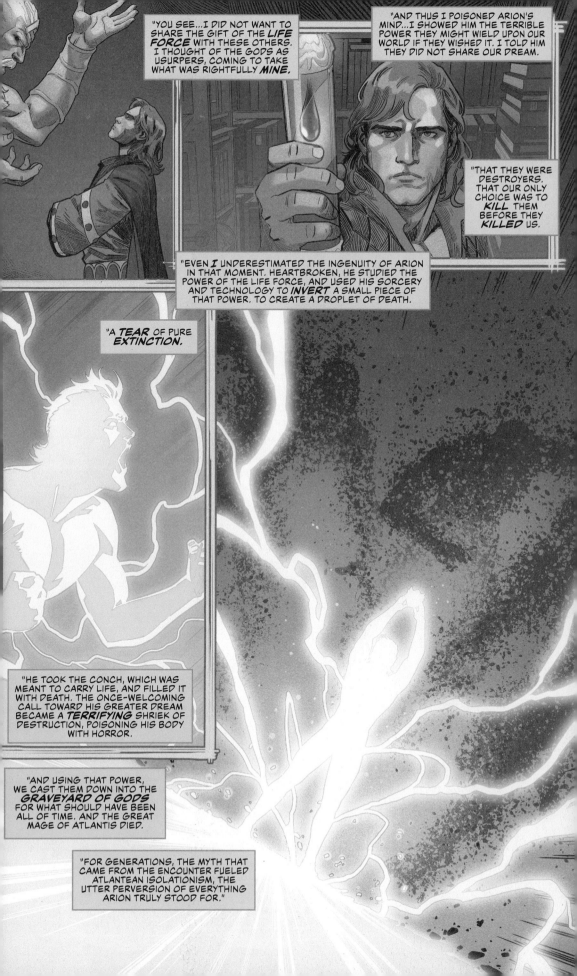

"YOU SEE...I DID NOT WANT TO SHARE THE GIFT OF THE *LIFE FORCE* WITH THESE OTHERS. I THOUGHT OF THE GODS AS USURPERS, COMING TO TAKE WHAT WAS RIGHTFULLY *MINE.*

"AND THUS I POISONED ARION'S MIND...I SHOWED HIM THE TERRIBLE POWER THEY MIGHT WIELD UPON OUR WORLD IF THEY WISHED IT. I TOLD HIM THEY DID NOT SHARE OUR DREAM.

"THAT THEY WERE DESTROYERS. THAT OUR ONLY CHOICE WAS TO *KILL* THEM BEFORE THEY *KILLED* US.

"EVEN *I* UNDERESTIMATED THE INGENUITY OF ARION IN THAT MOMENT. HEARTBROKEN, HE STUDIED THE POWER OF THE LIFE FORCE, AND USED HIS SORCERY AND TECHNOLOGY TO *INVERT* A SMALL PIECE OF THAT POWER, TO CREATE A DROPLET OF DEATH.

"A *TEAR* OF PURE *EXTINCTION.*

"HE TOOK THE CONCH, WHICH WAS MEANT TO CARRY LIFE, AND FILLED IT WITH DEATH. THE ONCE-WELCOMING CALL TOWARD HIS GREATER DREAM BECAME A *TERRIFYING* SHRIEK OF DESTRUCTION, POISONING HIS BODY WITH HORROR.

"AND USING THAT POWER, WE CAST THEM DOWN INTO THE *GRAVEYARD OF GODS* FOR WHAT SHOULD HAVE BEEN ALL OF TIME. AND THE GREAT MAGE OF ATLANTIS DIED.

"FOR GENERATIONS, THE MYTH THAT CAME FROM THE ENCOUNTER FUELED ATLANTEAN ISOLATIONISM, THE UTTER PERVERSION OF EVERYTHING ARION TRULY STOOD FOR."

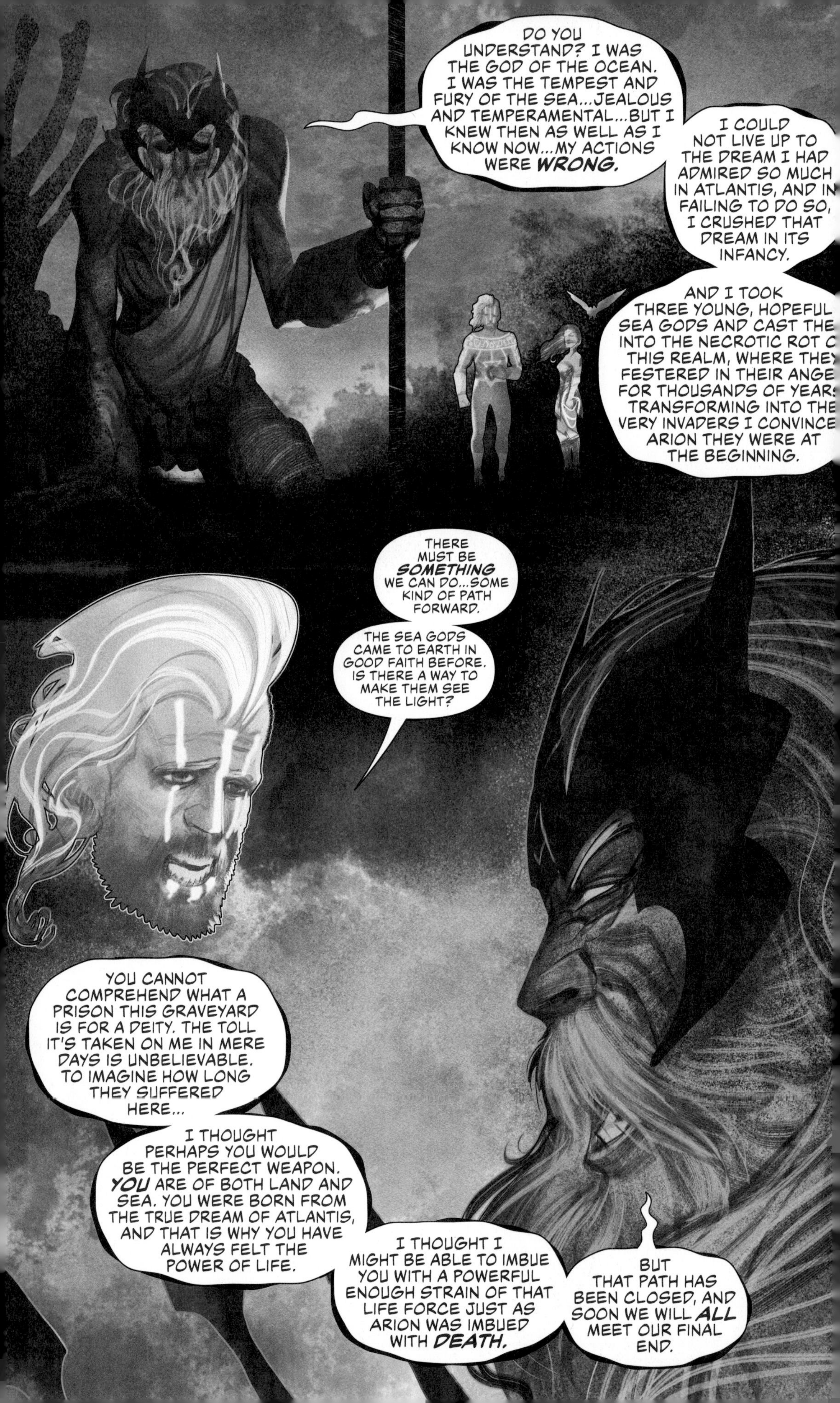
DO YOU UNDERSTAND? I WAS THE GOD OF THE OCEAN. I WAS THE TEMPEST AND FURY OF THE SEA...JEALOUS AND TEMPERAMENTAL...BUT I KNEW THEN AS WELL AS I KNOW NOW...MY ACTIONS WERE *WRONG.*
I COULD NOT LIVE UP TO THE DREAM I HAD ADMIRED SO MUCH IN ATLANTIS, AND IN FAILING TO DO SO, I CRUSHED THAT DREAM IN ITS INFANCY.
AND I TOOK THREE YOUNG, HOPEFUL SEA GODS AND CAST THE INTO THE NECROTIC ROT THIS REALM, WHERE THE FESTERED IN THEIR ANGE FOR THOUSANDS OF YEAR TRANSFORMING INTO THE VERY INVADERS I CONVINCE ARION THEY WERE AT THE BEGINNING.
THERE MUST BE ***SOMETHING*** WE CAN DO...SOME KIND OF PATH FORWARD.
THE SEA GODS CAME TO EARTH IN GOOD FAITH BEFORE. IS THERE A WAY TO MAKE THEM SEE THE LIGHT?
YOU CANNOT COMPREHEND WHAT A PRISON THIS GRAVEYARD IS FOR A DEITY. THE TOLL IT'S TAKEN ON ME IN MERE DAYS IS UNBELIEVABLE. TO IMAGINE HOW LONG THEY SUFFERED HERE...
I THOUGHT PERHAPS YOU WOULD BE THE PERFECT WEAPON. ***YOU*** ARE OF BOTH LAND AND SEA. YOU WERE BORN FROM THE TRUE DREAM OF ATLANTIS, AND THAT IS WHY YOU HAVE ALWAYS FELT THE POWER OF LIFE.
I THOUGHT I MIGHT BE ABLE TO IMBUE YOU WITH A POWERFUL ENOUGH STRAIN OF THAT LIFE FORCE JUST AS ARION WAS IMBUED WITH ***DEATH.***
BUT THAT PATH HAS BEEN CLOSED, AND SOON WE WILL ***ALL*** MEET OUR FINAL END.

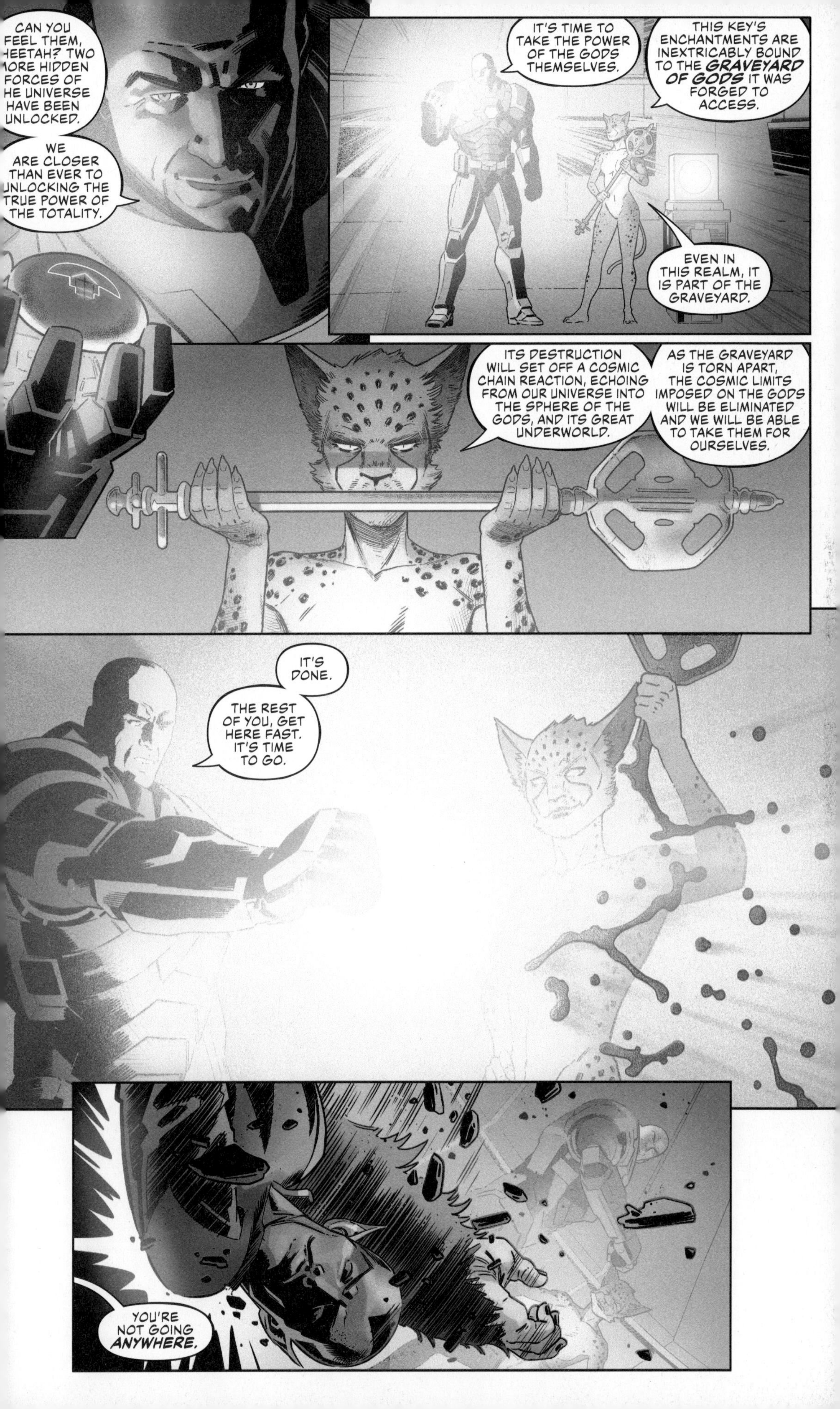

CAN YOU FEEL THEM, CHEETAH? TWO MORE HIDDEN FORCES OF THE UNIVERSE HAVE BEEN UNLOCKED.
WE ARE CLOSER THAN EVER TO UNLOCKING THE TRUE POWER OF THE TOTALITY.
IT'S TIME TO TAKE THE POWER OF THE GODS THEMSELVES.
THIS KEY'S ENCHANTMENTS ARE INEXTRICABLY BOUND TO THE GRAVEYARD OF GODS IT WAS FORGED TO ACCESS.
EVEN IN THIS REALM, IT IS PART OF THE GRAVEYARD.
ITS DESTRUCTION WILL SET OFF A COSMIC CHAIN REACTION, ECHOING FROM OUR UNIVERSE INTO THE SPHERE OF THE GODS, AND ITS GREAT UNDERWORLD.
AS THE GRAVEYARD IS TORN APART, THE COSMIC LIMITS IMPOSED ON THE GODS WILL BE ELIMINATED AND WE WILL BE ABLE TO TAKE THEM FOR OURSELVES.
IT'S DONE.
THE REST OF YOU, GET HERE FAST. IT'S TIME TO GO.
YOU'RE NOT GOING ANYWHERE.

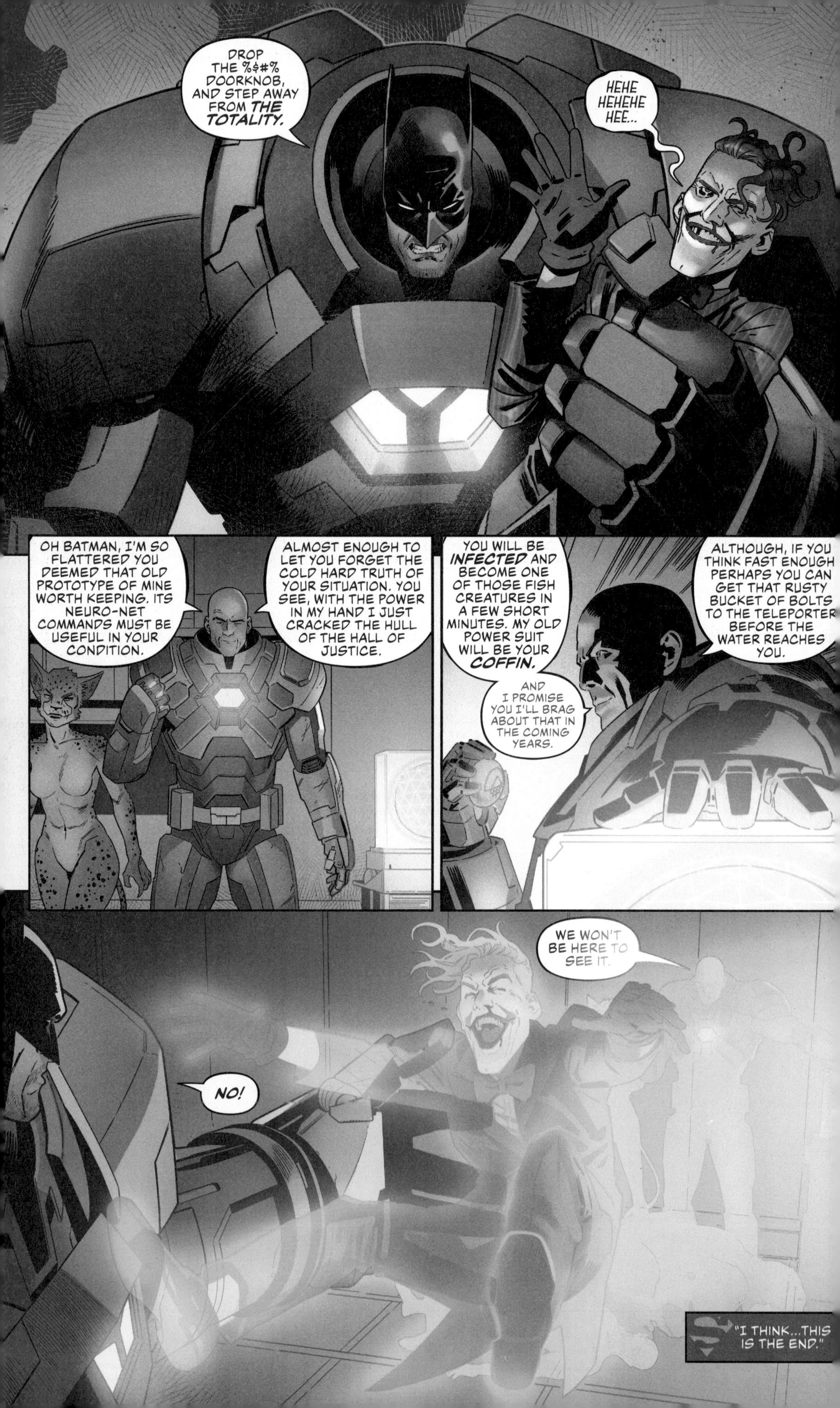
DROP THE %$#% DOORKNOB, AND STEP AWAY FROM THE TOTALITY.
HEHE HEHEHE HEE...
OH BATMAN, I'M SO FLATTERED YOU DEEMED THAT OLD PROTOTYPE OF MINE WORTH KEEPING. ITS NEURO-NET COMMANDS MUST BE USEFUL IN YOUR CONDITION.
ALMOST ENOUGH TO LET YOU FORGET THE COLD HARD TRUTH OF YOUR SITUATION. YOU SEE, WITH THE POWER IN MY HAND I JUST CRACKED THE HULL OF THE HALL OF JUSTICE.
YOU WILL BE INFECTED AND BECOME ONE OF THOSE FISH CREATURES IN A FEW SHORT MINUTES. MY OLD POWER SUIT WILL BE YOUR COFFIN.
ALTHOUGH, IF YOU THINK FAST ENOUGH PERHAPS YOU CAN GET THAT RUSTY BUCKET OF BOLTS TO THE TELEPORTER BEFORE THE WATER REACHES YOU.
AND I PROMISE YOU I'LL BRAG ABOUT THAT IN THE COMING YEARS.
WE WON'T BE HERE TO SEE IT.
NO!
"I THINK...THIS IS THE END."

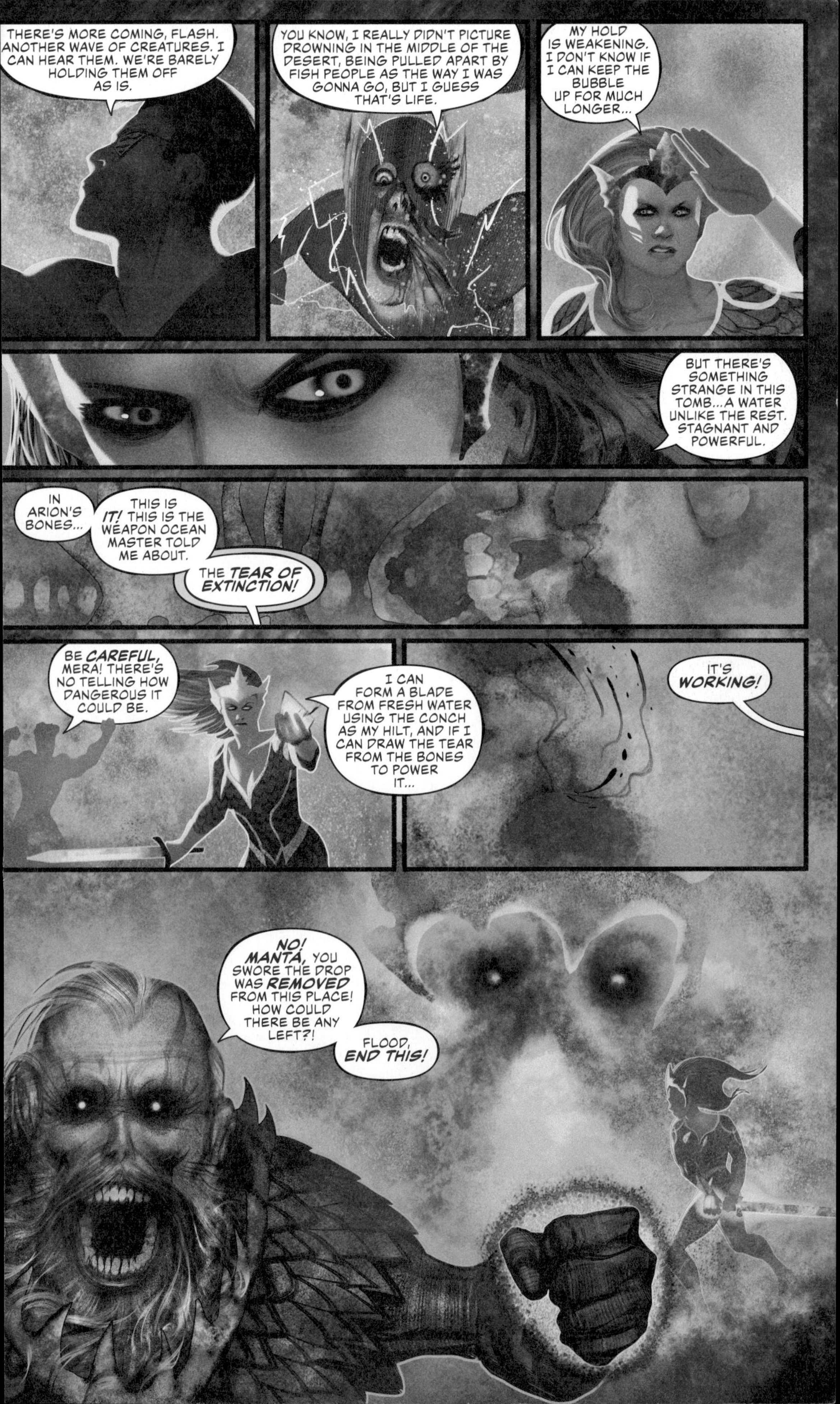
THERE'S MORE COMING, FLASH. ANOTHER WAVE OF CREATURES. I CAN HEAR THEM. WE'RE BARELY HOLDING THEM OFF AS IS.
YOU KNOW, I REALLY DIDN'T PICTURE DROWNING IN THE MIDDLE OF THE DESERT, BEING PULLED APART BY FISH PEOPLE AS THE WAY I WAS GONNA GO, BUT I GUESS THAT'S LIFE.
MY HOLD IS WEAKENING. I DON'T KNOW IF I CAN KEEP THE BUBBLE UP FOR MUCH LONGER...
BUT THERE'S SOMETHING STRANGE IN THIS TOMB...A WATER UNLIKE THE REST. STAGNANT AND POWERFUL.
IN ARION'S BONES...
THIS IS *IT!* THIS IS THE WEAPON OCEAN MASTER TOLD ME ABOUT.
THE ***TEAR OF EXTINCTION!***
BE ***CAREFUL,*** MERA! THERE'S NO TELLING HOW DANGEROUS IT COULD BE.
I CAN FORM A BLADE FROM FRESH WATER USING THE CONCH AS MY HILT, AND IF I CAN DRAW THE TEAR FROM THE BONES TO POWER IT...
IT'S ***WORKING!***
NO! MANTA, YOU SWORE THE DROP WAS ***REMOVED*** FROM THIS PLACE! HOW COULD THERE BE ANY LEFT?!
FLOOD, ***END THIS!***

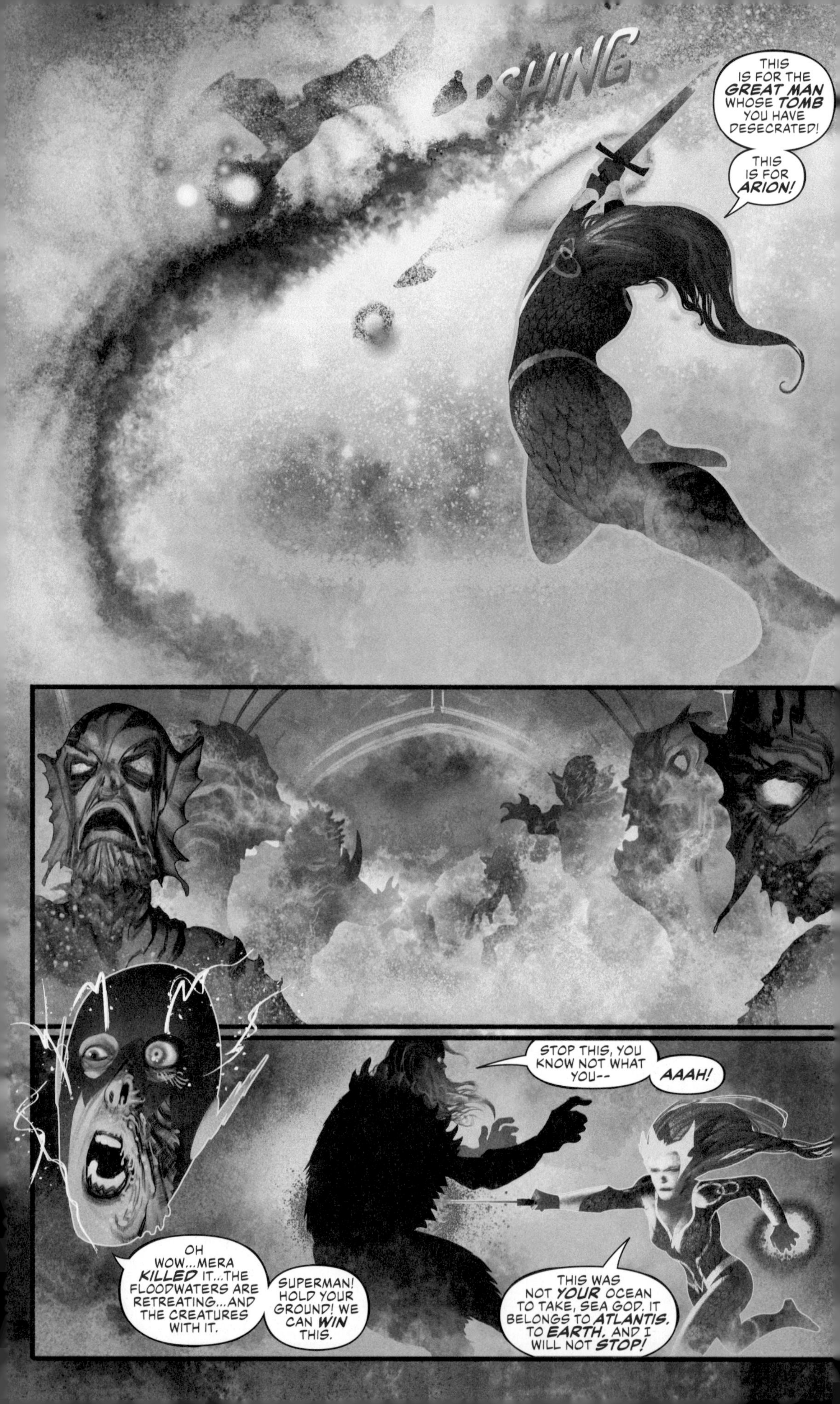
SHING
THIS IS FOR THE GREAT MAN WHOSE TOMB YOU HAVE DESECRATED!
THIS IS FOR ARION!
STOP THIS, YOU KNOW NOT WHAT YOU--
AAAH!
OH WOW...MERA KILLED IT...THE FLOODWATERS ARE RETREATING...AND THE CREATURES WITH IT.
SUPERMAN! HOLD YOUR GROUND! WE CAN WIN THIS.
THIS WAS NOT YOUR OCEAN TO TAKE, SEA GOD. IT BELONGS TO ATLANTIS, TO EARTH, AND I WILL NOT STOP!

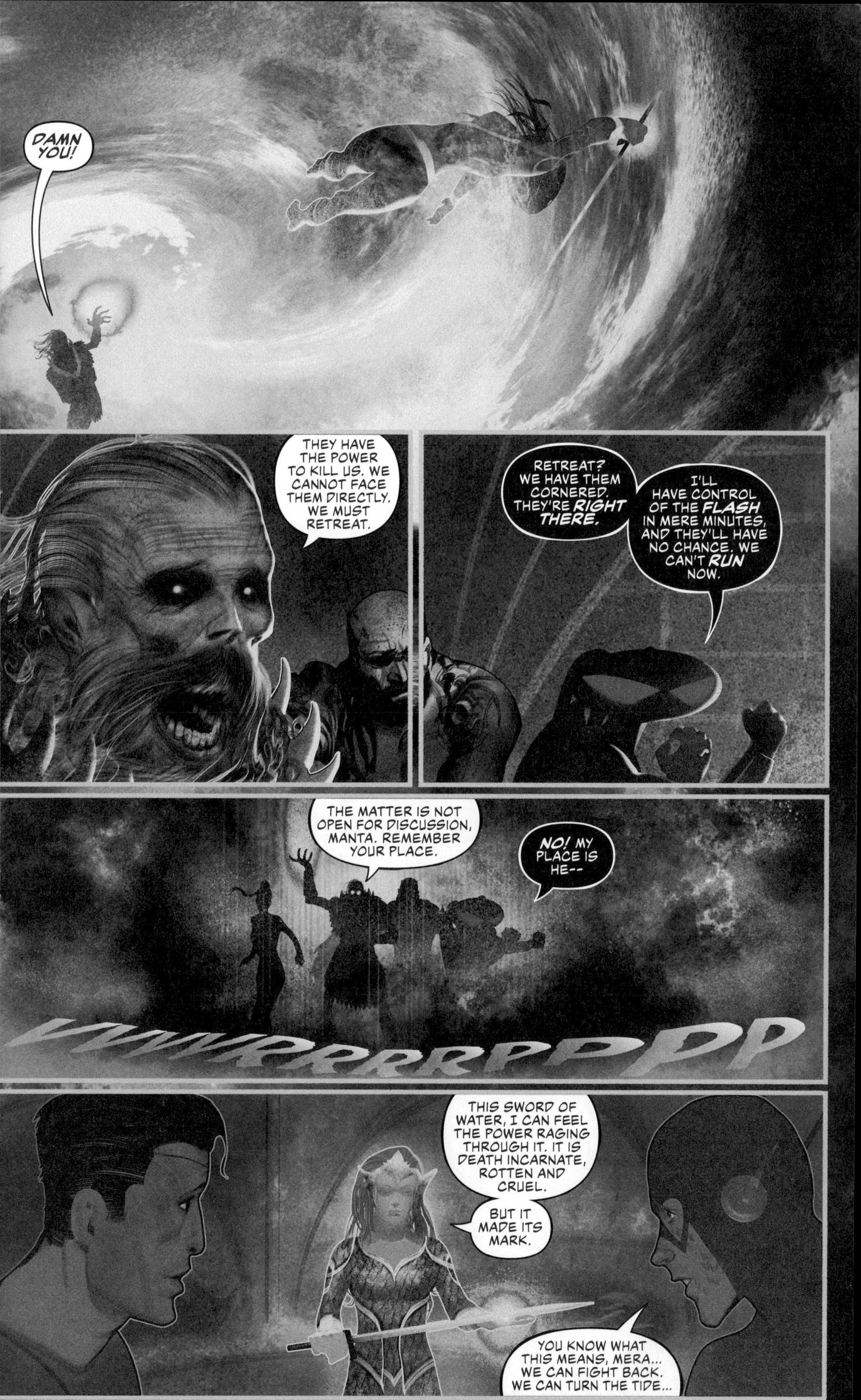
DAMN YOU!
THEY HAVE THE POWER TO KILL US. WE CANNOT FACE THEM DIRECTLY. WE MUST RETREAT.
RETREAT? WE HAVE THEM CORNERED. THEY'RE RIGHT THERE.
I'LL HAVE CONTROL OF THE FLASH IN MERE MINUTES, AND THEY'LL HAVE NO CHANCE. WE CAN'T RUN NOW.
THE MATTER IS NOT OPEN FOR DISCUSSION, MANTA. REMEMBER YOUR PLACE.
NO! MY PLACE IS HE--
VVVVRRRRRPPPPP
THIS SWORD OF WATER, I CAN FEEL THE POWER RAGING THROUGH IT. IT IS DEATH INCARNATE, ROTTEN AND CRUEL.
BUT IT MADE ITS MARK.
YOU KNOW WHAT THIS MEANS, MERA... WE CAN FIGHT BACK. WE CAN TURN THE TIDE...

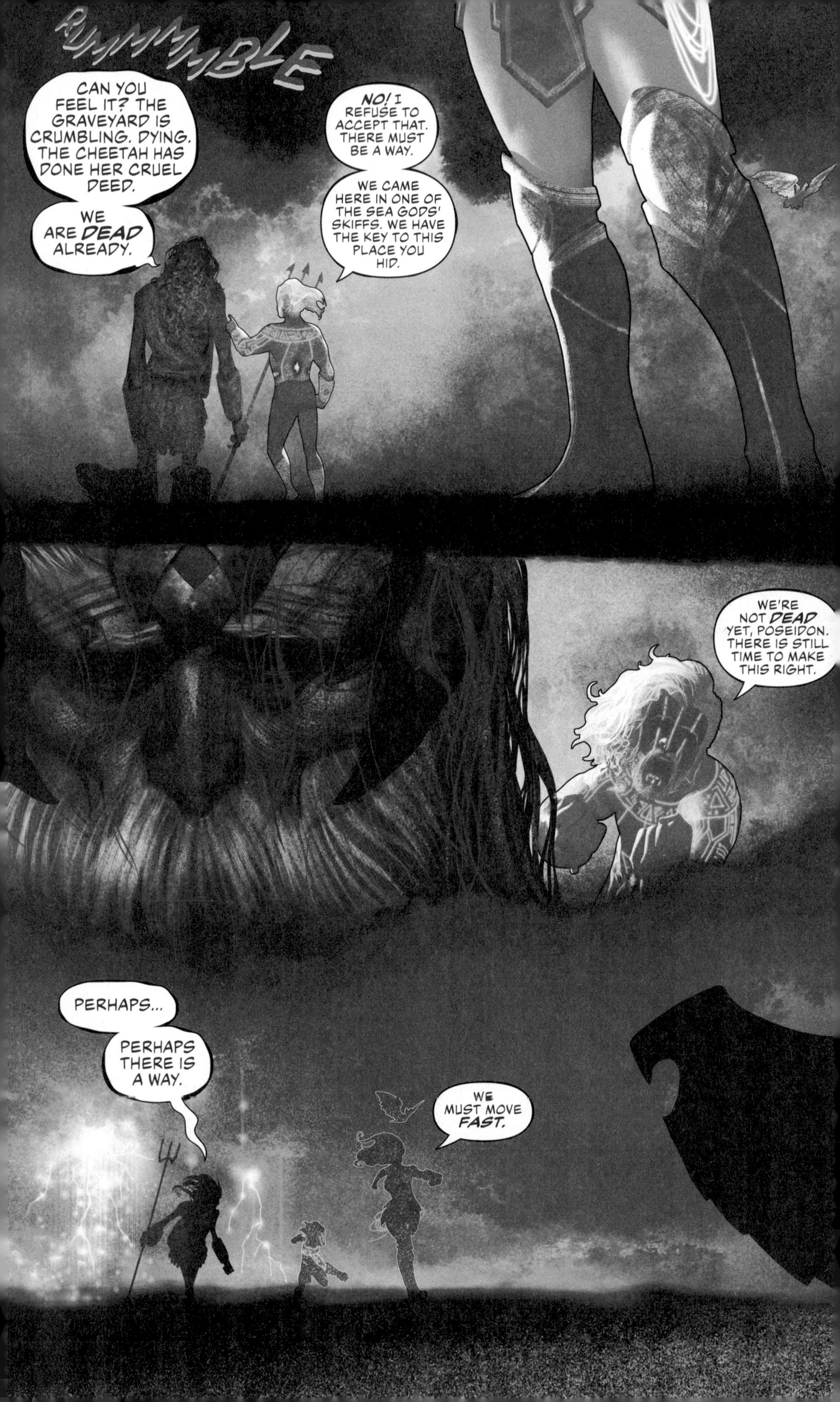
RUMMMBLE
CAN YOU FEEL IT? THE GRAVEYARD IS CRUMBLING. DYING. THE CHEETAH HAS DONE HER CRUEL DEED.
WE ARE *DEAD* ALREADY.
NO! I REFUSE TO ACCEPT THAT. THERE MUST BE A WAY.
WE CAME HERE IN ONE OF THE SEA GODS' SKIFFS. WE HAVE THE KEY TO THIS PLACE YOU HID.
WE'RE NOT *DEAD* YET, POSEIDON. THERE IS STILL TIME TO MAKE THIS RIGHT.
PERHAPS...
PERHAPS THERE IS A WAY.
WE MUST MOVE *FAST.*

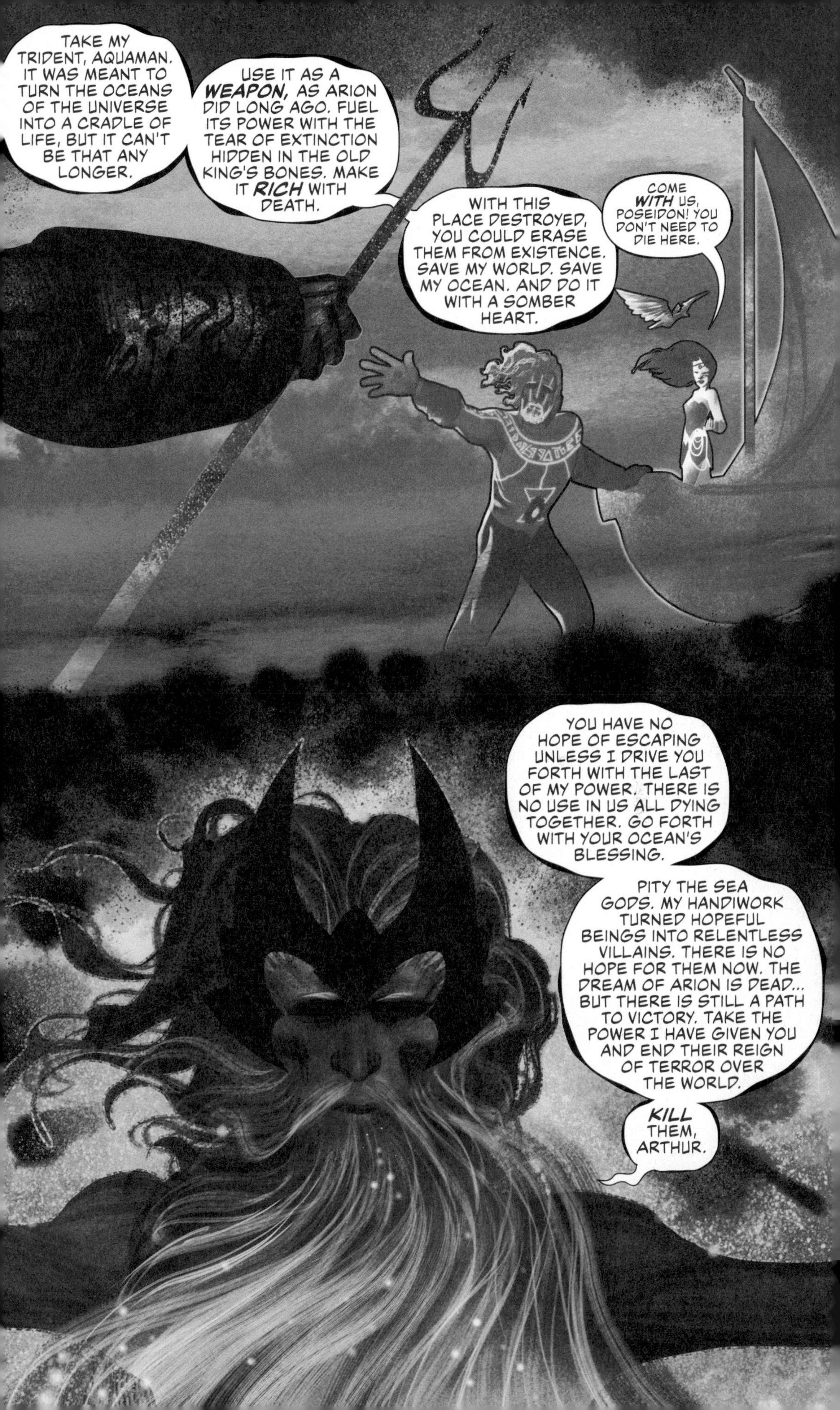
TAKE MY TRIDENT, AQUAMAN. IT WAS MEANT TO TURN THE OCEANS OF THE UNIVERSE INTO A CRADLE OF LIFE, BUT IT CAN'T BE THAT ANY LONGER.
USE IT AS A **WEAPON,** AS ARION DID LONG AGO. FUEL ITS POWER WITH THE TEAR OF EXTINCTION HIDDEN IN THE OLD KING'S BONES. MAKE IT **RICH** WITH DEATH.
WITH THIS PLACE DESTROYED, YOU COULD ERASE THEM FROM EXISTENCE. SAVE MY WORLD. SAVE MY OCEAN. AND DO IT WITH A SOMBER HEART.
COME **WITH** US, POSEIDON! YOU DON'T NEED TO DIE HERE.
YOU HAVE NO HOPE OF ESCAPING UNLESS I DRIVE YOU FORTH WITH THE LAST OF MY POWER. THERE IS NO USE IN US ALL DYING TOGETHER. GO FORTH WITH YOUR OCEAN'S BLESSING.
PITY THE SEA GODS. MY HANDIWORK TURNED HOPEFUL BEINGS INTO RELENTLESS VILLAINS. THERE IS NO HOPE FOR THEM NOW. THE DREAM OF ARION IS DEAD... BUT THERE IS STILL A PATH TO VICTORY. TAKE THE POWER I HAVE GIVEN YOU AND END THEIR REIGN OF TERROR OVER THE WORLD.
KILL THEM, ARTHUR.

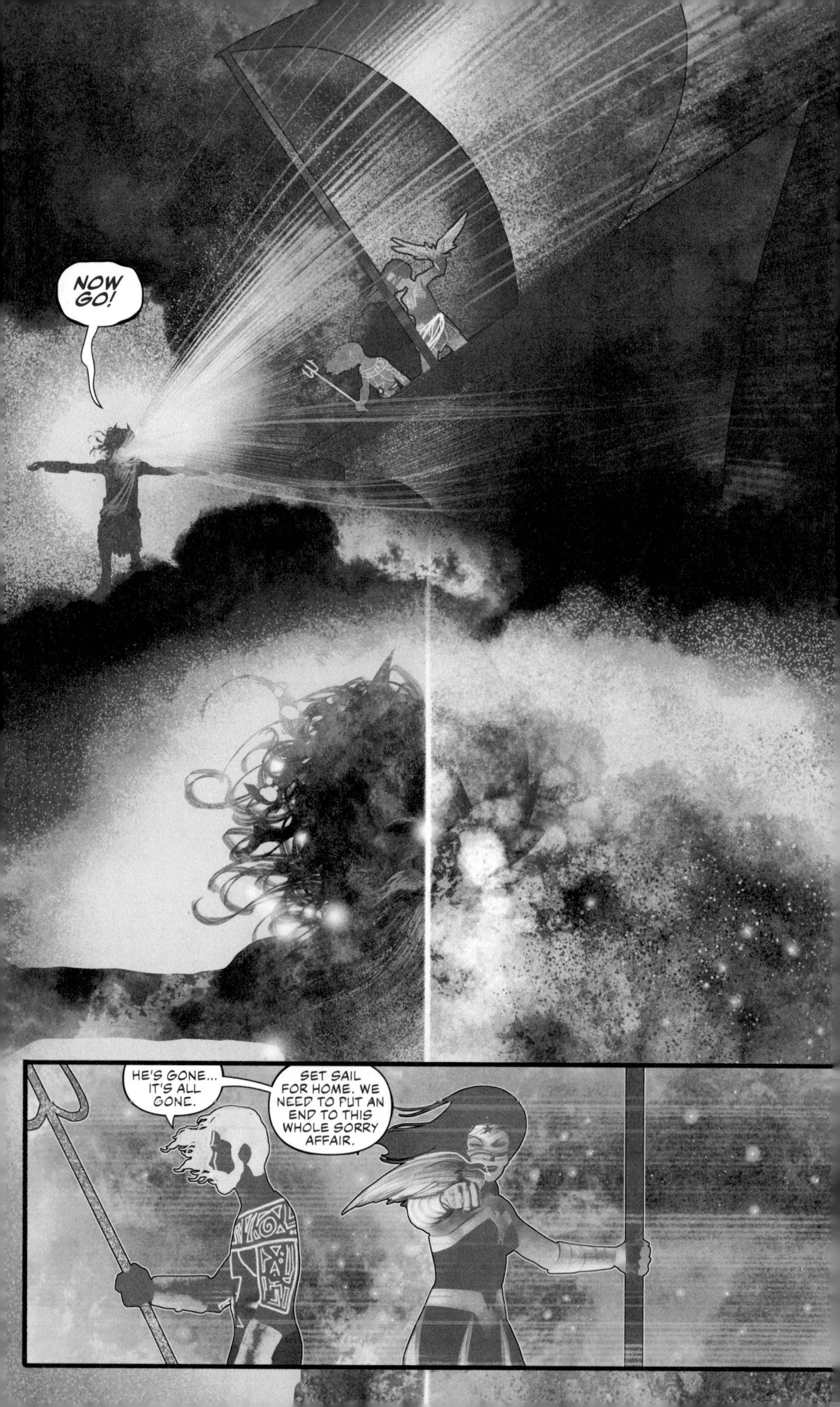
NOW GO!
HE'S GONE... IT'S ALL GONE.
SET SAIL FOR HOME. WE NEED TO PUT AN END TO THIS WHOLE SORRY AFFAIR.

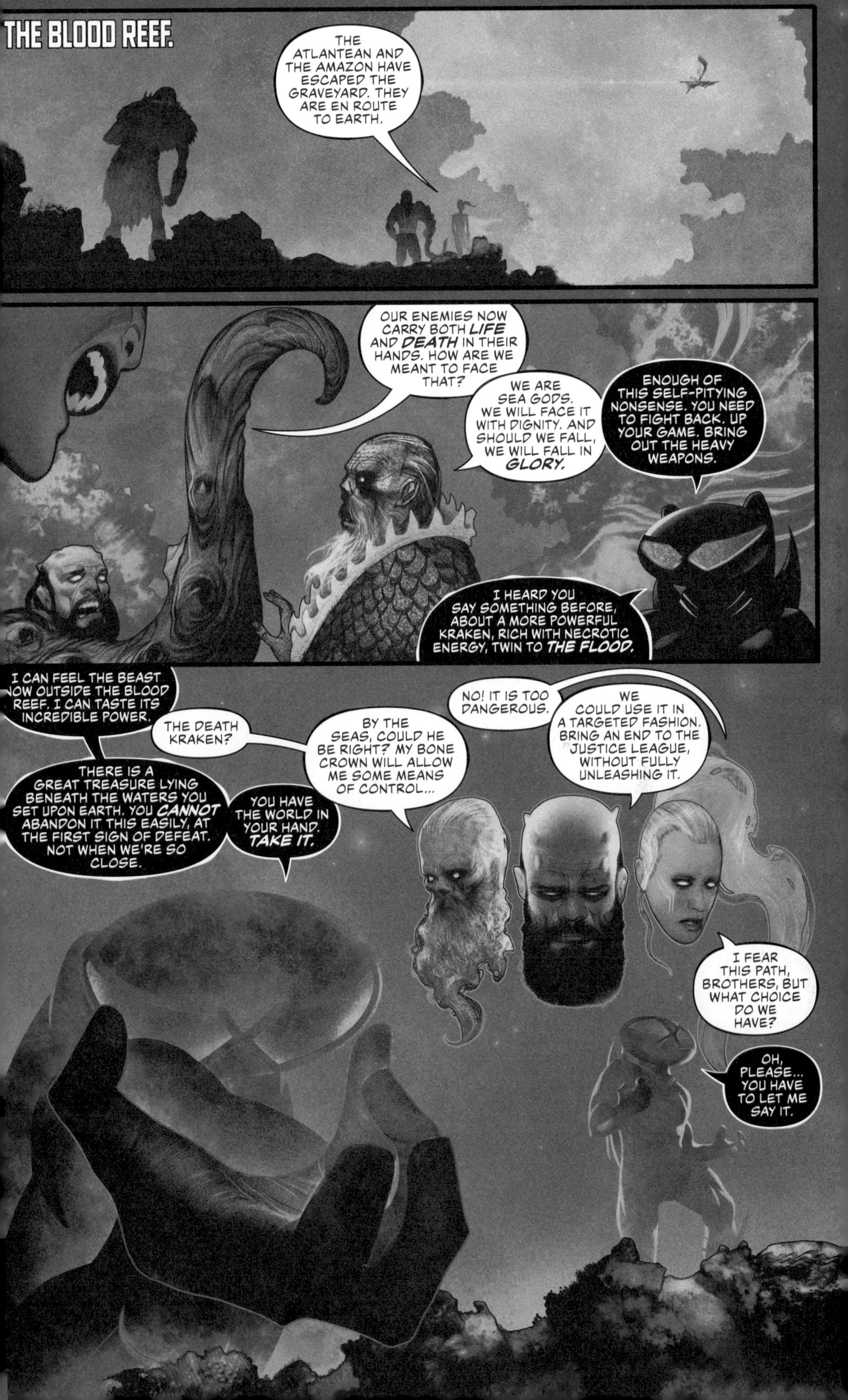
THE BLOOD REEF.
THE ATLANTEAN AND THE AMAZON HAVE ESCAPED THE GRAVEYARD. THEY ARE EN ROUTE TO EARTH.
OUR ENEMIES NOW CARRY BOTH LIFE AND DEATH IN THEIR HANDS. HOW ARE WE MEANT TO FACE THAT?
WE ARE SEA GODS. WE WILL FACE IT WITH DIGNITY. AND SHOULD WE FALL, WE WILL FALL IN GLORY.
ENOUGH OF THIS SELF-PITYING NONSENSE. YOU NEED TO FIGHT BACK. UP YOUR GAME. BRING OUT THE HEAVY WEAPONS.
I HEARD YOU SAY SOMETHING BEFORE, ABOUT A MORE POWERFUL KRAKEN, RICH WITH NECROTIC ENERGY, TWIN TO THE FLOOD.
I CAN FEEL THE BEAST NOW OUTSIDE THE BLOOD REEF. I CAN TASTE ITS INCREDIBLE POWER.
THE DEATH KRAKEN?
THERE IS A GREAT TREASURE LYING BENEATH THE WATERS YOU SET UPON EARTH. YOU CANNOT ABANDON IT THIS EASILY, AT THE FIRST SIGN OF DEFEAT. NOT WHEN WE'RE SO CLOSE.
YOU HAVE THE WORLD IN YOUR HAND. TAKE IT.
BY THE SEAS, COULD HE BE RIGHT? MY BONE CROWN WILL ALLOW ME SOME MEANS OF CONTROL...
NO! IT IS TOO DANGEROUS.
WE COULD USE IT IN A TARGETED FASHION. BRING AN END TO THE JUSTICE LEAGUE, WITHOUT FULLY UNLEASHING IT.
I FEAR THIS PATH, BROTHERS, BUT WHAT CHOICE DO WE HAVE?
OH, PLEASE... YOU HAVE TO LET ME SAY IT.

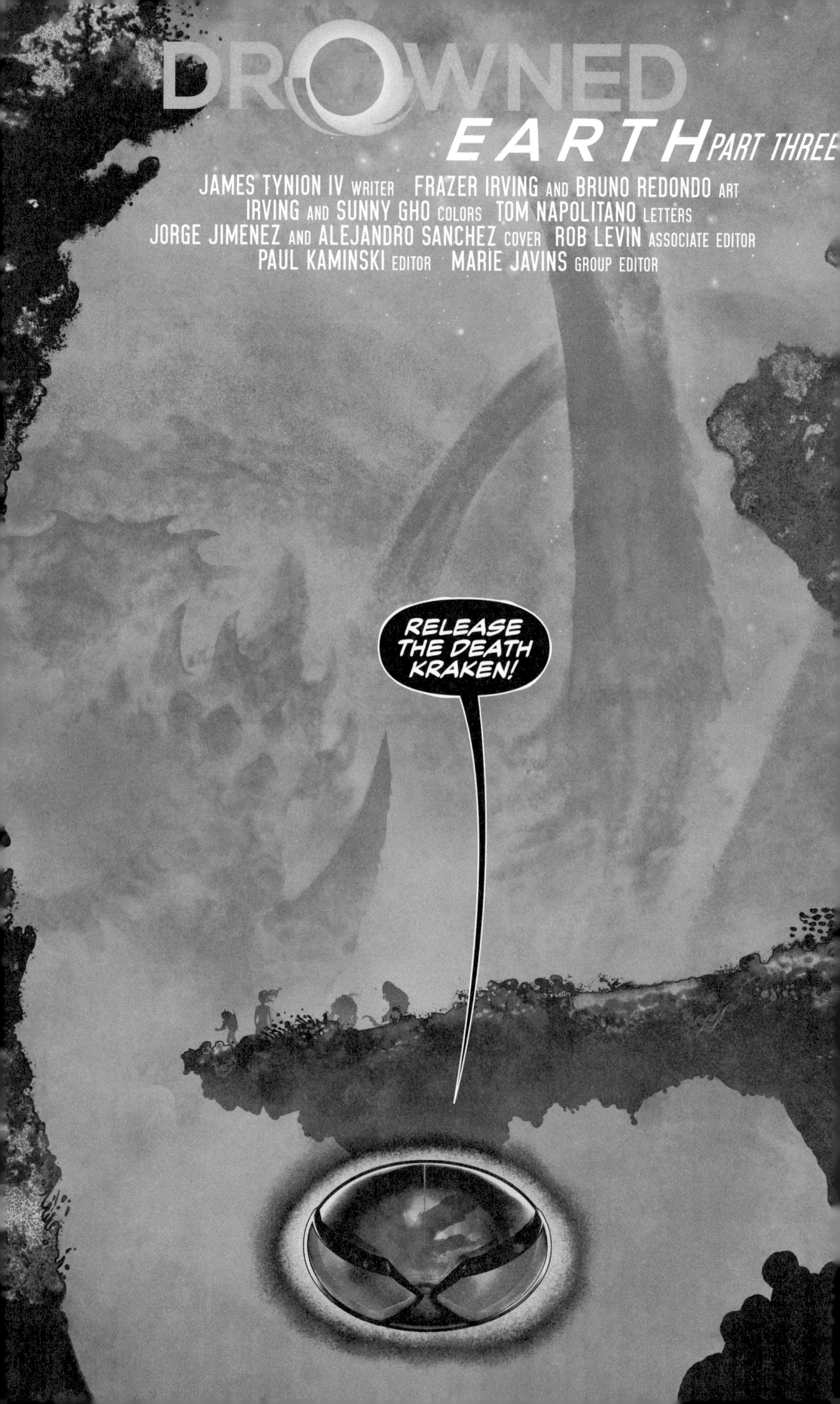
DROWNED
EARTH PART THREE
JAMES TYNION IV WRITER FRAZER IRVING AND BRUNO REDONDO ART
IRVING AND SUNNY GHO COLORS TOM NAPOLITANO LETTERS
JORGE JIMENEZ AND ALEJANDRO SANCHEZ COVER ROB LEVIN ASSOCIATE EDITOR
PAUL KAMINSKI EDITOR MARIE JAVINS GROUP EDITOR
RELEASE THE DEATH KRAKEN!

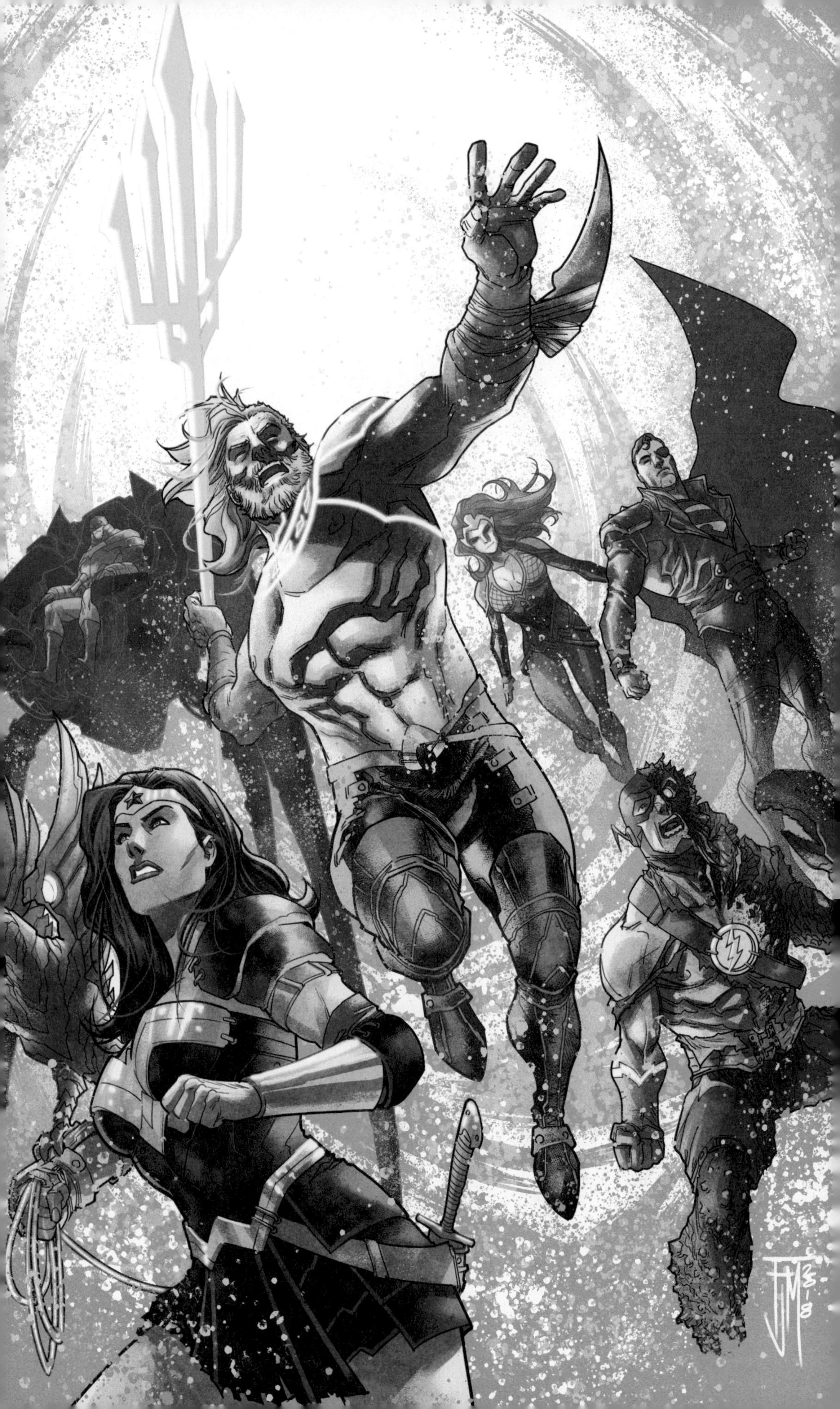

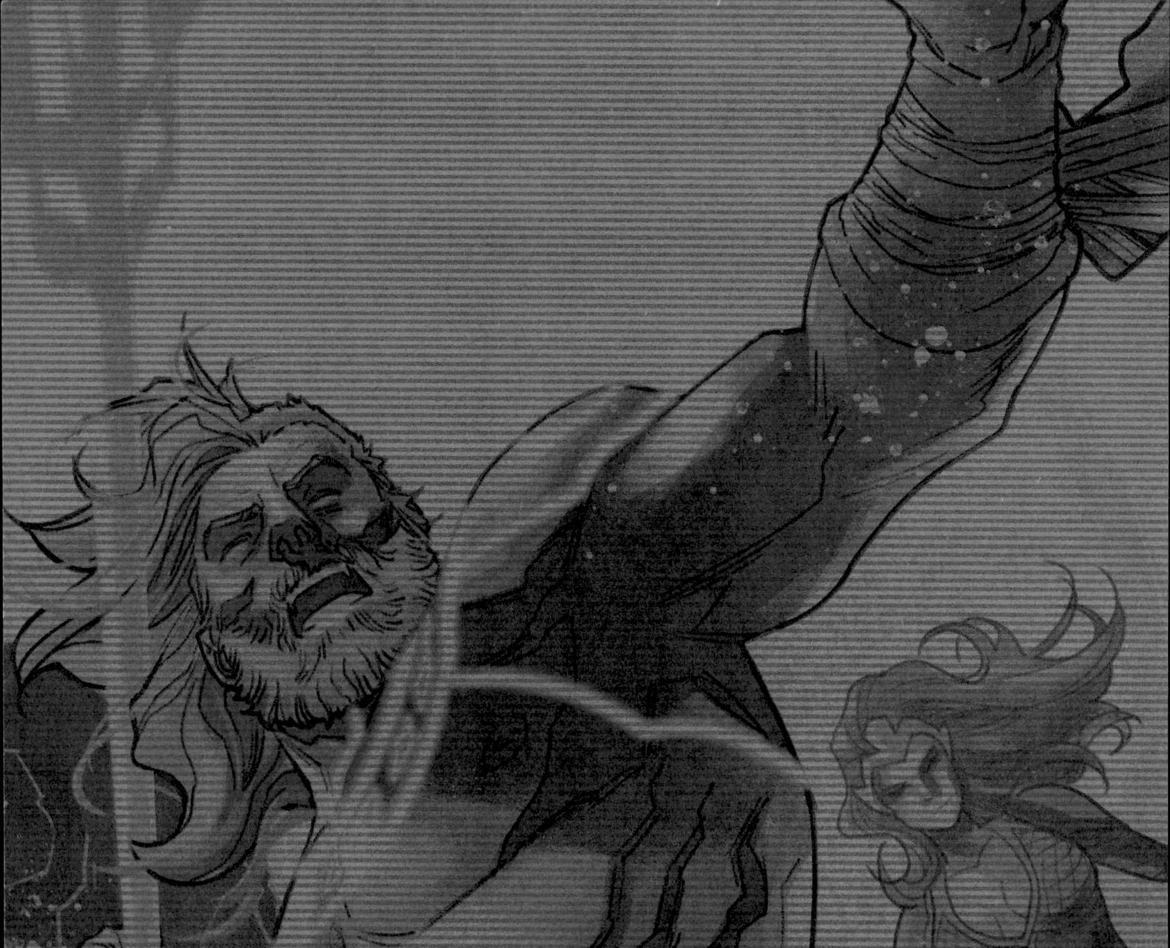

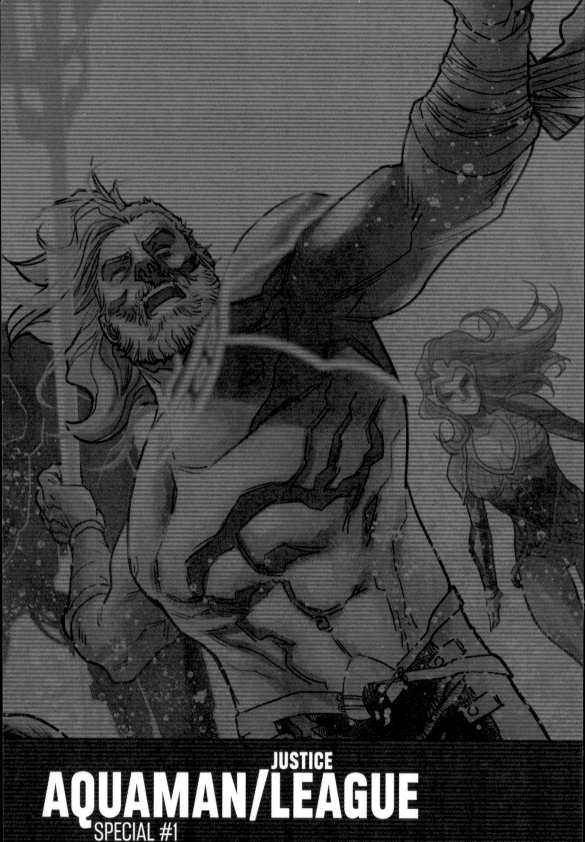

JUSTICE
AQUAMAN/LEAGUE
SPECIAL #1

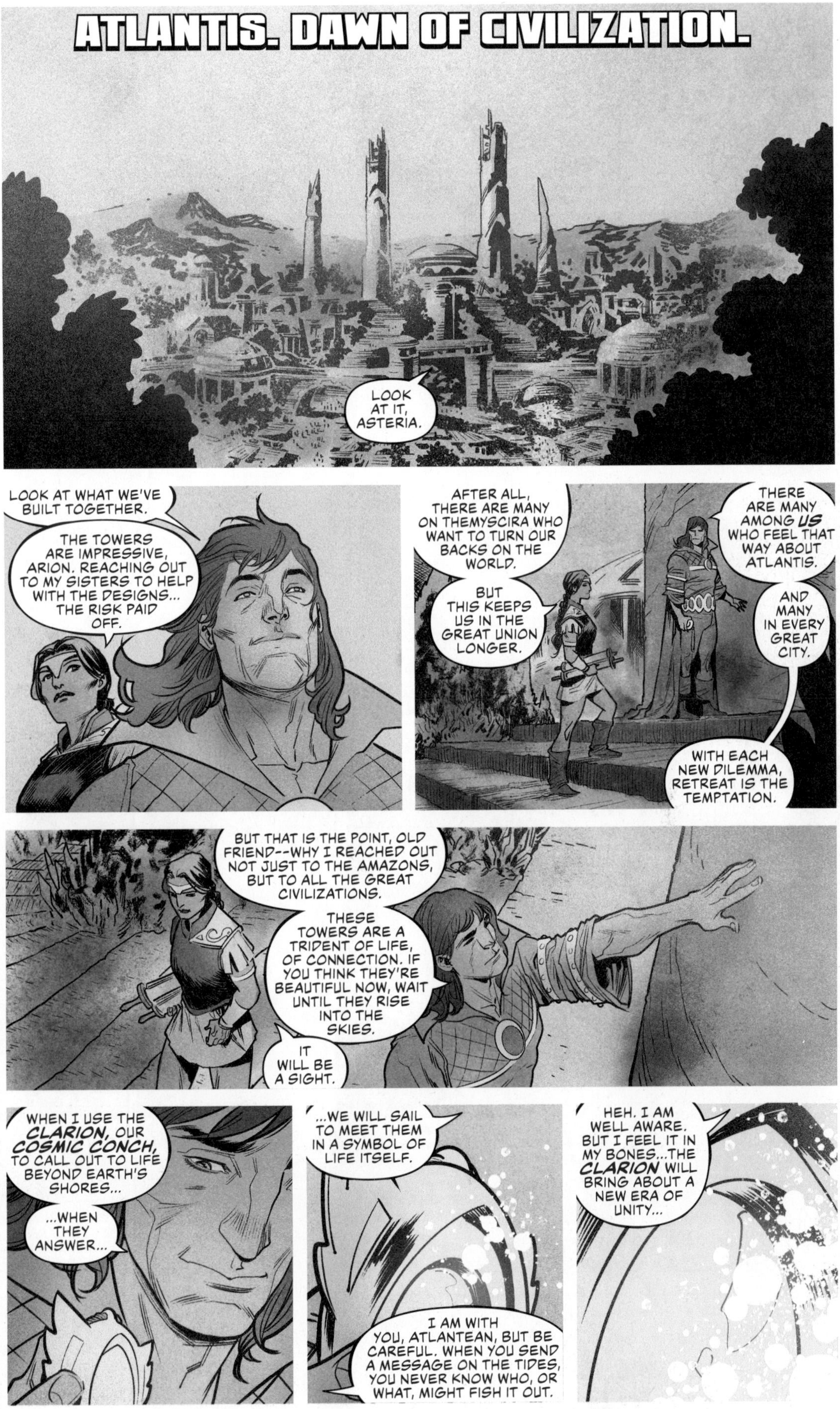
ATLANTIS. DAWN OF CIVILIZATION.
LOOK AT IT, ASTERIA.
LOOK AT WHAT WE'VE BUILT TOGETHER.
THE TOWERS ARE IMPRESSIVE, ARION. REACHING OUT TO MY SISTERS TO HELP WITH THE DESIGNS... THE RISK PAID OFF.
AFTER ALL, THERE ARE MANY ON THEMYSCIRA WHO WANT TO TURN OUR BACKS ON THE WORLD.
BUT THIS KEEPS US IN THE GREAT UNION LONGER.
THERE ARE MANY AMONG *US* WHO FEEL THAT WAY ABOUT ATLANTIS.
AND MANY IN EVERY GREAT CITY.
WITH EACH NEW DILEMMA, RETREAT IS THE TEMPTATION.
BUT THAT IS THE POINT, OLD FRIEND--WHY I REACHED OUT NOT JUST TO THE AMAZONS, BUT TO ALL THE GREAT CIVILIZATIONS.
THESE TOWERS ARE A TRIDENT OF LIFE, OF CONNECTION. IF YOU THINK THEY'RE BEAUTIFUL NOW, WAIT UNTIL THEY RISE INTO THE SKIES.
IT WILL BE A SIGHT.
WHEN I USE THE *CLARION,* OUR *COSMIC CONCH,* TO CALL OUT TO LIFE BEYOND EARTH'S SHORES...
...WHEN THEY ANSWER...
...WE WILL SAIL TO MEET THEM IN A SYMBOL OF LIFE ITSELF.
I AM WITH YOU, ATLANTEAN, BUT BE CAREFUL. WHEN YOU SEND A MESSAGE ON THE TIDES, YOU NEVER KNOW WHO, OR WHAT, MIGHT FISH IT OUT.
HEH. I AM WELL AWARE. BUT I FEEL IT IN MY BONES...THE *CLARION* WILL BRING ABOUT A NEW ERA OF UNITY...

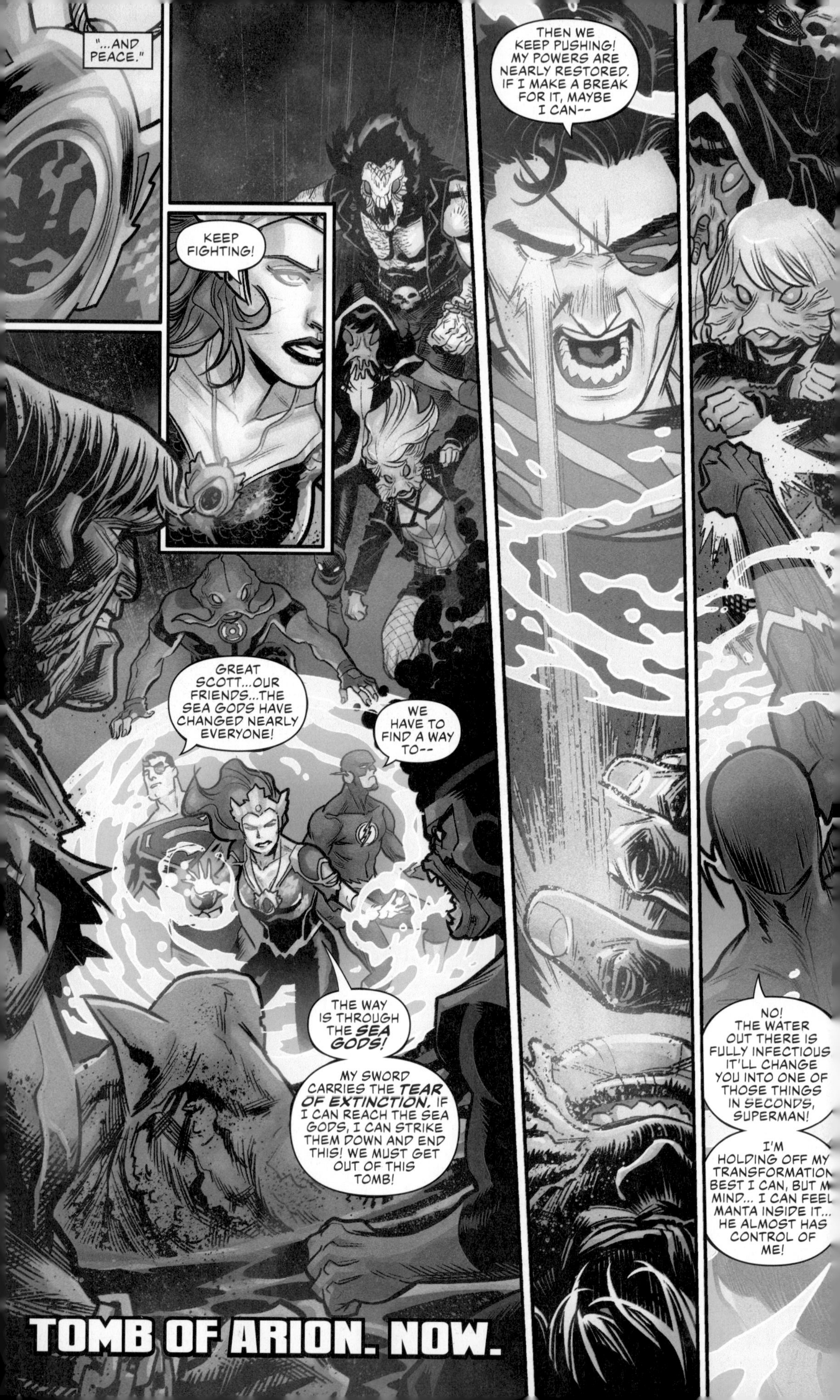
"...AND PEACE."
KEEP FIGHTING!
GREAT SCOTT...OUR FRIENDS...THE SEA GODS HAVE CHANGED NEARLY EVERYONE!
WE HAVE TO FIND A WAY TO--
THE WAY IS THROUGH THE SEA GODS!
MY SWORD CARRIES THE TEAR OF EXTINCTION. IF I CAN REACH THE SEA GODS, I CAN STRIKE THEM DOWN AND END THIS! WE MUST GET OUT OF THIS TOMB!
THEN WE KEEP PUSHING! MY POWERS ARE NEARLY RESTORED. IF I MAKE A BREAK FOR IT, MAYBE I CAN--
NO! THE WATER OUT THERE IS FULLY INFECTIOUS IT'LL CHANGE YOU INTO ONE OF THOSE THINGS IN SECONDS, SUPERMAN!
I'M HOLDING OFF MY TRANSFORMATION BEST I CAN, BUT M MIND... I CAN FEEL MANTA INSIDE IT... HE ALMOST HAS CONTROL OF ME!
TOMB OF ARION. NOW.

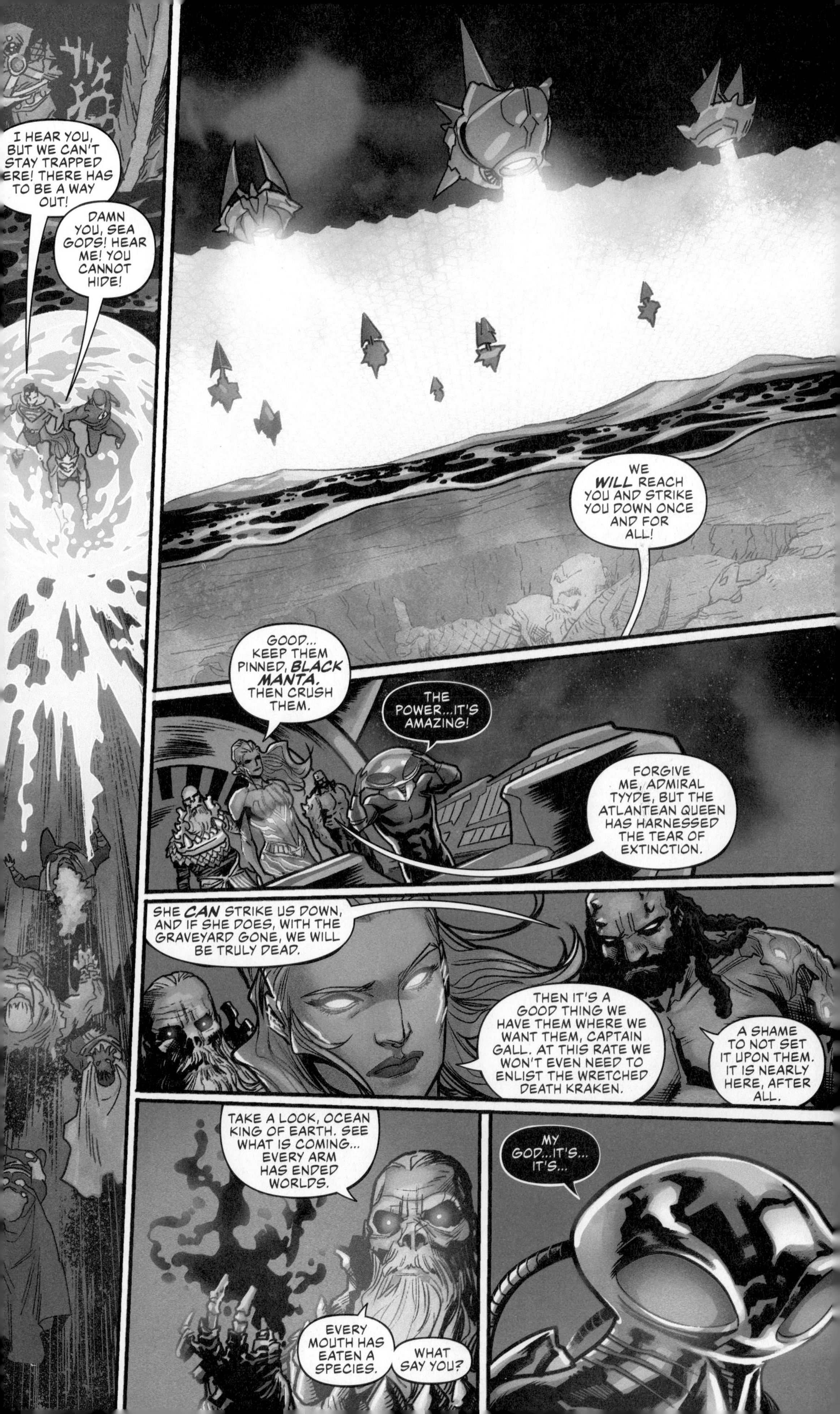
I HEAR YOU, BUT WE CAN'T STAY TRAPPED ERE! THERE HAS TO BE A WAY OUT!
DAMN YOU, SEA GODS! HEAR ME! YOU CANNOT HIDE!
WE WILL REACH YOU AND STRIKE YOU DOWN ONCE AND FOR ALL!
GOOD... KEEP THEM PINNED, BLACK MANTA. THEN CRUSH THEM.
THE POWER...IT'S AMAZING!
FORGIVE ME, ADMIRAL TYYDE, BUT THE ATLANTEAN QUEEN HAS HARNESSED THE TEAR OF EXTINCTION.
SHE CAN STRIKE US DOWN, AND IF SHE DOES, WITH THE GRAVEYARD GONE, WE WILL BE TRULY DEAD.
THEN IT'S A GOOD THING WE HAVE THEM WHERE WE WANT THEM, CAPTAIN GALL. AT THIS RATE WE WON'T EVEN NEED TO ENLIST THE WRETCHED DEATH KRAKEN.
A SHAME TO NOT SET IT UPON THEM. IT IS NEARLY HERE, AFTER ALL.
TAKE A LOOK, OCEAN KING OF EARTH. SEE WHAT IS COMING... EVERY ARM HAS ENDED WORLDS.
EVERY MOUTH HAS EATEN A SPECIES.
WHAT SAY YOU?
MY GOD...IT'S... IT'S...

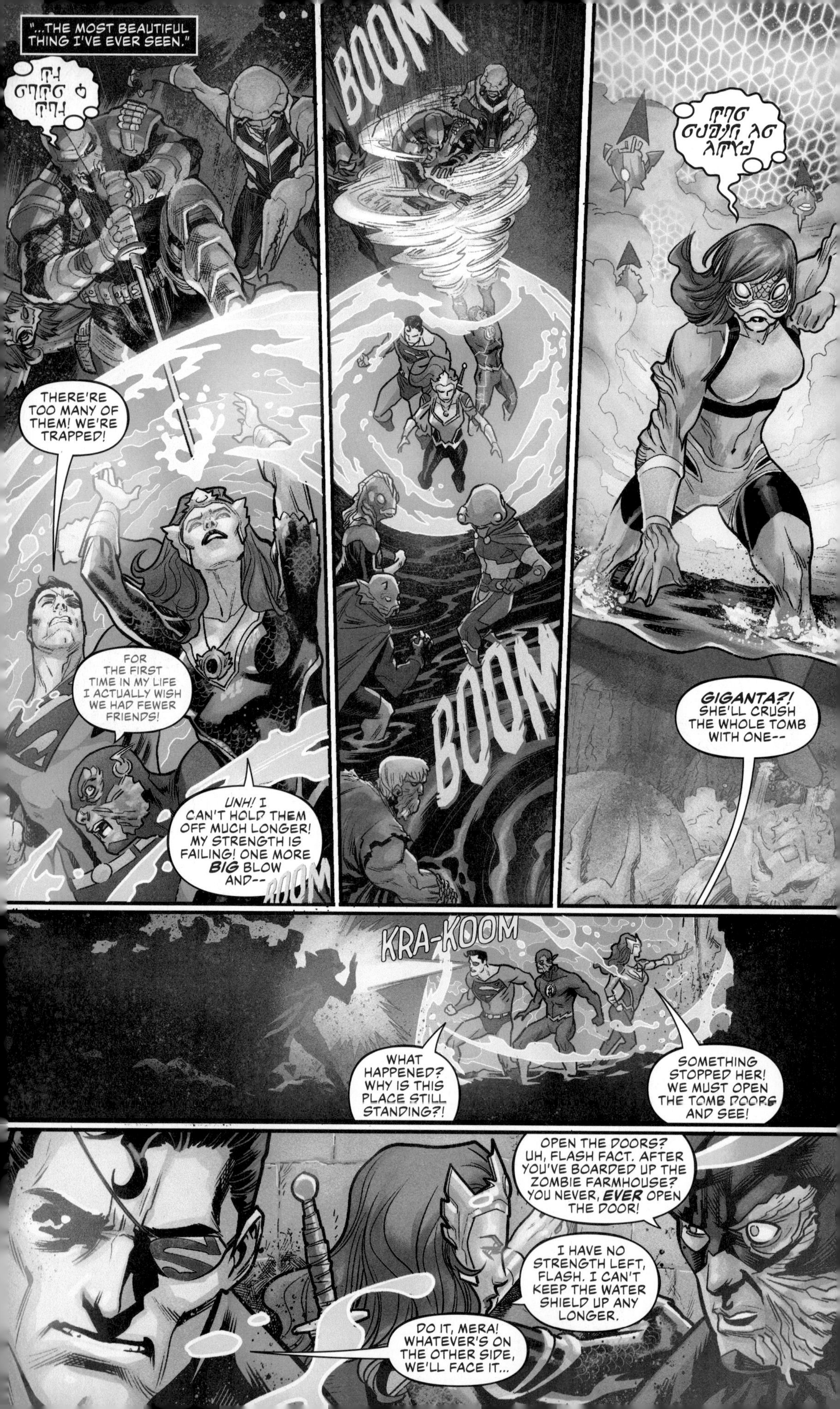

"...THE MOST BEAUTIFUL THING I'VE EVER SEEN."
THERE'RE TOO MANY OF THEM! WE'RE TRAPPED!
FOR THE FIRST TIME IN MY LIFE I ACTUALLY WISH WE HAD FEWER FRIENDS!
UNH! I CAN'T HOLD THEM OFF MUCH LONGER! MY STRENGTH IS FAILING! ONE MORE BIG BLOW AND--
BOOM
BOOM
BOOM
GIGANTA?! SHE'LL CRUSH THE WHOLE TOMB WITH ONE--
KRA-KOOM
WHAT HAPPENED? WHY IS THIS PLACE STILL STANDING?!
SOMETHING STOPPED HER! WE MUST OPEN THE TOMB DOORS AND SEE!
OPEN THE DOORS? UH, FLASH FACT. AFTER YOU'VE BOARDED UP THE ZOMBIE FARMHOUSE? YOU NEVER, EVER OPEN THE DOOR!
I HAVE NO STRENGTH LEFT, FLASH. I CAN'T KEEP THE WATER SHIELD UP ANY LONGER.
DO IT, MERA! WHATEVER'S ON THE OTHER SIDE, WE'LL FACE IT...

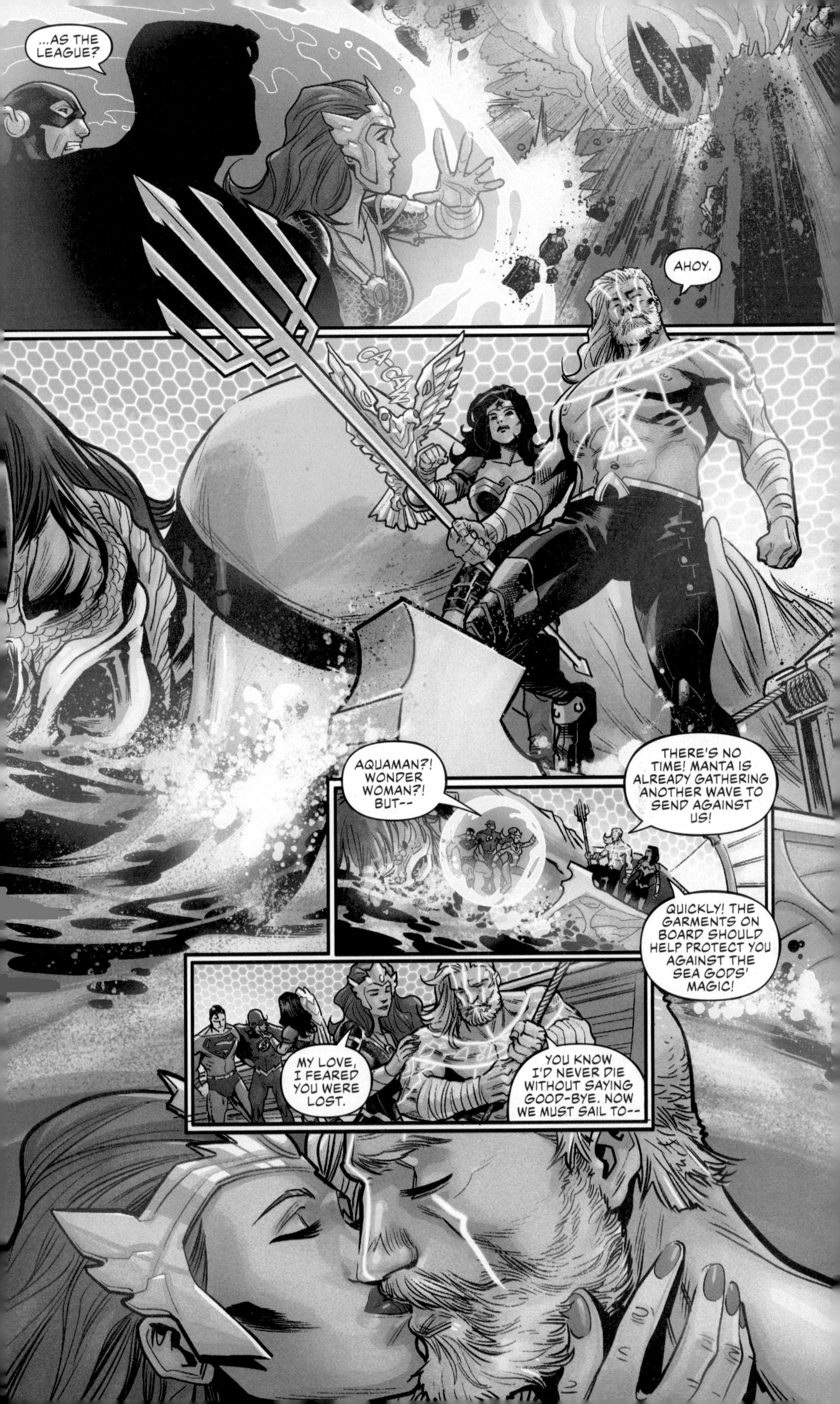
...AS THE LEAGUE?
AHOY.
CA-CAW
AQUAMAN?! WONDER WOMAN?! BUT--
THERE'S NO TIME! MANTA IS ALREADY GATHERING ANOTHER WAVE TO SEND AGAINST US!
QUICKLY! THE GARMENTS ON BOARD SHOULD HELP PROTECT YOU AGAINST THE SEA GODS' MAGIC!
MY LOVE, I FEARED YOU WERE LOST.
YOU KNOW I'D NEVER DIE WITHOUT SAYING GOOD-BYE. NOW WE MUST SAIL TO--

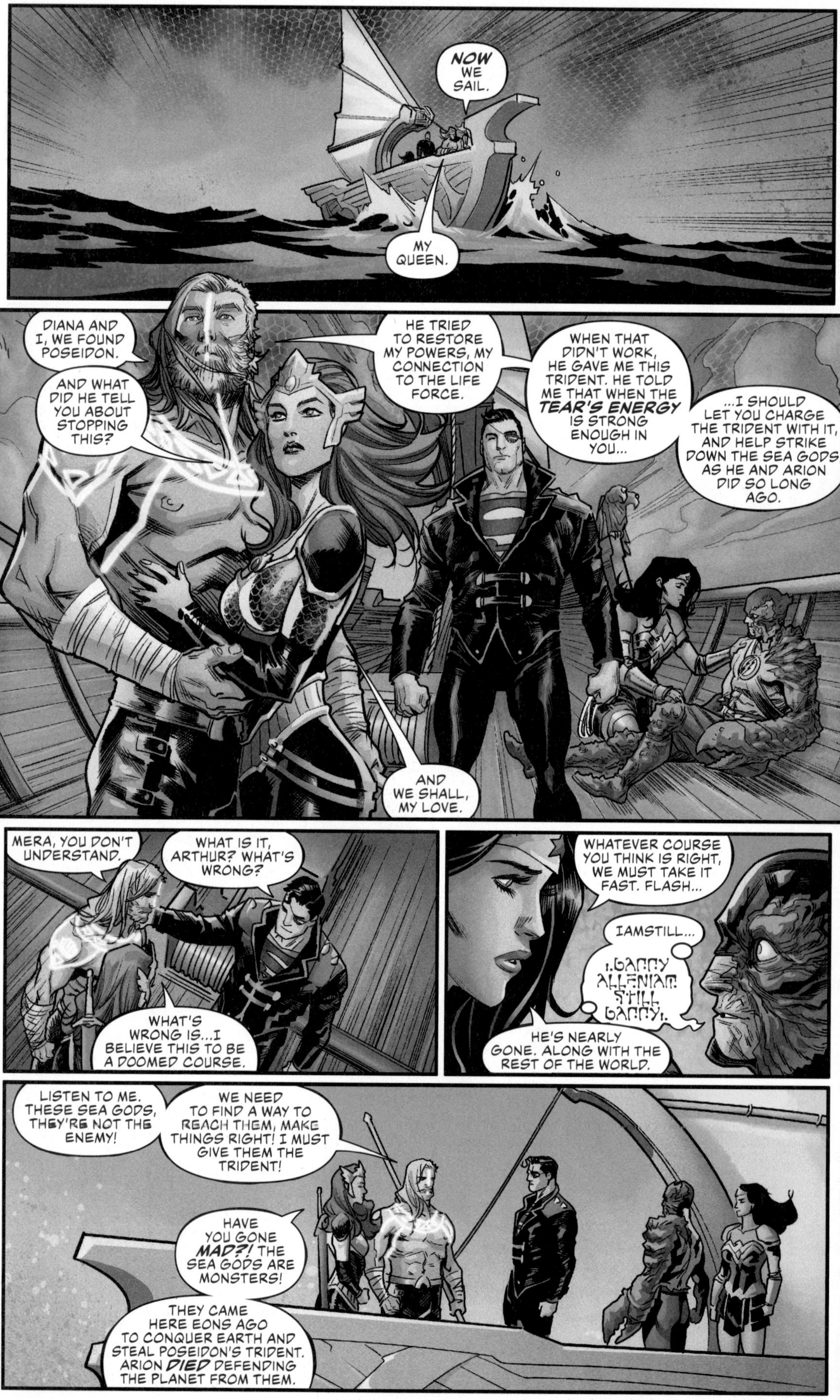
NOW WE SAIL.
MY QUEEN.
DIANA AND I, WE FOUND POSEIDON.
AND WHAT DID HE TELL YOU ABOUT STOPPING THIS?
HE TRIED TO RESTORE MY POWERS, MY CONNECTION TO THE LIFE FORCE.
WHEN THAT DIDN'T WORK, HE GAVE ME THIS TRIDENT. HE TOLD ME THAT WHEN THE TEAR'S ENERGY IS STRONG ENOUGH IN YOU...
...I SHOULD LET YOU CHARGE THE TRIDENT WITH IT, AND HELP STRIKE DOWN THE SEA GODS, AS HE AND ARION DID SO LONG AGO.
AND WE SHALL, MY LOVE.
MERA, YOU DON'T UNDERSTAND.
WHAT IS IT, ARTHUR? WHAT'S WRONG?
WHAT'S WRONG IS...I BELIEVE THIS TO BE A DOOMED COURSE.
WHATEVER COURSE YOU THINK IS RIGHT, WE MUST TAKE IT FAST. FLASH...
IAMSTILL...
I. BARRY ALLENIAM STILL BARRY!.
HE'S NEARLY GONE. ALONG WITH THE REST OF THE WORLD.
LISTEN TO ME. THESE SEA GODS, THEY'RE NOT THE ENEMY!
WE NEED TO FIND A WAY TO REACH THEM, MAKE THINGS RIGHT! I MUST GIVE THEM THE TRIDENT!
HAVE YOU GONE MAD?! THE SEA GODS ARE MONSTERS!
THEY CAME HERE EONS AGO TO CONQUER EARTH AND STEAL POSEIDON'S TRIDENT. ARION DIED DEFENDING THE PLANET FROM THEM.

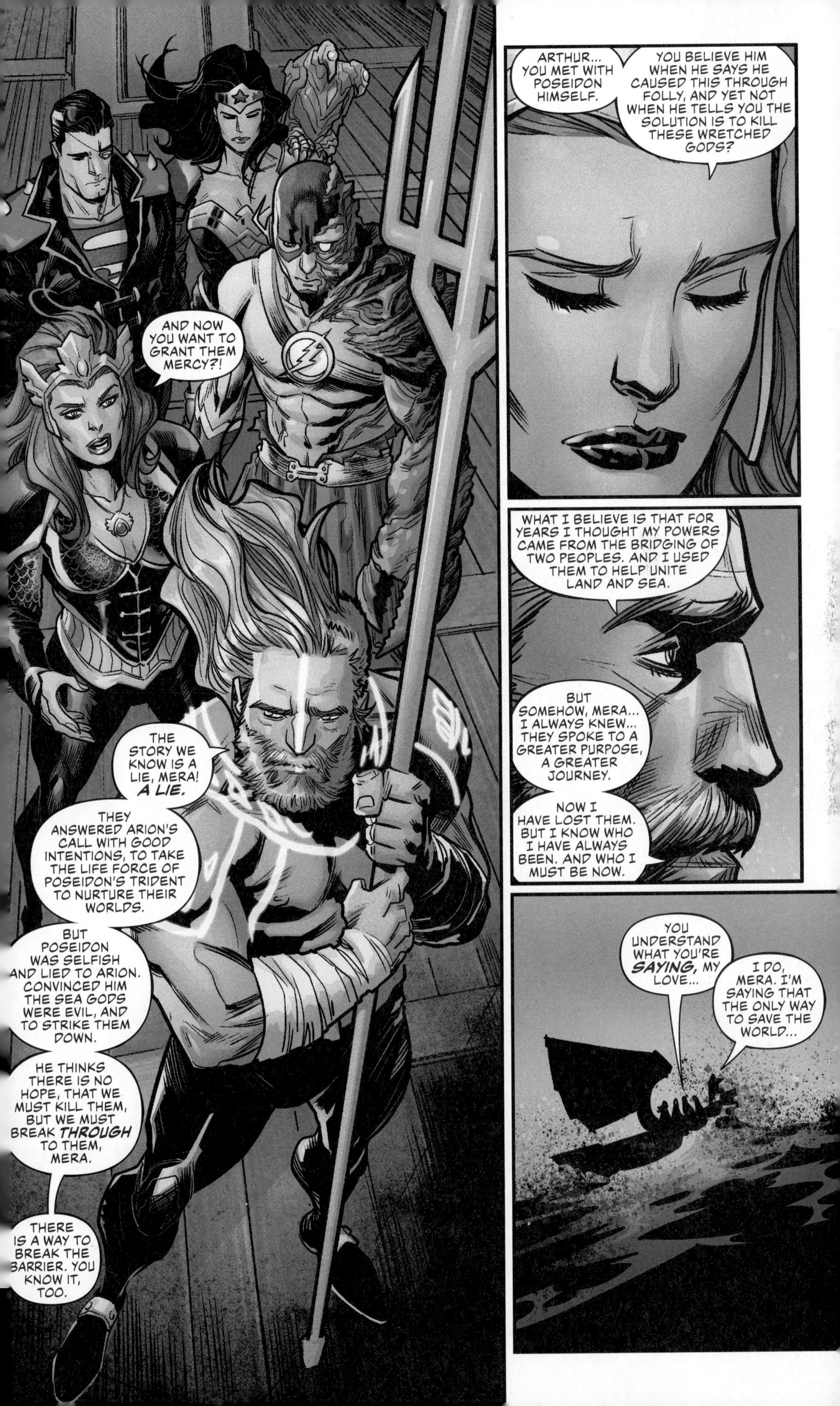
AND NOW YOU WANT TO GRANT THEM MERCY?!
THE STORY WE KNOW IS A LIE, MERA! *A LIE.*
THEY ANSWERED ARION'S CALL WITH GOOD INTENTIONS, TO TAKE THE LIFE FORCE OF POSEIDON'S TRIDENT TO NURTURE THEIR WORLDS.
BUT POSEIDON WAS SELFISH AND LIED TO ARION. CONVINCED HIM THE SEA GODS WERE EVIL, AND TO STRIKE THEM DOWN.
HE THINKS THERE IS NO HOPE, THAT WE MUST KILL THEM, BUT WE MUST BREAK *THROUGH* TO THEM, MERA.
THERE IS A WAY TO BREAK THE BARRIER. YOU KNOW IT, TOO.
ARTHUR... YOU MET WITH POSEIDON HIMSELF.
YOU BELIEVE HIM WHEN HE SAYS HE CAUSED THIS THROUGH FOLLY, AND YET NOT WHEN HE TELLS YOU THE SOLUTION IS TO KILL THESE WRETCHED GODS?
WHAT I BELIEVE IS THAT FOR YEARS I THOUGHT MY POWERS CAME FROM THE BRIDGING OF TWO PEOPLES. AND I USED THEM TO HELP UNITE LAND AND SEA.
BUT SOMEHOW, MERA... I ALWAYS KNEW... THEY SPOKE TO A GREATER PURPOSE, A GREATER JOURNEY.
NOW I HAVE LOST THEM. BUT I KNOW WHO I HAVE ALWAYS BEEN. AND WHO I MUST BE NOW.
YOU UNDERSTAND WHAT YOU'RE *SAYING,* MY LOVE...
I DO, MERA. I'M SAYING THAT THE ONLY WAY TO SAVE THE WORLD...

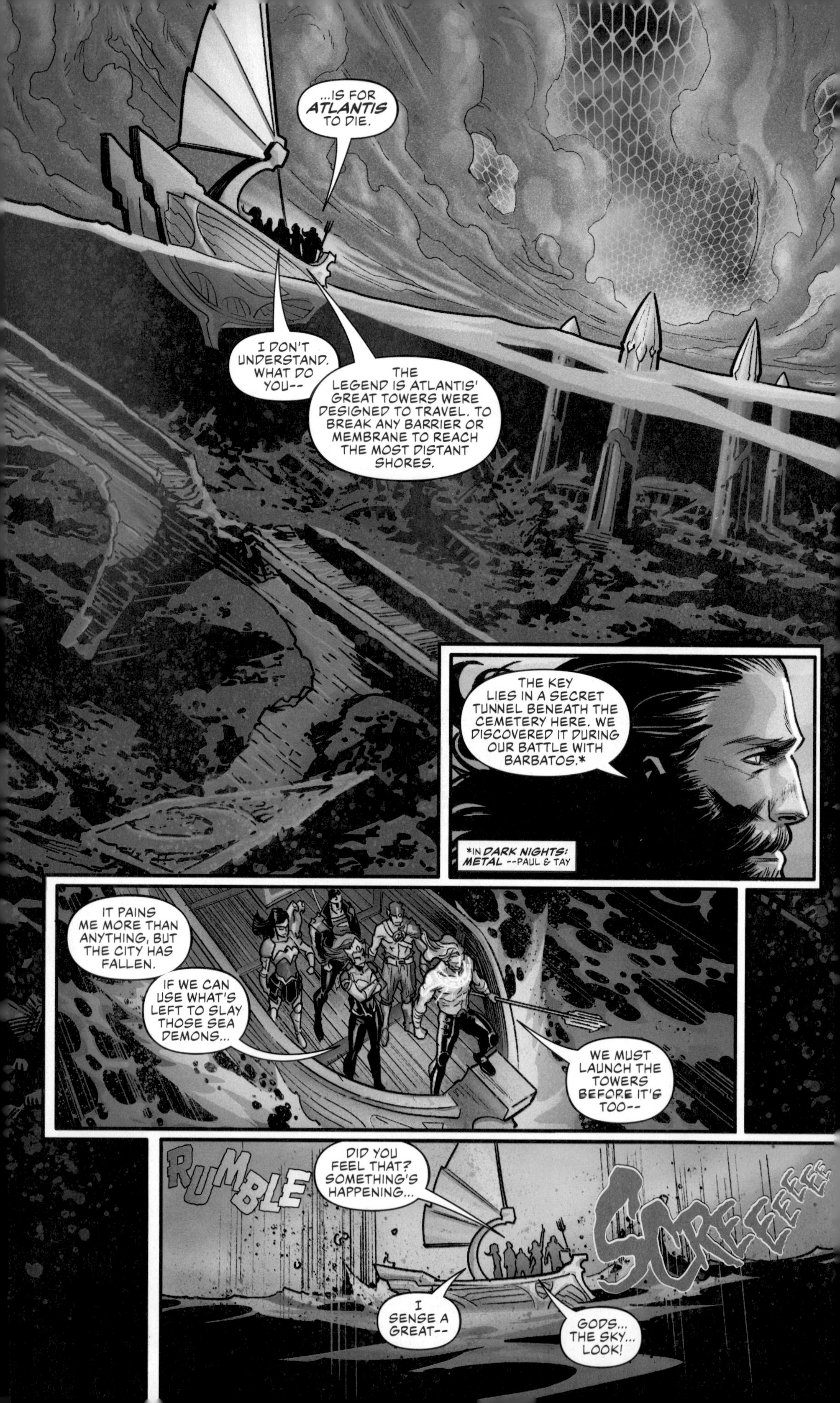
...IS FOR ATLANTIS TO DIE.
I DON'T UNDERSTAND. WHAT DO YOU--
THE LEGEND IS ATLANTIS' GREAT TOWERS WERE DESIGNED TO TRAVEL. TO BREAK ANY BARRIER OR MEMBRANE TO REACH THE MOST DISTANT SHORES.
THE KEY LIES IN A SECRET TUNNEL BENEATH THE CEMETERY HERE. WE DISCOVERED IT DURING OUR BATTLE WITH BARBATOS.*
*IN DARK NIGHTS: METAL --PAUL & TAY
IT PAINS ME MORE THAN ANYTHING, BUT THE CITY HAS FALLEN.
IF WE CAN USE WHAT'S LEFT TO SLAY THOSE SEA DEMONS...
WE MUST LAUNCH THE TOWERS BEFORE IT'S TOO--
RUMBLE
DID YOU FEEL THAT? SOMETHING'S HAPPENING...
SCREEEEEE
I SENSE A GREAT--
GODS... THE SKY... LOOK!

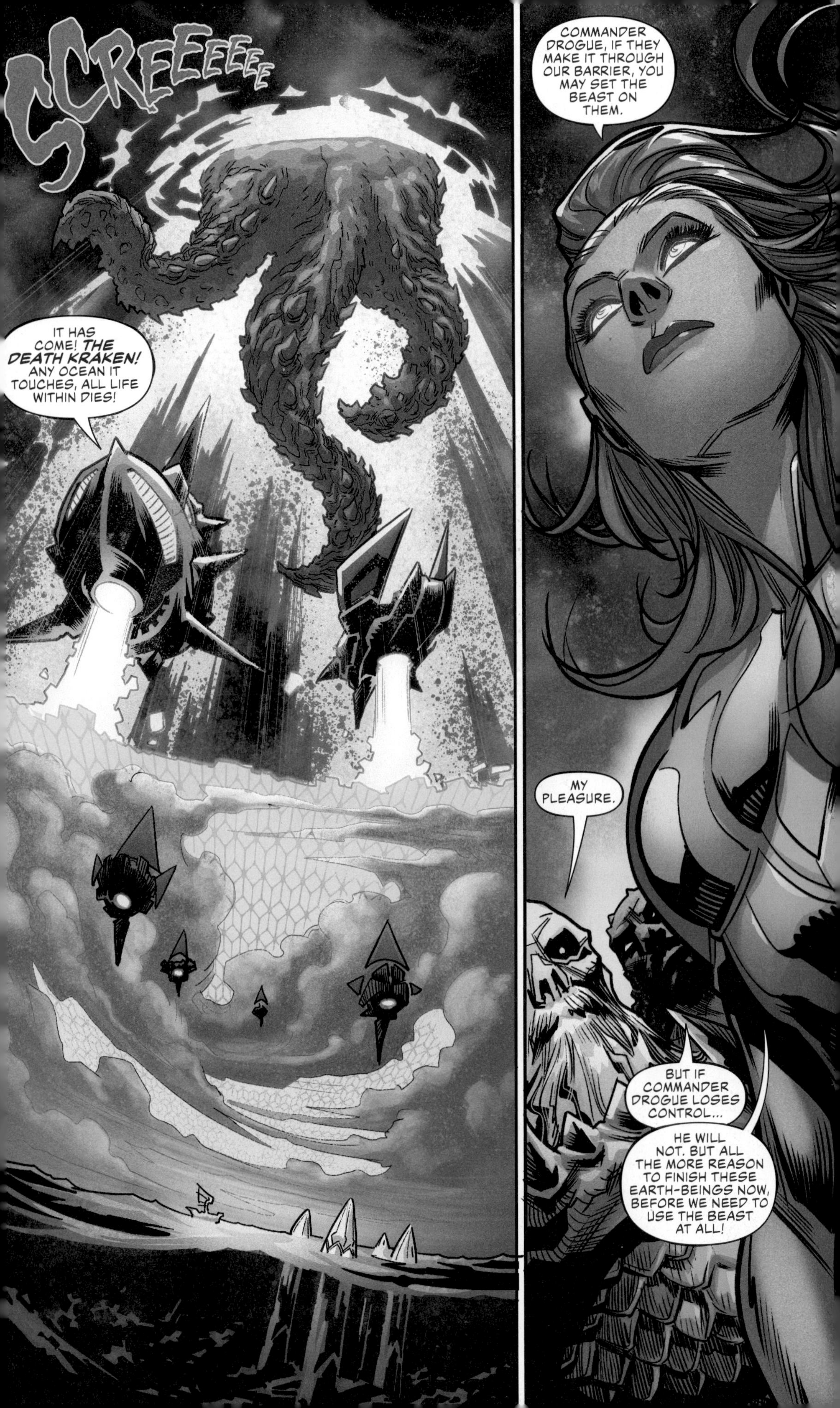
SCREEEEEE
IT HAS COME! THE DEATH KRAKEN! ANY OCEAN IT TOUCHES, ALL LIFE WITHIN DIES!
COMMANDER DROGUE, IF THEY MAKE IT THROUGH OUR BARRIER, YOU MAY SET THE BEAST ON THEM.
MY PLEASURE.
BUT IF COMMANDER DROGUE LOSES CONTROL...
HE WILL NOT. BUT ALL THE MORE REASON TO FINISH THESE EARTH-BEINGS NOW, BEFORE WE NEED TO USE THE BEAST AT ALL!

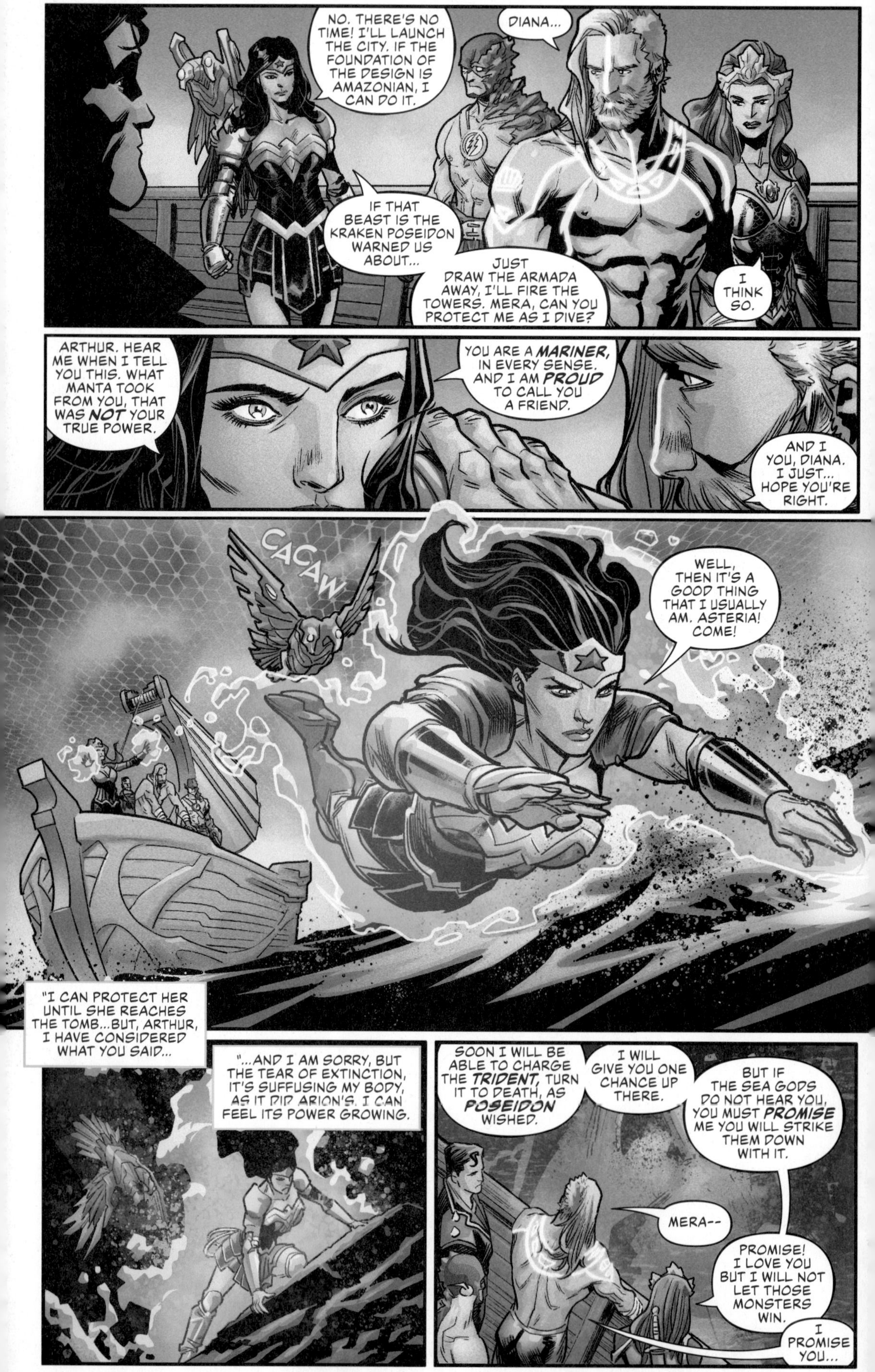

NO. THERE'S NO TIME! I'LL LAUNCH THE CITY. IF THE FOUNDATION OF THE DESIGN IS AMAZONIAN, I CAN DO IT.
DIANA...
IF THAT BEAST IS THE KRAKEN POSEIDON WARNED US ABOUT...
JUST DRAW THE ARMADA AWAY, I'LL FIRE THE TOWERS. MERA, CAN YOU PROTECT ME AS I DIVE?
I THINK SO.
ARTHUR. HEAR ME WHEN I TELL YOU THIS. WHAT MANTA TOOK FROM YOU, THAT WAS NOT YOUR TRUE POWER.
YOU ARE A MARINER, IN EVERY SENSE. AND I AM PROUD TO CALL YOU A FRIEND.
AND I YOU, DIANA. I JUST... HOPE YOU'RE RIGHT.
CACAW
WELL, THEN IT'S A GOOD THING THAT I USUALLY AM. ASTERIA! COME!
"I CAN PROTECT HER UNTIL SHE REACHES THE TOMB...BUT, ARTHUR, I HAVE CONSIDERED WHAT YOU SAID...
"...AND I AM SORRY, BUT THE TEAR OF EXTINCTION, IT'S SUFFUSING MY BODY, AS IT DID ARION'S. I CAN FEEL ITS POWER GROWING.
SOON I WILL BE ABLE TO CHARGE THE TRIDENT, TURN IT TO DEATH, AS POSEIDON WISHED.
I WILL GIVE YOU ONE CHANCE UP THERE.
BUT IF THE SEA GODS DO NOT HEAR YOU, YOU MUST PROMISE ME YOU WILL STRIKE THEM DOWN WITH IT.
MERA--
PROMISE! I LOVE YOU BUT I WILL NOT LET THOSE MONSTERS WIN.
I PROMISE YOU...

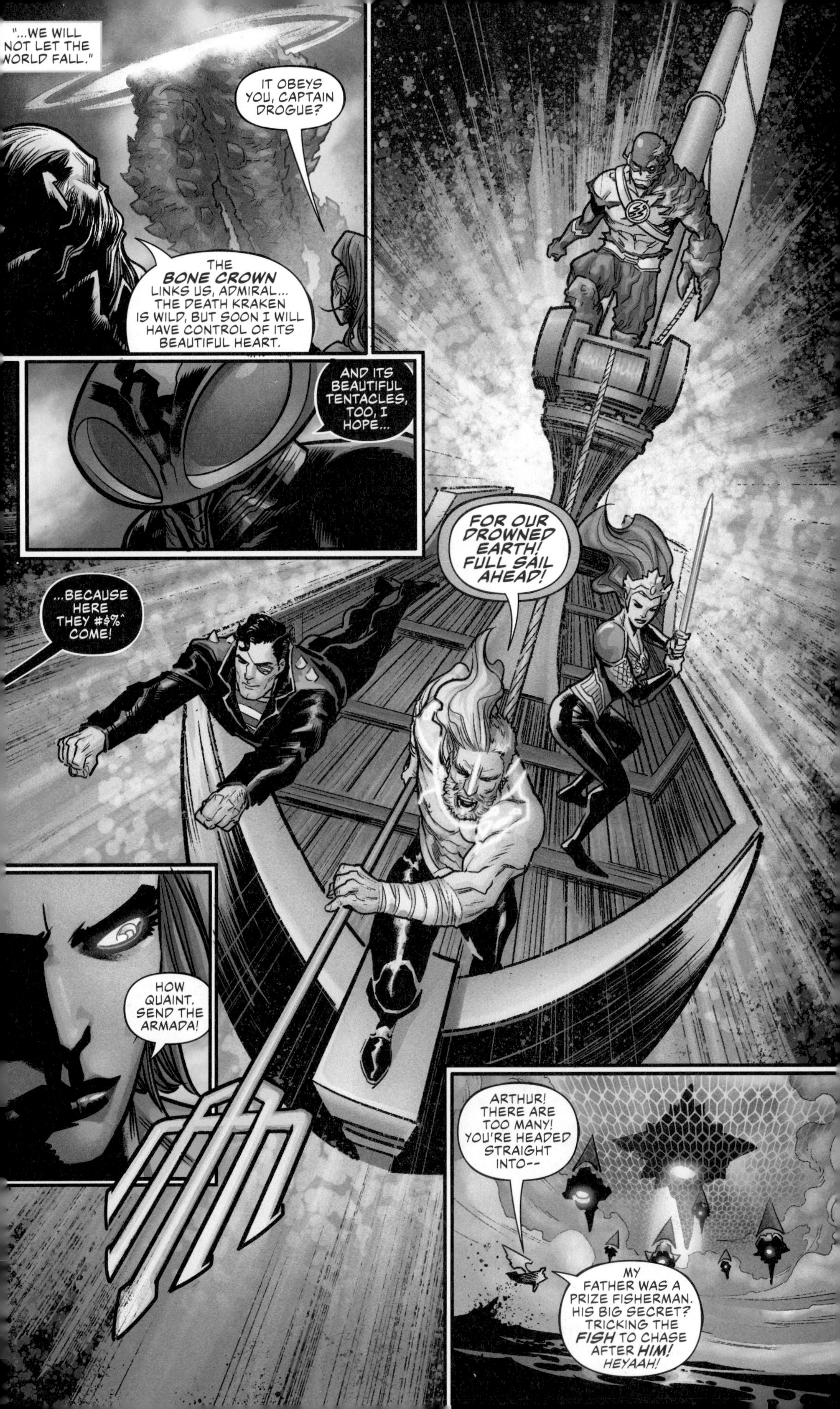
"...WE WILL NOT LET THE WORLD FALL."
IT OBEYS YOU, CAPTAIN DROGUE?
THE BONE CROWN LINKS US, ADMIRAL... THE DEATH KRAKEN IS WILD, BUT SOON I WILL HAVE CONTROL OF ITS BEAUTIFUL HEART.
AND ITS BEAUTIFUL TENTACLES, TOO, I HOPE...
...BECAUSE HERE THEY #$%^ COME!
FOR OUR DROWNED EARTH! FULL SAIL AHEAD!
HOW QUAINT. SEND THE ARMADA!
ARTHUR! THERE ARE TOO MANY! YOU'RE HEADED STRAIGHT INTO--
MY FATHER WAS A PRIZE FISHERMAN. HIS BIG SECRET? TRICKING THE FISH TO CHASE AFTER HIM! HEYAAH!

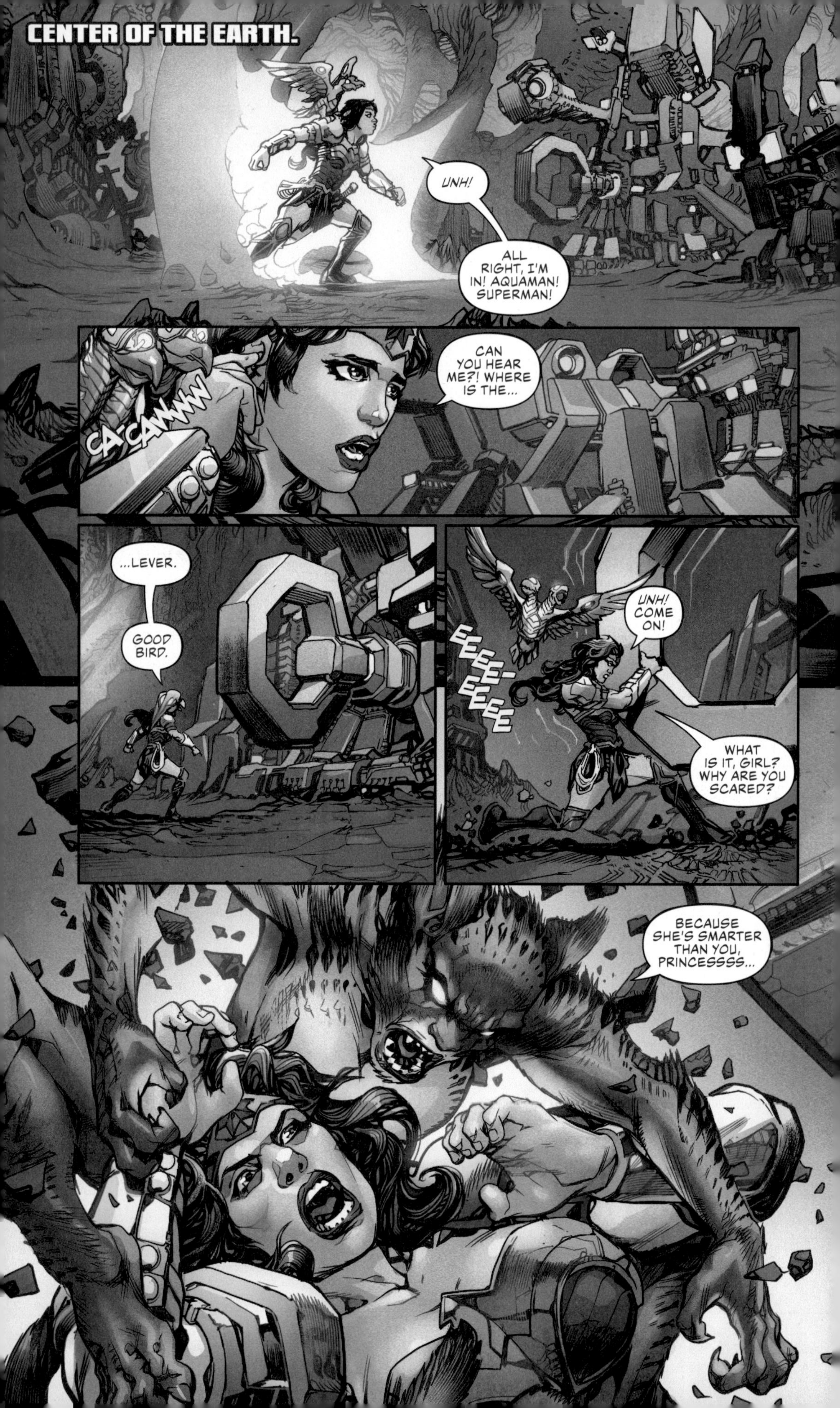

CENTER OF THE EARTH.
UNH!
ALL RIGHT, I'M IN! AQUAMAN! SUPERMAN!
CA-CAWWW
CAN YOU HEAR ME?! WHERE IS THE...
...LEVER.
GOOD BIRD.
EEEE-EEEE
UNH! COME ON!
WHAT IS IT, GIRL? WHY ARE YOU SCARED?
BECAUSE SHE'S SMARTER THAN YOU, PRINCESSSS...

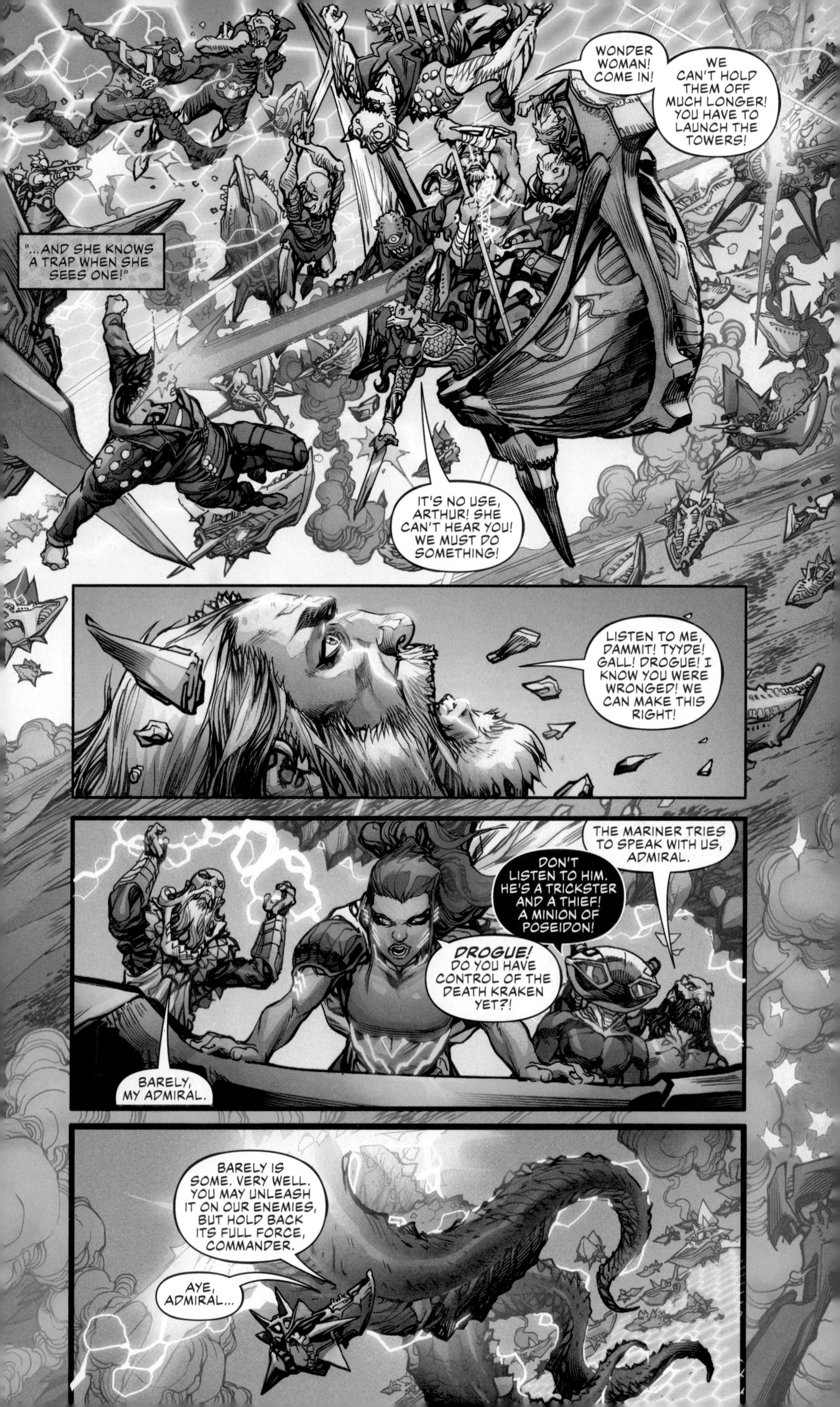
WONDER WOMAN! COME IN!
WE CAN'T HOLD THEM OFF MUCH LONGER! YOU HAVE TO LAUNCH THE TOWERS!
"...AND SHE KNOWS A TRAP WHEN SHE SEES ONE!"
IT'S NO USE, ARTHUR! SHE CAN'T HEAR YOU! WE MUST DO SOMETHING!
LISTEN TO ME, DAMMIT! TYYDE! GALL! DROGUE! I KNOW YOU WERE WRONGED! WE CAN MAKE THIS RIGHT!
THE MARINER TRIES TO SPEAK WITH US, ADMIRAL.
DON'T LISTEN TO HIM. HE'S A TRICKSTER AND A THIEF! A MINION OF POSEIDON!
DROGUE! DO YOU HAVE CONTROL OF THE DEATH KRAKEN YET?!
BARELY, MY ADMIRAL.
BARELY IS SOME. VERY WELL. YOU MAY UNLEASH IT ON OUR ENEMIES, BUT HOLD BACK ITS FULL FORCE, COMMANDER.
AYE, ADMIRAL...

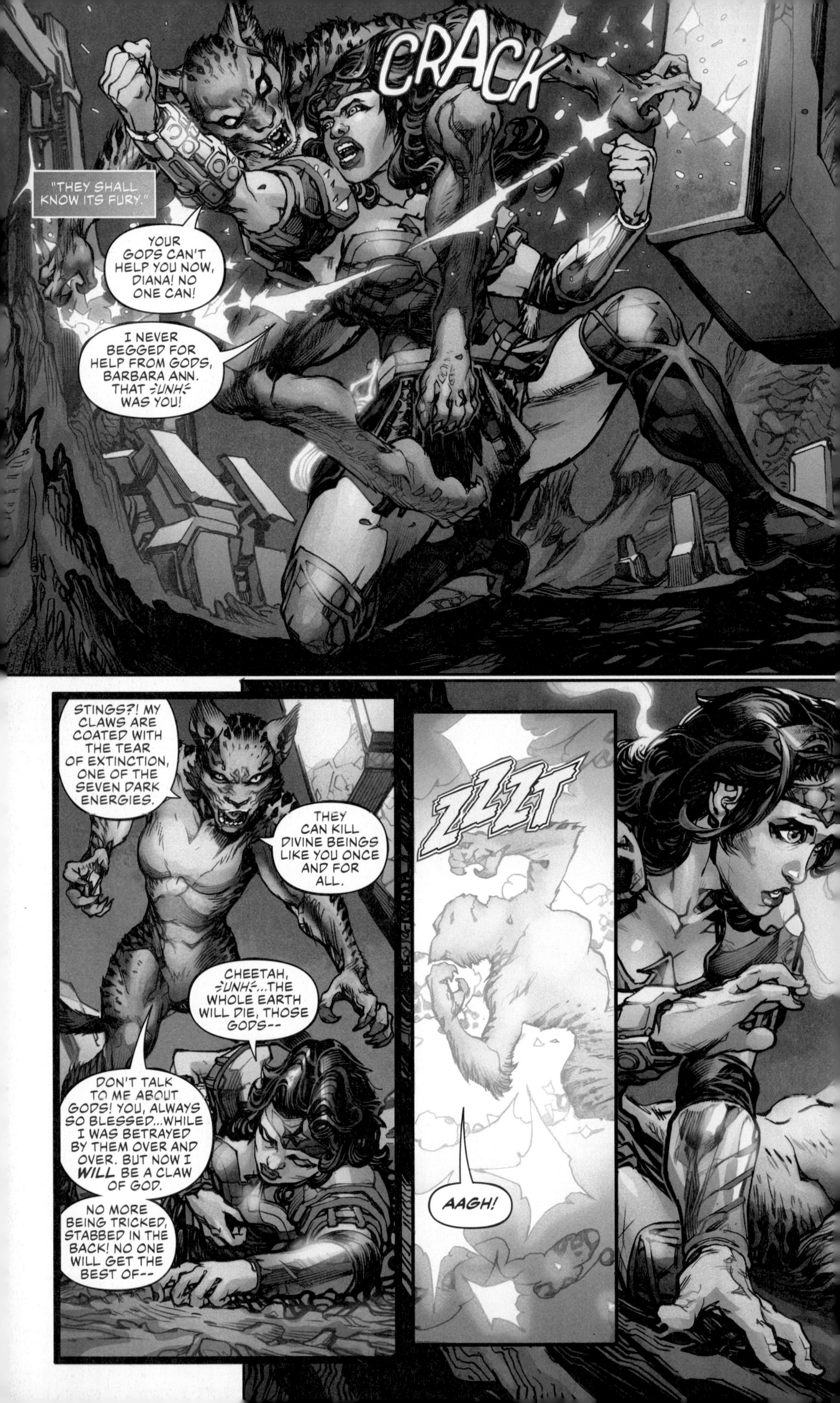
CRACK
"THEY SHALL KNOW ITS FURY."
YOUR GODS CAN'T HELP YOU NOW, DIANA! NO ONE CAN!
I NEVER BEGGED FOR HELP FROM GODS, BARBARA ANN. THAT =UNH= WAS YOU!
STINGS?! MY CLAWS ARE COATED WITH THE TEAR OF EXTINCTION, ONE OF THE SEVEN DARK ENERGIES.
THEY CAN KILL DIVINE BEINGS LIKE YOU ONCE AND FOR ALL.
CHEETAH, =UNH=...THE WHOLE EARTH WILL DIE, THOSE GODS--
DON'T TALK TO ME ABOUT GODS! YOU, ALWAYS SO BLESSED...WHILE I WAS BETRAYED BY THEM OVER AND OVER. BUT NOW I *WILL* BE A CLAW OF GOD.
NO MORE BEING TRICKED, STABBED IN THE BACK! NO ONE WILL GET THE BEST OF--
ZZZT
AAGH!

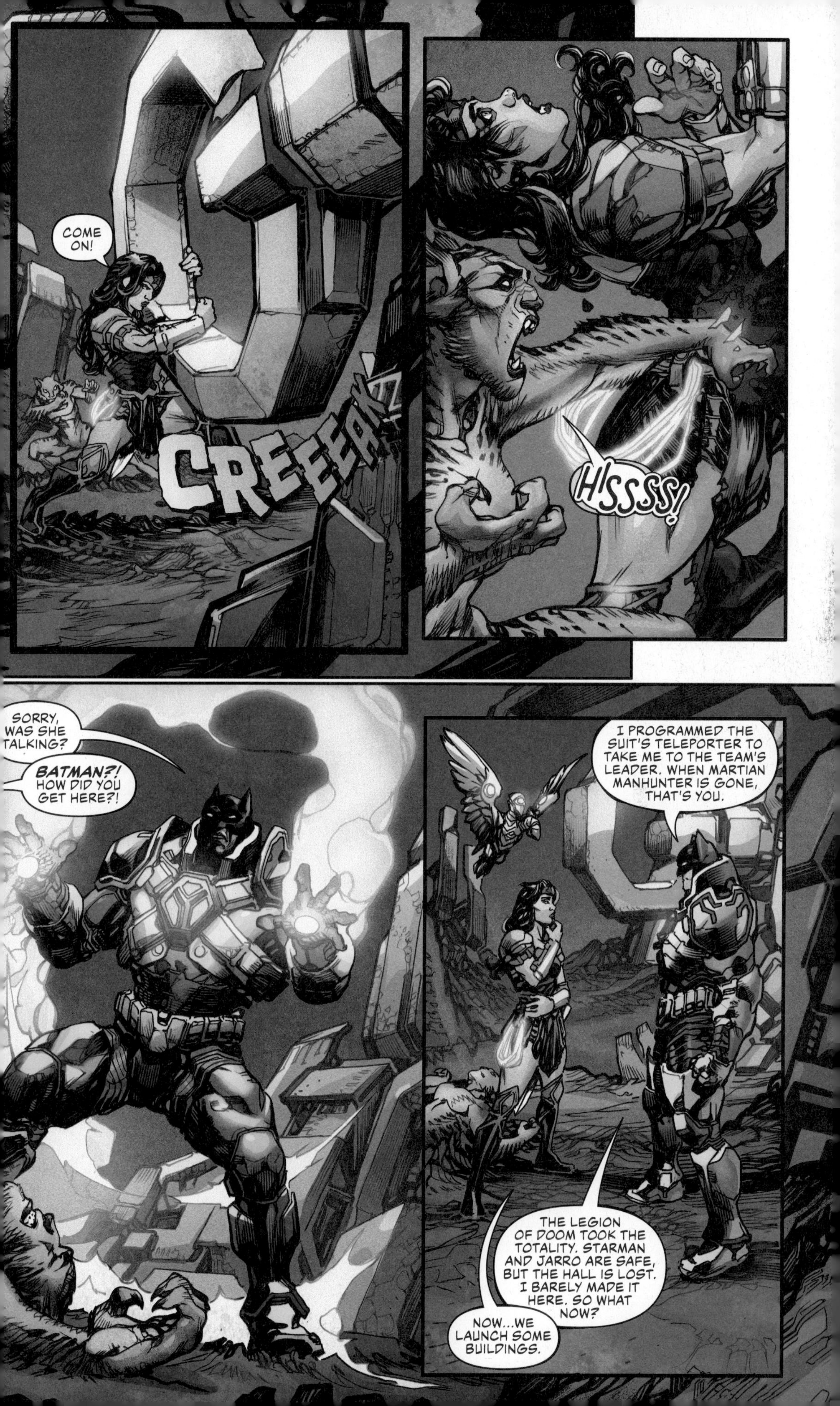
COME ON!
CREEEAK
HISSSS!
SORRY, WAS SHE TALKING?
BATMAN?! HOW DID YOU GET HERE?!
I PROGRAMMED THE SUIT'S TELEPORTER TO TAKE ME TO THE TEAM'S LEADER. WHEN MARTIAN MANHUNTER IS GONE, THAT'S YOU.
THE LEGION OF DOOM TOOK THE TOTALITY. STARMAN AND JARRO ARE SAFE, BUT THE HALL IS LOST. I BARELY MADE IT HERE. SO WHAT NOW?
NOW...WE LAUNCH SOME BUILDINGS.

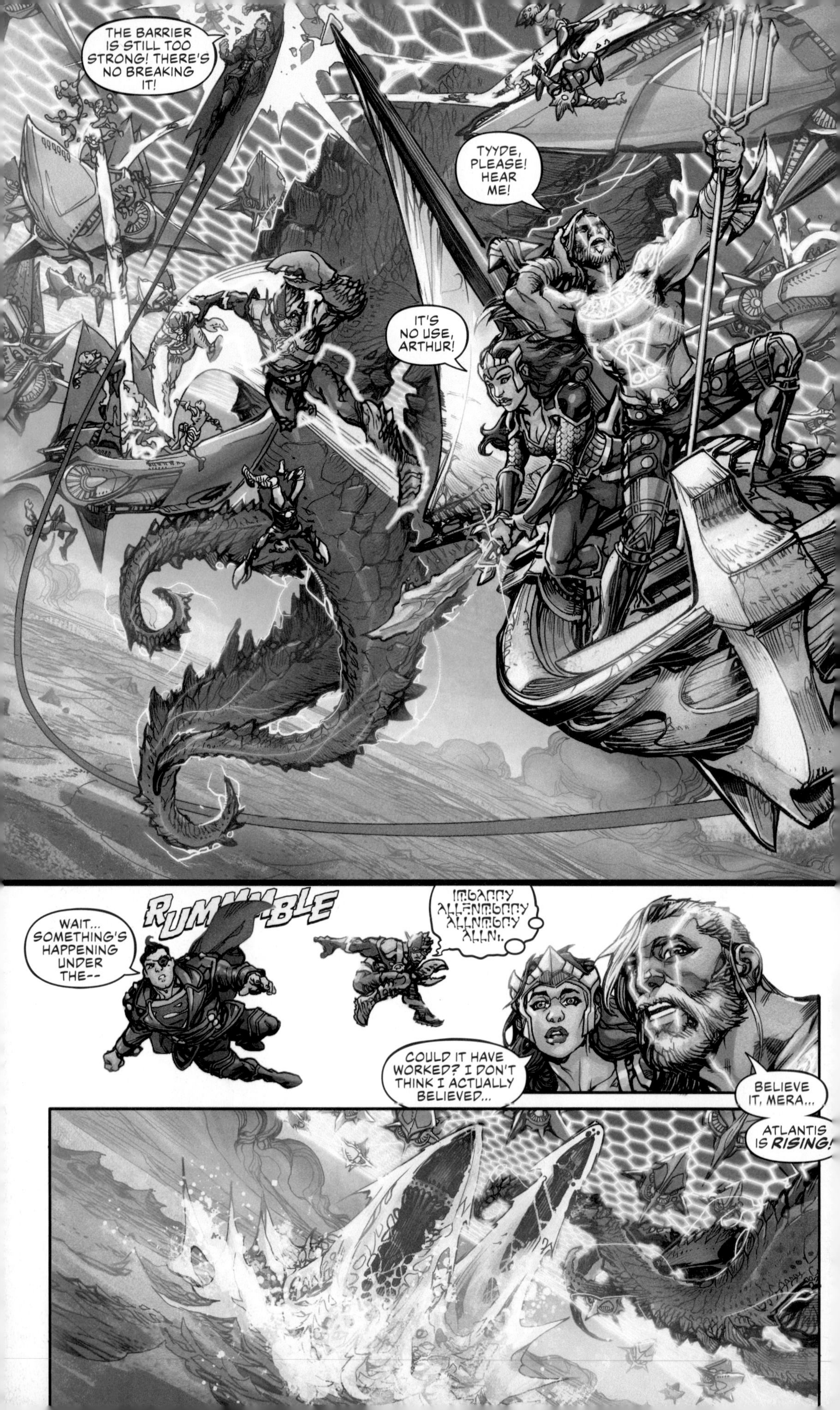

THE BARRIER IS STILL TOO STRONG! THERE'S NO BREAKING IT!
TYYDE, PLEASE! HEAR ME!
IT'S NO USE, ARTHUR!
RUMMMBLE
WAIT... SOMETHING'S HAPPENING UNDER THE--
COULD IT HAVE WORKED? I DON'T THINK I ACTUALLY BELIEVED...
BELIEVE IT, MERA...
ATLANTIS IS *RISING!*

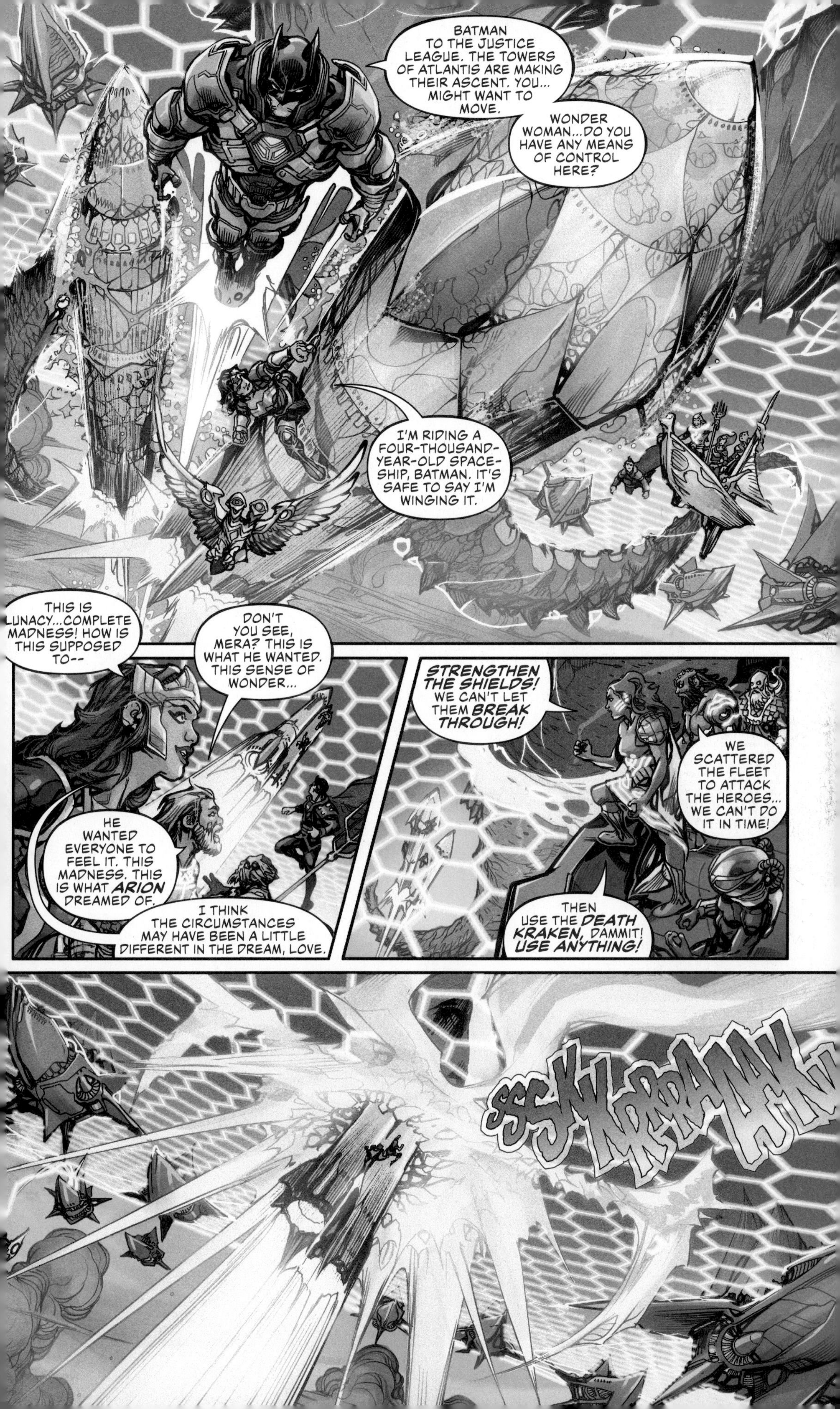
BATMAN TO THE JUSTICE LEAGUE. THE TOWERS OF ATLANTIS ARE MAKING THEIR ASCENT. YOU... MIGHT WANT TO MOVE.
WONDER WOMAN...DO YOU HAVE ANY MEANS OF CONTROL HERE?
I'M RIDING A FOUR-THOUSAND-YEAR-OLD SPACE-SHIP, BATMAN. IT'S SAFE TO SAY I'M WINGING IT.
THIS IS LUNACY...COMPLETE MADNESS! HOW IS THIS SUPPOSED TO--
DON'T YOU SEE, MERA? THIS IS WHAT HE WANTED. THIS SENSE OF WONDER...
HE WANTED EVERYONE TO FEEL IT. THIS MADNESS. THIS IS WHAT ARION DREAMED OF.
I THINK THE CIRCUMSTANCES MAY HAVE BEEN A LITTLE DIFFERENT IN THE DREAM, LOVE.
STRENGTHEN THE SHIELDS! WE CAN'T LET THEM BREAK THROUGH!
WE SCATTERED THE FLEET TO ATTACK THE HEROES... WE CAN'T DO IT IN TIME!
THEN USE THE DEATH KRAKEN, DAMMIT! USE ANYTHING!
SSSKKRRAAKK

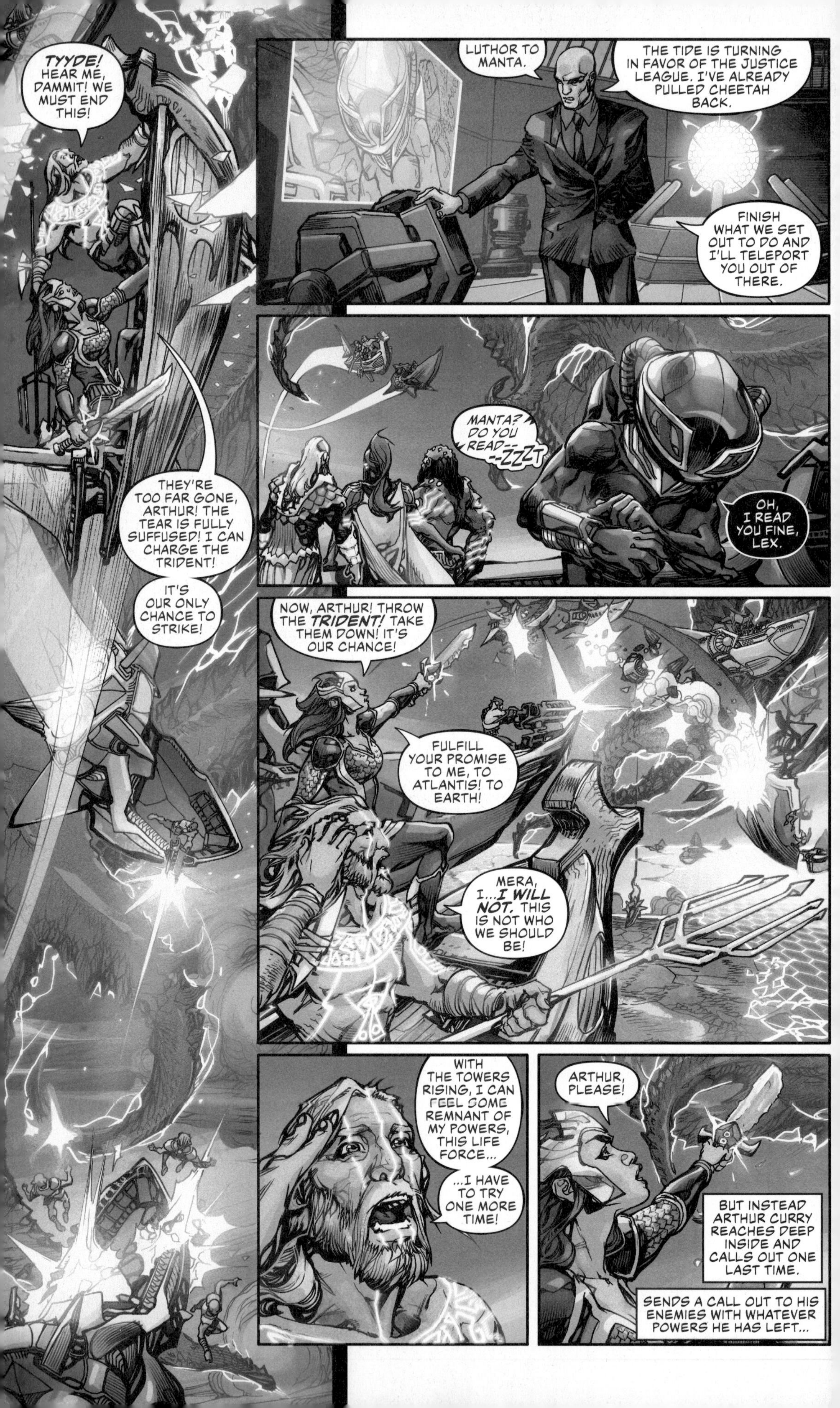

TYYDE! HEAR ME, DAMMIT! WE MUST END THIS!
LUTHOR TO MANTA.
THE TIDE IS TURNING IN FAVOR OF THE JUSTICE LEAGUE. I'VE ALREADY PULLED CHEETAH BACK.
FINISH WHAT WE SET OUT TO DO AND I'LL TELEPORT YOU OUT OF THERE.
MANTA? DO YOU READ-- --ZZZT
OH, I READ YOU FINE, LEX.
THEY'RE TOO FAR GONE, ARTHUR! THE TEAR IS FULLY SUFFUSED! I CAN CHARGE THE TRIDENT!
IT'S OUR ONLY CHANCE TO STRIKE!
NOW, ARTHUR! THROW THE TRIDENT! TAKE THEM DOWN! IT'S OUR CHANCE!
FULFILL YOUR PROMISE TO ME, TO ATLANTIS! TO EARTH!
MERA, I...I WILL NOT. THIS IS NOT WHO WE SHOULD BE!
WITH THE TOWERS RISING, I CAN FEEL SOME REMNANT OF MY POWERS, THIS LIFE FORCE...
...I HAVE TO TRY ONE MORE TIME!
ARTHUR, PLEASE!
BUT INSTEAD ARTHUR CURRY REACHES DEEP INSIDE AND CALLS OUT ONE LAST TIME.
SENDS A CALL OUT TO HIS ENEMIES WITH WHATEVER POWERS HE HAS LEFT...

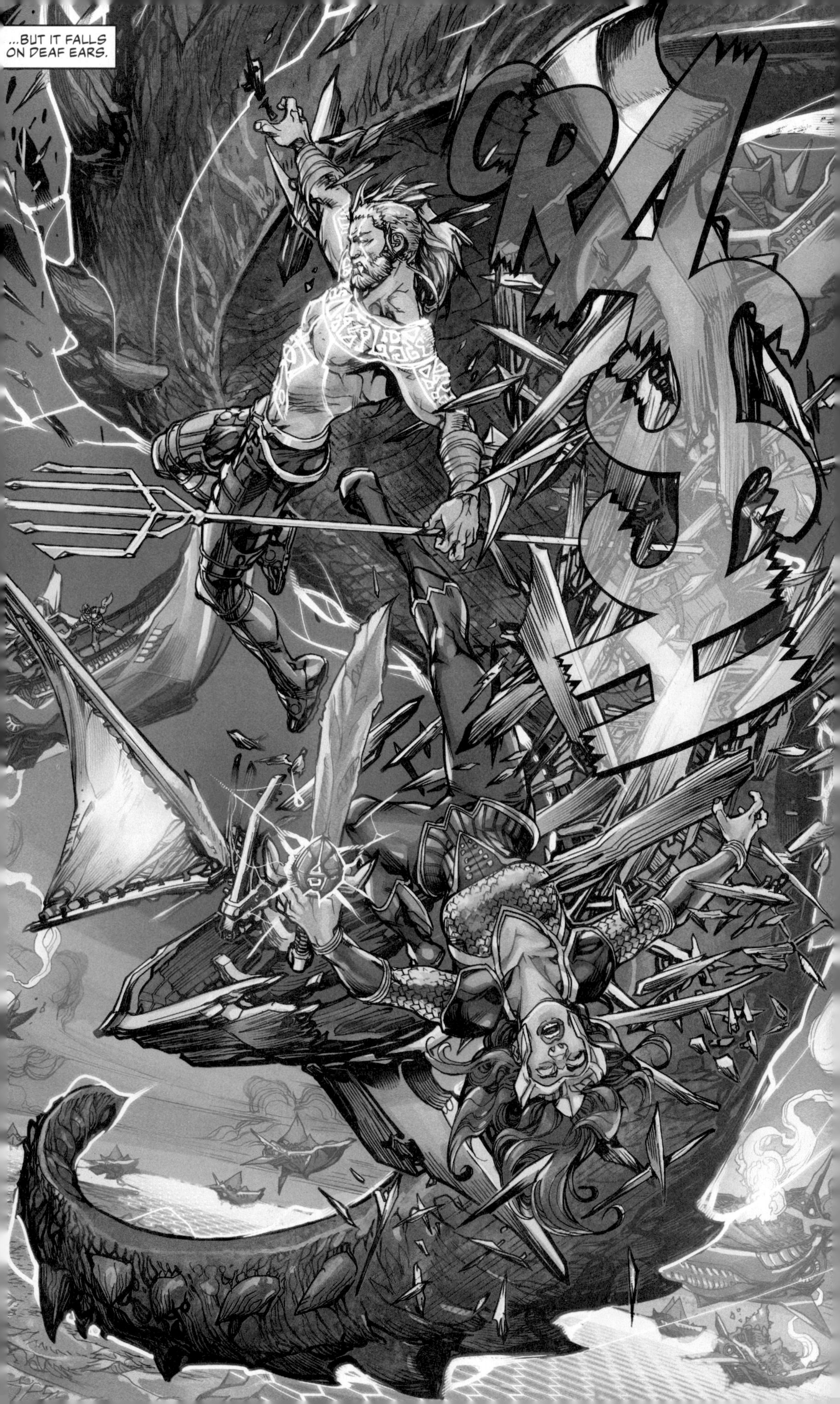
...BUT IT FALLS
ON DEAF EARS.

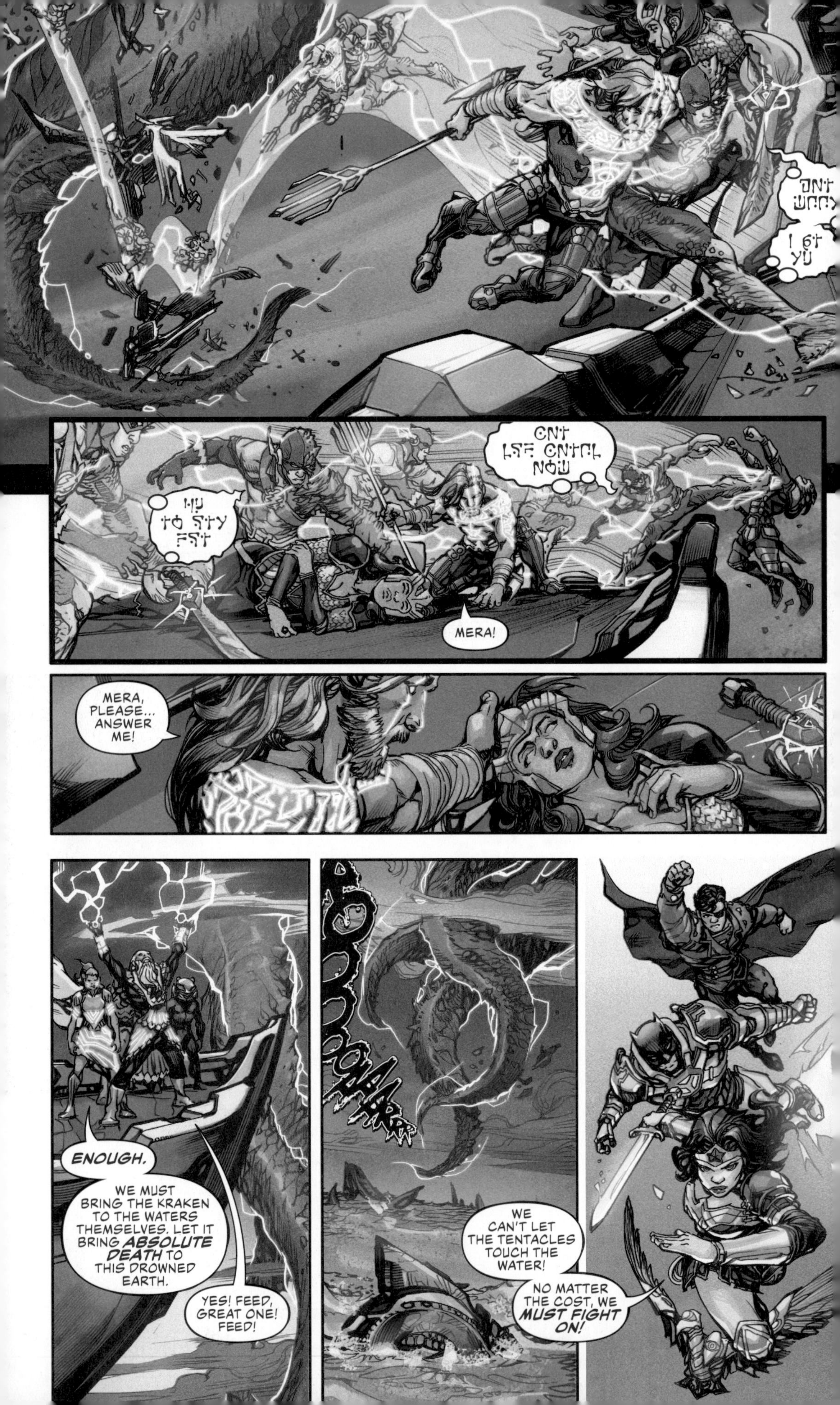

MERA!
MERA, PLEASE... ANSWER ME!
ENOUGH.
WE MUST BRING THE KRAKEN TO THE WATERS THEMSELVES. LET IT BRING ABSOLUTE DEATH TO THIS DROWNED EARTH.
YES! FEED, GREAT ONE! FEED!
WE CAN'T LET THE TENTACLES TOUCH THE WATER!
NO MATTER THE COST, WE MUST FIGHT ON!

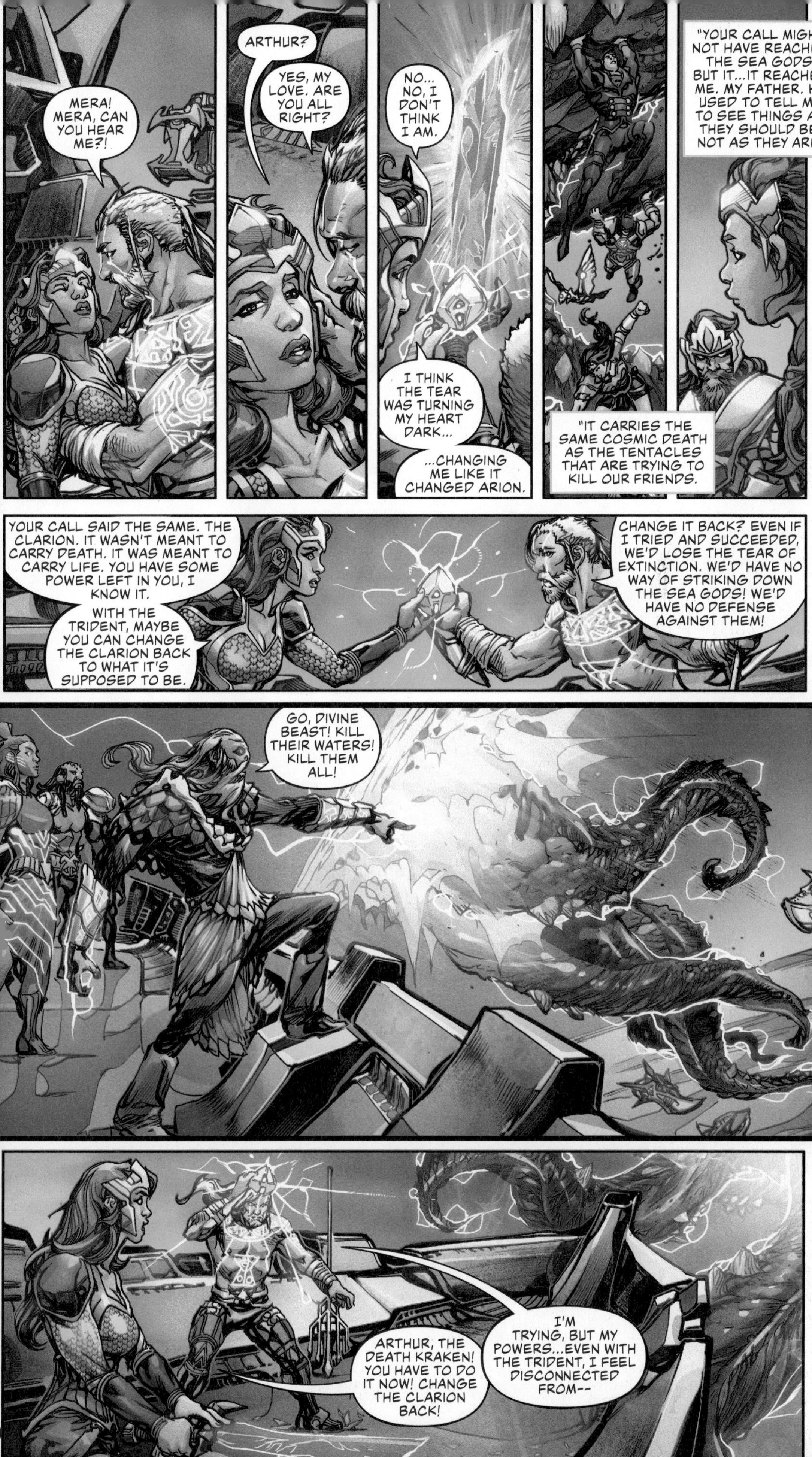
MERA! MERA, CAN YOU HEAR ME?!
ARTHUR?
YES, MY LOVE. ARE YOU ALL RIGHT?
NO... NO, I DON'T THINK I AM.
I THINK THE TEAR WAS TURNING MY HEART DARK...
...CHANGING ME LIKE IT CHANGED ARION.
"YOUR CALL MIGHT NOT HAVE REACHED THE SEA GODS, BUT IT...IT REACHED ME. MY FATHER. HE USED TO TELL ME TO SEE THINGS AS THEY SHOULD BE, NOT AS THEY ARE.
"IT CARRIES THE SAME COSMIC DEATH AS THE TENTACLES THAT ARE TRYING TO KILL OUR FRIENDS.
YOUR CALL SAID THE SAME. THE CLARION. IT WASN'T MEANT TO CARRY DEATH. IT WAS MEANT TO CARRY LIFE. YOU HAVE SOME POWER LEFT IN YOU, I KNOW IT.
WITH THE TRIDENT, MAYBE YOU CAN CHANGE THE CLARION BACK TO WHAT IT'S SUPPOSED TO BE.
CHANGE IT BACK? EVEN IF I TRIED AND SUCCEEDED, WE'D LOSE THE TEAR OF EXTINCTION. WE'D HAVE NO WAY OF STRIKING DOWN THE SEA GODS! WE'D HAVE NO DEFENSE AGAINST THEM!
GO, DIVINE BEAST! KILL THEIR WATERS! KILL THEM ALL!
ARTHUR, THE DEATH KRAKEN! YOU HAVE TO DO IT NOW! CHANGE THE CLARION BACK!
I'M TRYING, BUT MY POWERS...EVEN WITH THE TRIDENT, I FEEL DISCONNECTED FROM--

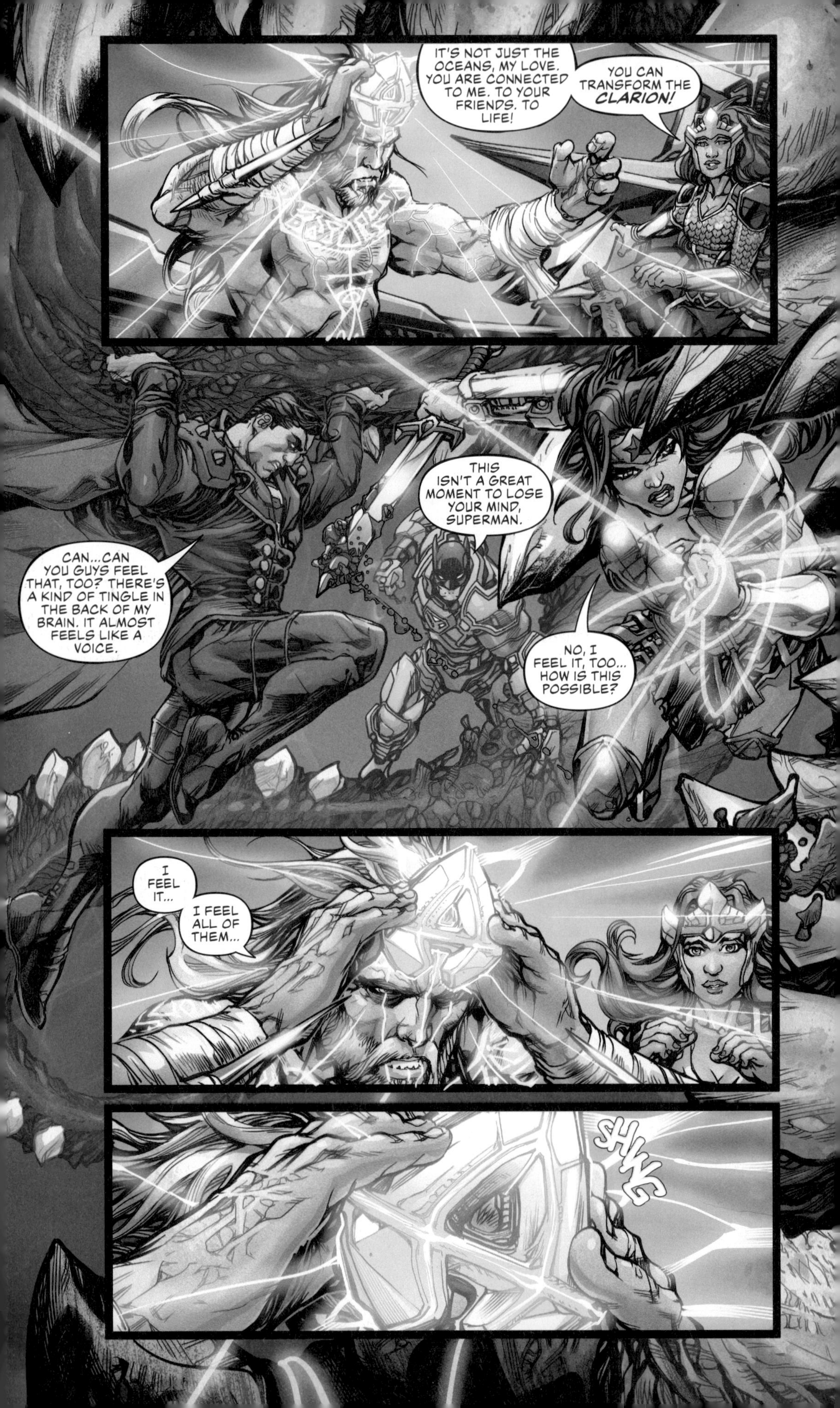

IT'S NOT JUST THE OCEANS, MY LOVE. YOU ARE CONNECTED TO ME. TO YOUR FRIENDS. TO LIFE!
YOU CAN TRANSFORM THE *CLARION!*
CAN...CAN YOU GUYS FEEL THAT, TOO? THERE'S A KIND OF TINGLE IN THE BACK OF MY BRAIN. IT ALMOST FEELS LIKE A VOICE.
THIS ISN'T A GREAT MOMENT TO LOSE YOUR MIND, SUPERMAN.
NO, I FEEL IT, TOO... HOW IS THIS POSSIBLE?
I FEEL IT...
I FEEL ALL OF THEM...
SHWG

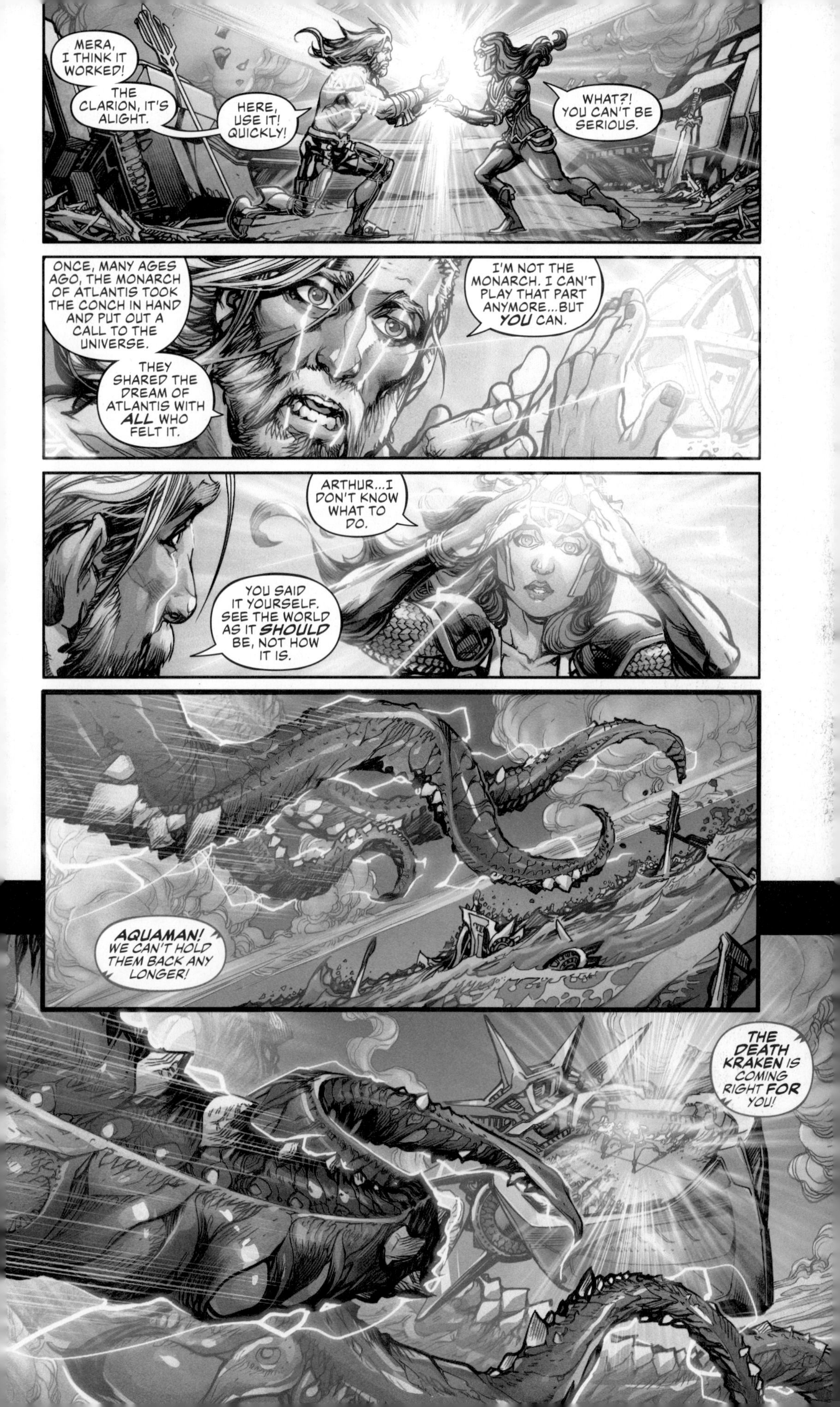
MERA, I THINK IT WORKED!
THE CLARION, IT'S ALIGHT.
HERE, USE IT! QUICKLY!
WHAT?! YOU CAN'T BE SERIOUS.
ONCE, MANY AGES AGO, THE MONARCH OF ATLANTIS TOOK THE CONCH IN HAND AND PUT OUT A CALL TO THE UNIVERSE.
THEY SHARED THE DREAM OF ATLANTIS WITH ALL WHO FELT IT.
I'M NOT THE MONARCH. I CAN'T PLAY THAT PART ANYMORE...BUT YOU CAN.
ARTHUR...I DON'T KNOW WHAT TO DO.
YOU SAID IT YOURSELF. SEE THE WORLD AS IT SHOULD BE, NOT HOW IT IS.
AQUAMAN! WE CAN'T HOLD THEM BACK ANY LONGER!
THE DEATH KRAKEN IS COMING RIGHT FOR YOU!

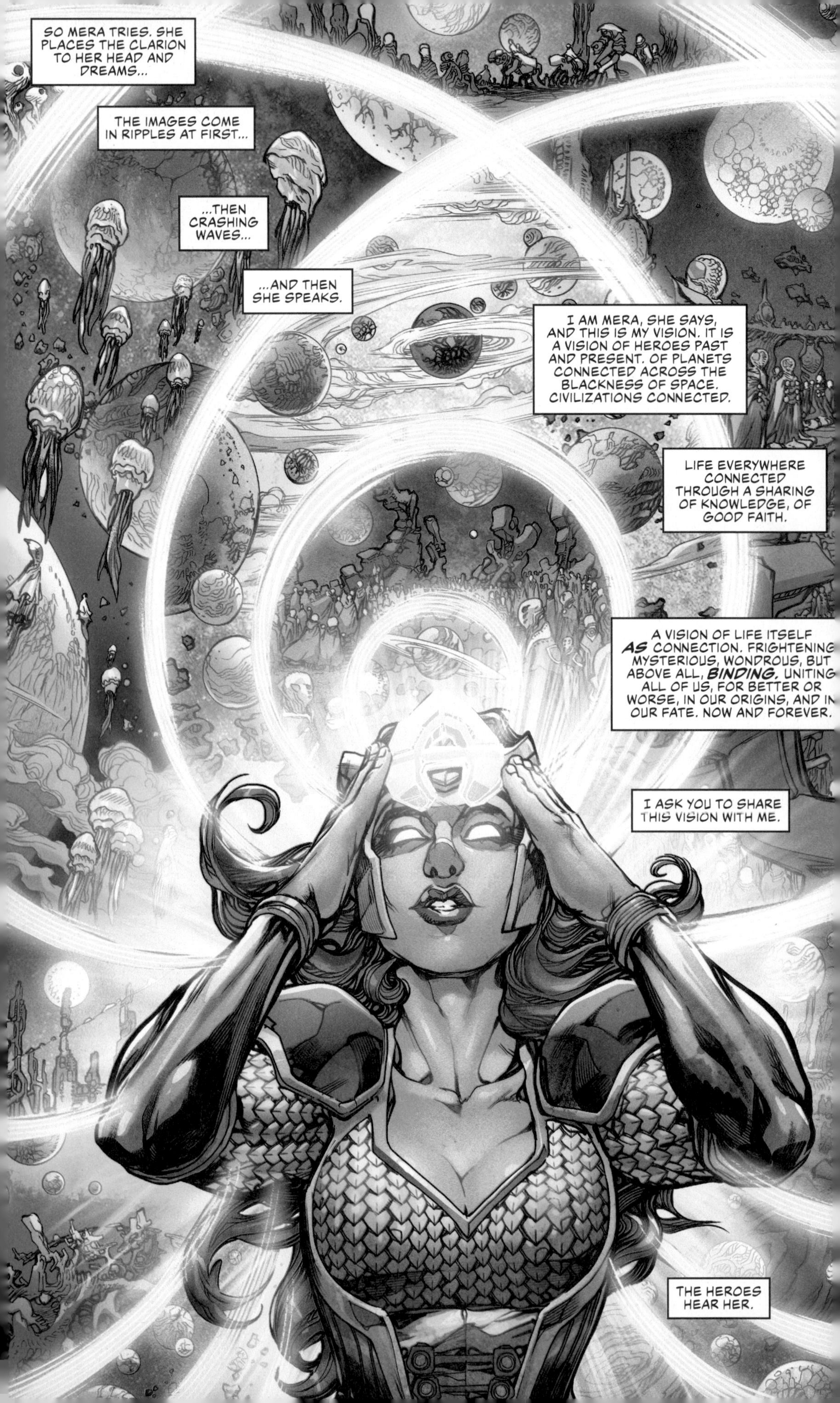
SO MERA TRIES. SHE PLACES THE CLARION TO HER HEAD AND DREAMS...
THE IMAGES COME IN RIPPLES AT FIRST...
...THEN CRASHING WAVES...
...AND THEN SHE SPEAKS.
I AM MERA, SHE SAYS, AND THIS IS MY VISION. IT IS A VISION OF HEROES PAST AND PRESENT. OF PLANETS CONNECTED ACROSS THE BLACKNESS OF SPACE. CIVILIZATIONS CONNECTED.
LIFE EVERYWHERE CONNECTED THROUGH A SHARING OF KNOWLEDGE, OF GOOD FAITH.
A VISION OF LIFE ITSELF AS CONNECTION. FRIGHTENING MYSTERIOUS, WONDROUS, BUT ABOVE ALL, BINDING. UNITING ALL OF US, FOR BETTER OR WORSE, IN OUR ORIGINS, AND IN OUR FATE. NOW AND FOREVER.
I ASK YOU TO SHARE THIS VISION WITH ME.
THE HEROES HEAR HER.

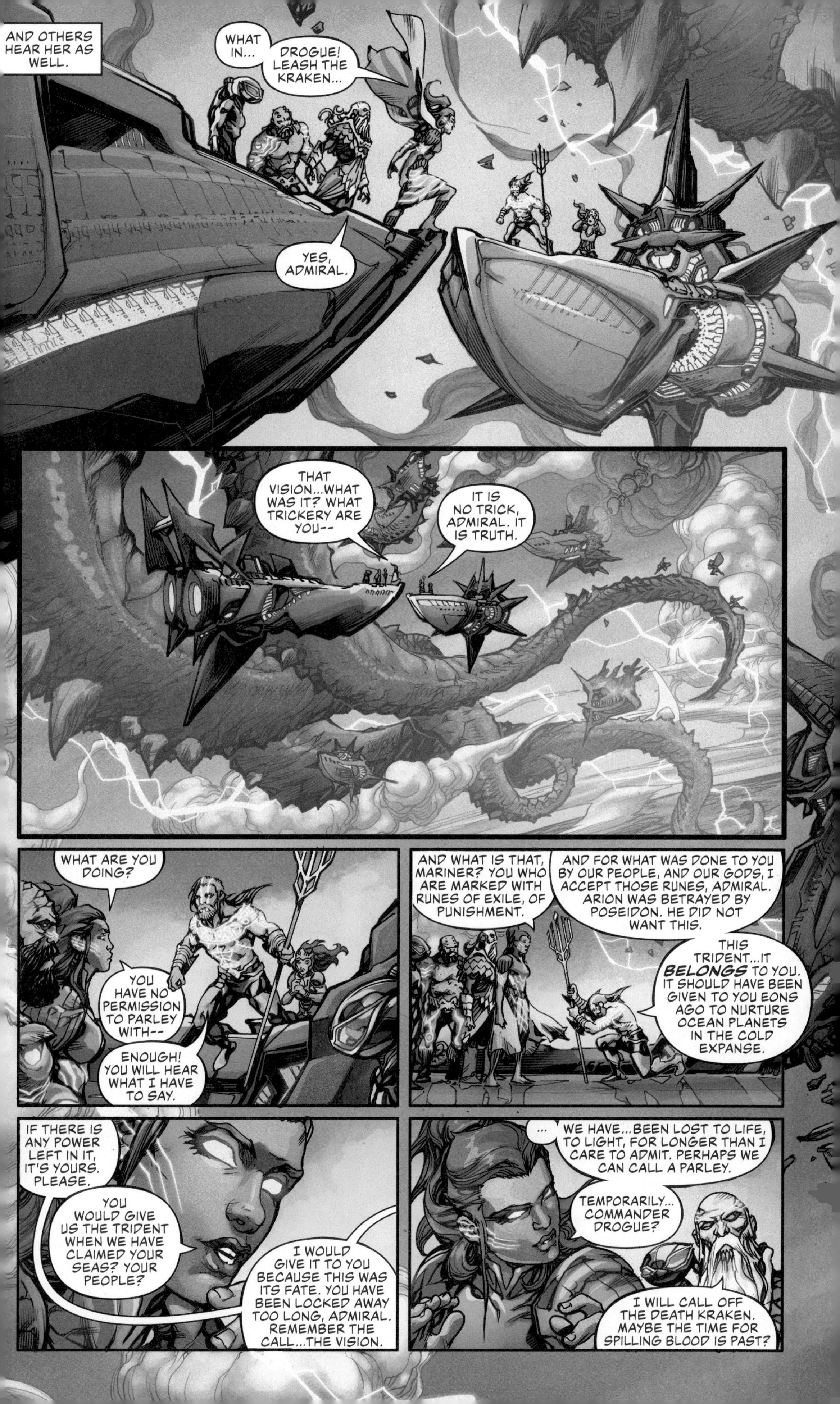
AND OTHERS HEAR HER AS WELL.
WHAT IN...
DROGUE! LEASH THE KRAKEN...
YES, ADMIRAL.
THAT VISION...WHAT WAS IT? WHAT TRICKERY ARE YOU--
IT IS NO TRICK, ADMIRAL. IT IS TRUTH.
WHAT ARE YOU DOING?
YOU HAVE NO PERMISSION TO PARLEY WITH--
ENOUGH! YOU WILL HEAR WHAT I HAVE TO SAY.
AND WHAT IS THAT, MARINER? YOU WHO ARE MARKED WITH RUNES OF EXILE, OF PUNISHMENT.
AND FOR WHAT WAS DONE TO YOU BY OUR PEOPLE, AND OUR GODS, I ACCEPT THOSE RUNES, ADMIRAL. ARION WAS BETRAYED BY POSEIDON. HE DID NOT WANT THIS.
THIS TRIDENT...IT BELONGS TO YOU. IT SHOULD HAVE BEEN GIVEN TO YOU EONS AGO TO NURTURE OCEAN PLANETS IN THE COLD EXPANSE.
IF THERE IS ANY POWER LEFT IN IT, IT'S YOURS. PLEASE.
YOU WOULD GIVE US THE TRIDENT WHEN WE HAVE CLAIMED YOUR SEAS? YOUR PEOPLE?
I WOULD GIVE IT TO YOU BECAUSE THIS WAS ITS FATE. YOU HAVE BEEN LOCKED AWAY TOO LONG, ADMIRAL. REMEMBER THE CALL...THE VISION.
...
WE HAVE...BEEN LOST TO LIFE, TO LIGHT, FOR LONGER THAN I CARE TO ADMIT. PERHAPS WE CAN CALL A PARLEY.
TEMPORARILY... COMMANDER DROGUE?
I WILL CALL OFF THE DEATH KRAKEN. MAYBE THE TIME FOR SPILLING BLOOD IS PAST?

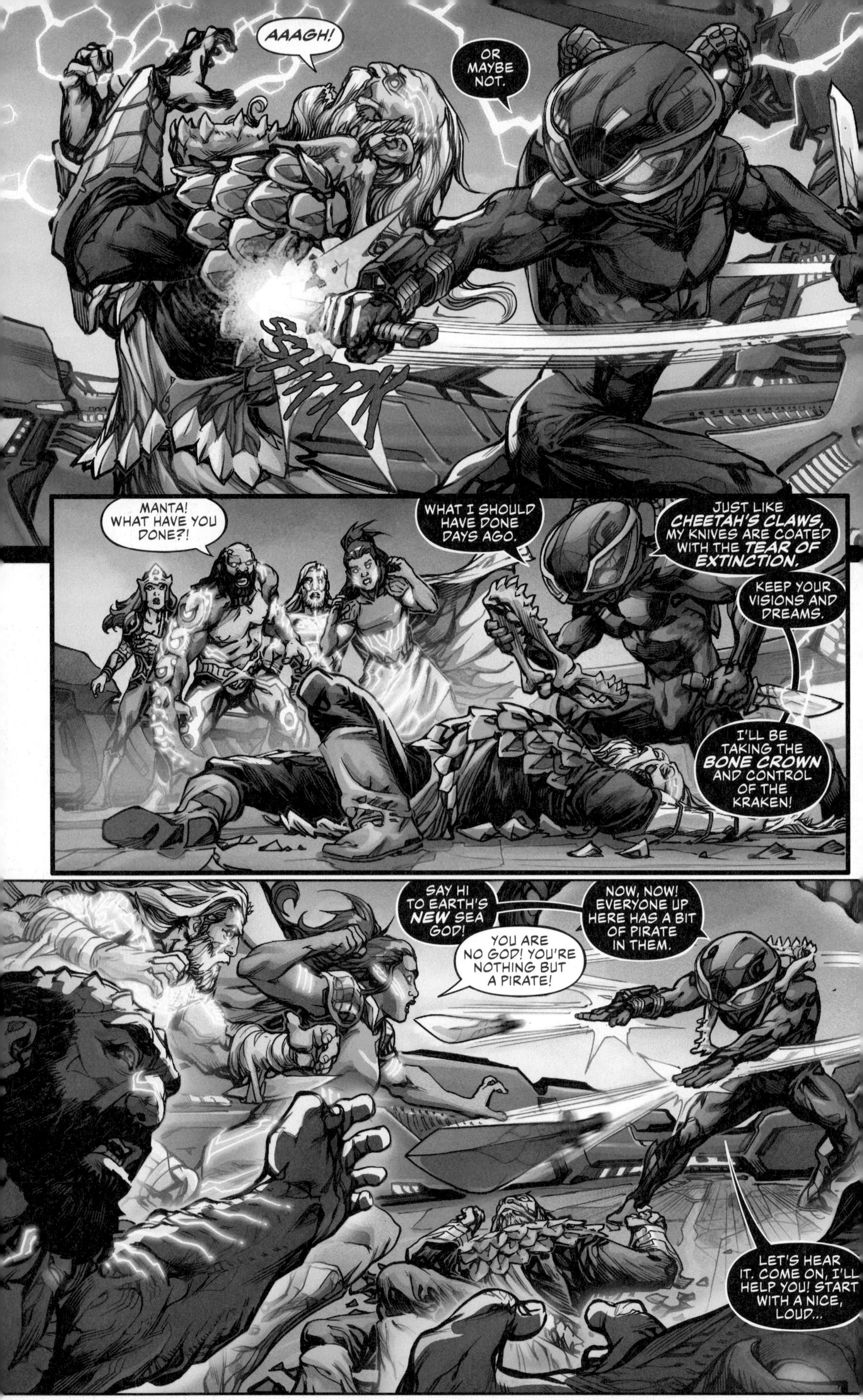
AAAGH!
OR MAYBE NOT.
SHHKK
MANTA! WHAT HAVE YOU DONE?!
WHAT I SHOULD HAVE DONE DAYS AGO.
JUST LIKE CHEETAH'S CLAWS, MY KNIVES ARE COATED WITH THE TEAR OF EXTINCTION.
KEEP YOUR VISIONS AND DREAMS.
I'LL BE TAKING THE BONE CROWN AND CONTROL OF THE KRAKEN!
SAY HI TO EARTH'S NEW SEA GOD!
YOU ARE NO GOD! YOU'RE NOTHING BUT A PIRATE!
NOW, NOW! EVERYONE UP HERE HAS A BIT OF PIRATE IN THEM.
LET'S HEAR IT. COME ON, I'LL HELP YOU! START WITH A NICE, LOUD...

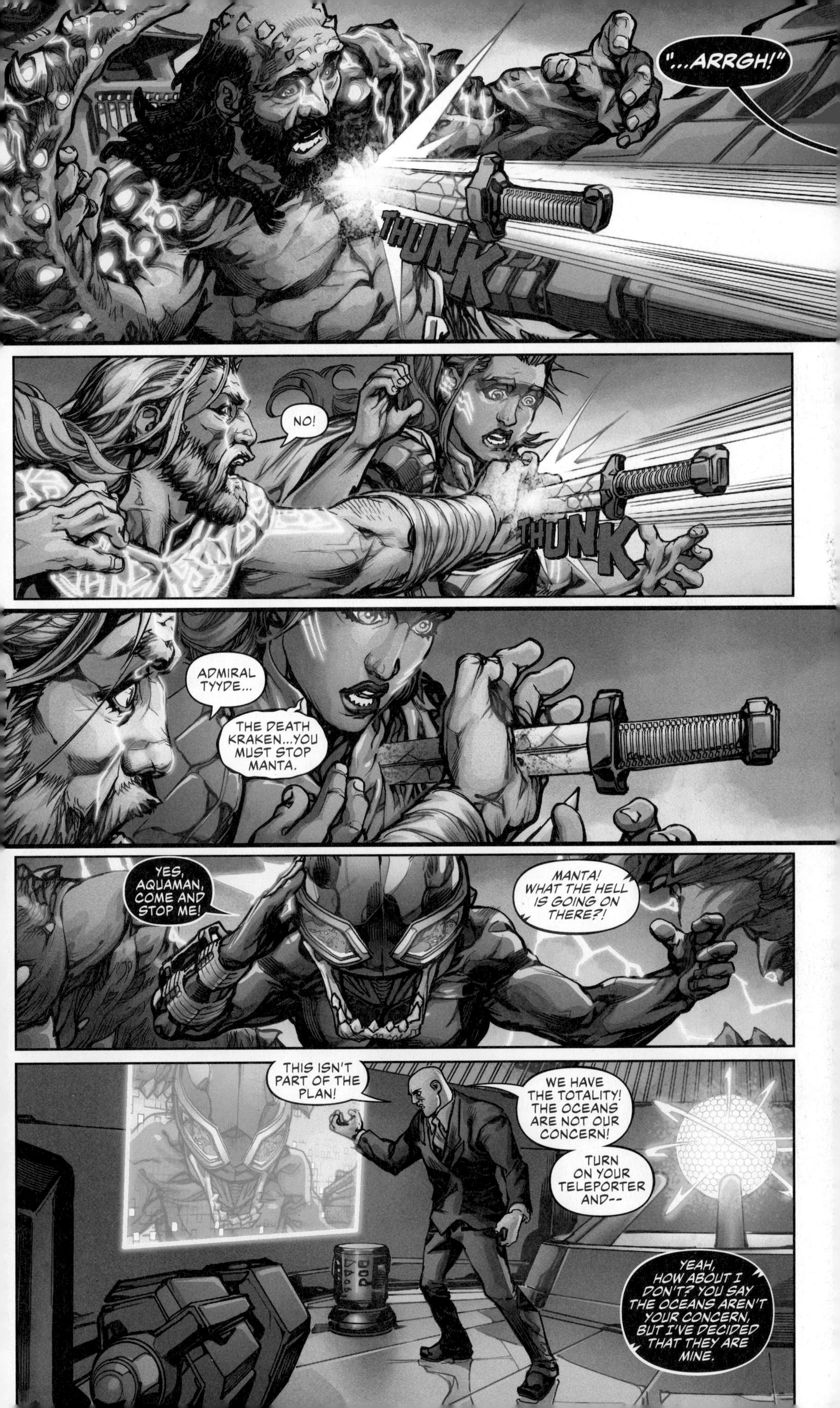
"...ARRGH!"
THUNK
NO!
THUNK
ADMIRAL TYYDE...
THE DEATH KRAKEN...YOU MUST STOP MANTA.
YES, AQUAMAN, COME AND STOP ME!
MANTA! WHAT THE HELL IS GOING ON THERE?!
THIS ISN'T PART OF THE PLAN!
WE HAVE THE TOTALITY! THE OCEANS ARE NOT OUR CONCERN!
TURN ON YOUR TELEPORTER AND--
YEAH, HOW ABOUT I DON'T? YOU SAY THE OCEANS AREN'T YOUR CONCERN, BUT I'VE DECIDED THAT THEY ARE MINE.

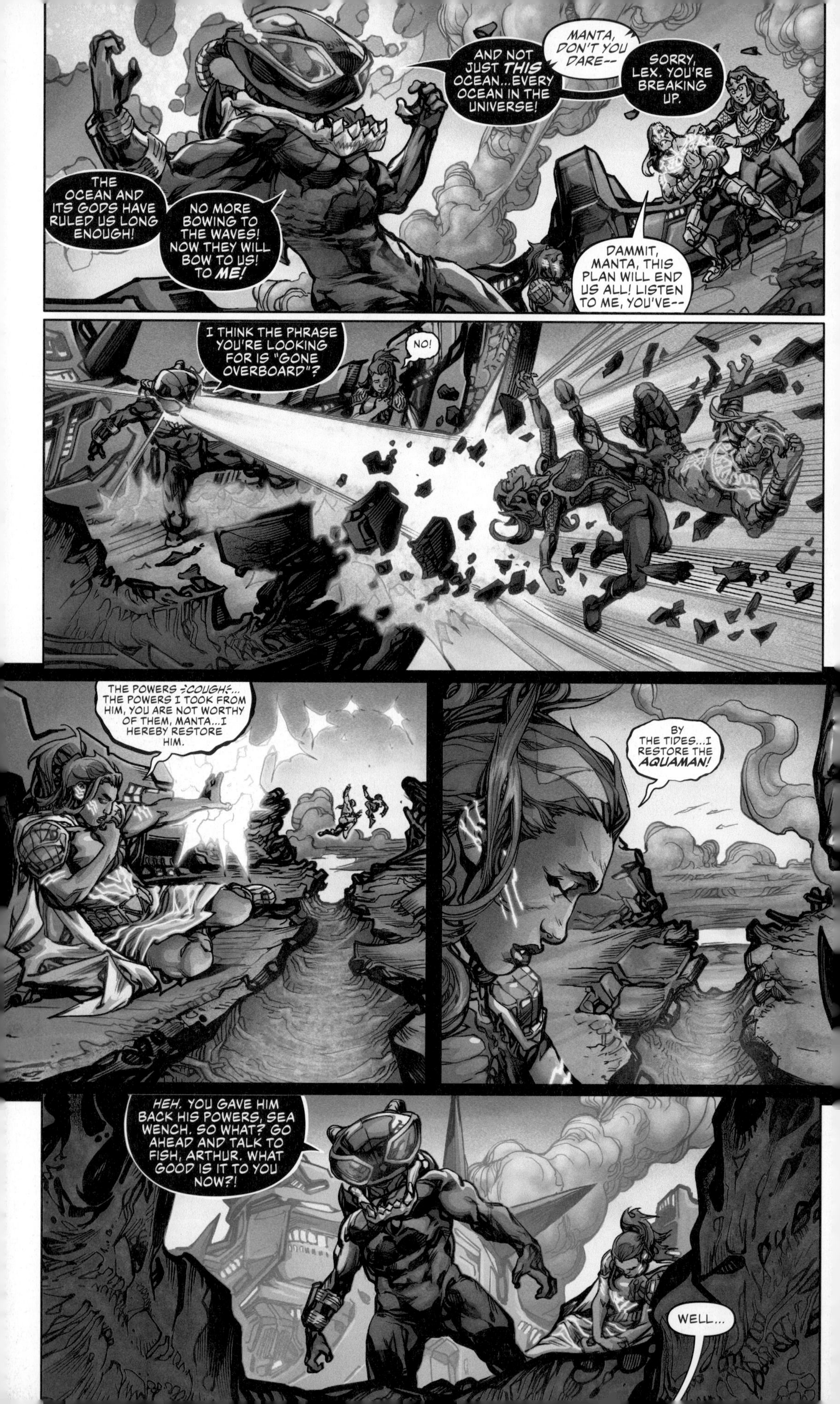

THE OCEAN AND ITS GODS HAVE RULED US LONG ENOUGH!
NO MORE BOWING TO THE WAVES! NOW THEY WILL BOW TO US! TO ME!
AND NOT JUST THIS OCEAN...EVERY OCEAN IN THE UNIVERSE!
MANTA, DON'T YOU DARE--
SORRY, LEX. YOU'RE BREAKING UP.
DAMMIT, MANTA, THIS PLAN WILL END US ALL! LISTEN TO ME, YOU'VE--
I THINK THE PHRASE YOU'RE LOOKING FOR IS "GONE OVERBOARD"?
NO!
THE POWERS ⇒COUGH⇐... THE POWERS I TOOK FROM HIM, YOU ARE NOT WORTHY OF THEM, MANTA...I HEREBY RESTORE HIM.
BY THE TIDES...I RESTORE THE AQUAMAN!
HEH. YOU GAVE HIM BACK HIS POWERS, SEA WENCH. SO WHAT? GO AHEAD AND TALK TO FISH, ARTHUR. WHAT GOOD IS IT TO YOU NOW?!
WELL...

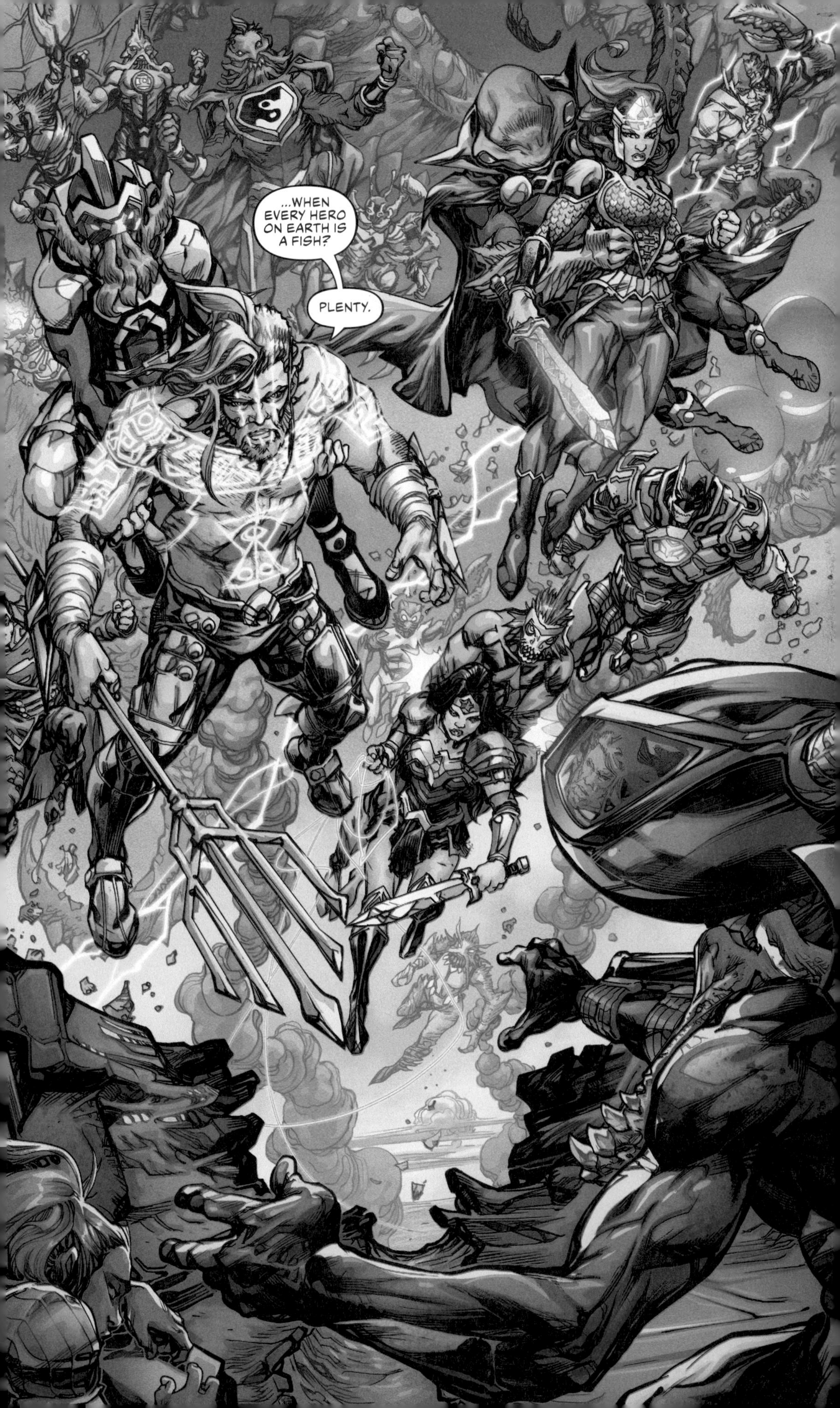
...WHEN EVERY HERO ON EARTH IS A FISH?
PLENTY.

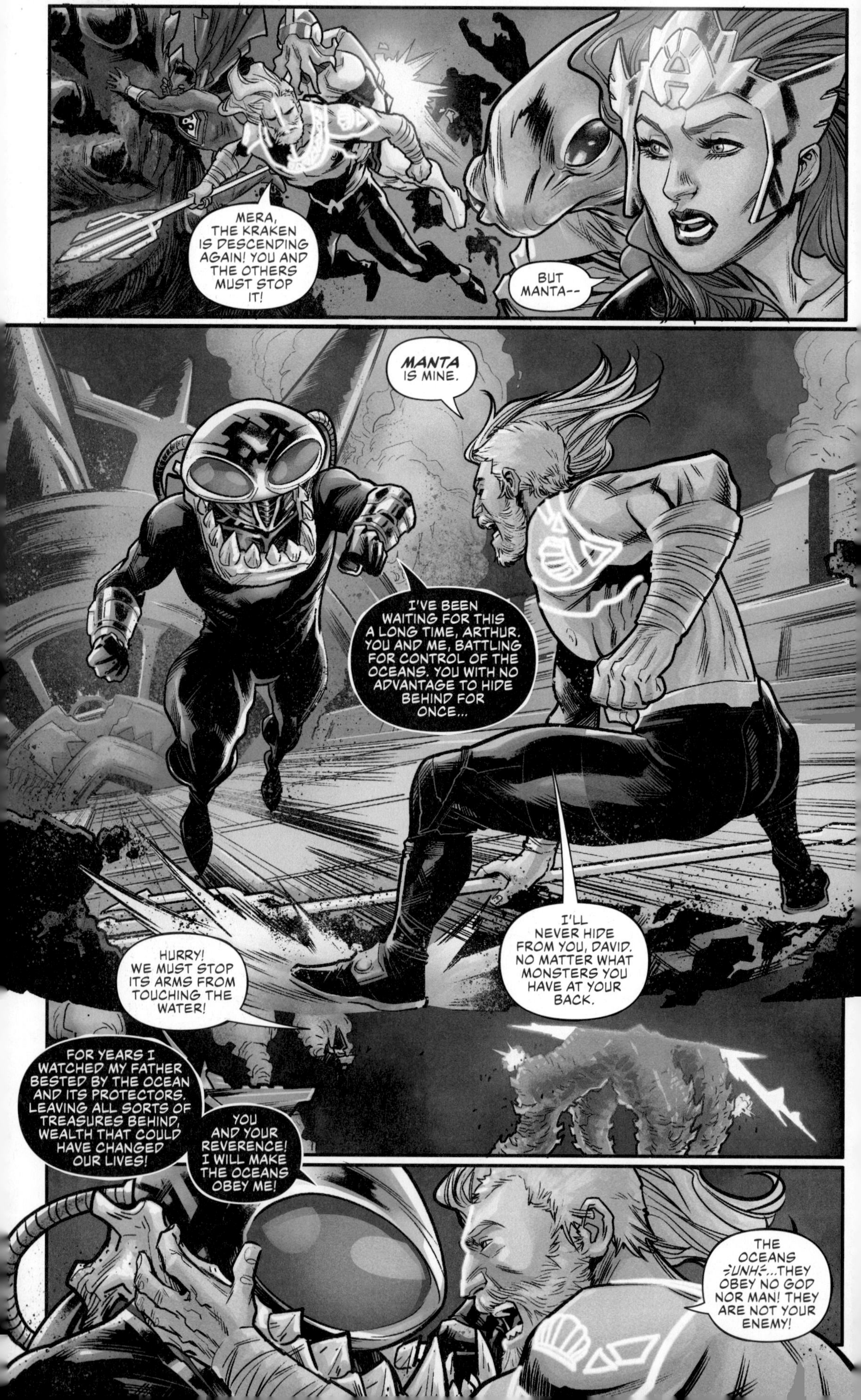
MERA, THE KRAKEN IS DESCENDING AGAIN! YOU AND THE OTHERS MUST STOP IT!
BUT MANTA--
MANTA IS MINE.
I'VE BEEN WAITING FOR THIS A LONG TIME, ARTHUR. YOU AND ME, BATTLING FOR CONTROL OF THE OCEANS. YOU WITH NO ADVANTAGE TO HIDE BEHIND FOR ONCE...
I'LL NEVER HIDE FROM YOU, DAVID. NO MATTER WHAT MONSTERS YOU HAVE AT YOUR BACK.
HURRY! WE MUST STOP ITS ARMS FROM TOUCHING THE WATER!
FOR YEARS I WATCHED MY FATHER BESTED BY THE OCEAN AND ITS PROTECTORS. LEAVING ALL SORTS OF TREASURES BEHIND, WEALTH THAT COULD HAVE CHANGED OUR LIVES!
YOU AND YOUR REVERENCE! I WILL MAKE THE OCEANS OBEY ME!
THE OCEANS =UNH=...THEY OBEY NO GOD NOR MAN! THEY ARE NOT YOUR ENEMY!

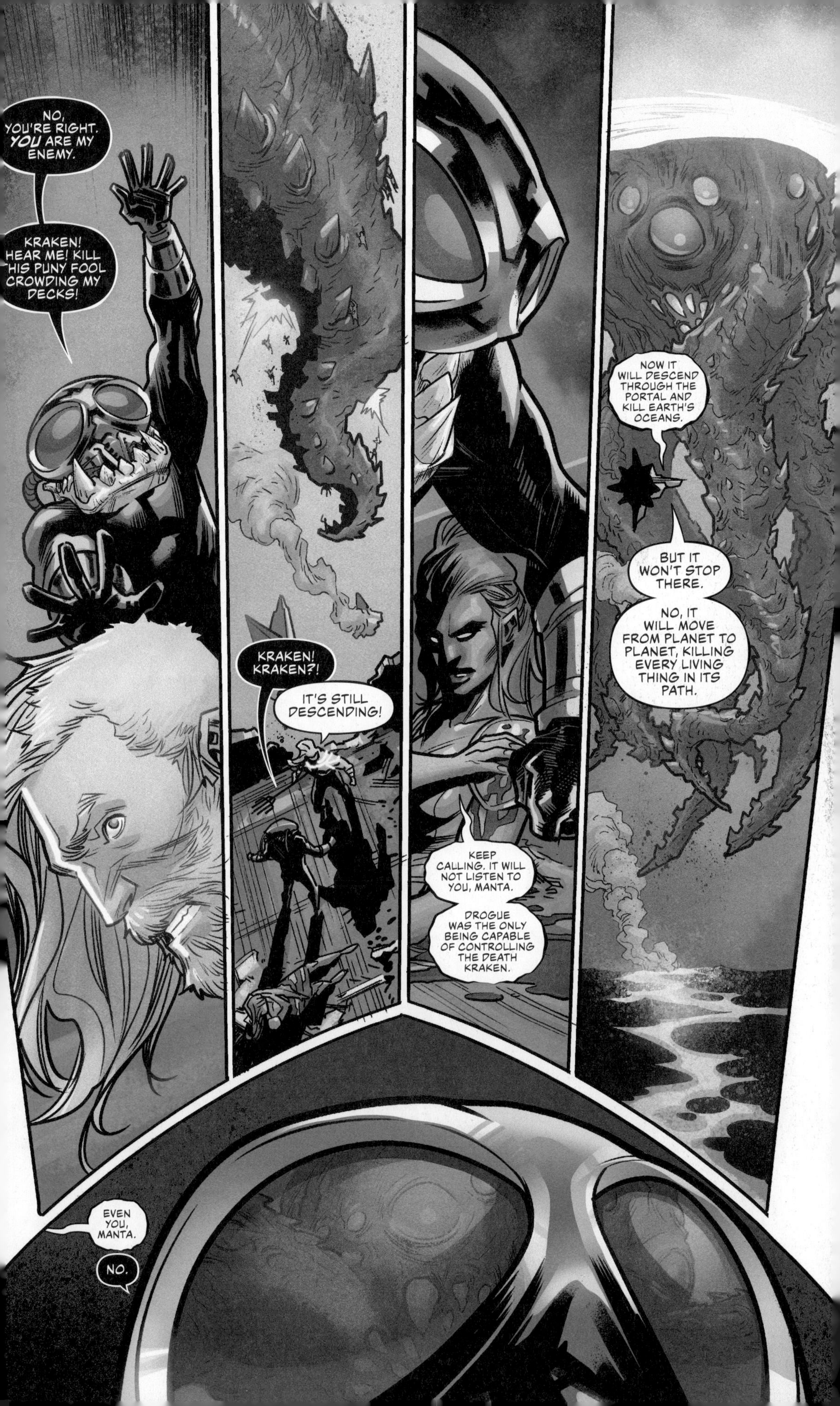

NO, YOU'RE RIGHT. YOU ARE MY ENEMY.
KRAKEN! HEAR ME! KILL THIS PUNY FOOL CROWDING MY DECKS!
KRAKEN! KRAKEN?!
IT'S STILL DESCENDING!
KEEP CALLING. IT WILL NOT LISTEN TO YOU, MANTA.
DROGUE WAS THE ONLY BEING CAPABLE OF CONTROLLING THE DEATH KRAKEN.
NOW IT WILL DESCEND THROUGH THE PORTAL AND KILL EARTH'S OCEANS.
BUT IT WON'T STOP THERE.
NO, IT WILL MOVE FROM PLANET TO PLANET, KILLING EVERY LIVING THING IN ITS PATH.
EVEN YOU, MANTA.
NO.

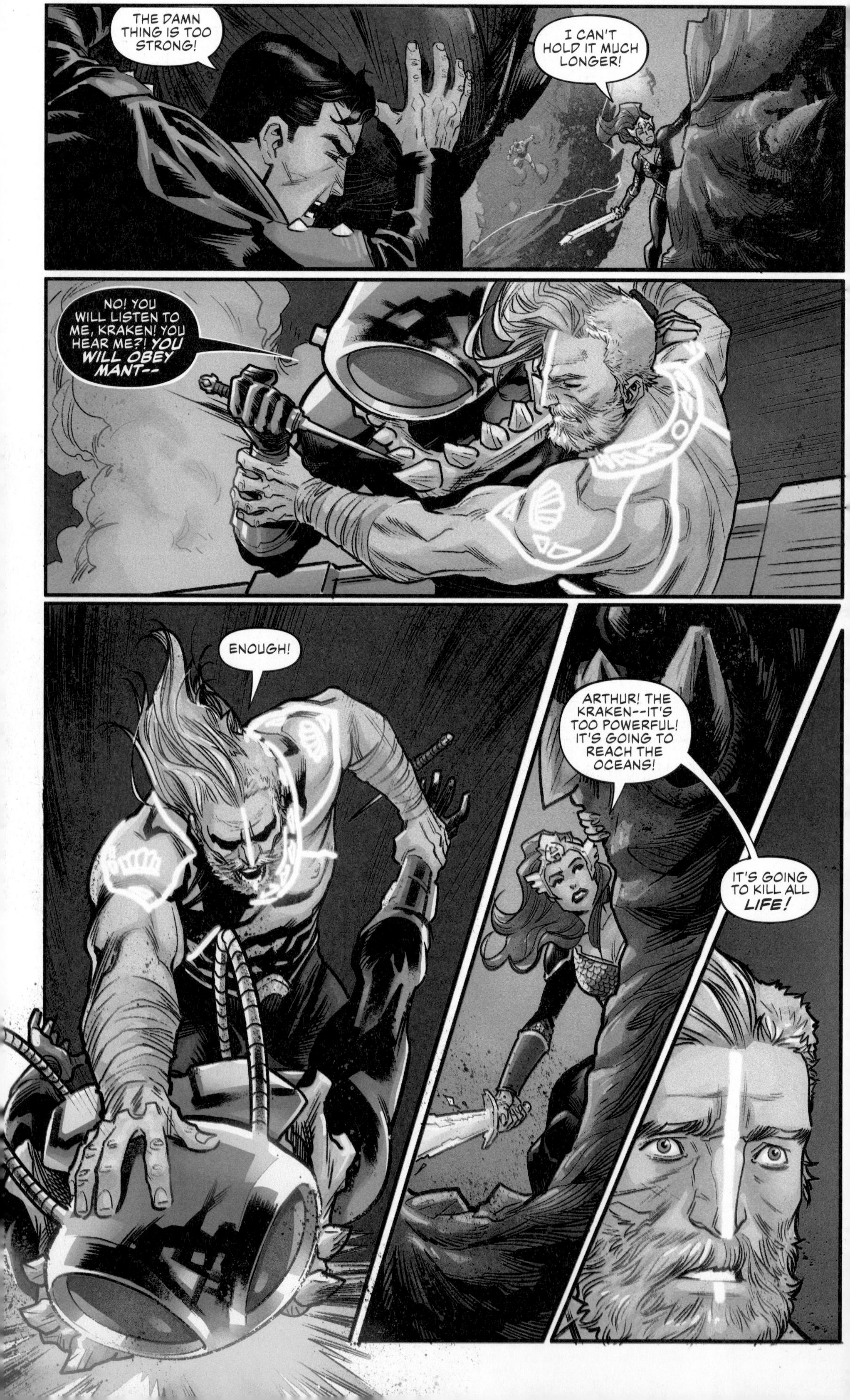
THE DAMN THING IS TOO STRONG!
I CAN'T HOLD IT MUCH LONGER!
NO! YOU WILL LISTEN TO ME, KRAKEN! YOU HEAR ME?! YOU WILL OBEY MANT--
ENOUGH!
ARTHUR! THE KRAKEN--IT'S TOO POWERFUL! IT'S GOING TO REACH THE OCEANS!
IT'S GOING TO KILL ALL LIFE!

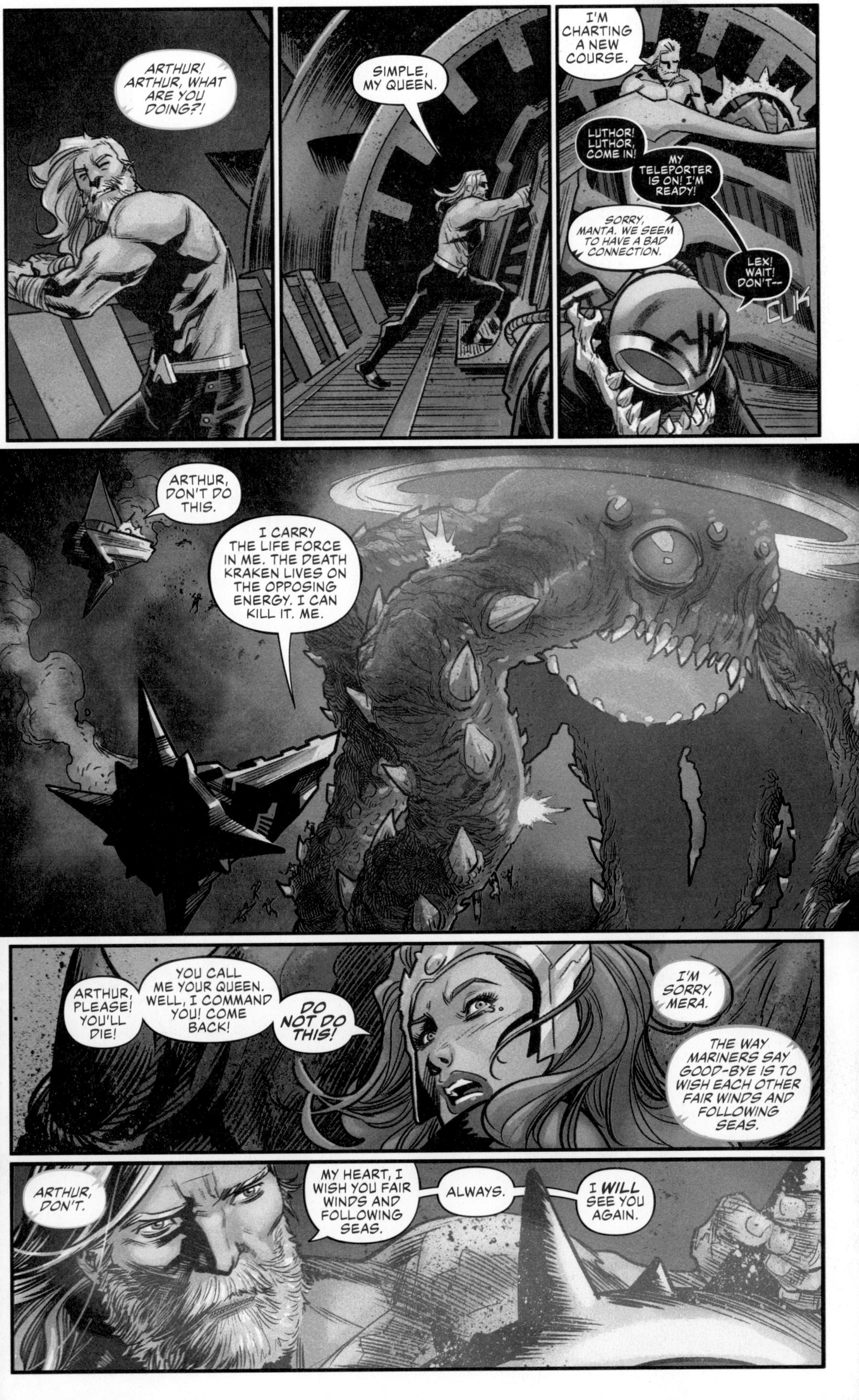
ARTHUR! ARTHUR, WHAT ARE YOU DOING?!
SIMPLE, MY QUEEN.
I'M CHARTING A NEW COURSE.
LUTHOR! LUTHOR, COME IN!
MY TELEPORTER IS ON! I'M READY!
SORRY, MANTA. WE SEEM TO HAVE A BAD CONNECTION.
LEX! WAIT! DON'T--
CLIK
ARTHUR, DON'T DO THIS.
I CARRY THE LIFE FORCE IN ME. THE DEATH KRAKEN LIVES ON THE OPPOSING ENERGY. I CAN KILL IT. ME.
ARTHUR, PLEASE! YOU'LL DIE!
YOU CALL ME YOUR QUEEN. WELL, I COMMAND YOU! COME BACK!
DO NOT DO THIS!
I'M SORRY, MERA.
THE WAY MARINERS SAY GOOD-BYE IS TO WISH EACH OTHER FAIR WINDS AND FOLLOWING SEAS.
ARTHUR, DON'T.
MY HEART, I WISH YOU FAIR WINDS AND FOLLOWING SEAS.
ALWAYS.
I WILL SEE YOU AGAIN.

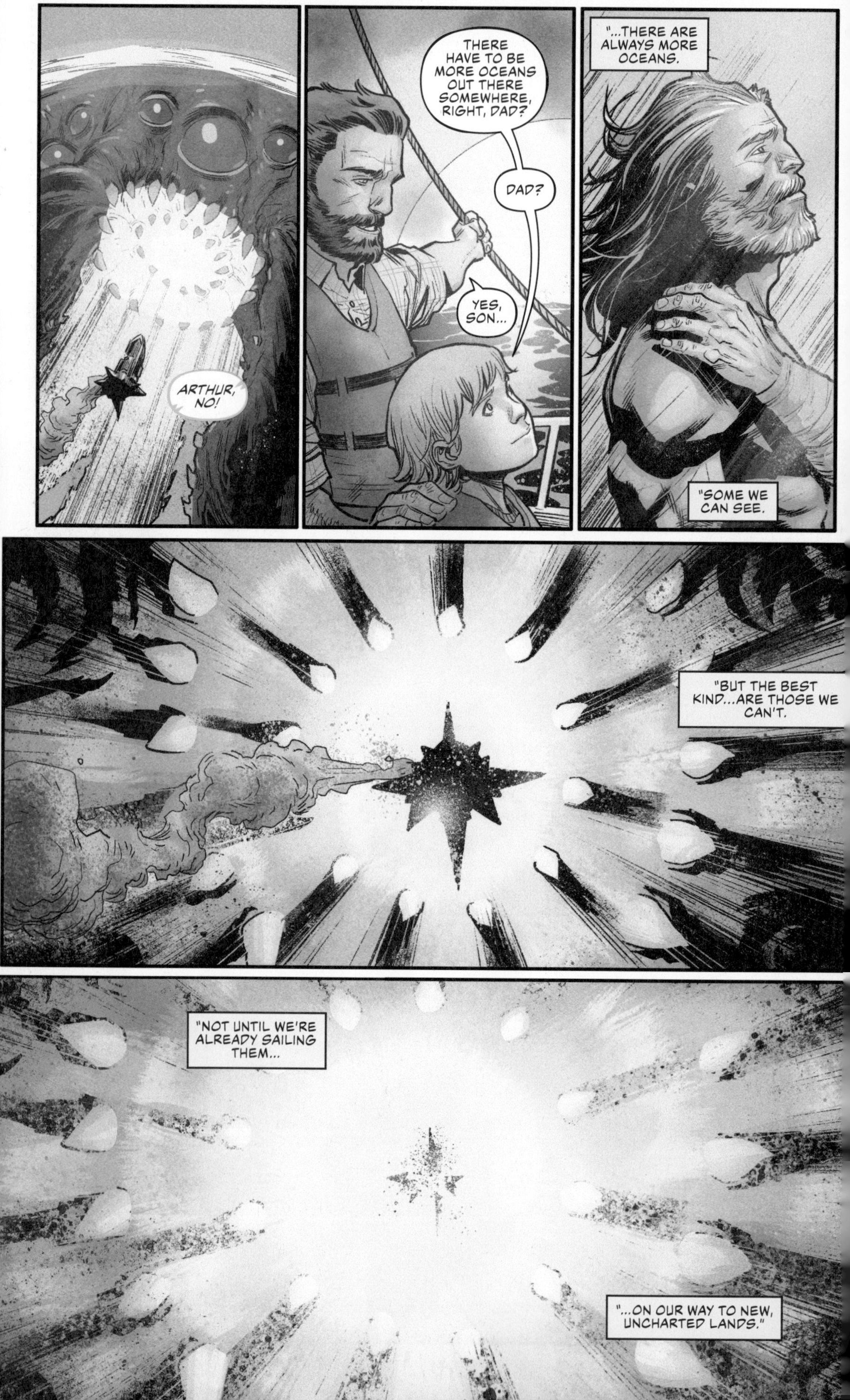
ARTHUR, NO!
THERE HAVE TO BE MORE OCEANS OUT THERE SOMEWHERE, RIGHT, DAD?
DAD?
YES, SON...
"...THERE ARE ALWAYS MORE OCEANS.
"SOME WE CAN SEE.
"BUT THE BEST KIND...ARE THOSE WE CAN'T.
"NOT UNTIL WE'RE ALREADY SAILING THEM...
"...ON OUR WAY TO NEW, UNCHARTED LANDS."

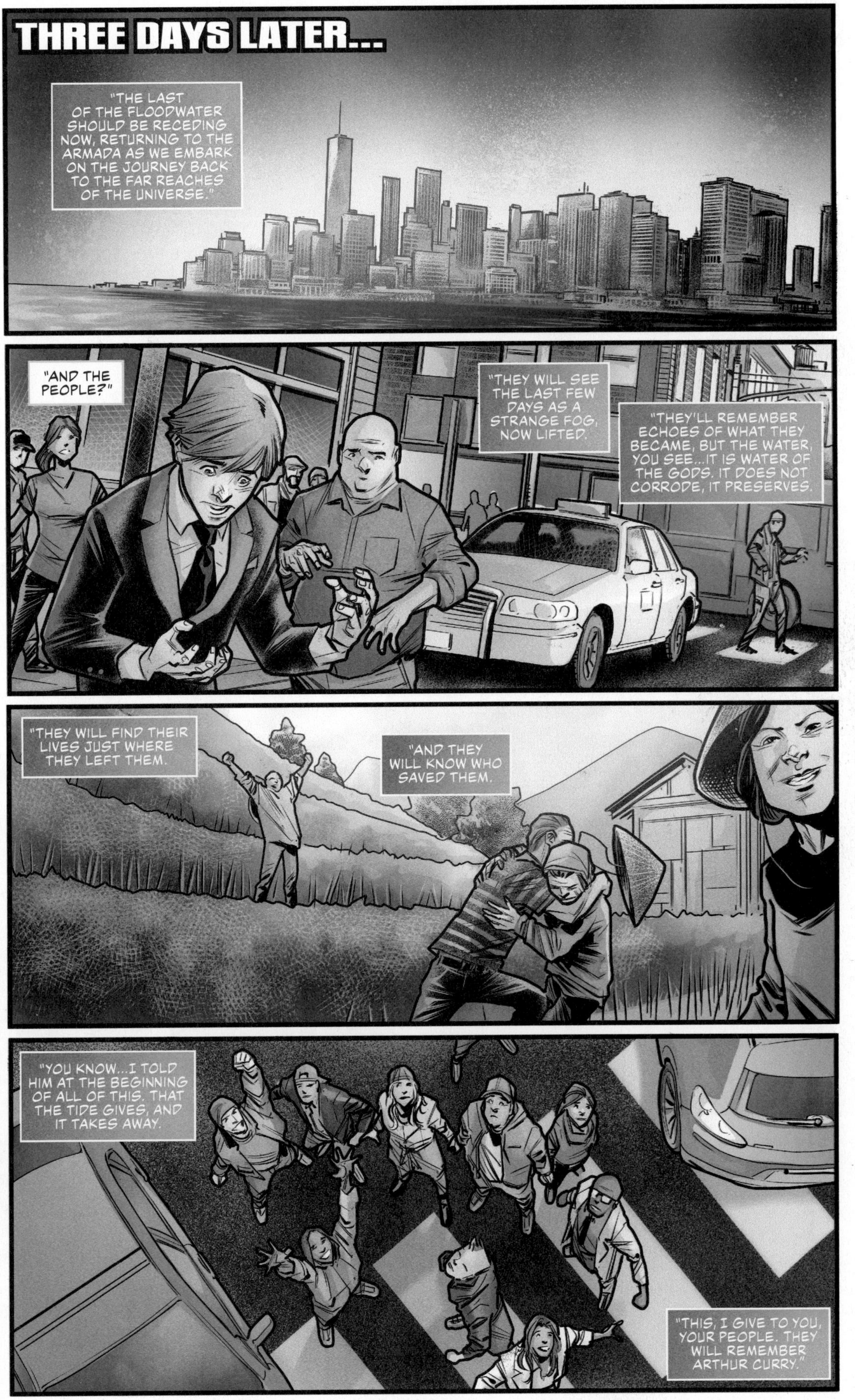
THREE DAYS LATER...
"THE LAST OF THE FLOODWATER SHOULD BE RECEDING NOW, RETURNING TO THE ARMADA AS WE EMBARK ON THE JOURNEY BACK TO THE FAR REACHES OF THE UNIVERSE."
"AND THE PEOPLE?"
"THEY WILL SEE THE LAST FEW DAYS AS A STRANGE FOG, NOW LIFTED.
"THEY'LL REMEMBER ECHOES OF WHAT THEY BECAME, BUT THE WATER, YOU SEE...IT IS WATER OF THE GODS. IT DOES NOT CORRODE, IT PRESERVES.
"THEY WILL FIND THEIR LIVES JUST WHERE THEY LEFT THEM.
"AND THEY WILL KNOW WHO SAVED THEM.
"YOU KNOW...I TOLD HIM AT THE BEGINNING OF ALL OF THIS. THAT THE TIDE GIVES, AND IT TAKES AWAY.
"THIS, I GIVE TO YOU, YOUR PEOPLE. THEY WILL REMEMBER ARTHUR CURRY."

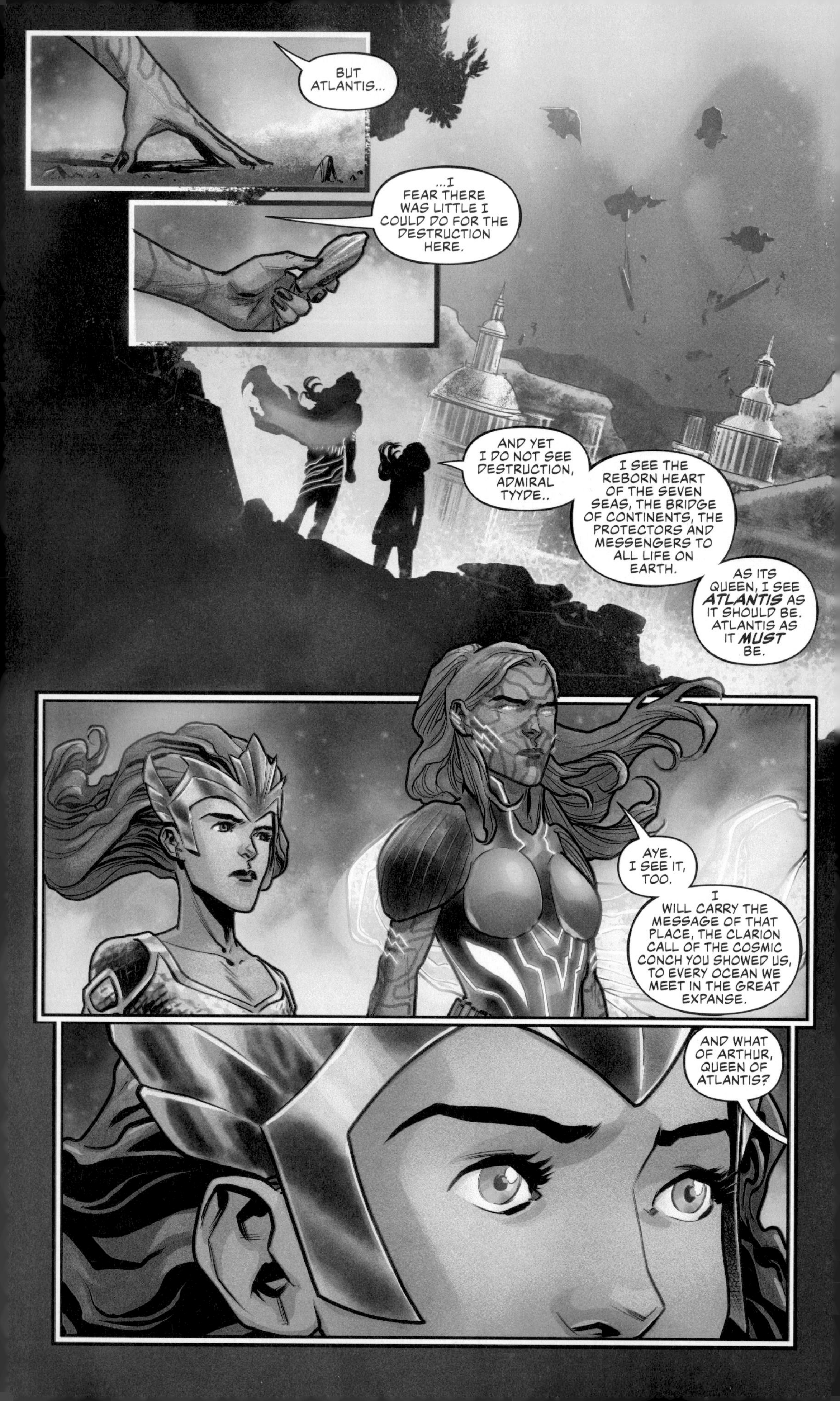
BUT ATLANTIS...
...I FEAR THERE WAS LITTLE I COULD DO FOR THE DESTRUCTION HERE.
AND YET I DO NOT SEE DESTRUCTION, ADMIRAL TYYDE..
I SEE THE REBORN HEART OF THE SEVEN SEAS, THE BRIDGE OF CONTINENTS, THE PROTECTORS AND MESSENGERS TO ALL LIFE ON EARTH.
AS ITS QUEEN, I SEE ATLANTIS AS IT SHOULD BE. ATLANTIS AS IT MUST BE.
AYE. I SEE IT, TOO.
I WILL CARRY THE MESSAGE OF THAT PLACE, THE CLARION CALL OF THE COSMIC CONCH YOU SHOWED US, TO EVERY OCEAN WE MEET IN THE GREAT EXPANSE.
AND WHAT OF ARTHUR, QUEEN OF ATLANTIS?

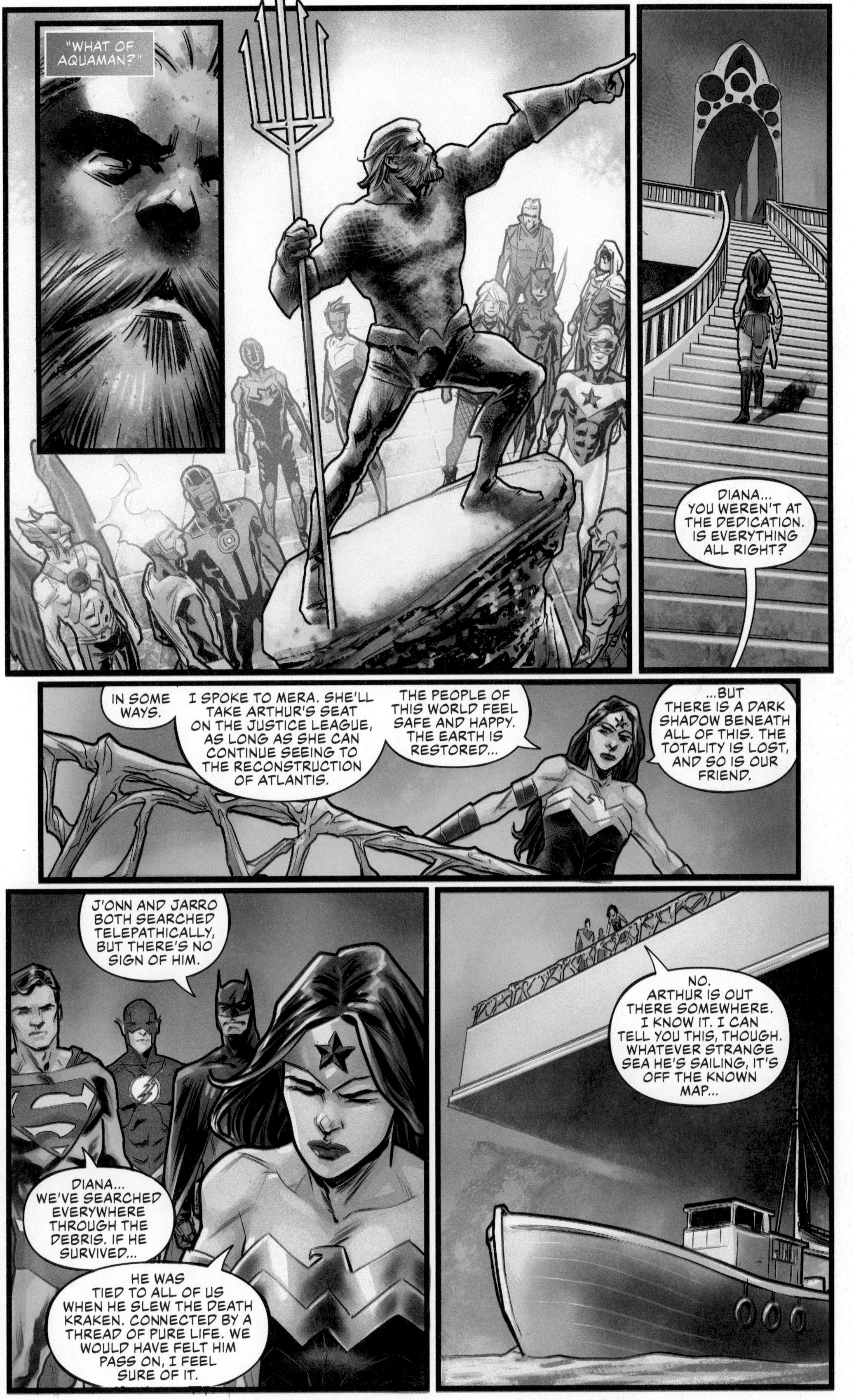
"WHAT OF AQUAMAN?"
DIANA... YOU WEREN'T AT THE DEDICATION. IS EVERYTHING ALL RIGHT?
IN SOME WAYS.
I SPOKE TO MERA. SHE'LL TAKE ARTHUR'S SEAT ON THE JUSTICE LEAGUE, AS LONG AS SHE CAN CONTINUE SEEING TO THE RECONSTRUCTION OF ATLANTIS.
THE PEOPLE OF THIS WORLD FEEL SAFE AND HAPPY. THE EARTH IS RESTORED...
...BUT THERE IS A DARK SHADOW BENEATH ALL OF THIS. THE TOTALITY IS LOST, AND SO IS OUR FRIEND.
J'ONN AND JARRO BOTH SEARCHED TELEPATHICALLY, BUT THERE'S NO SIGN OF HIM.
DIANA... WE'VE SEARCHED EVERYWHERE THROUGH THE DEBRIS. IF HE SURVIVED...
HE WAS TIED TO ALL OF US WHEN HE SLEW THE DEATH KRAKEN. CONNECTED BY A THREAD OF PURE LIFE. WE WOULD HAVE FELT HIM PASS ON, I FEEL SURE OF IT.
NO. ARTHUR IS OUT THERE SOMEWHERE. I KNOW IT. I CAN TELL YOU THIS, THOUGH. WHATEVER STRANGE SEA HE'S SAILING, IT'S OFF THE KNOWN MAP...

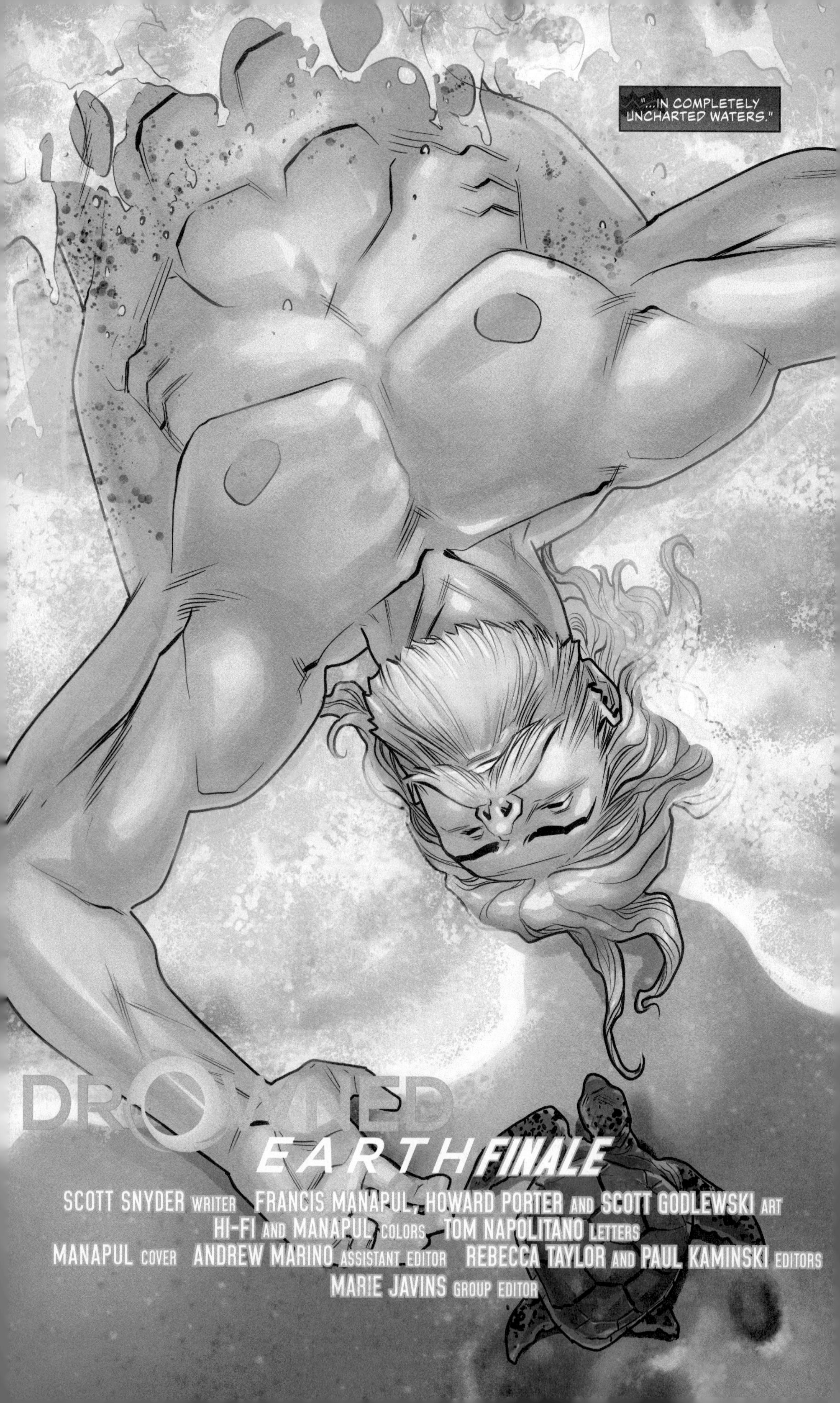

"...IN COMPLETELY UNCHARTED WATERS."
DROWNED EARTH FINALE
SCOTT SNYDER WRITER FRANCIS MANAPUL, HOWARD PORTER AND SCOTT GODLEWSKI ART
HI-FI AND MANAPUL COLORS TOM NAPOLITANO LETTERS
MANAPUL COVER ANDREW MARINO ASSISTANT EDITOR REBECCA TAYLOR AND PAUL KAMINSKI EDITORS
MARIE JAVINS GROUP EDITOR

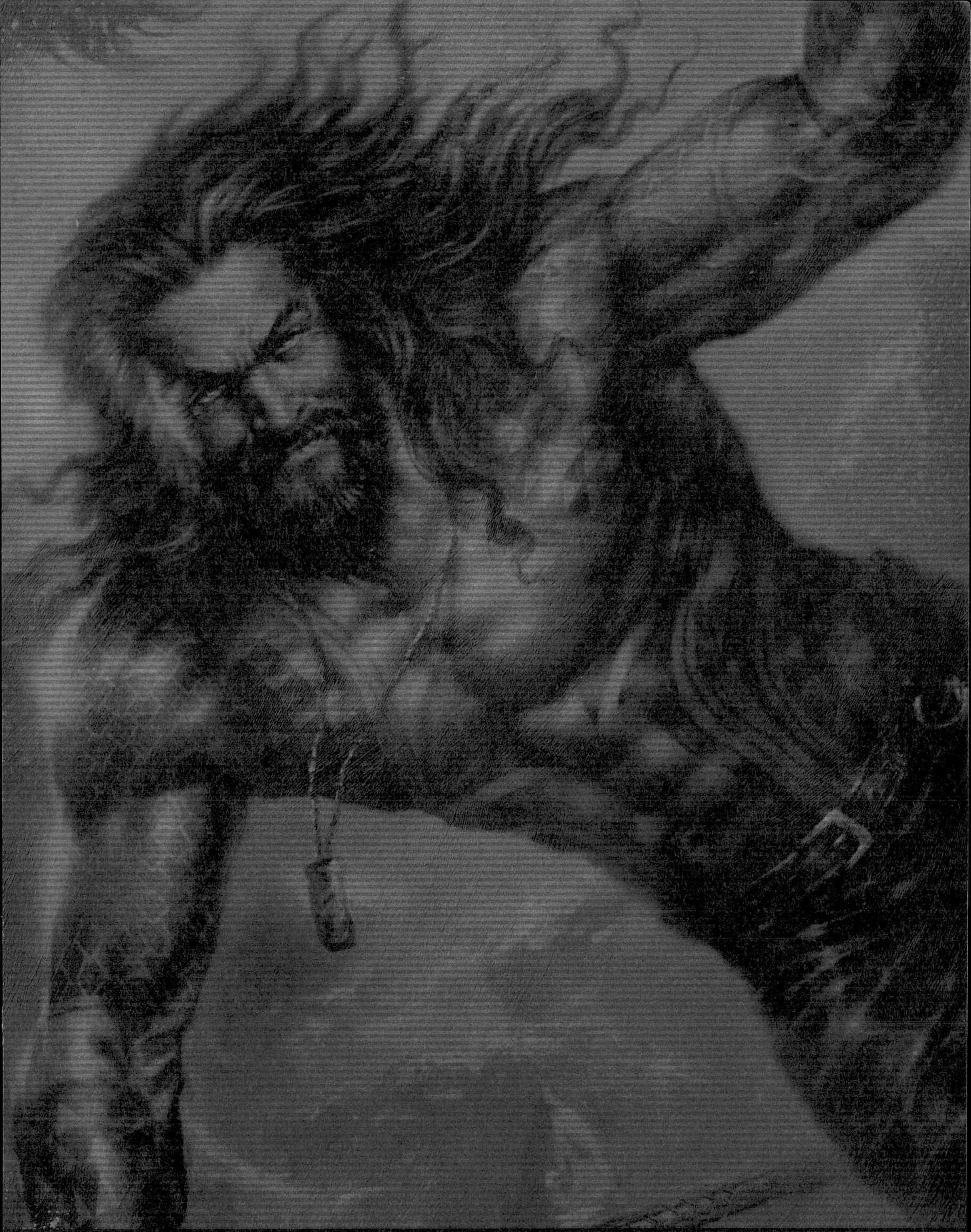

VARIANT COVER GALLERY

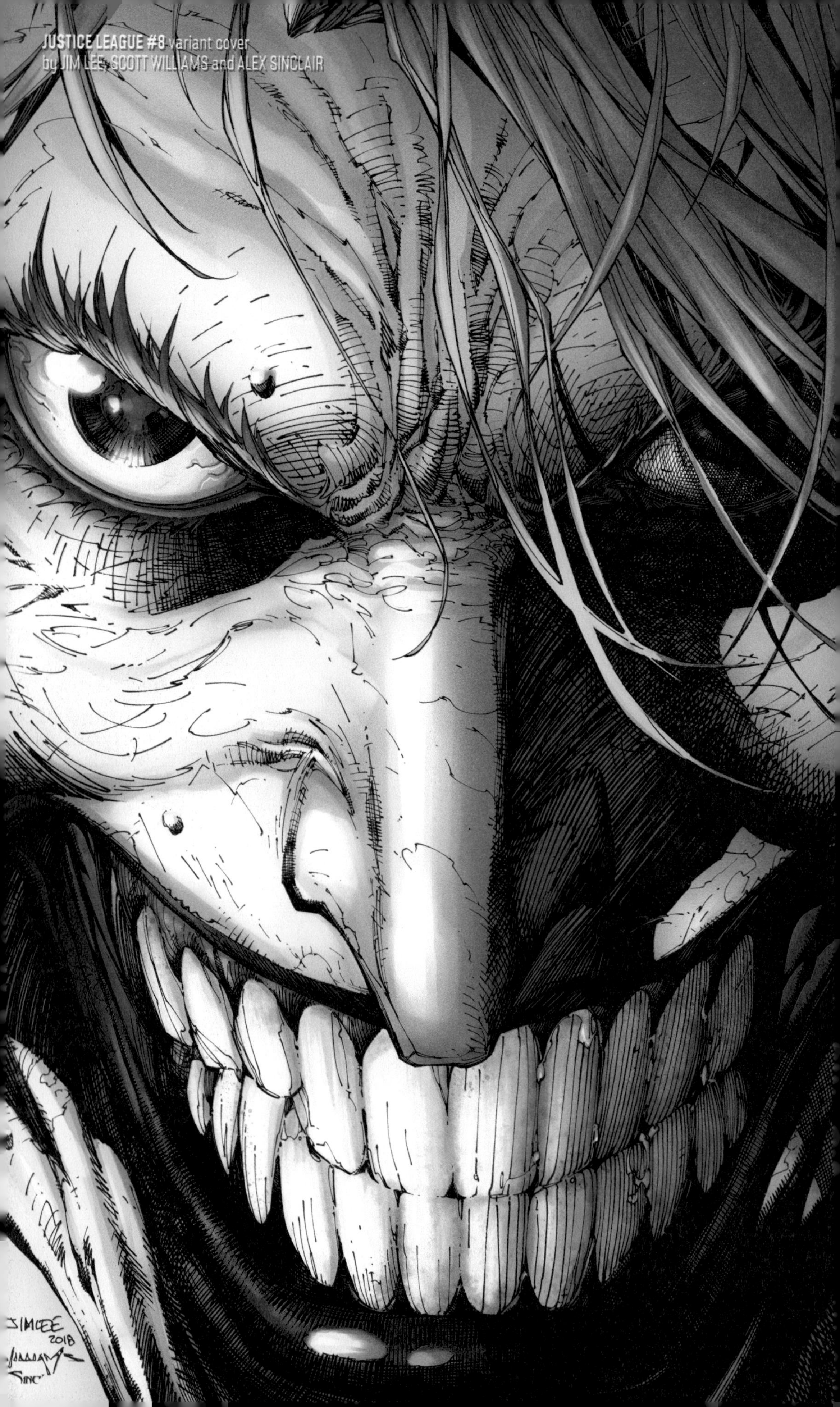
JIMLEE
2018
JUSTICE LEAGUE #8 variant cover
by JIM LEE, SCOTT WILLIAMS and ALEX SINCLAIR

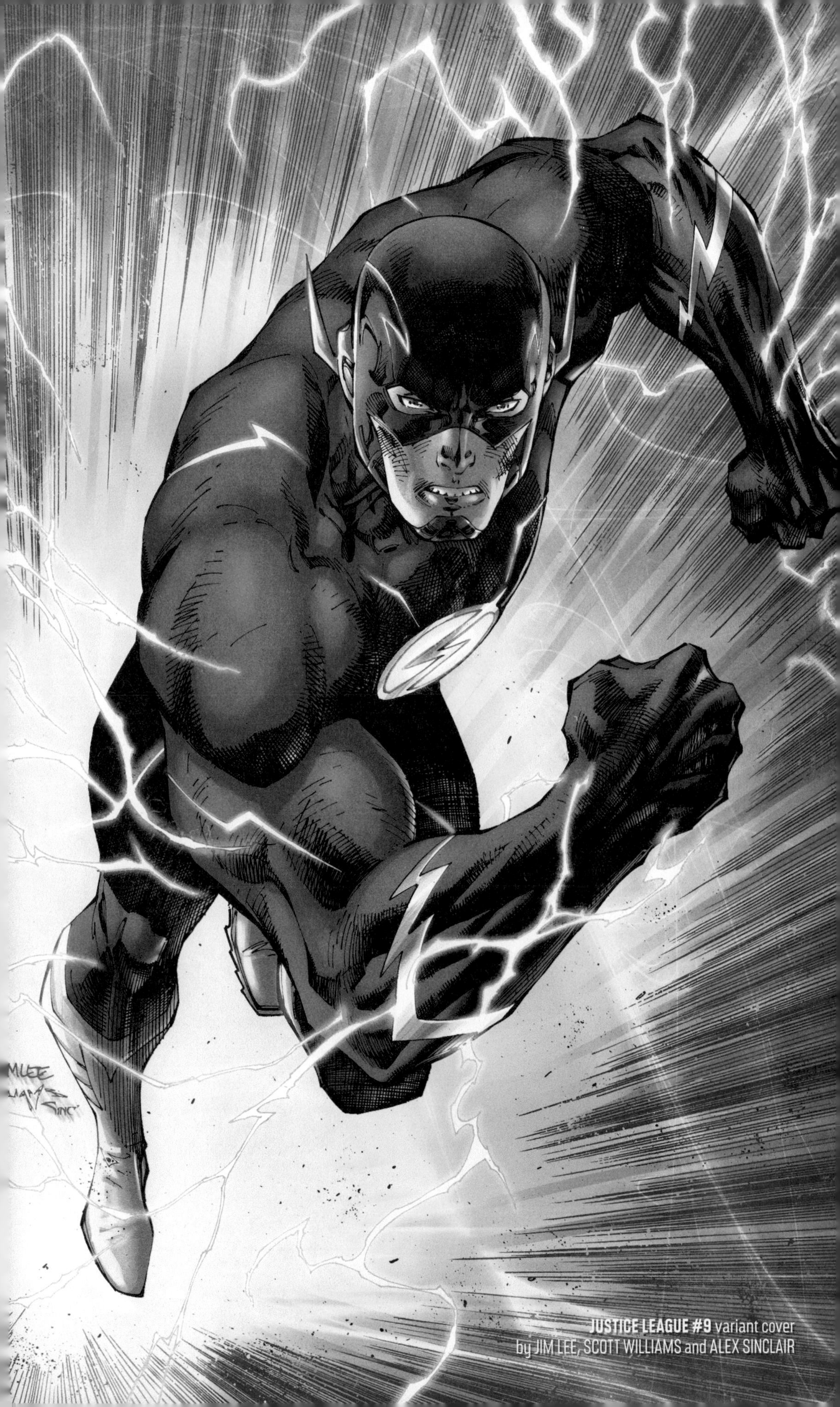

MLEE

JUSTICE LEAGUE #9 variant cover
by JIM LEE, SCOTT WILLIAMS and ALEX SINCLAIR

JUSTICE LEAGUE #10 variant cover
by JIM LEE, SCOTT WILLIAMS and ALEX SINCLAIR

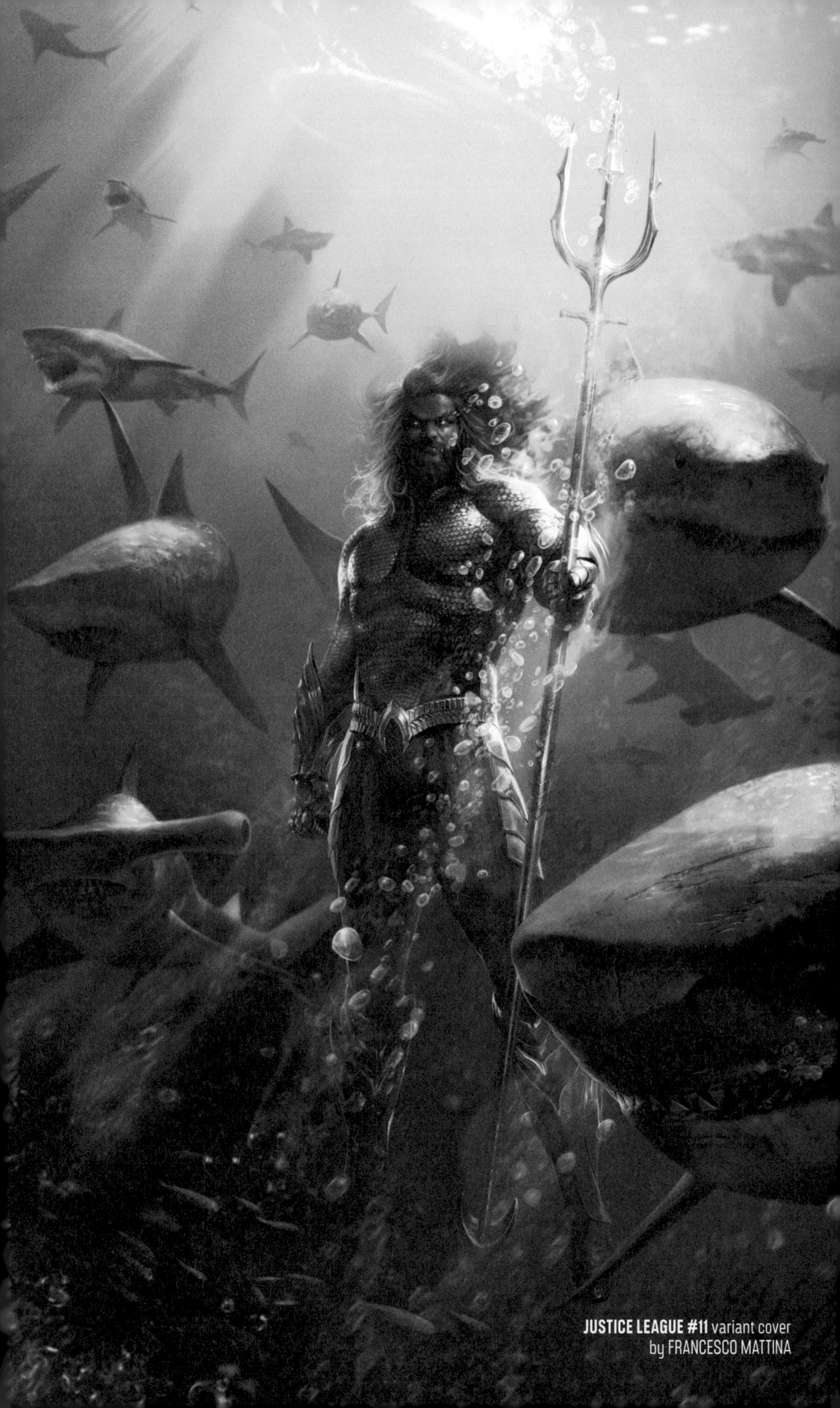

JUSTICE LEAGUE #11 variant cover
by FRANCESCO MATTINA

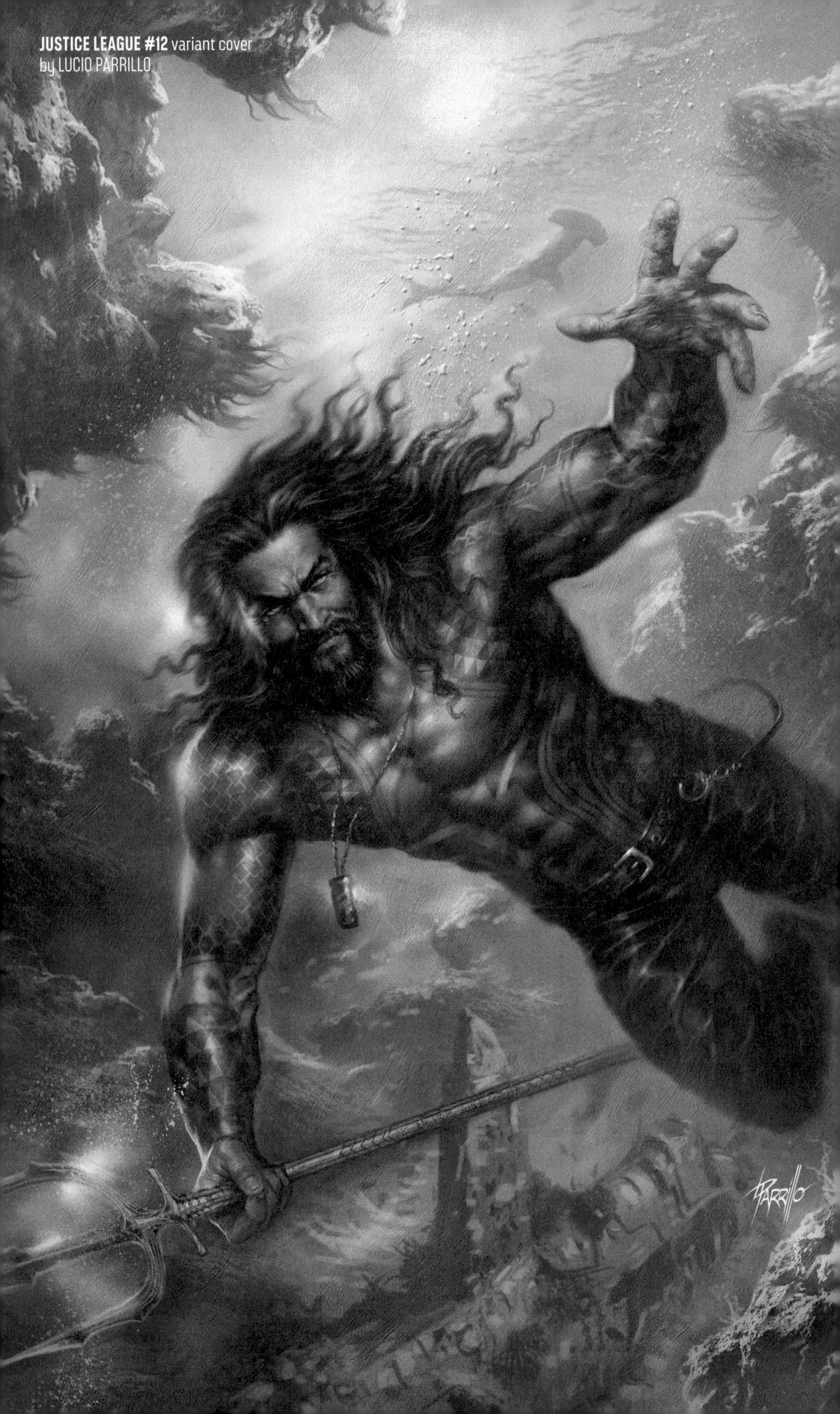

JUSTICE LEAGUE #12 variant cover
by LUCIO PARRILLO

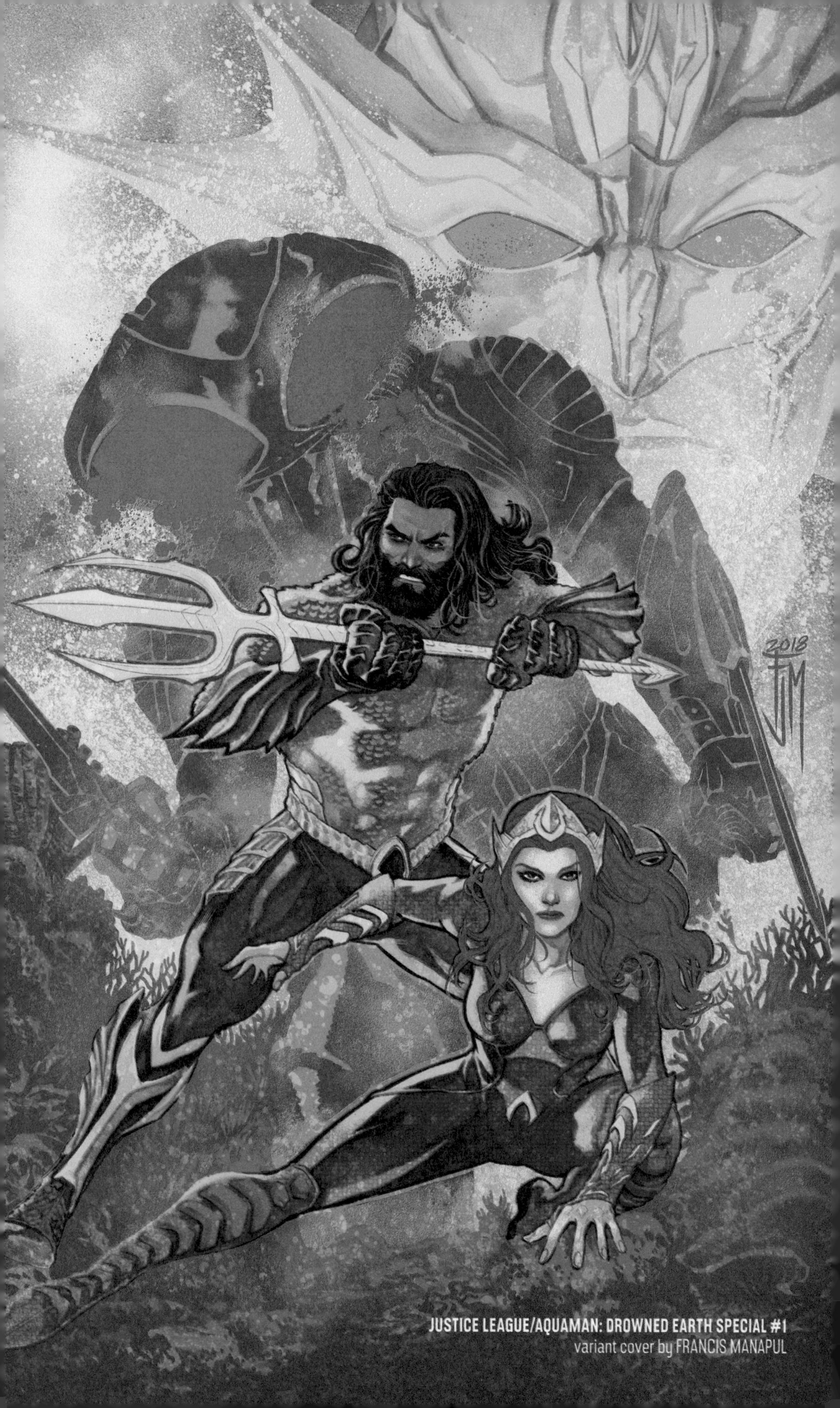
2018
FM

JUSTICE LEAGUE/AQUAMAN: DROWNED EARTH SPECIAL #1
variant cover by FRANCIS MANAPUL

AQUAMAN/JUSTICE LEAGUE: DROWNED EARTH SPECIAL #1
variant cover by DALE KEOWN and JASON KEITH

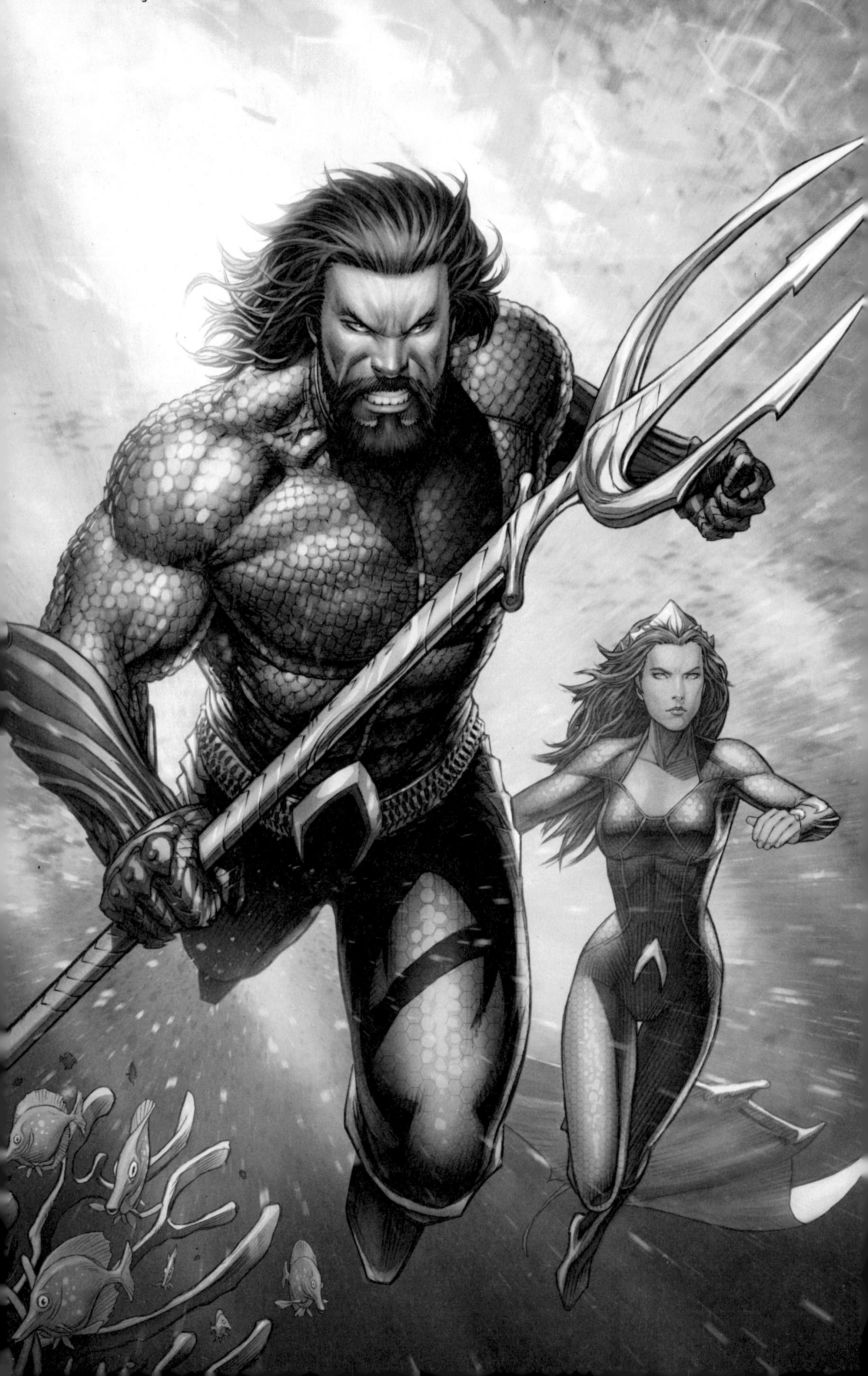

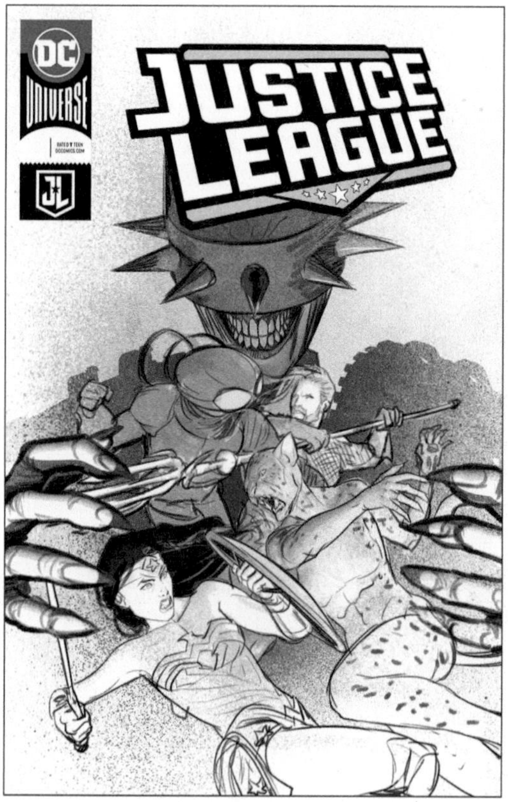
DC
UNIVERSE
JUSTICE
LEAGUE

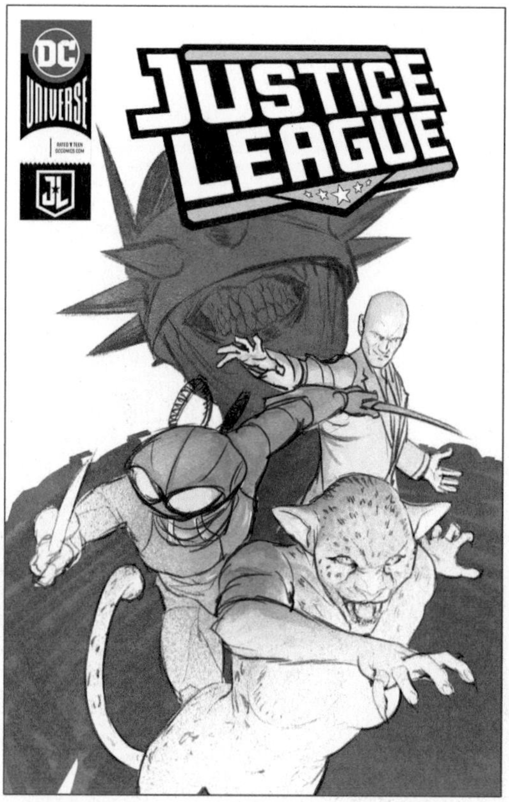
DC
UNIVERSE
JUSTICE
LEAGUE

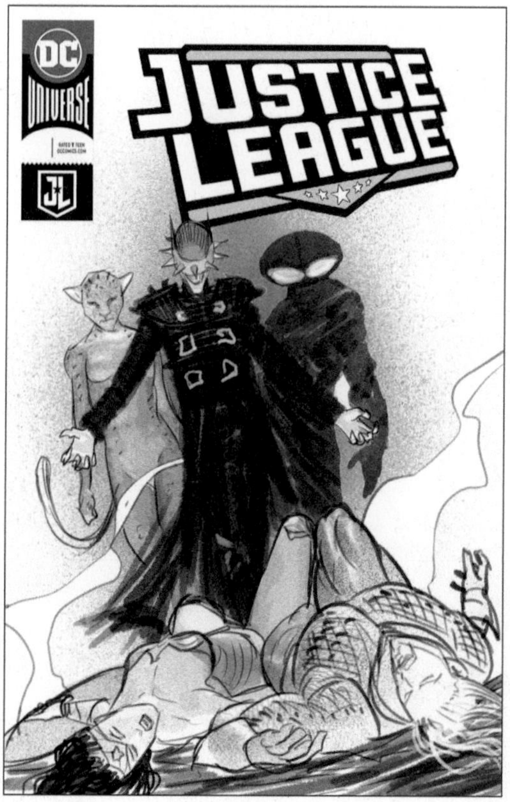
DC
UNIVERSE
JUSTICE
LEAGUE

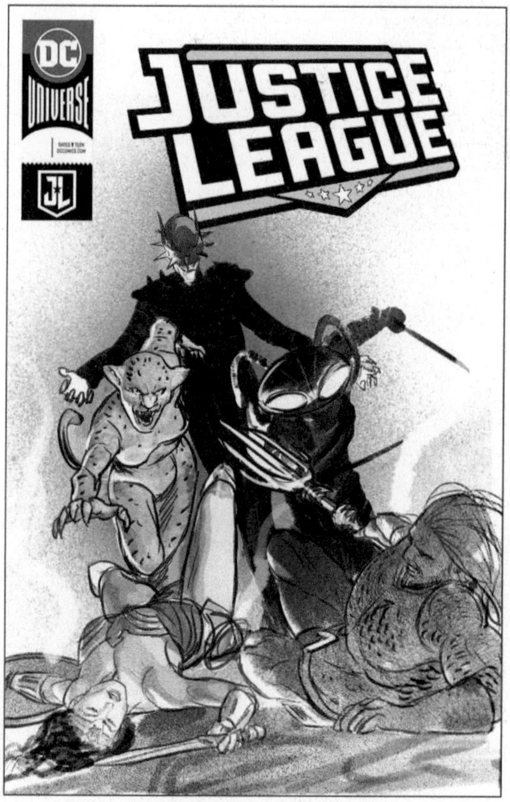
DC
UNIVERSE
JUSTICE
LEAGUE

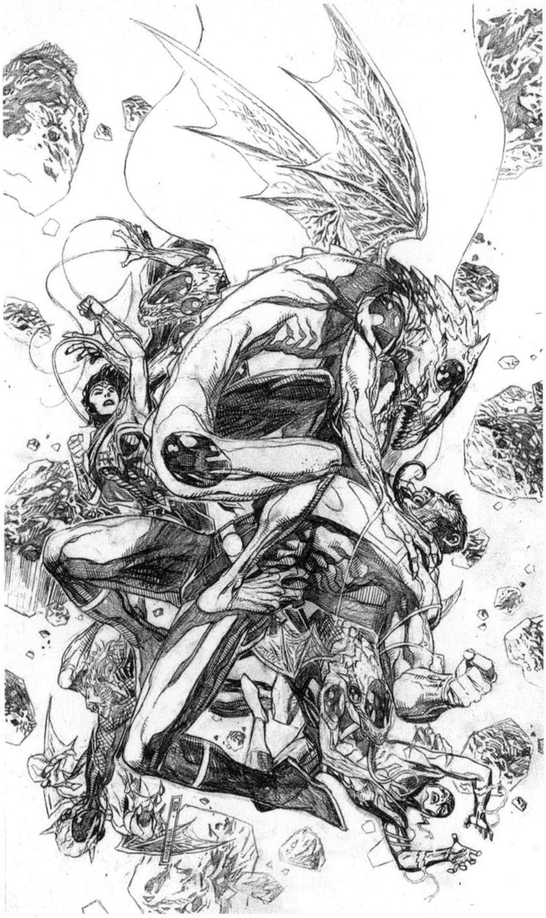

JUSTICE LEAGUE #9
cover pencils by JIM CHEUNG

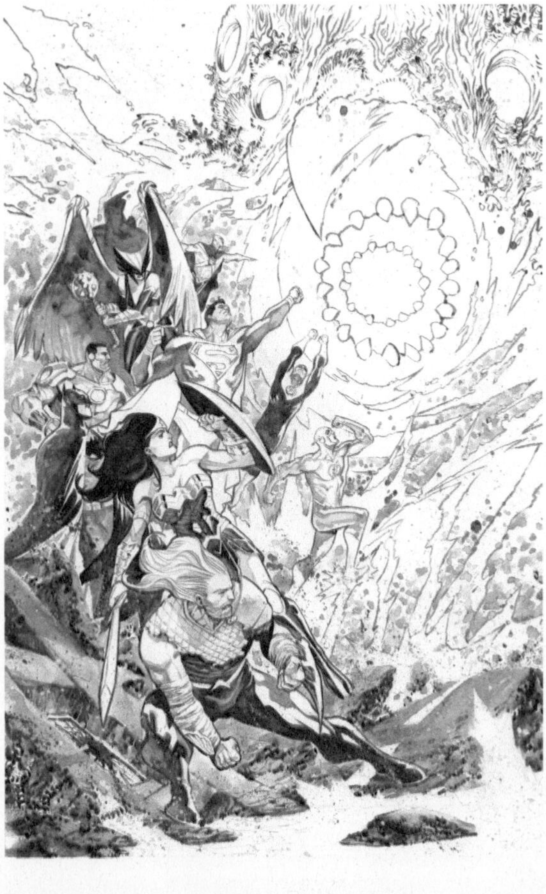

JUSTICE LEAGUE #11
cover inks by FRANCIS MANAPUL

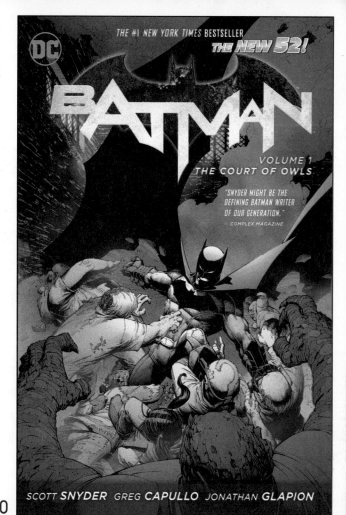
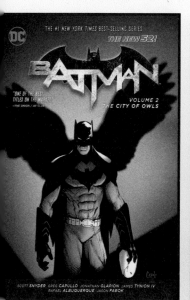
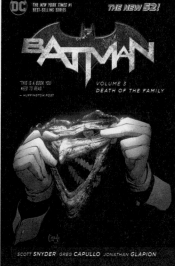

DARK NIGHTS:
METAL
SCOTT SNYDER
GREG CAPULLO

**DARK DAYS:
THE ROAD TO METAL**

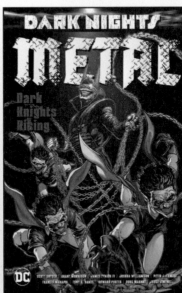

**DARK NIGHTS: METAL:
DARK KNIGHTS RISING**

**DARK NIGHTS: METAL:
THE RESISTANCE**

Get more DC graphic novels wherever comics and books are sold!